The EDUCATIONAL SYSTEM of the

United Kingdom

The ADMISSION and PLACEMENT of STUDENTS from the UNITED KINGDOM and STUDY ABROAD OPPORTUNITIES

A WORKSHOP REPORT
Sponsored by
Projects for International Education Research
1991

Sylvia K. Higashi, *PIER Workshop Co-Director and Co-Editor*
University of Hawaii at Manoa

Richard Weaver, *Workshop Co-Director*
University of Maryland-College Park

Alan Margolis, *Co-Editor*
CUNY-Queens College

Placement Recommendations Approved by the
National Council on the Evaluation of Foreign Educational Credentials

AMERICAN ASSOCIATION
of COLLEGIATE REGISTRARS
and ADMISSIONS OFFICERS
Washington, DC

NAFSA: ASSOCIATION
of INTERNATIONAL EDUCATORS
Washington, DC

#24627411

Library of Congress Cataloging-in-Publications Data

United Kingdom: a special report of the Projects for International Education Research Committee, cosponsored by the American Association of Collegiate Registrars and Admissions Officers and NAFSA: Association of International Educators, Washington, DC: placement recommendations approved by the National Council on the Evaluation of Foreign Educational Credentials / Sylvia K. Higashi, co-director, Richard Weaver, co-director; Alan Margolis, editor.

       p.   cm.

  Includes bibliographical references and index.

  ISBN 0-910054-96-7

  1. Education--Great Britain. 2. Education--Great Britain--Curricula. 3. Education--Scotland--Curricula. 4. College credits--Great Britain. 5. College credits--Scotland. 6. School credits--Great Britain. 7. School credits--Scotland. 8. Vocational qualifications--Great Britain. I. Higashi, Sylvia K. II. Weaver, Richard Madison, 1947- III. Margolis, Alan M. IV. Projects for International Education Research (U.S.) V. American Association of Collegiate Registrars and Admissions Officers. VI. NAFSA: Association of International Educators (Washington, D.C.) VII. National Council on the Evaluation of Foreign Educational Credentials (U.S.)

LA632.U56   1991

370'.941--dc20

                                                  91-37795

                                                    CIP

American Association
of Collegiate Registrars
and Admissions Officers
One Dupont Circle, Suite 330
Washington, DC 20036-1171
Telephone (202) 293-9161
FAX (202) 872-8857

NAFSA: Association of
International Educators
1875 Connecticut Avenue
Suite 1000
Washington, DC 20009-5728
Telephone (202) 462-4811
FAX (202) 667-3419

Additional copies of this report may be obtained from AACRAO or NAFSA for $25 ($40 nonmembers). For more information on available volumes in the World Education Series, contact the Publications Order Desk, c/o the respective association.

About Projects for International Education Research (PIER)

The Projects for International Education Research (PIER) Committee is a joint committee of the American Association of Collegiate Registrars and Admissions Officers (AACRAO) and NAFSA: Association of International Educators (see list of representatives below).

PIER is charged with providing information on foreign educational systems that can be used by U.S. admissions officers in the admission and placement of students entering institutions of higher education in the United States.

Three types of volumes comprise PIER's World Education Series: full country studies, workshop reports and special reports. Among the topics covered are the different levels of education, admission and program requirements, grading systems, credentials awarded, study abroad programs, and institutions. Placement recommendations, when included, are approved by the National Council on the Evaluation of Foreign Educational Credentials (see page v for an explanation of the role of the Council and a list of Council representatives and page 47 for a guide to understanding placement recommendations). The PIER committee oversees the selection of countries, authors and reviewers.

Projects for International Education Research Committee (PIER)

A joint committee of the American Association of Collegiate Registrars and Admissions Officers and NAFSA: Association of International Educators

PIER Chairperson:

Rebecca N. DIXON, Asociate Provost for University Enrollment, Northwestern University, Evanston, IL.

AACRAO Members:

Arunas J. ALISAUSKAS, Registrar and Director of Admissions, Mount Royal College, Calgary, Canada

Margit A. SCHATZMAN, Vice President, Educational Credential Evaluators, Inc., Milwaukee, WI

Richard N. ELKINS, Director of Admissions, Kansas State University, Manhattan, KS

NAFSA Members:

Michael HOLCOMB, Associate University Director-Graduate and Professional Admissions, Rutgers University, New Brunswick, NJ.

William PAVER, Associate Director of Admissions, University of Texas-Austin, Austin, TX.

The College Board:

Sanford C. JAMESON, Director, International Education Office, The College Board, Washington, DC.

Observers:

Agency for International Development–Hattie JARMON, Educational Specialist, AID, Washington, DC

United States Information Agency–Sheldon AUSTIN, USIA, Washington, DC

Association of Universities and Colleges in Canada–Desmond BEVIS, Director of Admissions, University of Manitoba, Winnipeg, Canada

American Association of Collegiate Registrars and Admissions Officers–Wayne E. BECRAFT, Executive Director, AACRAO, Washington, DC (ex-officio); Henrianne K. WAKEFIELD, Director of Communications, AACRAO, Washington, DC (ex-officio).

NAFSA: Association of International Educators–John F. REICHARD, Executive Vice President, NAFSA, Washington, DC (ex-officio); Jeanne-Marie DUVAL, Senior Director, Educational Programs, NAFSA, Washington, DC (ex-officio).

Participants in the PIER United Kingdom Workshop

Note: Team leaders for specific chapters are listed below their names.

Larry Ballinger, GMAC Observer
University of Notre Dame
College of Business Administration
Notre Dame, IN 46556

Joanne Berridge
College of Notre Dame
1500 Ralston Avenue
Belmont, CA 94002

James Donnen
University of Washington
Mail Stop PC-30
Seattle, WA 98195

David Green
Acadia University
Wolfville, Nova Scotia
Canada B0P 1X0
(chapter IV on Scotland)

Paulette Grotrian
Washtenaw Community College
Box D-1
Ann Arbor, MI 48106

Sylvia Higashi, Co-Director and Co-Editor
University of Hawaii at Manoa
College of Continuing Education and
Community Service
2530 Dole Street, Sakamaki C104
Honolulu, HI 96822

Margery Ismail
Purdue University
Schleman Hall
West Lafayette, IN 47907
(chapter II on Secondary Education)

Alan Margolis, Co-Editor
Queens College
65-30 Kissena Boulevard
Flushing, NY 11367-0904

John Pearson
Stanford University
Graduate Admission Building 590 209
Stanford, CA 94305
(chapter I on Study Abroad)

Peter Pelham
Pelham Associates
384 Magothy Road
Severna Park, MD 21146

Jasmin Saidi
International Education Research Foundation
PO Box 66940
Los Angeles, CA 90066
(chapter III on Higher Education)

Ellen Silverman
World Education Services, Inc.
PO Box 745
Old Chelsea Station
New York, NY 10113-0745

James Sullivan
SUNY Binghamton
Office of Academic Advising
Binghamton, NY 13901

Timothy Thompson
Office of International Services
University of Pittsburgh
708 William Pitt Union
Pittsburgh, PA 15260
(chapter V on Professional Qualifications)

Solveig Turner
Center for Education Documentation
Box 326
Boston, MA 02130

Richard Weaver, Co-Director
University of Maryland-College Park
International Education Services
3125 Mitchell Building
College Park, MD 20742

The National Council on the Evaluation of Foreign Educational Credentials

The National Council on the Evaluation of Foreign Educational Credentials is an interassociational group that establishes standards for interpreting foreign educational credentials for the placement of holders of these credentials in U.S. educational institutions. Its main purpose is to review, modify, and approve placement recommendations drafted for publications used by the U.S. admissions community. The Council also helps establish priorities, research guidelines, and review procedures for international admissions publications. The Council participates in international meetings that involve foreign educational credentials.

The Council is composed of representatives from the following organizations: the American Association of Collegiate Registrars and Admissions Officers (AACRAO), the American Association of Community and Junior Colleges (AACJC), the American Council on Education (ACE), The College Board, the Council of Graduate Schools (CGS), the Institute of International Education (IIE), and NAFSA: Association of International Educators. Also participating in Council meetings are observers from U.S. organizations with interests in international education, such as the United States Information Agency (USIA), the Agency for International Development (AID), and the New York State Education Department. The membership of the Council reflects the diversity of U.S. educational institutions for which recommendations are made.

The placement recommendations approved by the Council identify the level or stage of education represented by an educational credential and thus the appropriate placement of the holder of the credential in U.S. educational instituitons. Council recommendations are not directives, nor do they make judgments about the quality of programs and schools. Quality indicators may be provided by the author in the text. The effective use of placement recommendations depends on careful review of the supporting text in the publication and consideration of individual institutional policies and practices.

The Council suggests that institutions apply the same standards for a foreign applicant as for a U.S. applicant with a similar educational background. Recommendations reflect U.S. philosophy and structure of education and may differ from practices within the educational system being reviewed.

Chairperson–William H. SMART, Associate Director, International Education, Oregon State University, Corvallis, OR

Vice Chair/Secretary–Ann FLETCHER, Assistant Dean, Graduate Studies, Stanford University, Stanford, CA

REPRESENTATIVES OF MEMBER ORGANIZATIONS

AACRAO–Rebecca N. DIXON, Associate Provost of University Enrollment, Northwestern University, Evanston, IL; Caroline ALDRICH-LANGEN, Associate Director of Admissions, California State University-Chico, Chico, CA; Andrew J. HEIN, AACRAO-AID Project Director, Washington, DC.

AACJC–Yukie TOKUYAMA, Director of International Services, AACJC, Washington, DC.

ACE–Barbara TURLINGTON, Director, Office of International Education, ACE, Washington, DC.

College Board–Sanford C. JAMESON, Director, Office of International Education, The College Board, Washington, DC.

CGS–Ann FLETCHER, Assistant Dean, Graduate Studies, Stanford University, Stanford, CA

IIE–James O'DRISCOLL, Director, Placement and Special Services Division, IIE, New York, NY

NAFSA–William H. SMART, Associate Director, International Education, Oregon State University, Corvallis, OR; Liz A. REISBERG, Director of Public Relations, Arthur D. Little Management Education Institute, Cambridge, MA; Richard B. TUDISCO, Director, International Student Office, Columbia University, New York, NY.

REPRESENTATIVES OF OBSERVER ORGANIZATIONS

USIA–Sheldon AUSTIN, Chief, Advising and Student Services Branch, USIA, Washington, DC.

AID–Hattie JARMON, Education Specialist, Office of International Training, U.S. Department of State/AID, Washington, DC.

NY Education Department–Mary Jane EWART, Chief, Bureau of Comparative Education, State Education Department, The University of the State of New York, Albany, NY.

AACRAO–Henrianne K. WAKEFIELD, Director of Communications, AACRAO, Washington, DC.

ACKNOWLEDGEMENTS

Developing and planning a PIER project is like piecing together a giant jigsaw puzzle. It involves finding the right pieces: organizations to fund the project; professionals with the experience, dedication and perseverance to undertake a major research project above and beyond their normal work responsibilities; team leaders to find and organize the pieces into sections; and an editor to insure that all sections of the puzzle form a uniform whole. To all of you who helped us find the right pieces to finish our puzzle, we thank you and appreciate the years of support and assistance.

We were extremely fortunate to have a superb group of professionals to work with: not only were they excellent researchers and hard workers, but also wonderful individuals who worked harmoniously as a group. We are especially indebted to our diligent team leaders who led their teams until the very end: David Green, Margery Ismail, John Pearson, Jasmin Saidi and Timothy Thompson. Our editor and mentor, Alan Margolis, provided us with wise counsel throughout and taught us the true meaning of professionalism.

One of the greatest initial challenges in making this workshop a reality was finding the funds necessary to organize the research trip and then publish the report. The following individuals and organizations provided the requisite support that made this whole project possible: the Student Support Services Division of the United States Information Agency; The British Council; American Institute of Foreign Study Scholarship Fund; Beaver College; The College Board; Educational Credentials Evaluators, Inc.; Foundation for International Services; The Graduate Management Admissions Council; International Consultants of Delaware, Inc.; International Education Research Foundation; International Humanities Foundation; The University of Lancaster; Study in the U.S.A.; Test of English as a Foreign Language.

Special thanks are extended to the British Council officers and staff who provided indispensable support for the PIER project and especially to Dr. Tom Craig-Cameron who took a special interest in this workshop and paved the way for The British Council to provide significant financial, logistical and research support. Theo Addy, Judy Frankl and Isobel Ascherson are sincerely appreciated for their roles in making the requisite logistical arrangements for our planning trip and group research visits. Olga Stanojlovic, our central resource person in London who assisted us in all aspects of our program and especially with identifying and then arranging meetings with key resource people, was instrumental in ensuring the success of this project.

The number of British and Scottish professionals who assisted with this project is too large to mention. However, special recognition must be given to Malcolm Deere, the Committee of Vice Chancellors and Principals and Professor B. Saul, Vice-Chancellor, University of York, who provided guidance during our initial planning trip and advised us throughout the workshop. Nigel Rogers, Stephen Lamley and the University of Lancaster also contributed immensely by providing all of the accommodations, food and support for the summary seminar. We also wish to thank Dr. Derek Pollard and the Council for National Academic Awards (CNAA) for the innumerable resource materials provided, Janice Finn of the Fulbright Commission, and Nizam Mohammed of the University of London. In addition, the authors are indebted to the many Scottish educators who helped them in their study. All gave generously and graciously of their knowledge and time. In particular, we would like to mention Joy Wooton (Aberdeen), Douglas Osler (SED), Eddie Clarke (SCOTVEC) and both the SEB and SCOTVEC for permission to reprint their diplomas.

Our thanks to those universities and institutions who gave release time to the participants to undertake the research and writing of this report. We know this normally places an extra burden on other colleagues in the office and we thank all of those involved from: Acadia University, The Center for Educational Documentation, Queens College, University of Hawaii at Manoa, The International Education Research Foundation, Inc., University of Maryland, College of Notre Dame, University of Notre Dame, Pelham Associates, University of Pittsburgh, Purdue University, Stanford University, State University of New York at Binghamton, University of Washington, Washtenaw Community College, World Education Services, Inc. In addition, the Graduate Management Admissions Council is recognized for its consistent support for PIER workshops, and in particular, for sending an observer who provided invaluable assistance in the review and discussion of business programs.

To Jeanne-Marie Duval and Sarah Herr of NAFSA who ably administered the funds for this project, to Rebecca Dixon and Valerie Woolston, Chair and Past-Chair of the PIER Committee who believed in us and guided us, and to Henny Wakefield who provided the kind of technical editorial assistance that only a professional can–thank you.

A very special thank you to Mrs. Nell Johnson, Administrative Assistant in the Office of the Registrar at Queens College, whose editorial assistance smoothed the way for this project. Finally, to Les, Roy, and Anne, our families, staff and colleagues who assumed additional responsibilities in our absence–we gratefully acknowledge and thank you for your unwaivering support throughout the five years we've worked on this project.

Sylvia Higashi
Co-Director

Richard Weaver
Co-Director

INTRODUCTION

The U.K. PIER workshop report is unique among other workshop reports. Since much is already known about the U.K. educational system and institutions based on the 1976 World Education Series volume *United Kingdom* by Stephen Fisher and the *Commonwealth Universities Yearbook*, this report focuses on the areas of significant change in the educational system since 1976. Special attention is focused on areas outside the university sector as well as the changing examination, admission and grading policies.

Due to the continuing impact of educational reform policies, many of the conclusions must be considered tentative. The volume identifies the sources and pressure for change in the United Kingdom to enable the reader to better understand the probable directions for future change. Although it appears likely that major reforms will continue into the twenty-first century, there already has been significant change. Hence, this publication which updates education in the U.K. will provide valuable, if interim, information.

There are five main chapters: study abroad; secondary education; polytechnics and colleges of higher education; Scotland; and professional qualifications.

The study abroad chapter provides an overview of educational change in Britain and should be of interest to all readers. Given the large number of U.S. students studying in the U.K., it was felt that study abroad advisers and transfer credit evaluators would welcome an analysis of opportunities for study in U.K. higher education institutions. This is the first PIER volume to include a section on study abroad. This chapter focuses on the more problematic issue of assisting students who might

want or need to study in the U.K. for less then a full academic year since placing students in full year programs in the U.K. is relatively easy.

The chapter on secondary education examines the major changes in school curriculums with the implementation of the new National Curriculum and the introduction of new examinations, the GCSE and AS-level exams. The changes instituted at the secondary level will likely impact and force changes to occur later in higher education.

The chapter on polytechnics and colleges and institutes of higher education examines one of the largest areas of growth in British higher education since Fisher's 1976 publication. This sector now almost equals the university sector in number of graduates and is playing a major role in changing the nature of higher education.

A separate chapter on Scotland is provided because the Scottish system is quite different from that in England and Wales. While earlier publications have noted this difference, this chapter will deal in detail with the structure of education in Scotland.

One of the most difficult problems for American educators is how to evaluate U.K. professional qualifications. This chapter will focus on qualifications in engineering, accountancy, management, and nursing. These qualifications are presented as examples to provide a general framework for approaching British professional qualifications.

Contents

Tables

Figures

Charts

Sample Documents

AN UP-FRONT GLOSSARY

Accreditation of Prior Learning (APL) - The measurement of all skills, knowledge and achievement acquired up to the point of assessment. The specific skill is assessed against National Certificate modules by college staff through interviews and testing.

Associate Membership (or Associateship) - A level of membership in a professional society usually superior to student or ordinary membership but inferior to fellowship. Associate membership is an earned rather than an honorary status and is, in certain fields, the professional level required for registration.

Attainment Targets - Objectives for each foundation subject in the National Curriculum.

Block Release Scheme - A pedagogic timetable used for the formal classroom component of lower- and middle-level technical, commercial and vocational programs. This scheme consists of a release from employment for the purpose of study for a period varying from several weeks to several months, depending upon the program. The employment is in the same field as is the training program. Usually, the employment is a prerequisite for the program, and the program is a prerequisite for advancement in the profession. The block release scheme is used as an alternative to the day release scheme (see below).

Business and Technician Education Council (BTEC) - An organization which offers diploma and certificate courses at the post-compulsory school level.

Certificate of Pre-Vocational Education (CPVE) - A one-year course for those 16 or older which serves as an alternative to GCE Advanced level examinations.

Certificate of Secondary Education (CSE) - An examination system offered by 11 regional examining bodies for those completing the Fifth Form of secondary school. This system is an alternative to the General Certificate of Education (GCE). It differs from the GCE in that there is no requirement that schools follow external syllabuses or an external examination system. Schools may opt for completely external assessment (both syllabus and examinations), for totally internal assessment, or a combination of internal syllabuses and external examination. The syllabus is practically based.

The grading system ranges from 1 (highest) to U (ungraded/failure), with 5 being the lowest passing grade. Although geared somewhat lower than the GCE in expectation of student attainment, a grade of 1 on the CSE may be said to be marginally comparable with a pass on the GCE Ordinary level examinations.

Chartered Universities - Postsecondary institutions which have official government charters to offer university-level degrees. University degrees differ from individually approved programs which are offered at nonuniversity, but postsecondary, institutions with the approval of the Council on National Academic Awards (see below).

City Technology Colleges - New, independent schools for the 11 - 18 age group established by the Department of Education and Science as joint ventures with local industry. The curriculum emphasis technology.

College - An educational institution at the secondary or postsecondary level, or an institute or association (e.g., the College of Speech Therapists, the professional association in the field of speech therapy). The term does not define the level of education.

Comprehensive Schools - Secondary schools catering to students of mixed academic ability.

Core Subjects - Within the National Curriculum (see below), English, mathematics and sciences.

Council for National Academic Awards (CNAA) - A quasi-official agency chartered in 1964 and charged with awarding degrees for programs taken in nonuniversity institutions. The CNAA must approve the specific program for the degree; it does not approve the institution for the purpose of granting degrees.

Cross-Curricular Themes - Skills and themes which are to be integrated into the subject curriculums of the National Curriculum.

CCW - Curriculum Council for Wales

Day Release Scheme - A pedagogic timetable for the formal classroom component of lower- and middle-level technical, commercial and vocational programs.

1

This scheme consists of a release from employment of one day a week for several months to a year or more, depending on the program, for the purpose of study. Employment in the same field as the training program usually is a prerequisite for the program and the program is a prerequisite for advancement in the profession. This pattern is used by teaching institutions as an alternative to the block release scheme (see above).

ERA - Education Reform Act, passed by Parliament in 1988, which introduced the National Curriculum.

External Candidate - An individual who sits for an examination but is not coming directly from an academic program which prepared for that examination. Usually, external candidates study independently in order to prepare for the examination.

External Examination System - A testing system meant to standardize the teaching of a particular body of knowledge. The examining body may be an organization established for this purpose (e.g., the City and Guilds of London Institute) or a professional body such as the Institute of Medical Laboratory Sciences. Syllabuses for external examinations may be set externally or internally (at the school).

Fellowship - Usually the highest level of membership in a professional society. Fellowship may be earned or may be honorary and is, in certain fields, the professional level required for registration.

General Certificate of Education (GCE) - An external examination system which sets both syllabuses and examinations for three levels of pre-university education.

The lowest level is the **Ordinary** (O-level), normally given to those who have completed the Fifth Form. Passes in five academic subjects at this level normally may be considered as equivalent to the receipt of a U.S. academic high school diploma. (See placement recommendations.) Grades of A, B and C are passing.

The middle level is the relatively new **Advanced Supplementary** (AS-level), taken usually at the end of the two-year Sixth Form. It is at the same academic level as the Advanced level (see below), is graded in the same manner, but covers approximately half of the material.

The highest--**Advanced** or A-level--is administered to those who have completed the Sixth Form. Freshman-year credit in subjects passed at this level usually may be granted by U.S. colleges and univer-

sities. (See placement recommendations.) Grades of A through E are passes.

Those who may not have the formal educational background or who have been out of school several years may sit for all levels of examinations, at the discretion of the examining boards, as external candidates.

General Certificate of Secondary Education (GCSE) - An external examination system which replaced the General Certificate of Education and the Certificate of Secondary Education programs. It provides for syllabuses which are adaptable to a wide range of student ability and lends itself to internal assessment and criterion-referenced instruction.

Higher Grade - In Scotland, examinations taken at the end of the fifth year of secondary school (the twelfth year of schooling). These are required for entry into Scottish universities.

INSET - In-service training for teachers, including preparation for teaching the National Curriculum.

Institutes and Colleges of Technology/Polytechnics - Educational institutions which offer technical and other programs ranging from introductory, short-term courses to degree programs approved by the Council for National Academic Awards. The programs may meet external examination standards or be totally internal. Although polytechnics historically have offered a greater proportion of more advanced programs than institutes and colleges of technology, for North American readers the level and nature of the program, rather than where it is taught, is of prime importance.

Key Stages - The four stages identified by the National Curriculum, at the end of which students' progress is assessed.

LEA - Local Education Authority

LEAG - London and East Anglia Examining Group; one of the five examining groups for the GCSE.

Mature Applicant - An applicant for admission into an institution of higher education who, despite the fact that (s)he does not meet the stated admissions requirements, is eligible for consideration based on age. Usually, the minimum age for mature admission is 21; however, it sometimes is as high as 25.

MEG - Midland Examining Group; one of the five examining groups for the GCSE.

Membership - A relationship with a professional body which may take the form of Fellowship, Associateship, Student, etc. Depending on the professional body, the terminology for different levels of membership may vary.

National Council for Vocational Qualifications (NCVQ) - An organization which sets and monitors guidelines for vocational qualifications.

National Curriculum - A curriculum mandated by the Education Reform Act of 1988 which provides a uniform set of curriculums in 10 foundation subjects in England and Wales.

National Curriculum Council - An advisory body, established by the ERA in 1988, to advise schools in England and Wales, in 10 foundation subjects.

National or Group Awards (SCOTVEC) - A specific group of modules designed to provide competency in a specific area. If the qualification awarded consists solely of National Certificate modules, it will be called, for example, "National Certificate in Accounting/Business." If the qualification includes other types of modules, it might be called "Certificate in...." If it is awarded in collaboration with a specific industry, it might be called "Joint Certificate in...."

NEA - Northern Examining Association; one of the five examining groups for the GCSE.

Non-Advanced Further Education (NAFE) - Provided in Sixth Form colleges, tertiary colleges or other colleges of further education, serving, predominantly, those interested in entering the work force.

Ordinary Grade - In Scotland, a series of examinations taken usually at the end of the fourth year of secondary school (the eleventh year of 1 schooling); it has been replaced by the Standard Grade examinations.

Polytechnics. See Institutes and Colleges of Technology

Postgraduate - Academic work which generally requires a bachelor's degree or its equivalent for admission. Postgraduate programs may or may not be at a level higher than the anterior qualification.

Professional Qualifying Associations - Professional organizations which function both as learned societies and as the bodies that determine the requirements for practicing in the particular professions.

Qualification - A generic term in British education indicating a formally obtained educational attainment that prepares a person for further education, employment, etc.

Record of Education and Training (RET) - Started in 1990, the RET records all educational achievement within SCOTVEC's provision and will be awarded to anyone who has been successful in any SCOTVEC module or unit. It does not include the old (pre-1990) qualifications of HNC/HND, which were not modular.

Registration - Licensing; meeting the requirements for practicing a profession in the public sphere.

Regulated Professional Qualifications - Those professions in the United Kingdom which are regulated either by statute or common law.

Research Degrees - Advanced academic degrees which may be obtained mainly or solely through research. A major paper–a thesis or dissertation–which must be defended, usually is the basic requirement.

Royal Charter - A status granted to a professional organization by Her Majesty's Privy Council upon petition, after the Council has ascertained the reputation of the organization.

Sandwich Scheme - A pedagogic timetable used for the formal classroom component of higher level technical programs. This scheme consists of alternating periods of fulltime employment and fulltime class work (both the employment and the class work being in the same field). Usually, there is some articulation between the academic and practical training components.

Schools Examination and Assessment Council (SEAC) - A statutory body created in the 1988 Education Reform Act.

Scottish Vocational Qualifications (SVQs) - Similar to the British National Vocational Qualifications (NVQs), these qualifications for a particular occupational sector and the Certificate indicate SCOTVEC and the specific industry collaborating on the award.

Secondary Examinations Council (SEC) - Replaced by SEAC in 1988 (see above).

Secondary Modern School - A school introduced in 1944 whose intent was to provide a practical, applied, secondary school curriculum.

SEG - Southern Examining Group; one of the five examining groups for the GCSE.

Sixth Form College - A school offering a two-year curriculum which prepared students for the GCE A- and AS-level examinations. Other types of programs are offered also.

Standard Assessment Tasks (SATs) - Oral or written tests given at the end of each Key Stage of the National Curriculum.

Standard Grade - In Scotland, the examinations taken at the end of the fourth year of secondary school (eleventh year of total schooling); it replaced the Ordinary Grade examinations.

Student Membership - An entry level of membership in some professional societies requiring attendance in an approved training program. Student status usually leads to ordinary and/or associate membership (depending on the field) upon completion of appropriate formal training.

Taught Degrees - Advanced academic degrees which have classroom instruction as a major component of the academic program. This is distinguished from research degrees.

Technical and Vocational Education Initiative (TVEI) - An initiative to introduce technical and vocational education in the secondary curriculum, including a period of work experience.

Tertiary College - A school with a mission similar to the Sixth Form Colleges, but drawing students from a wider geographical area.

TGAT - Task Group on Assessment and Testing established to develop detailed recommendations on appropriate assessment methods for the National Certificate.

Unit-Based Certification - All students who are successful in one or more National Certificate modules have their achievement recorded on a single National Certificate, which is a cumulative record including all completed modules. From 1990 these modules have been certified on the new Record of Education and Training which will list National Certificate units, Higher National units, Work-Place-Assessed units, Scottish Vocational Qualifications (SVQs) and any national or industry Group Awards on one single RET. Previously, only the National Certificate units were listed.

Welsh Joint Education Committee - The GCSE examining group for Wales.

Work-Place Assessed Units - Competencies achieved in the workplace which are measured by SCOTVEC assessors based on industry-specified standards of competence within a specific occupational area. Each standard is compared in the workplace to a competency element that must be demonstrated by the person seeking the assessment to the assessor together with a set of performance criteria for each each competency element.

The glossary is based partially upon Chapter One, "An Up-Front Glossary," *United Kingdom: Medical Laboratory Science, Occupational Therapy, Physiotherapy* by Margolis and Monahan (1980).

I. STUDY ABROAD

Introduction

Until the 1980s, it was relatively easy to advise a U.S. student who wished to study in the United Kingdom. The U.K. higher education system was relatively uniform and it was possible to make generalizations with a reasonable degree of confidence. However, all sectors of higher education have undergone significant changes recently and appear to be on the threshold of even greater ones in the 1990s. Study abroad advisers and transfer credit evaluators need to understand how the system is changing for U.K. students to determine the most appropriate opportunities for U.S. students.

Two facts about information in this chapter need to be kept in mind: the material covers recent changes in higher education in England and Wales; Scotland is covered in chapter IV. "Higher education" is used to define universities, polytechnics and colleges/institutes of higher education; it does not refer to the colleges of further education which offer a wide range of programs including A-level preparation.

Traditionally education in England and Wales has four general characteristics:

1. The system was, and in many ways still is, elitist. Only the most talented proceed to higher education and the proportion of 18-year-olds doing so is still the lowest in Western Europe. In 1990 approximately 15% of 18-year-olds (a little over 500,000) entered higher education in the U.K.; the comparable figure in 1962 was 8.5% (200,000). In West Germany it is 28%.

2. The academic preparation and focus of students have been highly specialized, starting with a selection of Ordinary (O) and Advanced (A) levels, and continuing with a single honours degree–a concentration on one subject, with specialization increasing with each successive year of education. A single honours degree often required specific A-levels. Some specialization was required at O- level to ensure adequate preparation for A-levels.

3. University three-year degree programs were structured into year-long courses followed by degree exams in Year 3 and sometimes Year 2 as well.

4. Comprehensive exam results were the overwhelming determinant for the conferral and classification of degrees.

These realities set the standards for U.S. students interested in studying directly in U.K. universities and polytechnics. A prospective student had to be superior academically (at least a B average); able to focus on a single major subject rather than take a variety of subjects; and prepared to spend a full academic year in the U.K., taking end-of-year exams, in most cases, if offered.

For the student who qualified, it was relatively easy to arrange for a full year of study in the U.K. and for approval for transfer credit when the student returned to the home institution. However, many U.S. students were unable to or preferred not to go abroad for a full academic year for a combination of academic, financial and personal reasons. In light of these factors, until the late 1970s an increasing number of students studied in the U.K. on semester-based American college-sponsored study abroad programs rather than through direct enrollment (including direct reciprocal student exchange programs) in U.K. universities and polytechnics.

While this traditional divergence between the needs and interests of some U.S. students and the structure of the U.K. system was widely recognized, there was little concern about it in Britain until the Conservative government came to power in 1979, and introduced an economic policy to reduce inflation and increase the efficiency of British industry. In education, the government soon initiated a series of policies, two of which directly affected study abroad opportunities: budgets of universities were reduced over a period of several years; full-cost fees were introduced for overseas students, substantially raising the cost for degree as well as study abroad students.

The government allowed universities to obtain income from overseas students to offset their budget cuts. In fact, these policies prompted many U.K. institutions to become involved more actively in the North American study abroad market, albeit with wide differences in style, method, and intensity. This soon was followed by an emphasis on recruitment worldwide. Junior Year Abroad (JYA) offices were established, less than full-year study options were developed, a wider range of subjects was offered to prospective students and, in some instances, special programs were created by U.K. institutions for U.S. students which were not an integral part of the U.K. degree program.

American study abroad advisers, as well as those making transfer credit recommendations, responded in two ways. Many welcomed the changes and encouraged students to attend for less than a year on one- or two-term programs. Others were more cautious, questioning whether the visiting student would be assessed adequately or whether programs were being created especially for overseas students with standards of assessment different from those applied to regular courses offered to U.K. students. Many advisers feared that an option of less than one year prevented American students from experiencing fully the British approach to education which relies on year-end exams.

While many U.K. institutions created special options for American students in light of the financial pressure mentioned above, it soon became clear that there were other forces working to change U.K. secondary and higher education itself. For philosophical, political and economic reasons, British education underwent major changes in the 1980s and further major educational reforms are continuing in the 1990s.

This chapter discusses these educational changes and analyzes their potential impact on opportunities for American students. Since these educational reforms are still being developed and implemented, the conclusions are tentative. However, it appears that British degrees are becoming more flexible and diverse. Of particular interest are the development of modular programs offering term- or semester-based courses and utilizing more continuous assessment and the introduction of transfer credit schemes. U.S. students should increasingly be able to study in the U.K. for less then a full year and take part in the same educational program as the U.K. student.

The traditional British degree remains a dominant aspect of British higher education. It still will be relatively easy for students who wish to study for a full year in their major to find an appropriate placement in a British university or polytechnic. However, this chapter looks at the new opportunities that will potentially facilitate the placement of students who wish to study a somewhat wider range of subjects and participate in programs lasting less than a year.

The initial review focuses on the factors affecting change in U.K. higher education. Particular attention is given to the impact of these changes on the curriculum and pedagogy within U.K. degrees. The next section deals with central characteristics of the U.K. degree: its specialization, course structure and exams. It examines the U.K. degree as it has been and the changes that are now being implemented. Thus, the first two sections

focus on British education as it exists for British students. The last section provides suggestions on the best methods for advising and placing U.S. students in U.K. institutions based on the information and analysis of the first two sections.

Curricular and Pedagogic Changes in U.K. Higher Education, 1960 to Present

The Robbins Report of 1963 introduced two themes into U.K. higher education: higher education opportunities should be available to more school leavers, and such study should be more applicable to the needs of business and industry. The report recommended that colleges of advanced technology become universities, and that some degree work continue in the technical colleges. It also recognized the need for a degree-awarding and course-validating body and recommended the establishment of the Council for National Academic Awards (CNAA) to coordinate and oversee education in the nonuniversity sector of higher education, including the polytechnics and colleges of higher education. Robbins indicated that, "as an axiom, courses of higher education should be available for all those who are qualified...to pursue them and who wish to do so." The report was very firm in its belief that the expansion of higher education would not bring a lowering of standards.

These policies and recommendations were reinforced by the 1966 White Paper, *A Plan for Polytechnics and Other Colleges*, which suggested the creation of polytechnics as a separate and distinct sector of higher education; the incorporation, within the polytechnics, of fulltime, part-time and sandwich programs, both degree and nondegree; the introduction of curricular changes such as combined studies, accountability in curricula development, stated course objectives; an emphasis on applied research and technology; and finally an emphasis on local and regional cooperative arrangements between the 29 polytechnics and local industry. All of these contributed to a trebling of the number of students in higher education between 1950 and 1980, and the establishment of 20 universities and 30 polytechnics.

Another major influence on the increase of access to higher education and on the changing structure of degrees was the creation of the Open University (OU) in 1971. The Open University links radio and television instruction with residential tutorial services, awards its own degrees and offers admission without any specific entry requirement. In essence, OU created an opportunity for flexible part-time education unavailable previously in the U.K. It introduced both a degree built on credit modules that encouraged study in a wide range of subjects and the concept of responding to learning styles of nontraditional students (e.g., distance learning), which increased the acceptance of continuous assessment for much of the cumulative degree program. Many students wanted to use their OU credits in lieu of entrance qualifications to gain advanced standing for other more traditional degree programs. This led to an agreement between the OU and the CNAA in 1977 which provided a mechanism for transferring credit.

The creation of polytechnics and the Open University helped to introduce the concept of modular courses. Modules could be of less than a year's duration, contain more continuous assessment and result in less reliance on end-of-program degree exams.

In the late 1970s there was increased debate over education in the U.K., especially regarding secondary education. Prime Minister James Callaghan's Ruskin College speech (1976), calling for higher standards and an applied core curriculum to meet the needs of industry, led to what was called the Great Debate. In 1985 the Thatcher government produced a White Paper called *Better Schools* which led to the 1987 Education Act.

The movement to change secondary education produced three major reforms:

1. The General Certificate of Secondary Education (GCSE) examinations replaced the O-level and Certificate of Secondary Education (CSE) exams and emphasized the learning skills of numeracy, analysis and communication, with less reliance on facts. Students were expected to do project work, and continuous assessment formed a part of GCSE grades.

2. Advanced Supplemental (AS) exams were introduced and equated to half an Advanced-level exam, although at the same standard. The purpose of the AS exams was to encourage students to follow a broader range of courses.

3. A national curriculum was introduced requiring students to take a broader range of subjects and avoid the relatively high degree of secondary school specialization.

The first group of school leavers took the GCSE exams in 1988 and the AS-level in 1989. The first students to experience the full National Curriculum will graduate in the late 1990s. Currently, it is difficult to assess how fully these proposals will change secondary education and what additional reforms might be added or if the full national curriculum will be implemented. Nevertheless, the emphasis on skills development, a broader curriculum and the increased importance of continuous assessment are likely to significantly alter the kind of student entering higher education. Whether this will lead to wider use of a broad foundation year to create a less specialized degree and of modular courses and continuous assessment in higher education remains to be seen. Certainly, such approaches are being utilized increasingly in higher education.

Demographic Changes and Widening Access to Higher Education

There is much confusion over demographic changes and their effect on higher education. The Department of Education and Science's paper, *Higher Education into the 1990s*, first issued a warning about the effects of a demographic trough. Certainly the number of traditional-aged students is declining. The number of 18-year-olds already has declined by 10% since the early 1980s and is expected to drop an additional 20%-25% by the mid-1990s. This, however, is only half the story as universities will compete with employers who also will be more aggressively recruiting from this cohort.

The government has been concerned with this trend. One proposal suggests that a wider range of students must be attracted to higher education to make use of existing facilities. This view has given added impetus to those educators and government officials who think Britain must eliminate the elitism of the educational system by promoting greater access to higher education for mature students, women, minorities and working class youth. In 1989 the Secretary of State for Education called for a participation rate of 20% by 1995 and an increased rate of 30% (equalling 2,000,000 students) by the year 2000.

A second view holds that while the overall number of 18-year-olds is declining, a higher proportion is applying for higher education and the number of children from middle class families is not declining as rapidly as those from working class families. This argument suggests that demographic pressures may not be the cause of changes in higher education and that traditional entry requirements and degree programs will be maintained. As of 1990 this seems to be the case.

Access is a widely used term in U.K. higher education. The 1987 White Paper, *Meeting the Challenge*, defined access, first, as a philosophy for providing the means by which nontraditional students can enter higher education; and, second, as an Access Course specifically designed to provide nontraditional students with the skills to enter higher education. Access Courses, as defined by Professor M. Woodrow in 1988, are targeted towards groups traditionally underrepresented in higher education and are delivered by a process of collaboration between further and higher education. In many cases the course will be offered in the institution of further education but developed, delivered and monitored by staff in both institutions and offer clear progression to, not just preparation, for higher education (Wagner 1989, 33).

Attempts to create broader access to higher education have met with varying degrees of success by polytechnics, universities and colleges of higher education. The Polytechnics were founded, in part, to promote access to higher education. The demographic projections are giving some impetus to their efforts. In the 1980s fulltime enrollment in polytechnics increased nearly 40% while fulltime university enrollment rose by only 3%. Polytechnics also have a higher proportion of part-time students and fulltime women enrolled than the universities. See chapter III for more information on polytechnics and colleges/institutes of higher education. Universities in Scotland are discussed in chapter IV.

Historically, the polytechnics have been more assiduous than universities in their efforts to admit and provide for nontraditional entrants. They are the institutions developing modular structures that allow students to create more individualized programs, making part-time study more feasible. Half of the student population of 10,000 at Sheffield Polytechnic participate in sandwich courses. Part-time study, often designed to meet the professional training or retraining needs of local employers, is not completely absent, however, from the universities. The University of Warwick, for example, has 800 students in a distance learning MBA program, and also offers an MS in Engineering for students employed in industry.

Polytechnics and a few universities have introduced the "Associated Student Scheme" which provides individuals without formal, academic qualifications or recent educational experience with a chance to sample a module unit. Assessment is optional. For the student who elects to be assessed and is successful, this course can provide the basis for admission to a degree program and for credit accumulation. The idea of using experience, looking at the experiences of each individual outside the traditional educational setting as a guide to potential successful performance, is gaining ground.

The Credit Accumulation and Transfer Scheme (CATS) has contributed to the growth of the nonstandard entrant to higher education. Funded by the CNAA for an initial period of five years beginning October 1985, CATS was initiated to encourage and support the progress of nontraditional students; provide greater opportunities for continuing professional education; enable individual students to gain the maximum exemption for qualifications they already have; and allow students, through increased institutional flexibility, to put together programs to meet their own particular needs.

CATS establishes credit ratings of individual student qualifications; supports links between consortia of institutions to promote credit accumulation and continuing professional development (initially two types of consortia emerged: groups of institutions coming from the same geographic area and groups of institutions specializing in a common discipline); serves as an academic facilitator between higher education and the training needs of industry; and promotes continuing professional education.

Franchising, which has become an acceptable way to broaden access, can take two forms. A university or polytechnic validates a course or qualification at another institution, usually a further education college. The completion of the course, in some instances, leads to entrance to the institution of higher education. The second occurs when an institution of higher education enters into an agreement with a specific industrial firm whereby the institution offers a certificate or degree program specifically for the employees of that industrial firm (e.g., Portsmouth Polytechnic and ICI, Manchester Polytechnic and Sainsburys, and Lancaster University and British Airways).

The larger question is how and whether changing demographics will cause higher education as a whole, and universities in particular, to adapt curriculums, calendars and timetables, as well as teaching methods. There still is tremendous competition to enter higher education in the U.K. In 1989 Oxford Polytechnic received 27,000 applications for 1,500 places; 30% of the applicants for Manchester Medical School had four A grades at A-level. Also in that year the degree programs in English/American studies at Manchester University received 900 applications for 18 places.

Financing Higher Education

During the 1980s the government significantly cut its financial support to higher education. From 1980-81 to 1984-85 expenditures were reduced by about 3.5%, adjusted for inflation, although student enrollments increased approximately 10% within the polytechnics. A significant reduction of academic staff occurred: higher education lost one in seven teachers in universities and one in 12 teachers in the polytechnics and colleges (*The Development of Higher Education into the 1990s*, 1985, p. 39).

By the late 1980s, the government developed programs to reduce further its expenditure in higher education. The White Paper of 1987 had as one aim to make higher education institutions more efficient through the operation of market mechanisms. This approach was embodied in the Educational Reform Act of 1987 which removed polytechnics and most colleges of higher education from the control of local authority and replaced the National Advisory Body (NAB) for Public Sector Higher Education with a Polytechnics and Colleges Funding Council (PCFC). It also replaced the Universities Grants Committee (UGC) with the Universities Funding Council (UFC). These funding bodies were responsible for implementing a number of financial and educational objectives: encouraging institutions to attract contracts from other sources such as business as part of the goal of achieving greater commercial and industrial relevance in higher education; increasing accountability for the use of public funds; strengthening the commitment of institutions to deliver educational services; increasing the amount of funding brought in by student fees by raising the level of home country tuition while limiting funding from UFC and PCFC; and relating university and polytechnic funding levels to the successful performance of an institution in meeting stated objectives (e.g., in research). In addition, it abolished life tenured appointments for all new university academic appointments.

The government is pressuring institutions to accept more students. Since central funding is being cut, the government is allowing institutions to "bid" for more students. If they accept more students and at a lower price per capita than other institutions, they can compensate for the reduction in central funds by taking in sufficient numbers. This, however, means increasing class size and stretching resources for labs, advising and student services over a larger number of students.

In the autumn of 1988 the government introduced a loan scheme for students entering higher education in the fall of 1990. The proposal was to limit future maintenance grants (which covered students' living expenses) to those set for the 1988-89 academic year. As costs increased in future years, students would pay the differential themselves (Trythall). While there is some serious concern that the maintenance level of grants presently is insufficient, there is also concern that a system of loans might lead to increasing attrition after the start of a course; fewer minority and working class students; and a possible demand for, and move to, two-year degrees which could undermine educational quality.

The potential impact of these financial pressures on the institutions themselves could conceivably lead to mergers of universities, polytechnics and colleges to create economies of scale and to reduce duplication of programs. Some universities increasingly may become research institutions as a way of attracting grants from industry and government, leaving less distinction between the remaining universities and polytechnics. Market factors may make it increasingly difficult for institutions to teach a broad range of subjects if these subjects do not promise an immediate economic return to students. Increasing competition among universities and polytechnics for both traditional and nontraditional students may become prevalent, leading universities to develop more modular degrees which allow part-time study.

The European Factor

One of the principal objectives of "1992" is the creation of a single market within the European Economic Community (EEC) as of December 31. European cooperation exists in higher education and to a lesser extent in further and secondary education through the Community Action Program for Education and Training for Technology (COMETT) and European Community Action Scheme for the Mobility of University Students (ERASMUS) programs.

The COMETT program was adopted in July 1986 to encourage relations between business and higher education in the area of new technologies. It has five principal objectives (with 50% of the funding going to the second): the development of business/higher education networks for training; transnational exchanges of students and business personnel; development of joint business/higher education projects to promote continuing education; development of multilateral initiatives to perfect training in multimedia systems (satellite, radio, computers, etc.); and establishment of information and evaluation systems to promote the COMETT program.

The ERASMUS program was initiated formally in June 1987 to promote student and faculty exchanges among the EEC universities and schools of advanced study by encouraging them to identify common programs and allowing students to pursue their studies equally and without penalty in all EEC institutions. Its objectives include establishing a European higher education network with financial aid to students who spend a recognized period of study–normally three to 12 months–in another EEC country; providing scholarships for travel and language preparation; assisting in developing conferences, publications and inter-university cooperation in the EEC; and supporting the European Community Course Credit Transfer System (ECTS).

ECTS was introduced as a pilot project for six years in 1989. The scheme allows students at some 80 universities and other higher education institutions (including some in the U.K.) to study in more than one country and still obtain their degree in the recognized time period through a system of transfer of course units.

Conclusion

Many of the trends mentioned above will have a significant effect on the way education is presented. Taken together, they are of interest and probable benefit to U.S. students planning to study in the U.K. Due to changes in the secondary curriculum, students will be accustomed to a broader curriculum and the use of continuous assessment. Greater access to the system for nontraditional students is likely to produce a challenge to the traditional year-long courses. Modular structures, in whatever form, will increase student choice, part-time study, and course offerings of less than a year's duration. Within courses, there is likely to be a similar challenge to the comprehensive final exam. With a system that is providing for the needs of part-time students, as well as forging linkages with industry and exchanges with European institutions, it is likely that some form of continuous assessment will increase noticeably.

Curricular and Pedagogic Issues

Data for this section are based on questionnaires sent to universities and to polytechnics and colleges of higher education that are members of CAPTEC (Colleges and Polytechnics Transatlantic Exchange Committee) as well as interviews in March and April 1990 with administrators and faculty at selected institutions.

The following responses to the questionnaire from a polytechnic serve as an example of the changes that are occurring in U.K. higher education. At the same time, the answers indicate that traditional values still are very much evident. In answer to a question concerning changing age groups and traditional methods of evaluation, the respondent made three very revealing statements:

- Combined studies will be available but generally students will opt for degree programs specifically in one or two subjects--a single or joint honours degree;

- There will be more continuous assessment, but traditional exams will remain very important;

- More modularity will occur but there will not be the "cafeteria" selection process as exists in the U.S.

Specialization

Historically, students specialized by the age of 16 when they began to study for A-level exams. For entry into many courses in higher education, specifically in mathematics, the sciences, and engineering, students had to complete specific A-level courses. In contrast, for some subjects (e.g., anthropology, business, politics, sociology and psychology), students had to complete two or three nonspecific A-levels to gain admission.

The A-level still dominates entry to higher education. In the early 1980s, approximately 90% of those obtaining university degrees and close to 75% obtaining CNAA degrees had two or more A-levels on entry. Even among mature students the figures were remarkable: 95% of mature students in universities, 83% of those in polytechnics and 77% of Open University students had A-level qualifications. However, various changes within the U.K. educational system are likely to have an impact on the A-level courses and exams.

The abolition of O-levels and the introduction of the GCSE have changed secondary education greatly. Students are taking a broader range of subjects. Emphasis is placed on skills development and the study of applied subjects; continuous assessment is being introduced widely. These changes are detailed in the chapter on secondary education. It is critical to note that secondary students now will follow a broader, less specialized, program. As these students pursue A-levels, there will be pressure to reform the A-levels to match the curricular and pedagogical approaches of the GCSE.

The 1988 Higginson Report recognized that, as single honors subjects cease to be the norm in higher education, and as secondary education is changing, the A-level becomes a problem reflecting neither the developments going on below it or above it (Wagner 1989, 32). Hence, there is an increasing acceptance of qualifications other than A-levels. Both universities and polytechnics are willing to accept access qualifications often taught by further education colleges linked to universities and polytechnics in the local region and validated by the accepting institution. However, this route to entrance into higher education may be more prevalent in the nonuniversity sector.

One change affecting A-levels is the introduction of AS-levels in 1987. The first examinations were held in 1989, alongside traditional A-levels, and both systems will operate side by side. AS exams, introduced to broaden the curriculums of 17- and 18-year-olds, are of the same standard as A-levels but require half the teaching and learning time, and are aimed at allowing A-level students to broaden their studies through a choice of contrasting AS-levels (English for science students) or by complementing other subjects (adding a language for humanities).

Whether students will in fact use AS-levels to broaden their studies remains to be seen. What is important is the response to AS-levels by the higher education selection process, especially in the universities. Institutions of higher education equate two AS-levels with one A-level such that certain prerequisites for university study can be met by AS exams. For example, at Essex University some mathematics and language requirements now can be satisfied by AS-levels instead of A-levels. This approach underscores the central issue with AS-levels: what effect will these new qualifications have on the curriculums in higher education? Essex, for example, is undergoing curricular review to ensure that students with various educational backgrounds can benefit equally from the institution's courses.

One of the effects of a changing secondary system is in foundation/introductory year programs. Some of these programs add a year to the degree but are not part of the degree program itself. These programs help students bridge the gap between prior academic learning and university-level work. Other programs do not add a year to the degree but allow a student to choose which degree to pursue from an initial year's study, usually of three subjects. Some newer universities (e.g., Keele, Lancaster) have introduced broad-based first-year programs consisting of a number of courses.

A similar change is evidenced in Combined or Joint Honours degrees whereby a student takes a program of study in two or more major subjects. Such changes indicate more fluidity and greater flexibility in the system. In many institutions there is increasing support for students who take courses outside their major department. While traditionally the second and third years have been specialized, there now appears to be a trend towards combined studies. "Most undergraduates," reported one institution, "are required to attend and pass examinations in some subject other than that indicated by the title of their honours programme." Another reported that students are "increasingly being encouraged to acquire computing skills and competence in a second language." However a cautionary note should be added: in many instances, the "other subjects" are closely allied to the major.

Whether the impetus for these changes is internal or a response to external forces, a number of institutions are encouraging cross-disciplinary programs. Even if these fall short of the general education requirements found in U.S. institutions, U.S. students can more readily pursue studies in the U.K. beyond their major/minor as British students have the option to pursue a broader curriculum.

Year-Long Courses and Exams

The structure of courses into year-long units and the examination system are interrelated phenomena. While year-long courses with end-of-year exams remain the dominant pattern, especially in universities, there are significant exceptions.

Traditionally, the vast majority of courses are taught through the full academic year with a course beginning in October and ending in June. Each course runs through three terms, each approximately 10 weeks long. Terms I and II tend to be teaching terms while Term III can vary between further lectures, review of the course material, or revision for exams. Differences occur in Term III depending on the year of study as degree exams usually are given at the end of the third year. Thus, Term III of the second year might consist of more teaching than in Year Three.

Degree classifications–First, Upper Second, Lower Second, Third, or Pass–are determined in a variety of ways. For most students the heaviest weight is placed on performance in degree exams. These may come only at the end of the third year, some may be taken after the second year and the remainder after Year Three. In only a few institutions are the first-year exams counted. The following examples illustrate these patterns and are just a sample of the many responses to the questionnaire that strongly indicated the wide variety in the relative importance of the final exam.

UNIVERSITY OF BRISTOL: 80%-90% of degree classification is based on exams; 60% of the total is based on third-year exams.

UNIVERSITY OF ESSEX: In Chemistry, 80% of degree classification is based on exams while in History and Literature, only 45% is based on exams.

HUMBERSIDE POLYTECHNIC: 60% by exams with 70% weighted toward year three.

KINGSTON POLYTECHNIC: 80% by exams with 70% weighted toward year three.

The UNIVERSITY OF NEWCASTLE responded that "degree classification is based on the results of written examinations taken at the end of the final year, although other elements also contribute to the final classification. These elements vary...but typically include the results of written examinations taken at the end of the second year, the marks obtained for submitted course work, and the mark obtained for dissertation."

Final examinations, especially in the arts and sciences, are typically of three hours duration for each course and require students to write three or four essays from a selection of up to 15. Exams are graded by at least two faculty members, often a third, and a selection of exams is marked by an outside examiner (except at Oxford and Cambridge) whose role is to ensure that the grades at one institution are comparable to those at another institution.

In the U.S., students graduate by accumulating credits for each course. The faculty member is the sole determiner of the grade and provides clear guidelines on course content, readings, exams, and projects. In the U.K., students are graded on their knowledge of an entire program of study. The instructor is never the sole determiner of a final grade. Furthermore, in the arts and humanities, as opposed to the sciences, there is not a set body of knowledge to be studied and assessed. Given that there is a wide choice of questions on the exams, students are allowed to select what they will read and study. Lectures and tutorials cover key topics; faculty do not concern themselves with ensuring that students are keeping up with their work.

The importance of this is that it is the prevalent form of assessment which has conditioned alternative methods. Changes in assessment, especially in the universities, merely are variations of this traditional system. Continuous assessment, as a truly innovative alternative to the traditional system, presents issues of its own. How much continuous assessment should there be in degree classification? Degree exams are still the dominant form of assessment in most universities and polytechnics; however, with increasing interest in older students, many institutions find that mature students learn better with a more continuous form of assessment. The move to modular courses, described in the next section, is also increasing the interest in continuous assessment; however, institutions define continuous assessment differently.

Many institutions assign essays and projects to students throughout the course. However, in many cases the marks count only minimally in the final grade for the course as a part of the degree classification. These approaches to continuous assessment have little impact on how courses are taught. Yet, increasingly, continuous assessment is playing a more important role in degree classification. Where this occurs, faculty give students more specific course requirements and feedback. Students are forced to keep up with their work and cannot wait until the end of Term II to cram for exams in Term III. For example, Essex University's courses in arts consist of 50% continuous assessment; Sunderland Polytechnic's courses are 40% continuously assessed; and at Sheffield Polytechnic, there is an element in each course that is continuously assessed. This is not to indicate that institutions always are consistent internally about their application of continuous assessment.

Modularity

In U.K. higher education, continuous assessment is related to modular programs. Previously described changes in the system have made it increasingly important to offer programs consisting of independent units that are assessed separately. This is important for part-time, older students and for European students who may come to the U.K. as part of the ERASMUS scheme. Modular courses also help institutions create economies of scale. Since courses are broken into smaller components, institutions can allow some units to be taught in large classes but retain tutorials in other parts of the course. Some units, such as sociology and psychology, also can be taught as a common core for students in different disciplines.

The CNAA defines a module as a "self-contained block or unit of study which has a standard size or some method of agreeing on a standard value. Each module has specified prerequisites and distinct aims and objectives and is assessed and examined separately, normally during and immediately following its completion."

Oxford Polytechnic offers a highly developed modular degree program. Other institutions having extensive modular programs are City of London Polytechnic and Middlesex Polytechnic. In the publication, *Managing The Modular Course: Perspectives From Oxford Polytechnic*, David Watson explains the notion of a modular degree.

1. Credit Accumulation: Students may achieve passes in individual modules which will lead to a specific degree or award. "Frequently the student will study these modules alongside students with other qualification aims [in terms of both title (of award) and level (of study)]";

2. Progressive Assessment: Credit accumulated as passes in individual modules are built up progressively towards a final award. External examiners also evaluate modular progress. In such a system of credit accumulation, it is possible for part-time students to build towards an award in the same way as a fulltime student and to make frequent adjustments to their programs as interests and abilities develop;

3. Responsibility and Choice: Students can choose subjects to study; qualifications at which to aim; a choice of modules within a subject or field; and selected modules from other subjects to complete the requirements for the award.

Thus far, the greatest momentum for modular programs has occurred in the polytechnics and colleges, which were developed in part to create wider access to higher education. It is logical that they would have experimented first.

If the idea of modular units prevails and if final year exams lose their significance, then the concept of credit accumulation can gain wider acceptance. The CNAA CAT Scheme has established credit quantification in which one year's work is equivalent to 120 credits and a three-year degree is equivalent to 360 credits.

Even within the universities there has been some move towards modularity. In November 1989, seven universities (Bradford, Brunel, City, Keele, Sheffield, Warwick and Oxford's Department of External Studies) agreed to take part in the CAT Scheme by dividing their courses into modular units. Other universities are considering modular programs. As the *Times Higher Education Supplement* reported about the decision of the seven universities:

"Students will be able to register with a single university but also to attend and obtain credits for courses taken elsewhere...Under the scheme...these institutions (can) liaise with CATS about admitting students into the second or third year of a degree course taking account of points already earned by following courses elsewhere. Universities will also allocate credit ratings to their own courses."

While more institutions are creating module units, these are not necessarily modular programs involving greater student choice and responsibility. For example, some institutions may label all second- and third-year courses as modules. Students, however, may not be given a greater choice in the units they may take and may still be assessed with the typical second- and third-year degree exams.

The concept of building credits also is gaining ground in part because of ERASMUS, as visiting students will need to have their work quantified and assessed so that their work can be recognized by their home institutions. Another credit program is being created as part of ERASMUS. The European Community Course Credit Transfer Scheme (ECTS) works on the basis of 60 credits per year of work. The CAT Scheme and ECTS can be made compatible by multiplying ECTS credits by 2 to get CATS credits. Document 1.1 is an example of a proposed ECTS transcript. Under the leadership of CATS two large consortiums have been created to enable students to transfer work from one institution to another.

SOUTH EAST ENGLAND CONSORTIUM

Brighton Polytechnic
Cambridgeshire College of Art and Technology
City of London Polytechnic
Ealing College of Higher Education

Essex Institute of Higher Education
Harrow College of Higher Education
Hatfield Polytechnic
Hillcroft College
Middlesex Polytechnic
North East London Polytechnic
Oxford Polytechnic
Polytechnic of Central London
Polytechnic of North London
Portsmouth Polytechnic
Thames Polytechnic
West London Institute of Higher Education

MIDLANDS CONSORTIUM

Birmingham Polytechnic
Coventry Polytechnic
Derbyshire College of Higher Education
Harper Adams Agricultural College
Leicester Polytechnic
Loughborough College of Art and Design
Nottingham Polytechnic
Staffordshire Polytechnic
Wolverhampton Polytechnic

If there is a move to modularity, the programs are likely to contain these elements:

1. Most modular schemes will divide a degree into component parts that will be independently assessed. Thus, final year exams will become less common.

2. The role of external examiners will change as they will no longer be needed to assess end-of-year exams. If the examiner is retained to assess individual modules, financial and logistical as well as educational problems are likely to develop.

3. Units will be given credit values as with CATS and ECTS. A trial program called the Educational Counselling and Credit Transfer Information Service (EC-CTIS, PO Box 88, Walton Hall, Milton Keynes MK7 6DB, ENGLAND) will consolidate information on credit values for all U.K. institutions which will help students know to which institution they can transfer work.

4. While modular courses may give students greater flexibility to design an individualized academic program, that choice probably will be limited within carefully defined guidelines. Thus the U.S. concept of university general requirements and electives probably will not be an outcome.

5. More courses are likely to be offered on a semester or term basis; however, patterns will vary greatly.

6. With the division of degree programs into smaller units, more continuous assessment will probably be introduced.

U.S. Students Studying in the U.K.

Study abroad advisers or transfer credit evaluators who have a traditional view of U.K. higher education are likely to be surprised by the extent of change. A description of these changes provides the context and relevancy for the advice and recommendations given in this section. The guidance offered to study abroad advisers is based on generalizations, for which many exceptions exist, especially in light of the dynamic changes in U.K. education. The remainder of this section addresses the most important issues for U.S. students planning to study in the United Kingdom.

Factors Determining Institution Type

The majority of American students attend a relatively small number of U.K. institutions. Advisers should be familiar with the broader range and diversity of U.K. institutions and be aware of the following.

First, Oxbridge and the older universities are most likely to follow the traditional pattern of year-long courses and comprehensive exams. While it is difficult to be exact, "older universities" in England and Wales include Oxford, Cambridge, Birmingham, Bristol, Durham, Leeds, Liverpool, London, Manchester, Nottingham, Sheffield and some colleges of the University of Wales. Age, however, does not always equate with traditional educational practices.

Second, newer universities and the technical universities are more likely to offer flexible degree programs with foundation year courses and to experiment more with modular structures and continuous assessment. Technical universities also offer more applied subjects which may include internships.

Examples of newer and technical universities are, respectively, Bradford, Essex, Kent, Lancaster, Keele, East Anglia, Stirling, Surrey, Sussex; and Bath, Aston, Salford, Strathclyde, and Heriot-Watt.

Third, the Scottish system of education differs from that of England and Wales (see Chapter IV, Scotland). However, it is safe to say that four-year degrees and a broader-based first year are common in Scotland.

Example of a transcript of records with additional ECTS grading scale (supplement to 4.5.)

University of . . . .
Address . . . .
. . . .
Tel . . . .
Tlx . . . .   Department of History
Fax . . . . '. . . . . . .   *Transcript of Records*

Grading System

A (+ or −) excellent
B (+ or −) good
C (+ or −) satisfactory
D (+ or −) fair (lowest passing grade)

F   failure

ECTS Grading Scale

1 = top 25% of succesful students
2 = second quarter of succesful students
3 = third quarter of succesful students
4 = fourth quarter of succesful students

Student: MILLER James
Birth date: 03 09 1967
Address: 65 Moon Crescent, London, SW2A 4GM
Entrance qualifications: A-levels History/ English/ German (1985)
Institutions attended: —
Degrees held: —
Matriculation date: 01 09 1985
Matriculation number: 85-265

Course	Number	Short title of course	Taken in	Grade	ECTS credits	ECTS grading scale	Examinations taken
UK-LSUD 1	Hist 111	Introduction to History	1/2/3 1985/86	B+	6	1	
UK-LSUD 1	Hist 121	British historians	1 1985/86	C	2	3	
UK-LSUD 1	Phil 101	Philosophy	1/2/3 1985/86	A−	6	1	Title of
UK-LSUD 1	Lat 131	University Latin I	1/2/3 1985/86	A	6	1	thesis
UK-LSUD 1	ArHi 142	Art History I	1 1985/86	C	2	3	
UK-LSUD 1	SoHi 134	Introduction Social Hist	2 1985/86	C−	2	4	
UK-LSUD 1	MeHi 136	Medieval History	3 1985/86	C	2	3	Diplomas
UK-LSUD 1	AnHi 126	Ancient History	1 1985/86	C	2	3	awarded
	Hist 112		2/3 1985/86	B	4	2	
	Hist 113		2/3 1985/86	B−	4	2	
	Germ 201		1/2/3 1985/86	A−	6	1	Degrees
	Germ 202		1/2 1985/86	B+	4	1	awarded
	Hist 122		1/2/3 1985/86	B	6	2	
	SoHi 132		3 1985/86	A	2	1	ECTS credits
	PhEd 111		1/2/3 1985/86	B−	6	2	First year 60
					60	30	Second year
							Third year
							Fourth year
							Fifth year

Date: Signature of registrar/administration officer: Stamp of institution

Document 1.1. European Community Course Credit Transfer System Transcript

Fourth, the polytechnics and colleges historically have been neglected as a study abroad option despite the assurance of academic quality through CNAA accreditation. Many of these institutions are responding quickly to the pressures for modular programs and offer an excellent opportunity for North American students.

Background Needed by U.S. Students

If a specific A-level is required prior to beginning the study of a subject, the U.S. student should have the equivalent of a two-semester sequence course at freshman level. This generally would be true in mathematics, physics, chemistry, most other sciences, appropriate pre-engineering courses, languages and economics. If an institution is trying to expand language study in response to opportunities under ERASMUS, there might be increasing possibilities for beginning language study. In subjects that do not require specific A-levels– for example, the social sciences, business and the humanities--beginning study is possible.

Role of Exams

U.S. students should be required to take any available end-of-year exams. If study abroad students are exempt from the final exams, there is no way of knowing if they are doing less work than their U.K. counterparts. This consideration is increasingly important as U.K. institutions adapt their programs to meet study abroad students' needs.

In an absence of final exams, two items need to be examined. First, in the specific course the student hopes to take, is continuous assessment, a significant element in the final degree classification for U.K. students? If it is, there is a greater likelihood that the student will be doing the appropriate amount of work. However, it is important to note that in some departments continuous assessment in the form of essays is used primarily to give students feedback and may not carry much weight in degree classification, as the final exam still is the most important factor.

There are a number of questions that need to be asked. What is the exact role and scope of continuous assessment in the department and institution a student plans to attend? If a student goes to an institution or department which has no, or limited, continuous assessment and does not stay to take the end-of-course exams,

how and by what standard is this student assessed in the U.K.? American institutions should be looking for the same assessment that is offered to a U.K. student. Second, if continuous assessment is not part of the final course classification, are special assessment arrangements possible for a student who does not take the final exam? While take-home essays may be graded, some type of unseen exam is needed to approximate the degree exams. Some universities set up special unseen exams that are graded by committees, thus mirroring the process and standards used for U.K. students.

It is possible to get evaluative comments from the tutor that reflect a student's progress in terms of U.K. expectations. These are good supplemental comments but are not a prime basis for judgment.

Term or Semester Options

There is widespread agreement that a full year at a U.K. institution offers a more complete experience, giving the student time to adjust to the different expectations of British faculty and to the academic and social climate. Therefore, a semester-based U.K. institution, or a Term II and Term III option (where Term III is predominantly a teaching term), presents the best options, that is, ones which would enable a student to attend 15 to 20 weeks of study.

Semester-Based Institutions. With the move to modularity more institutions will be developing semester-based programs. Listed below are those institutions having semester-based programs for at least part of their degrees as of Spring 1991. Study abroad advisers should inquire whether a semester-based program is designed for U.K. students or just for U.S. students.

University of Aberdeen
Brighton Polytechnic
Polytechnic of Central London
City of London Polytechnic
Hatfield Polytechnic
Middlesex Polytechnic
Oxford Polytechnic
Queen Mary College, University of London
Stirling University
University of Strathclyde
Thames Polytechnic
University of Wales-Bangor

A semester calendar divides the academic year into two terms of roughly 15 weeks each. These semesters run from October to February and from February to

June, with vacations at Christmas and Easter. Many institutions give final assessment at the end of each semester but some hold exams only at the end of the year.

Even if an institution has a semester-based program, it does not mean that the American student stays the whole 15 weeks and takes the normal British exams. Several institutions allow students to leave by Christmas, thus cutting the length of study, or before the exams are given at the end of spring semester. It is recommended that students be required to stay the full semester.

Term I Programs. Each U.S. institution must decide how valuable it is to have a student study for Term I only, since it is 10 weeks in length.

Term II and III Programs. Prior to approving a Term II and Term III program, a study abroad adviser should ask the U.K. Junior Year Abroad Office whether Term III is a teaching term, rather than a period when students prepare for exams. It is not possible to list institutions where Term III is predominantly a teaching term as this often varies among departments within an institution. If a student wishes to attend Terms II and III, advisers must assess how easy it will be to enter a course that is already in progress.

Additional inquiries on assessment procedures should be addressed to the Junior Year Abroad Office at the institution. In general, American students should be evaluated under the same or similar procedures used to determine degree classifications of U.K. students. Unless continuous assessment is a significant part of degree classification, unseen exams are the major quality control of students' work and the pressure that keeps the workload of U.K. students appropriately rigorous. Therefore unless continuous assessment is a significant portion of the U.K. student's degree classification, whenever possible the U.S. student should be faced with unseen exams which are the same as those set for U.K. students. If this is not possible, special unseen exams should be available. Given the move to modularity, continuous assessment and the administration of more frequent unseen exams are likely to be made a part of many U.K. programs. Thus, some U.K. institutions will be able to provide these forms of assessment more readily.

Transfer Credit

Regular courses taken at a U.K. university, CNAA-accredited institution or one participating in a CNAA-validated program should be considered for transfer credit. Evaluators must address the method by which assessment is reported, the number of credits granted, and the comparability of grades between the U.K. and U.S. systems.

The transcript, in the U.S. sense, has not been common in the U.K. However, the move to modular programs will necessitate some form of transcript. Some institutions within CATS and ECTS already are issuing transcripts. Many U.K. institutions also prepare a transcript-like document for study abroad students which provides information such as the name of the course, grade for the course with an explanation of the U.K. institution's grading system, the institution's interpretation of the British grade in terms of U.S. grading, and comments from the instructor. Documents 1.2 and 1.3 are examples of study abroad transcripts. Note that the conversion charts on the transcripts have been created by the institutions for U.S. study abroad students.

Quantifying Credits and Contact Hours

Contact hours cannot be equated with credits as is the common practice in the U.S. as the concept is not part of the U.K. system. U.K. students are expected to do considerable out-of-class study to prepare for exams or term essays. Typically there is more out-of-class preparation in the U.K. than in the U.S. For example, at Sheffield University, a year-long class meeting for a two-hour lecture and a two-hour tutorial weekly might constitute half of the student's fulltime load. In other words, much of a U.K. student's time is devoted to independent study and exam preparation (even if the program is modular). However, U.S. evaluators should not be concerned about contact hours as long as the study abroad student is assessed in the same manner as the U.K. student.

A more appropriate method for assigning credits is to determine the percentage of a fulltime load that a course represents. An evaluator can then define the normal credit load for a student at the U.S. institution and calculate the transfer credits. For example, if 32 credits is the normal credit load at the American institution and a student takes a U.K. course that is one fourth the fulltime U.K. course load, then the U.K. course equals 8 credits (.25 x 32 credits = 8 credits). However, with the increase in modular programs and the introduction of credit accumulation (through CATS and ERASMUS/ECTS), more U.K. institutions will become familiar with assigning credit units. These credit units will indicate the relative weight of a course as a proportion of a fulltime load. For example, under CATS, each year's work is assigned a total of 120 credits. Consequently, 1 U.S. semester credit equals approximately 4 CATS credits or units. Under the ECTS scheme, each year's work is assigned a total of 60 credits. Thus, 1 U.S. semester credit approximates 2 ECTS credits.

Comparability of Grades

A great deal has been written comparing U.K. and U.S. grades. David Rex and Tom Roberts (1986) articulated the process by which grades are determined in the U.K. and how this might be translated into U.S. credit grades. Most U.K. students study for honours degrees. The designation "honours" has two meanings. First, it refers to a course of study specializing in a subject. This may be single honours or a joint or combined honours, focusing on two or, in some combined honours programs, three subjects. Second, it refers to the attainment of a certain level of quality of performance. A student may receive a First, Upper Second, Lower Second or Third Class Honours Degree. The student who follows an honours curriculum, but scores below Third Class, receives a Pass degree or Ordinary degree. Below this is a fail and no degree is awarded.

The distribution of classification by percentage of students receiving each class of degree provides an indication of grade comparability. U.K. higher education currently offers admission to the top 15% of an age cohort. This represents a student population comparable to most selective American institutions. Listed below is the percentage of U.K. students receiving each classification based on 1988 degree results provided by CNAA through its Transbinary Student Database.

CLASSIFICATION

U.K.	% Receiving	
	CNAA	University
First Class	4	8
Upper Second	31	38
Lower Second	40	33
Third Class	6	8
Pass/Non-Honours	19	12

No recommendation is given equating U.K. grades with U.S. grades. Since U.S. grades vary in meaning, depending on the institution awarding the grade, the above data should enable U.S. institutions to determine grade comparabilities based on the U.S. school's own selectivity in admission and grade distribution policy or practice.

There is no U.K. grade of D in the American sense of the term. In the U.S. a student must have a C average to receive a degree. A Pass classification which still leads to the conferral of a degree (though not an honours degree), is comparable to the lowest C for which a student can still receive a degree in the U.S. Most Pass degrees are awarded within a non-honours program. In 1988, for example, 17% of CNAA degrees were Pass degrees awarded to students within non-honours programs. Thus, only a small percentage of CNAA non-honours degrees is awarded to students in honours programs who receive such low results as to receive a Pass degree. In 1988 only 2% of CNAA degrees were Pass degrees awarded to students pursuing honours programs.

Conclusion

The above guidelines should enable advisers to better counsel students about opportunities in the U.K. These guidelines also enable those responsible for transfer credit to specify what the North American student must do to gain the academic experience comparable to that of U.K. students.

However, these guidelines should be applied with an understanding of the increasingly diverse U.K. educational system. The chapters on secondary education, polytechnics and colleges of higher education, and Scotland describe the changes more fully. While it is difficult to speculate where U.K. higher education is heading, there is no doubt that the traditional generalizations are no longer universally valid. Modular programs, credit transfer, access opportunities, continuous assessment, European links and other developments are leading to a system that will offer greater opportunities for study abroad students to enter directly in the system and experience what a U.K. student experiences.

Middlesex Polytechnic

TRANSCRIPT OF ACADEMIC RECORD: Academic Year 1989/90
                                   SEMESTER 1

Surname:

Given name(s):

Student Number (UK):   971336

Student Number (US):   049-64-6236

Home Institution: University of Rhode Island

Course Code	Course Title	*Grade (UK)	*Grade (USA)	Credit(Unit)
SS325	Issues in Contemporary Social Structure	C 14	C	4
ED310	Education and Values	B1 6	A	4
ED360	Children, Education and the Law	B1 8	A-	4

I certify that the above details of courses and grades as given are correct for the above-named student who was registered as a full-time study-abroad/exchange student at this institution.

....
Coordinator of Overseas Students' Programmes   Date

*For conversion chart please see overleaf

Document 1.2a. Academic Transcript, Middlesex Polytechnic

Note: This page shows Middlesex Polytechnic's own grade conversion chart.

<u>GRADE CONVERSION CHART</u>

UK letter grade		UK numerical grade	UK%	USA letter grade
		1	80+	
First class honours	A	2	75-79	
		3	71-74	A
		4	70	
		5	67-69	
Second class honours First division	B1	6	64-66	
		7	61-63	A-
		8	60	
		9	57-59	B+
Second class honours Second division	B2	10	54-56	B
		11	51-53	
		12	50	B-
		13	48-49	C+
Third class honours	C	14	45-47	C
		15	42-44	C-
Pass	D	16	38-41	D
		17	34-37	
		18	30-33	
Fail	F	19	21-29	F
		20	0-20	
Incomplete	I			I
Withdrew from course	W/D			W/D

Document 1.2b. page 2

University of
LANCASTER
North American Office

S A M P L E

University House, Lancaster, United Kingdom LA1 4YW
Telephone: (0524) 65201 Telex: 65111 Lancul G

Name of Student:
Home address:
Date of Birth:

Home School:
Year: Terms attended:

I hereby certify that the above-named was registered as a student at the University of Lancaster for the period stated. The courses taken, and grades awarded, are shown below. Students are recommended to undertake a workload of no more than 32 credits for a full year's work, and pro rata for shorter periods. Term dates:
Michaelmas (M) -   Lent (L) -
Summer (S) -

Course No. and Title	Terms	Grade	% Mark	Recommended Credit	Class Size	Position
CHEM 102 Organic Chemistry	MLS	A	82 -	8	82	= 2
HIST 255 Europe 1815 0 1914	M	B	57	4		
PHIL 201 Philosophy in the 17th and 18th Centuries	ML	B+	63	6	8	Top ¼
R.ST 233 Life of Muhammed	L	C	48	4	10	Below av.
SOCL 101 Introduction to Sociology	M	B	55	4	43	34
IND. ST Please see the attached samples:						
How the nature of self-help literature reflects the changing definition of success in the United States	S	A-	67	4		
Experiments with luminous bacteria	S	A	85	6		

Please see second sheet for tutor's comments and grading system

S. A. C. LAMLEY

Document 1.3a. Transcript, University of Lancaster, North American Office

S A M P L E

Continuation sheet for ----------------------   (Name of University)

TUTORS' COMMENTS:

CHEM 102
An outstanding performance; the student did not find the subject easy but intelligent application
and enthusiasm have earned this excellent result. Assessment on coursework and examination.

HIST 255
Conscientious and interested; the student contributed well and purposefully; wrote well and
showed genuine interest. The written work was clear and concise although somewhat light in
substance.

PHIL 201
The student worked diligently and the written assignments gave evidence of wide reading.
Assessment based on coursework.

R.ST 233
The written work was very superficial, error-ridden and clearly assembled in haste. Lectures
were missed which would have allowed the student to avoid certain errors.

SOCL 101
Conscientious student; regular attender. Quiet at first, but contributed later as confidence grew.
Given unfamiliarity with system the marks were good. Assessment based on coursework.

IND.ST
Please see the attached report.

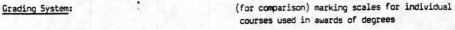

Grading System:		(for comparison) marking scales for individual courses used in awards of degrees	
A	70% or higher	1st class	70% or higher
A-	65 - 69%	2nd class div. 1	60 - 69%
B+	60 - 64%	2nd class div. 2	50 - 59%
B	55 - 59%	3rd class	40 - 49%
B-	50 - 54%	Pass (not Honours)	35 - 39%
C	40 - 49%	Fail	below 35%
D	35 - 39%		
F	below 35%		

Document 1.3b. page 2 with Tutor's Comments, grading system and marking scales

II. SECONDARY EDUCATION

Introduction

The Education Reform Act 1988 (ERA) was a major landmark in the history of secondary education, reminiscent of the impact made by the 1944 Education Act. In order to clarify the development of secondary education up to 1988, a brief review of the major changes which have occurred as a result of the 1944 Act and subsequent reforms follows.

The major impact of the 1944 Act was the introduction of universal free secondary education. Until then, only primary (elementary) education was free, although with the raising of the school leaving age to 14 in 1902, a form of extended elementary education already existed. Students paid tuition to attend the state maintained secondary schools, known as grammar schools, although some scholarships were available for those who passed a special examination.

The 1944 Act swept all this away. Education through the first six years of schooling was designated as primary education and all school children then moved on to four more years of free compulsory education called secondary education. The legal school leaving age was raised to 15.

Although the 1944 Education Act was promulgated by the wartime coalition government, it enjoyed the support both of the Labour and the Conservative parties in the post-war period, and successive governments strove to implement it. Prior to the 1944 Act, a series of influential reports, the Haddow Reports of 1926 and 1931, the Spens Report of 1938 and the Norwood Report of 1943, had advanced the idea that secondary education should have several tracks. This thinking was based on the theory held by some educational psychologists that "types of mind" could be distinguished at an early age by certain testing instruments such as I.Q. tests. Hence, following the passage of the 1944 Education Act, the Local Education Authorities (LEAs) introduced the "11+" examination which consisted of a series of objective tests in arithmetic and English language as well as an intelligence test. Teachers submitted their assessment of the student's abilities to the Local Education Authority, and these were considered along with the examination results in determining into which secondary school track a student would proceed–grammar (the title given the academic track), technical or modern.

The existing secondary high and grammar schools became the academic track schools, in most cases with little discernible difference in mission from that of their previous existence. The curriculums were developed with university entrance in mind. Most students took the external School Certificate examinations after five years, in five to nine subjects. The academically abler students progressed into the Sixth Form, where they followed a two-year specialized program in three or four subjects leading to the examinations for the Higher School Certificate. The syllabuses for both of these certificates were established by examination boards associated with the universities, and the examinations were set and marked by external examiners selected by the boards. These examinations were graded by subject as "distinction," "credit" or "pass."

In reality, a minority of students in the academic track were interested in attending university. Many left at 16 or earlier, usually after taking the School Certificate examinations. Others left after completing the Sixth Form curriculum and taking the Higher School Certificate examinations. These students went directly into the work force where many employers required or preferred School Certificate passes or credits in selected subjects. For certain types of employment such as local government positions, lower civil service jobs and many entry level management positions in private business, Higher School Certificate examination passes were required.

The concept of secondary technical schools never was realized fully. Technical education was conducted either in existing postsecondary technical institutions such as local technical colleges designed for the post 14-year-old population or as a special stream in the academic or secondary modern schools. Very few new facilities were constructed.

The third track represented by the secondary modern schools served the remainder of the 11-15 age group. The sponsors of the 1944 Education Act intended to provide a practical curriculum geared to the needs of the workplace. In spite of the rhetoric of equal but different, parents and the general public viewed the secondary modern schools as both academically and socially inferior to the other two tracks.

In response to this perception, the secondary modern schools modeled themselves more closely after the academic secondary or grammar schools, which in turn mirrored the so-called "public" schools–private, fee-paying grammar schools. Secondary modern schools began to offer foreign languages and to enter some of their more academically able students for the School Certificate examinations, and later for its successor, the General Certificate of Education, Ordinary level (GCE O). This three-track system was the subject of great debate. As a result, some moves were made towards a form of comprehensive or multilateral education as early as 1946. However, the firmly entrenched examination system was a barrier to general comprehensive education.

In 1951 the School Certificate and Higher School Certificate were replaced by the General Certificate of Education (GCE) which could be taken at two levels: Ordinary (O) level taken generally after Form Five, and Advanced (A) level taken after the two-year Sixth Form. Unlike the previous School Certificate group and Higher School Certificate examinations, the GCEs were organized so that the examinations could be taken in any number of subjects, singly or in groups, at any time or stage of life. As a result, GCE examinations and opportunities for further education became accessible to a broader pool of students than previously.

While most students took GCE O-level examinations in several subjects at age 16, many students, some of them mature students taking adult education courses, sat for one or more single subject exams to advance their careers, improve their marks, or simply for self-improvement. The GCE A-level examinations generally were taken after two years of study in the Sixth Form when three subjects, occasionally four, were studied. The syllabuses, as with the earlier examinations, were developed by the various examining boards with some participation by specialist teachers, always with university entrance requirements in mind.

The establishment of new and technical universities in the 1950s and 1960s created more places for students with acceptable combinations of A-level subjects and grades. Admission to a wide range of other higher educational programs, such as those offered at polytechnics, teacher training colleges and technical colleges, also was determined by GCE A-level results.

Meanwhile, new developments were occurring in the secondary modern schools. As noted earlier, many of them began entering their most academically able students for external examinations. GCE streams in these schools became quite common and the original intention of the 1944 Education Act–to provide a practical rather than an academic education in these schools–became obscured.

In an effort to redress this situation a whole new examination system was introduced in 1965, known as the Certificate of Secondary Education (CSE), specifically targeting the secondary modern student. Eleven new regional examining boards, not related to the universities, were established with significant representation from secondary modern teachers. They developed curriculums adapted to the abilities of the secondary modern student and monitored examinations. Teacher assessment and objective testing played a significant role in the examination process. Comparability of sorts developed between the GCE O-level and the CSE, as there was general agreement that a Grade 1 on the CSE scale of 1-5 could be equated to a pass in the GCE O-level examination despite the fact that the CSE used more skills-oriented syllabuses than the predominantly knowledge-based GCE O-level examination syllabuses.

The General Certificate of Education (GCE) system and the Certificate of Secondary Education are described very thoroughly in the World Education Series volume, *United Kingdom of Great Britain and Northern Ireland*, by Stephen Fisher, 1976, pp. 37-61.

A few experimental comprehensive schools were established in the late 1940s but the comprehensive school movement grew slowly during the 1950s, when even the Labour Party continued to support the tripartite secondary system. Disenchantment with the 11+ examination and the selectivity inherent in the system, which first surfaced soon after the implementation of the 1944 Act, began to gain momentum. A new generation of educational psychologists challenged the basic tenets of the "type of mind" theories on which the system was based. Encouraged by this ferment, the newly elected Labour government in 1965 introduced a system of comprehensive secondary education. Implementation was left in the hands of the LEAs, some of which already had opted for comprehensive schools as the most economical solution to the rapid increase in the number of school age children in the expanding suburbs of the 1950s and 1960s.

When the Conservative government was elected in 1979, it did not address this trend but turned its attention instead to the existing two-tier examination system and to the content of the curriculum. Hence, comprehensive secondary schools still are not universal. In 1989, 28 out of 162 LEAs retained the 11+ examination and the selective tripartite system of secondary schooling. Most comprehensive secondary schools continued to offer both the GCE O-level and the CSE curriculum with students streamed into different ability groups as late as the fourth and fifth years.

Changes in secondary education began to accelerate in the mid-1970s, following a landmark speech by Prime Minister James Callahan at Ruskin College, Oxford, in which he called on "parents, teachers, learned and professional bodies, representatives of higher education and both sides of industry, together with the government" to determine the purpose of education and challenged the effectiveness of the existing system. This speech opened the door to the possibility of the central government and other elements of society, especially industry, employers and parents, playing a larger role in the formulation of educational policy. This trend is manifested clearly in the Technical and Vocational Education Initiative (TVEI), a project conducted by the Training Agency of the Department of Employment formerly known as Manpower Services. TVEI was begun in 1982 to introduce technical and vocational education into the curriculum for the 14-16 year age group. Among its objectives were preparation for employment and adult life and provision for a period of planned work experience.

In 1984 the Secondary Examinations Council (SEC) was established to develop a single examination to replace the existing two-tier GCE/CSE system. The result was the General Certificate of Secondary Education (GCSE). The intent of this new examination is to foster positive rather than negative assessment and to test what students know, understand and can do. The GCSE was administered for the first time in the summer of 1988. The GCE A-level remained with the addition of an Advanced Supplementary (AS) level syllabus.

A great debate was waged in the decade following Mr. Callahan's Ruskin speech over the components of a "core curriculum." From this debate the notion of a centrally controlled or national curriculum began to emerge culminating in the passage of the 1988 Education Reform Act. (ERA) which introduced just such central control.

One of the major provisions of the Act was the establishment of a National Curriculum, being phased in over several years beginning in 1989 with English, math and science as the core subjects. Working groups were appointed to develop the curriculums for 10 foundation subjects. Another major thrust of the ERA was a drastic reorganization of the administration of primary and secondary education: the power of the LEAs diminished and fiscal responsibility for primary and secondary educational programs shifted from the LEAs to the schools. This new fiscal management system is known as Local Management of Schools (LMS).

Secondary Schools

A brief listing of the types of institutions which provide secondary education in England and Wales follows:

Comprehensive Secondary Schools have open admission and are the most numerous of all the secondary schools. Some offer a broad range of programs for those aged 11 to 16, including preparation for the GCSE examinations, as well as preparatory programs for the BTEC or CGLI courses. These schools are linked with Sixth Form colleges or tertiary colleges to which their students have access at age 16. Other comprehensive secondary schools cover the 11 to 18 age range, and, in addition to the programs already mentioned, offer courses leading to the GCE A- and AS-level examinations and the Certificate of Pre-Vocational Education (CPVE) offered jointly by BTEC and the CGLI.

County Grammar Schools still are maintained as selective secondary schools by a few Local Education Authorities. Entry to a selective county grammar school is by examination at age 11 or 12.

The courses offered are preparatory to the GCSE and the GCE A- and AS-level examinations. Even in areas where comprehensive education is the model, an occasional selective grammar school survives, frequently for some historical reason.

Secondary Modern Schools, like selective grammar schools, are operated by a few LEAs. A wide range of courses, including the GCSE curriculum, is offered for students who are less academically oriented than those attending the grammar schools.

Voluntary Secondary Schools are of two types: controlled and aided. The controlled schools have been funded primarily by the LEA with a proportion of their support coming from a religious organization, typically the Church of England, whose representatives sit on the Board of Governors. The aided schools, on the other hand, derive most of their financial support from the religious organization and establish their own selective admission policies. The Roman Catholic voluntary schools are of this type.

City Technology Colleges, authorized by the 1988 Act, are a type of urban magnet school that provides a broad curriculum for students ages 11 through 18. Their admission policies are academically highly selective.

The government's expectation that private industry would provide generous contributions has not been realized on a large scale. Several have opened with the main financial burden falling on the Department of Education and Science. These colleges are not required to follow the National Curriculum.

Independent Schools in England and Wales serve about 6% of the school age population. They range from the famous "public schools" to less prestigious establishments. All charge tuition and provide secondary education through the Sixth Form, offering the GCE A- and AS-level curriculums. Many of them append "college" to their name, but they are secondary schools.

All independent schools have selective entrance policies. Most have an entrance examination while others rely on recommendations from preparatory schools. Some specialize in university entrance preparation; others are oriented to future careers in the military or the church. Independent schools are not required to follow the National Curriculum, but a small sampling indicates that many of them will do so.

Higher Secondary Schools

Sixth Form Colleges have been established by a number of LEAs. Admission is open to students from those comprehensive secondary schools with no Sixth Form program. Some LEAs view these colleges as an economical and efficient way of providing the more specialized programs leading to the GCE A- or AS-levels. These colleges offer a wide range of BTEC, CGLI and CPVE courses. In addition, students may take GCSE examinations to obtain improved results or passes in subjects not taken previously.

Tertiary Colleges offer both GCE A- and AS-level preparation and also pre-vocational courses for the 16-18 age group. In administrative structure they resemble colleges of further education but academically are more like Sixth Form colleges.

Colleges of Further Education

The term "Further Education" (FE) was introduced in 1944 with the Education Act. It is defined as a system of schools for persons 16 and over at a standard up to and including the GCE A-level examinations. It is a flexible system in which students may enter at any level and progress in accordance with their abilities.

Colleges of further education (CFE) replaced the technical colleges and are often called "second-chance" institutions. Their level of instruction overlaps with secondary and higher education and provides an alternative to the Sixth Form programs offered in comprehensive schools or Sixth Form colleges and in tertiary colleges.

Coursework may be both vocational and academic. Offerings include preparation for the GCSE, the GCE AS-Level, and the GCE A-Level examinations; and awards from the BTEC Certificate of Pre-vocational Studies, First, National, and Higher; City and Guilds of London Institute (CGLI); London Chamber of Commerce and Industry (LCCI); the Royal Society of Arts (RSA); and Pitman Examinations Institute (PEI); some professional qualifications; adult education; and recreation. Training for various trades is offered, including the building trades, automobile repair and printing. Many of the students taking vocational courses are employed by factories and firms and are given day releases several hours each week to attend classes. The attraction of many CFE programs is that they are part-time or sandwich, pursued in conjunction with employment. Hence, the courses attract many mature students.

Although the greatest numbers of CFE students are taking terminal vocational courses, in 1984-85, 12% of candidates in England and Wales accepting university placements came from the colleges of further education. Some of these are students who had "opted out" of the school system at 16, others who wanted to study subjects which the secondary school could not provide, and others who may be re-entering the academic world after a period of work or participation in an Employment Training Program, a government program for the unemployed.

Most colleges of further education work closely with colleges or institutes of higher education offering "franchised" or "access" courses. Franchising means offering the first two years of a degree program at a local college of further education. This allows mature students to enroll through an alternative entry scheme if they do not meet standard entry requirements of the colleges and institutes of higher education or polytechnics. The government's 1987 White Paper, *Higher Education: Meeting the Challenge,* lists three generally recognized routes to higher education: A- and AS-levels, vocational qualifications and access courses.

Access courses have been developed formally to prepare students from a specific college of further education to enter a polytechnic, college or institute of higher education with a guaranteed place. They have been devised specially to provide study skills resulting in a more rapid route to higher education than through the traditional A-levels. The current practice is to allow students to transfer their access courses to a Higher National Diploma (HND) or degree program at any number of polytechnics, colleges, or institutes of higher education. These often are targeted toward underrepresented groups of students–women or ethnic minorities.

For more information about CFEs, write to the Council for National Academic Awards, 344-354 Gray's Inn Road, London, England, WC1X 8BP.

The LEA is the control board for most colleges of further education, although there are a few direct grant institutions. The Education Reform Act of 1988 requires every LEA to prepare a plan outlining procedures for developing further education, setting college budgets and delegating control over budgets to college governing bodies. The LEAs are obligated to ensure adequate training facilities. With the change in funding to a per capita formula has come the creation of short courses meant to produce revenue. These are nonacademic, designed for a targeted market. Examples are the Employment Training Program (courses developed for business and industry), and English as a second language courses.

The colleges of further education are different from polytechnics and colleges or institutes of higher education in that they have a broader mandate, a greater variety of courses and levels of study. In formal education, every level of student is provided for, from those of modest ability who have just left secondary school at 16 to postgraduate students. Almost every subject or skill is provided for as well.

Similarly, in informal education many leisure time activities find a place, too. Further education may be divided into the following broad areas of interest: vocational, academic, formal adult, and social and recreational activities. These generally are distinguished from one another, but there is overlap. In a modern language class, for example, one might find a student there for strictly vocational purposes, one learning a foreign language as a course that can be transferred into a degree program and one studying a foreign language just for fun.

The classification of courses in the colleges of further education is comprised of four levels:

1. operative (semiskilled workers carrying out specific operations involving machinery or plant);

2. craftsman (people who have been craft apprentices and use the course to advance through various stages of craftsmanship);

3. technicians (people working in a wide range of responsible jobs involving mathematics, scientific, and technical knowledge) and technologists (those with technical knowledge who are fully qualified professional engineers or applied scientists); and

4. academic transfer (designed as preparation for a bachelor's degree).

With the exception of recreational courses, many of the courses in the colleges of further education lead to external examinations and the award of certificates accepted widely in commerce, industry, and education. The most important and best known examining board is the City and Guilds of London Institute which has six regional branches. These qualifications are being standardized through the National Council for Vocational Qualifications. (For descriptions of the National Council for Vocational Qualifications [NCVQ], CGLI, RSA, LCCI and PEI, see chapter III.) The National Vocational Qualification (NVQ) ratings will appear on the already established awards. The ratings will be indicated in terms of the levels of achievement I through IV, I being the highest. A growing number of students now are using these awards for alternative entry into higher education.

Adult education has been available in England for the past 80 years. The scope of adult and continuing education has widened in recent years and now includes, in addition to the development of the individual through cultural, physical and craft pursuits, such subjects as basic education, education for disadvantaged groups and for those with special needs such as ethnic minorities or the disabled, consumer education, health education, and pre-retirement education. In 1982 the government launched the Professional, Industrial and Commercial Updating Program (PICKUP), designed to broaden the skills of those in mid-career. In 1984 REPLAN, a program designed to expand opportunities for unemployed adults, was launched. A list of the colleges of further education appears in Appendix C.

City and Guilds of London Institute

The City and Guilds of London Institute (CGLI) is the largest independent testing and qualifying body in Britain. Its business is to produce schemes of technical education, set examinations and establish national standards of expertise. The regulations and syllabuses for its schemes are drawn up by specialist committees consisting of representatives from industry, technical education and government departments. Qualifications are offered in more than 300 subjects from aeronautical engineering to yacht and boat building.

Programs leading to these qualifications are provided by schools, colleges of further education and training centers in every major town in the British Isles. Most are part-time, day-release programs with students being granted release by their employers in order to attend. Fulltime and evening programs also may be available.

Most CGLI students are in the 16 to 20 age group and are following programs of further education (usually at operative or craft level) to complement their industrial training and experience. These are career qualifications which recognize the various standards or technical skills and knowledge needed for the various levels within an occupation. The CGLI also provides schemes and certificates for technicians in the other Commonwealth countries.

In partnership with the BTEC, the CGLI has developed foundation programs of pre-vocational studies for 14 to 16 year olds and programs leading to the Certificate of Pre-Vocational Education. The CPVE is awarded jointly to those who complete an approved one-year program after reaching the statutory school-leaving age.

The address of the CGLI is 76 Portland Place, London, England W1N4AA.

For more information concerning the CGLI, its awards and their analysis, refer to the World Education Series volume, *United Kingdom*, 1976, by Stephen Fisher, pp. 101-102 and 224-225.

CGLI works closely with 10 regional examining boards in England and Wales. These bodies have changed from examining bodies in their own right to a unified system of regional offices of CGLI. They now function as regional advisory councils and examination sites. For more information, write to the CGLI's main address.

The Royal Society of Arts

The Royal Society of Arts (RSA) Examining Boards are part of the Royal Society of Arts for the Encouragement of Arts, Manufactures and Commerce, founded in 1754. The Society conducts examinations in commercial subjects and also offers general and modern language examinations. The examinations are designed mainly to provide qualifications for prospective secretaries and information processors. Other qualifications offered are road transport and teaching training, primarily certifying teachers who already have Qualified Teacher Status (QTS) in learning delivery systems and extracurricular activities.

Certificates awarded by the RSA are in single subject areas or in groups of subjects. The examinations are offered at the following three levels: Stage I (Elementary), Stage II (Intermediate), Stage III (Advanced). The RSA certificates are not academic qualifications but rather represent a statement of an individual's level of skill and practical ability.

For most of its programs there are no specific entry requirements. The institutions that prepare students to test for the award, however, may have their own entry standards. Similarly, the duration of the program is determined by the institution offering preparation for the award.

The Single-Subject examinations are generally classified as follows:

Stage I indicates that a basic course in the subject has been completed and the successful candidate has sufficient knowledge or skill to begin employment although further study would be beneficial;

Stage II indicates a sound understanding and competence in the subject and a recommendation for employment. It also suggests that someone who holds such a certificate may well benefit from advanced studies.

Stage III indicates an all-around knowledge and understanding of the subject and in the practical skills at a very high degree of proficiency.

Results for shorthand-transcription, audio-typewriting, shorthand-typewriting and typewriting skills are graded Pass with Distinction, Pass or Fail. Bookkeeping and accounting have no Pass with Distinction grade. Bronze or silver medals are awarded for outstanding work in Stages I and II.

For more information, write to RSA Examinations Board, Westwood Way, Coventry, England, CV48HS and also refer to the World Education Series volume, *United Kingdom*, 1976, by Stephen Fisher, pp. 106-107 and p. 225.

London Chamber of Commerce and Industry

The London Chamber of Commerce and Industry (LCCI) conducts examinations similar in general standard and nature to the Royal Society of Arts. Its examinations are categorized as elementary, intermediate and higher. It awards certificates in single or group subject areas which may be rated "with distinction." There are no LCCI entry requirements to the examinations; the administering centers create their own standards and program length. Like the RSA, LCCI certificates are not academic qualifications.

The following assessment is used:

Stages I and II	Pass with Distinction (75%)
	Pass (50%)
	Fail (below 50%)
Stage III	Pass with Distinction (75%)
	Pass with Credit (60%)
	Pass (50%)
	Fail (below 50%)

For further information, write the London Chamber of Commerce and Industry, Marlowe House, Station Road, Sidcup, Kent, England, DA157BJ and also refer to the World Education Series volume, *United Kingdom*, 1976, by Stephen Fisher, pp.107-108 and p.225.

Pitman Examinations Institute

The Pitman Examinations Institute (PEI) offers a higher secretarial certificate that includes typewriting, shorthand and some general subjects. Single subject certificates in secretarial skills are awarded also. The certificates are awarded at elementary, intermediate and advanced levels.

Overseas examinations in English as a second language also are offered by the PEI but they should not be considered to satisfy U.S. institution's English proficiency requirements.

In early 1991 the City and Guilds of London Institute acquired Pitman Examinations Institute. City and Guilds will maintain the separate identity of PEI, which will continue to offer its worldwide examination services in their present form. The acquisition of PEI by CGLI means that between them they now provide comprehensive assessment services for both technical and business occupations.

The following assessment is used: Elementary–Pass (60%), Intermediate and Advanced–First Class (75%), Pass (60%).

For further information, write Pitman Examinations Institute, Catteshall Manor, Godalming, Surrey, England, GU71UU and also refer to the World Education Series volume, *United Kingdom*, 1976, by Stephen Fisher, pp. 108 and 225.

The National Council for Vocational Qualifications

With the exception of the CNAA, all of the validating examining bodies work in collaboration with the National Council for Vocational Qualifications (NCVQ) which was set up following the 1986 White Paper, *Working Together: Education and Training*, to standardize the system of vocational qualifications. Ratings of levels of achievement (I-IV) are determined by faculty and awarded by the CNAA and appear as National Vocational Qualifications (NVQs) on the certificates jointly awarded by the examining bodies and the CNAA. The main features of NVQs are that they are competence-based and employment-led. In other words, they are ratings of skills as required by the employers.

NCVQ has established four levels of achievement which indicate clear routes of progression:

Level I indicates the ability to perform basic activities which provide the broad foundation for progression;

Level II recognizes competence in a more demanding range of activities which require a degree of individual responsibility;

Level III denotes skilled work of a complex nature and the ability to undertake a supervisory role;

Level IV demands specialist or technical expertise and the ability to undertake professional work.

For more information, write the National Council for Vocational Qualifications, 222 Euston Road, London, England NW1 2B2.

General Certificate of Secondary Education

One of the concerns of the Conservative government was the existence of two different examination systems which resulted in too many examining boards and syllabuses. The purpose of the General Certificate of Secondary Education (GCSE) was to merge the GCE O-level and the CSE systems examinations taken by students at the end of the fifth year of secondary education. The GCSE syllabuses were organized to be covered in the fourth and fifth years, with the first examination administered in 1988.

The examination boards for the GCE and CSE were merged into five groups:

1. The Northern Examining Association consisting of one GCE board (the Joint Matriculation Board) and three CSE boards (the Associated Lancashire Schools Examination Board, the North West Regional Examination and the Yorkshire and Humberside Regional Examination Board);

2. The Midland Examining Group consisting of three GCE boards (the Cambridge University Local Examinations Syndicate, the Oxford and Cambridge Schools Examination Board, the Southern Universities Joint Board) and two CSE boards (the East Midland Regional Examination Board and the West Midlands Examination Board);

3. The London and East Anglia Examining Group consisting of one GCE board (the University of London Schools Examination Board) and two CSE boards (the East Anglian Examination Board and the London Regional Examination Board);

4. The Southern Examining Group consisting of two GCE boards (the Oxford Delegacy of Local Examinations and the Associated Examining Board) and three CSE boards (the Southern Regional Examination Board, the South East Regional Examination Board, and the South Western Examination Board); and

5. The Welsh Joint Education Committee.

The syllabuses and the assessment system for the GCSE were developed by the examining groups using a set of national criteria produced by the Joint Council of the GCE O-level and CSE Boards. The national criteria include both general and subject-specific standards.

The general criteria consist of the title; general aim of the syllabus; assessment objectives; proportion of marks to be allocated to the various assessment objectives; scheme of assessment; and descriptions of standards that are likely to be achieved by the candidates.

The subject-specific national criteria include detailed aims, assessment objectives and content requirements. They may be obtained by writing to HMSO (Her Majesty's Stationery Office) 49, High Holborn, London WC 1V 6HB, UK and asking for the publication: *GCSE, The National Criteria* plus the subject or subjects required.

The responsibilities of the examining groups include the development of subject syllabuses, assurance that the requirements for both the national general and subject-specific criteria are met, and that the format of the examinations is such that students across a wide ability range will be able to succeed on some part of them.

Before the enactment of the Education Reform Act of 1988, all new syllabuses were submitted to the Secondary Examinations Council (SEC) for approval. The SEC was established in 1982 to ensure that each subject area followed the national criteria and to implement in-service training programs for teachers who would be using the new GCSE syllabuses. In addition, the SEC was charged with the responsibility of advising the Secretary for Education and Science on all matters pertaining to the GCSE and with ensuring that the subject examinations of the five examining boards were comparable in content and difficulty.

The 1988 Act created a new statutory group, the School Examination and Assessment Council (SEAC), which replaced the SEC. It is responsible for developing the system of assessment at ages 7, 11, 14 and 16 of the new National Curriculum as well as approving the GCE A-level and AS-level examination syllabuses and promoting the adoption of the AS-level syllabus as a means of broadening the Sixth Form curriculum.

Assessment and Syllabuses

One of the priorities of the new examination system is the concept of positive assessment. This gives students the opportunity to show what they know, understand and can do. The GCE O-levels used a norm-referenced system of assessment whereby an individual's performance was compared with that of others taking the same examinations. The GCSE examination assessments, on the other hand, are criterion-referenced whereby the student's mastery of a specific skill is assessed.

With a single examination system and students of a variety of abilities taking the same examinations, the concept of differentiation comes into play. Each subject examination must be designed to test students with differing abilities. Depending on the subject and the examining group, the examination may take one of the following forms:

1. questions of increasing difficulty;

2. a common paper completed by all students in addition to either an easier or more difficult paper;

3. a common paper completed by all candidates. Those who wish for a higher grade have the opportunity to complete an additional examination paper at a more difficult level;

4. four papers of increasing difficulty with students selecting an adjacent pair of papers. Each pair of papers determines the range of grades a student can receive.

Paper	Achievement level	Grade range
1-2	High	A-C
2-3	Intermediate	C-E
3-4	Low	D-G

The GCSE system has incorporated into its grading structure a substantial component of teacher-assessed coursework, an element present in CSE syllabuses. Examples of teacher-assessed activities include laboratory exercises, field work, research techniques, application of motor skills and interactive skills either with people or materials. No standard percentage of the grade is allocated to teacher assessed coursework; variation from subject to subject and among the examining groups ranges from 20% to 100%. Schools may select a syllabus for each subject from among the five examining groups.

In one school, for example, an English syllabus from an examining group was selected because it was 100% teacher-assessed while at another school a mathematics syllabus was chosen by the head of the department because it contained only 20% teacher assessment, 80% being derived from the external examination. The department head felt this best matched the teaching strengths of the staff.

Most schools choose syllabuses from several of the examining groups, creating an element of competitive-

ness among the groups. Hence, a student who has been examined in different subjects by different examining groups will present GCSE certificates from each of these groups. (See documents 2.1 through 2.3 for certificates issued to a single student). The teacher assessments are compared for consistency either by the submission of samples of work to an external moderator or by a system known as consensus moderation in which the teachers meet to decide what the standards will be.

GCSE Grading

The GCSE grading scheme uses a 7-point scale, A-G. In lieu of failing grades, unsatisfactory results are listed as "unclassified." With the introduction of the National Curriculum, the grading scale will change to a 10-point scale. This will be phased in by subject beginning with math and the sciences in 1994. A grading comparison among the GCE O-level, the CSE, the GCSE (current) and the GCSE National Curriculum (NC) as proposed by SEAC is as follows.

1963-1987	1965-1987	1988-	Proposed
GCE-O	CSE	GCSE (current)	GCSE (NC)
A		A	9-10
B		B	8
C	1	C	7
D	2	D	
E	3	E	6
	4	F	5
	5	G	4
N and U			1-2-3

Note: Between 1951 and 1963 GCE O-level was assessed as Pass/Fail. After 1963 a letter grading system was introduced in which A-C were considered comparable to the previous GCE O-level pass but D and E were recorded grades and not viewed as comparable to Fail but to achievement at a lower level. A failure was not recorded. In the proposed GCSE (NC) grading scale, 7 and 6 replace the GCSE grades C, D and E.

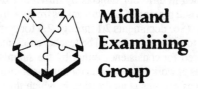

Midland Examining Group

East Midland Regional Examinations Board
Oxford and Cambridge Schools Examination Board
Southern Universities' Joint Board for School Examinations
The West Midlands Examinations Board
University of Cambridge Local Examinations Syndicate

GENERAL CERTIFICATE
OF SECONDARY EDUCATION

This is to certify that in the examination held in the

SUMMER of 1989

Date of Birth 13 August 1973

achieved the following results in 4 (four) subjects

MATHEMATICS	B (b)
ENGLISH LITERATURE	C (c)
HISTORY	C (c)
PHYSICS	C (c)

••

The Midland Examining Group is recognised by the Secretary of State for Education and Science
as an approved examining body for the General Certificate of Secondary Education.

For the Department of Education and Science   For the Midland Examining Group

Document 2.1. GCSE from the Midland Examining Group

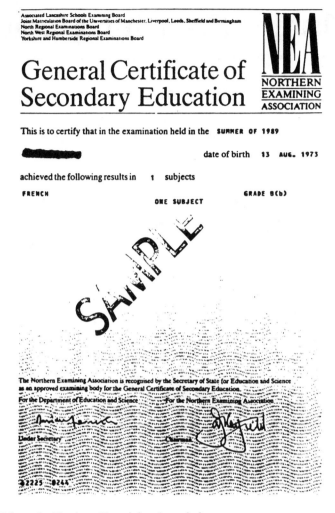

Associated Lancashire Schools Examining Board
Joint Matriculation Board of the Universities of Manchester, Liverpool, Leeds, Sheffield and Birmingham
North Regional Examinations Board
North West Regional Examinations Board
Yorkshire and Humberside Regional Examinations Board

General Certificate of Secondary Education

NEA
NORTHERN
EXAMINING
ASSOCIATION

This is to certify that in the examination held in the **SUMMER OF 1989**

date of birth **13 AUG. 1973**

achieved the following results in **1** subjects

FRENCH

ONE SUBJECT

GRADE B(b)

The Northern Examining Association is recognised by the Secretary of State for Education and Science as an approved examining body for the General Certificate of Secondary Education.

For the Department of Education and Science

For the Northern Examining Association

Under Secretary

Chairman

Document 2.2. GCSE from the Northern Examining Association

The General Certificate of Education Advanced level (GCE A-level) provides a two-year syllabus with examinations taken at the end of the thirteenth year of school. These two optional years, known historically as the Sixth Form, are divided into Lower (Year 12) and Upper (Year 13).

Sixth Form programs are offered at the secondary school in some LEAs; in others, Sixth Form or tertiary colleges offer a variety of educational opportunities to the over-16 population from a number of secondary schools in a city borough or sector of a county. Students planning to take the GCE A-level examinations select courses in which they are likely to continue at the university or polytechnic–generally two or three subjects–and study them intensively for both years.

There has been general concern in England and Wales that students are specializing too early in their academic careers. In 1988 the Higginson Report reviewed the existing GCE A-level curriculum and made recommendations for the syllabuses and methods of assessment. The A-level syllabuses were compared with the French *Baccalaureat* which requires seven subjects and the German *Abitur* which requires four. The committee concluded that the syllabuses were too narrow and that early specialization was a problem. Their report, eventually rejected by the Secretary of State for Education and Science, recommended that the

Southern Examining Group

THE ASSOCIATED EXAMINING BOARD   THE OXFORD SCHOOL EXAMINATIONS BOARD

GENERAL CERTIFICATE OF SECONDARY EDUCATION

This is to certify that in the examination held in the Summer of 1989

at:-

BURFORD SCHOOL AND COMMUNITY COLLEGE

date of birth   13th AUGUST 1973

achieved the following results in FOUR subjects

*ENGLISH	GRADE B(b) 2(ii)
HOME ECONOMICS (FOOD)	GRADE B(b)
BIOLOGY	GRADE C(c)
COMPUTER STUDIES	GRADE C(c)

Number of subjects obtained at each Grade:

B(b)=2; C(c)=2

CENTRE No./CANDIDATE No. 62225   0244   CERTIFICATE No. B461332

Signed on behalf of
THE ASSOCIATED EXAMINING BOARD

Secretary General

Signed on behalf of
THE DEPARTMENT OF EDUCATION AND SCIENCE

Signed on behalf of
THE OXFORD SCHOOL EXAMINATIONS BOARD

Secretary

Signed on behalf of
SOUTHERN EXAMINING GROUP

Chief Executive

Document 2.3. GCSE from the Southern Examining Group

Their report, eventually rejected by the Secretary of State for Education and Science, recommended that the syllabuses be broadened and streamlined to enable students to take five courses rather than three. The content of each syllabus should articulate with the content and skills of other subjects. The emphasis should be on learning concepts and their application rather than on memorization. Instead, as a compromise, the Advanced Supplementary examinations (GCE AS-levels) were introduced.

The GCE AS syllabuses require that a subject be studied to the same depth and with the same degree of academic rigor as the A-level course but with half the content, class time and study time. These syllabuses are designed, like the A-levels, to be completed over two years. They are intended to give students more flexibility in their program, as well as a chance to experience a subject outside their major area of interest. For example, a student concentrating on chemistry and biology might elect to take English literature at the AS-level.

Schools are experiencing problems integrating the AS-levels with the existing A-levels. Some schools have neither money, time nor teachers to offer both curriculums. As a result some schools are not offering AS-levels at all; others have scheduled them into existing free elective or general studies time slots; still others have attempted to fit them into their current timetable by having students attend only half the classes of the regular A-level timetable and do only half of the assignments.

While the universities in England and Wales have gone on record as welcoming the new AS examinations, in some subjects (e.g., mathematics, sciences), preference for admission still is given to the A-level examination results. The University of London states it will accept the following combinations: two A-levels; four AS-levels; one A-level and two AS-levels. It should be noted, however, that most students are continuing along the more traditional path to the universities with at least two A-levels.

Many of the changes in England and Wales have occurred very rapidly and have generated problems which have yet to be worked out. For example, the first group of students who moved from the GCSE into the GCE A-level curriculum found a gap between the two teaching methodologies and learning styles. Students who followed the GCSE curriculum have had difficulty adjusting from the emphasis on the skills orientation of the GCSE curriculum to the predominantly knowledge-based approach of the GCE A-level curriculum. In mathematics and science subjects, students may need bridging courses to adapt to the GCE A-level curriculum to proceed to the GCE A-level course. In one school visited, such a bridging course had been introduced.

This dilemma is a result of the shift in emphasis from the academically selective approach of the GCE O-level syllabuses, set by the GCE Examining Boards, to the broad based, real life approach of the GCSE syllabuses, which incorporate much of the thinking behind the CSE examination syllabuses. This shift is mandated by the requirement that the examining groups follow the national criteria, both general and subject specific.

Approximately 40% of the 15- to 16-year age cohort in the United Kingdom followed the GCE O-level syllabuses while now almost the entire cohort follows the GCSE syllabuses and takes the examinations. The examining groups are challenged to maintain a high academic standard while allowing for a much greater range of achievement than was possible with GCE O-levels, as reflected by the broader grade range. This shift in focus has been the basis for the difficulties experienced by students who proceed to the GCE A-level syllabus from GCSE work. The A-level syllabuses, academically specialized and narrowly focused, were developed by the GCE examining boards with university entrance requirements in mind. The critical need to develop an alternative to A-level syllabuses or to broaden them to include a more technological, vocational component, is being addressed. The development of the AS-level syllabuses was an attempt to introduce more breadth into the Sixth Form curriculum but it does not represent a change in the basic approach to the subject matter.

As of Fall 1990, the whole issue has been under intensive study by a working committee formed under the auspices of the SEAC to study the problem and determine how the GCE A-levels can be aligned better with the GCSE. It is possible that a more comprehensive examination syllabus will emerge, either as part of an extension of the National Curriculum or as a revised and expanded GCE A-level examination system.

The National Curriculum

The Education Reform Act of 1988 mandated the creation of a National Curriculum in England and Wales in all publicly funded, "maintained" schools. In the past, the secondary school curriculums have been driven by the established syllabuses of the GCE O-level or the CSE examination and more recently by those of the GCSE examination. While there was not a wide variation in either content or level of difficulty among the syllabuses of the GCE O-level examining boards, there was considerable choice among alternative syllabuses from which teachers could select. Some boards incorporated more teacher assessment than others into their grading systems. The CSE examining boards maintained similar standards among themselves, although the CSE examinations all contained a greater element of teacher assessment than the GCE O-level examinations.

Since the introduction of the GCSE, the SEAC has been charged with approving syllabuses and ensuring that they meet the national criteria. While considerable variation still exists among them, especially with regard to the ratio of teacher assessment to written examination, there is a move towards more uniform and inclusive syllabuses than before. The GCSE syllabuses are so constructed that almost all students can achieve at some level.

The concept of a national curriculum stems in part from the demands of the market place for stronger technical and vocational preparation and the perception of successive governments that the GCE/CSE system in England and Wales was not meeting these demands adequately. It represents a move towards greater uniformity in the entire school curriculum throughout England and Wales for students aged 5 through 16.

The 1988 Act established three new councils: the National Curriculum Council (NCC); the Curriculum Council for Wales (CCW); and the School Examination and Assessment Council (SEAC). Each of these has 10 to 15 members appointed by the Secretary of State for Education and Science. The NCC and the CCW are charged with oversight of the curriculum in all schools, advising the Secretary on all curricular matters and with carrying out research and disseminating information.

The major curricular provisions of the 1988 Act are that the national curriculum will be followed by all registered students of compulsory school age at a maintained school and that religious education will be provided at every maintained school.

Implementation

This curriculum consists of 10 foundation subjects. The three core subjects are mathematics, English and science, plus Welsh in Welsh-speaking schools in Wales; the additional subjects are history, geography, technology, music, art, physical education, plus, at the secondary level, a modern foreign language (in Wales, Welsh in non-Welsh-speaking schools).

Central to the implementation of the National Curriculum are four key educational stages, through which students, beginning at age 5, progress.

Stage (Abbreviation)	Length	Age
1 (KS1)	2	5 - 7
2 (KS2)	4	7 - 11
3 (KS3)	3	11 - 14
4 (KS4)	2	14 - 16

Related to these four key stages are three central components:

1. **Attainment Targets** - the knowledge, skills and understanding the student should have acquired by the end of each key stage. The number of attainment targets varies by subject; for example, mathematics has 14 and science 17. Each target can be attained at ten levels of increasing difficulty. A student who has mastered all 14 attainment targets in mathematics at Level 10 will have completed the National Curriculum in mathematics at the highest level of achievement.

2. **Programs of Study** - the subject matter, skills and processes to be taught at each key stage in each foundation subject to enable students to meet the attainment targets at the 10 levels for each key stage. They are not curriculums but are designed to provide guidance to the teachers in the development of their teaching strategies. In addition to the subject specific skills and concepts, certain common skills (reading, writing, and numeracy) must be integrated into each subject.

3. **Assessment Arrangements** - assessment of the level of achievement at the end of each key stage.

Subject area working groups have been established by the Secretary of State for Education and Science to produce programs of study, attainment targets and assessment arrangements. The members, appointed by the Secretary, are drawn from the universities, institutes of education, Her Majesty's Inspectors (HMI), the heads of schools and classroom teachers. Implementation of the National Curriculum is being phased in over a number of years and should be completed by 1997. The provisional timetable for introduction of the National Curriculum appears below.

Assessment

The GCSE will be the assessment instrument at Key Stage 4. The syllabuses will be modified to conform to the National Curriculum attainment targets, and the grading scale will change from A-G to 10-1 as each subject is completed.

In addition to the subject working groups, a Task Group on Assessment and Testing (TGAT) was established to develop detailed recommendations on appropriate assessment methods. The TGAT report acknowledged that a fundamental responsibility for any assessment system must continue to rest with the teachers who must be given the proper support in the form of diagnostic tests. Beyond that, TGAT proposed the following guidelines:

1. assessment should be formative, determining how both individuals and groups of students can progress to higher levels of learning. For the 16-year-old group, assessment should also be summative and should provide a comprehensive record of achievement for each student;
2. assessment should be criterion-referenced, with each student's progress assessed relative to what has been taught;
3. a profile for each student, as well as for classes or other teaching groups, should be developed, illustrating progress across the curriculum towards the achievement of the attainment targets;
4. a system for arriving at some common agreement on assessment between the teaching staffs of different schools should be introduced.

TGAT's proposals concerning this last guideline are well developed and focus on the use of external oral and written tests given at the end of each key stage. These are referred to as Standard Assessment Tasks or SATs. At Key Stages 1 and 2, the SATs will be task oriented with a wide range from which teachers will be able to select. At the secondary level, Key Stages 3 and 4, the SATs will be subject related.

The contracts for developing SATs for Key Stage 3 have been awarded to the Consortium for Assessment and Testing in Schools, a group of three University of London schools (King's College, Goldsmiths' College and the Institute of Education), the London East Anglian Examining Group, and a publisher; the East London and MacMillan Assessment Group; the Midland Examining Group; and the National Foundation for Educational Research for Assessment in Wales. The work of these groups will be supervised by the SEAC.

Beyond the four key stages of the National Curriculum are several alternatives available to those students who have completed 11 years of compulsory schooling at approximately age 16. Less than 50% of the 16 to 18 age cohort continue for advanced education. The Non-Advanced Further Education (NAFE) provision of the educational scheme for England and Wales serves this population, providing full- or part-time courses in practical subjects at colleges of further education and, formerly, at the technical colleges. Of this group approximately half will enter the work force after two or more years of schooling. The wide range of available courses includes those of the Business and

---

Provisional Timetable for Introduction of the National Curriculum

			KS1	*KS2*	*KS3*	*KS4*
Mathematics	Introduction	Autumn	1989	1990	1989	1992
and Science	Assessment	Summer	1992	1995	1993	1994
English	Introduction	Autumn	1989	1990	1990	1992
	Assessment	Summer	1992	1995	1994	1994
Technology	Introduction	Autumn	1990	1990	1990	1993
	Assessment	Summer	1993	1995	1994	1995
History and	Introduction	Autumn	1991	1991	1991	1994
Geography	Assessment	Summer	1994	1996	1995	1996
Art, Music	Introduction	Autumn	1992	1992	1992	1992
and PE	Assessment	Summer	1995	1997	1996	1994
Modern	Introduction	Autumn	–	–	1992	1992
Languages	Assessment	Summer	–	–	1996	1997

Source: Adapted from *NCC News*, June 1989, National Curriculum Council.

Technician Education Council (BTEC), City and Guilds of London Institute (CGLI) and Royal Society of Arts (RSA) courses. Those who are planning to continue their education at a university or polytechnic take the GCE A-/AS-level courses. The introduction of "access" courses has opened up an alternative route to higher education for those who have not followed the traditional route through the school system. A college of further education may offer access courses which prepare for admission to a polytechnic which in turn may offer courses giving access to a university degree program.

The SEAC has been charged with formulating plans for incorporating the curriculum for the 16 to 18 age group into an extension of the National Curriculum. Given the problems of articulation between the GCSE and the GCE A-level syllabuses and the criticism leveled at the GCE A-level curriculum, it is possible that a broader based, less specialized curriculum eventually may replace the current one.

Records of Achievement

Records of Achievement, detailing each student's achievement relative to the attainment targets for students in the same age group, will be maintained by the schools. For external purposes, the attainment targets will be grouped into profile components. As an example, in the English curriculum, the profile components are reading, writing, and speaking and listening. These records will be released to parents and, when circumstances warrant, to the LEAs when testing or special services are indicated for students with learning disabilities or other problems.

The results of assessments for individual classes and for schools will be published as part of a broader report by the LEAs. The character of the neighborhood in which the school is located and special populations will be taken into account in the formulation of these reports.

Cross-Curricular Issues

Certain cross-curricular issues were identified by the National Curriculum Council. These include personal and social adjustment; basic skills such as communication, problem solving, and studying; and other cross-cultural themes such as economic and industrial understanding, careers education, environmental educa-

tion, health education and citizenship. These must be integrated into the scheme of attainment targets, programs of study and assessment arrangements. A committee has been established by the NCC to study these issues.

Special Education

The 1981 Education Act required schools to develop a statement defining the specific needs of students with special educational requirements. The 1988 Act states that such "statemented" students may be exempted from the requirements of the National Curriculum or be permitted to participate in a modified curriculum, as appropriate. Previously, although mainstreamed, statemented students usually did not take GCE O-level or CSE examinations.

Pedagogy

The overall aim of the GCSE is to improve the quality of secondary education in England and Wales by making it more responsive to conditions in the real world and by placing more emphasis on skills and practical knowledge and less on memorization and the acquisition of facts. The student is required to take a more active role in the educational process through greater classroom participation than traditionally has been the custom and through the application of interactive teaching methods.

The GCSE examination was given first in 1988 but the syllabuses had been taught for two years previous. An intensive period of in-service training was provided to prepare teachers for the change in emphasis from the GCE O-level and the CSE curriculums to the GCSE.

It would be a misconception to view the introduction of the GCSE as having brought about a nationwide revolution in teaching methods, as a great deal of creative curriculum development already was occurring both at the local and national levels. Autonomy in curricular matters was left to the schools; individual initiative in teaching methodology was encouraged.

The GCE O-levels, the CSE and, at the higher level, the GCE A-levels, with their range of alternative syllabuses, offered a variety of approaches to individual subjects but also assured a degree of uniformity in content and academic level. Many of the GCE O-level syllabuses required a percentage of teacher assessment, often in science subjects, through experimental projects or field work records. The CSE examinations were designed to include a high percentage of teacher assessment. However, the concepts of classwork, individual projects, teacher assessment, the inquiry method and problem solving, while not new, were for the first time mandated for all examinations by the introduction of the GCSE.

The GCSE focuses on positive achievement: what the student knows, understands and can do. All teachers have had to adapt their methods to allow more active student participation, interaction in the classroom and individually paced learning. Some classes are organized in sets which group students of similar ability; others are in classes which are taught across the ability range. Several innovative curriculums already existed, such as the Nuffield Foundation Science Teaching project which stressed student participation and the inquiry mode of teaching.

On the whole, teachers have reacted positively to the GCSE curriculums and in many cases indicated that they already had moved away from the didactic teaching style to a more interactive, inquiring, and problem solving approach, and therefore did not need to change their methods drastically.

The concept of differentiation has created difficulties for classroom teachers, especially in classes organized across the ability range and not grouped. More emphasis on individual work, with the teacher as facilitator, is required. In the context of a national teacher-student ratio of 1:16.5, this may be manageable.

The introduction of the National Curriculum so quickly on the heels of the GCSE has created a high level of stress among the teachers in the U.K. The National Curriculum appears to be a response to market forces. Although some testing of materials in classrooms took place, the critical comments of academic educators suggest that insufficient research into the structure and content of the proposed curriculum was undertaken before the National Curriculum was introduced. The speed with which it was developed and introduced inhibited more indepth study.

As a result, teachers have struggled with the format and complexity of the curriculum. The consensus seems to be that now that implementation is underway and a number of modifications have occurred no new or dramatic changes in teaching methods are called for. What has changed most dramatically are the recordkeeping requirements and the degree of accountability both to parents and the general public.

Most schools are developing mechanisms to help teachers "map" the curriculum to include in each subject a course outline provision for incorporating common skills as well as course-specific skills and learning activities. Teachers are required to attend a series of in-service training sessions (INSET) to familiarize themselves with the new requirements. At the same time the attainment targets must be the central focus. Secondary school teachers who have been accustomed to teaching "to" a specific examination syllabus have been troubled by the lack of published standard assessment tasks (SATs).

The net result appears to be a significant increase in the amount of time each teacher must spend maintaining records and performing teacher assessments for the GCSE and a concomitant decrease in the time available for adequate class preparation and development of teaching materials. It is too early to say whether this will result in more effectively organized course outlines and new and imaginative teaching methodology or less effective classroom teaching or a compromise between the two.

Head teachers and university education specialists are concerned that teachers will be tempted to plan their classwork with too much focus on the SATs and not enough on their students' needs. The assessment schemes and reporting procedures, with publication of each school's achievement, are likely to encourage teachers to strive to "look good" by motivating their students to do well on the SATs at the expense of sound pedagogy.

The NCC issues nonstatutory guides for each of the published subject statutory curriculums and a series of circulars with both general and subject-specific advice. If these are followed by all teachers, a high degree of uniformity in general pedagogy and in subject teaching methodology will be achieved.

In advice to secondary school mathematics teachers, the NCC points out that the programs of study are not in themselves a scheme of work but should be used to develop activities which take into account a variety of learning and teaching styles. They list these 10 guidelines to schools from the Mathematics Working Group of the National Curriculum Council Secondary Mathematics:

1. activities should bring together different areas of mathematics;

2. the order of activities should be flexible;

3. activities should be balanced between tasks which develop knowledge, skills and understanding and those which develop the ability to tackle practical problems;

4. activities should be balanced between the application of mathematics and ideas which are purely mathematical;

5. activities should be balanced between activities which are short in duration and those which have scope for development over an extended period;

6. activities should, as appropriate, use pupils' own interests or questions either as starting points or as further lines for development;

7. activities should, as appropriate, involve both independent and cooperative work;

8. tasks should include those which have an exact result or answer and those which have many possible outcomes;

9. activities should be balanced between different modes of learning: doing, observing, talking and listening, discussing with teachers and other pupils, reflecting, drafting, reading and writing;

10. activities should encourage pupils to use mental arithmetic and paper and pencil methods, and to become confident in the use of a range of mathematical tools and new technology.

The use of computers in mathematics teaching is receiving special attention and is inferred in number 10. Most secondary schools in England and Wales have access to computers, but budgetary constraints under the Local Management of Schools (LMS) scheme may make this guideline difficult to follow in all schools.

One of the practical problems associated with implementation of the National Curriculum is the timetable for the 10 foundation subjects in addition to religious education, physical education and other elective courses. In a comprehensive school, where the student population may cover a wide range of academic ability, meeting all of the requirements of the National Curriculum provides a challenge. The less academically inclined students may be able to cover the syllabus in a limited number of subjects and would profit from more emphasis on practical subjects, while the university-bound students may be covering the full examination syllabus in all of the foundation subjects. In some schools, streaming or banding by academic ability is

practiced. In addition, the school timetable in secondary schools already is complicated; not all subjects are taught daily and science subjects and some practical subjects need to be taught in blocks. This additional layer of required classes may be difficult to accommodate.

The staff of one secondary grammar school, which enjoys an excellent academic reputation, felt it would have no difficulty adapting to the exigencies of the National Curriculum. There were no alternatives to the GCE A-level offered in the Sixth Form, and almost all the students were bound for the university. An inner city school, by contrast, with a much smaller percentage of its students continuing to university or polytechnic, is faced with a much more complex implementation problem, as many of the students would prefer to take pre-BTEC courses or other similar more practical, work-oriented courses.

Curricular Concerns and Comparisons

The general effect on curriculums of the change from the GCE O-level and CSE to the GCSE and more recently to the National Curriculum has been to produce a higher degree of uniformity in the secondary school curriculum. The change in approach between GCE O-level examination syllabuses and the GCSE has been discussed already as has the major impact of the National Curriculum.

Mathematics has been taken as a curricular model for comparison among three U.K. curriculums–the GCE O-levels and two GCSE syllabuses and also for comparison between U.S. first year college calculus, GCE A-levels and AS-levels and two programs with which U.S. educators are familiar, the International Baccalaureate (IB) and The College Board Advanced Placement (AP) tests. Table 2.1 compares the topics covered in the GCE O-level syllabuses of two of the examining boards in 1987, and those covered in the GCSE syllabuses for 1990. Table 2.2 provides a similar comparison among the topics covered in U.S. first year calculus, GCE A, GCE AS, IB and College Board AP. The GCE A- and AS-level syllabuses are those of the University of London for June 1991 and January 1992

The GCSE syllabus can be taken at three levels under the differentiation scheme: foundation, intermediate and higher. For comparative purposes, only the higher level syllabus was considered. This syllabus is more oriented to everyday living or the technical job market than the GCE O-level. There is less geometry than in the GCE O-level, but topics in statistics and probability have been added. Some additional topics may need to be covered either in the Sixth Form or alternative further education by students planning to pursue advanced courses in science or engineering.

Based on the program of study statements for Levels 7-10 and the sample problems in the attainment targets, the National Curriculum at Level 10 in all the attainment targets is roughly the same as the GCSE higher level syllabus. The National Curriculum, however, appears to be even less academic and more practically oriented than the GCSE higher level syllabus. Students who have completed all of the attainment targets at Levels 8, 9 or 10 may be prepared adequately for mathematics courses at the university but might require additional preparatory coursework before taking first-year calculus courses.

The GCE A-level syllabuses of two of the examining boards were studied, one for the 1987 examinations, the other for the June 1991/January 1992 examinations. These syllabuses approximate the U.S. first-year calculus syllabus as shown in Table 2.1. Some topics usually covered in that sequence, such as infinite series and polar coordinates, are missing. This is not a serious limitation, however.

The GCE AS-level syllabus covers almost all of the material in the first course of first year calculus and includes some topics not covered.

When compared with The College Board Advanced Placement tests, the GCE A-level goes beyond the AP/AB calculus syllabus but is not quite equivalent to the AP/BC syllabus because it fails to cover infinite series and polar coordinates. However, the GCE A-level syllabus covers elementary linear transformations and related matrix theory, both topics not covered usually in high school AP classes or in first-year calculus courses in the United States.

The International Baccalaureate syllabus at the higher level is comparable to the GCE A-level syllabus. Students who complete this syllabus will have covered the material in first-year science and engineering mathematics courses. The syllabus for the subsidiary level goes beyond the GCE O-level syllabus and is clearly oriented to the study of college-level mathematics. Students who have taken the compulsory core of the IB syllabus and covered topics 2 and 3 of the optional topics have covered the material in the first course of the first-year science and engineering mathematics sequence.

Advice to Admissions Officers

Change is the central theme in secondary education in England and Wales at the present time. This change in secondary education is a continuing evolutionary process. The following points should be noted.

1. The GCE O-level examination has not been offered in England and Wales since 1987. It is still being offered by the GCE examination boards in overseas schools; therefore, GCE O-level certificates will continue to appear. In format and syllabus content, they are the same as the GCE O-levels formerly offered in England and Wales. In some subjects, attempts have been made to make the subject matter more relevant to the students' environment. For example, the syllabuses for botany and geography may include course content covering local conditions. The GCE O-levels offered in overseas schools should be evaluated in the same way as the former GCE O-levels in Britain.

2. The CSE syllabus, offered between 1965-1987, focused on preparation for the job market and was practically oriented. Teacher assessment was central. The highest grade of 1 on the CSE was considered comparable in the U.K. to a C on the GCE O-level examination.

3. The GCSE syllabuses, first offered in 1986 and first examined in 1988, cover much the same range of material as the GCE O-levels but the orientation is more to the skills and activities which will be useful in real life situations (i.e., more problem solving, less compilation of information). Student preparation may be closer to that of a U.S. high school graduate. The GCE O-level examinations were taken by the more academically gifted, roughly 40% of the 16-year-olds, whereas the GCSE syllabuses are geared to the total age cohort. While GCSE passes in subjects appropriate to the desired degree program are adequate for admission purposes to U.S. colleges and universities, there may be some minor deficiencies in subject matter relative to the O-levels.

4. The differentiation schemes of the GCSE will present some difficulties for the U.S. admissions officer. At this time there is no consistency in the way differentiation is achieved. For admission, only the higher level grades (A-C) are recommended. The grades of A and B are awarded only at the higher level. The grade of C, however, is the lowest passing grade at the higher level (most difficult) and the highest passing grade at the intermediate level (less difficult) with D and E being the

other passing grades at the intermediate level. The syllabuses at the higher and intermediate levels are different but the GCSE certificate does not indicate at which level the examination was taken. To identify the syllabus followed, write to the examination group.

5. The National Curriculum is being phased in and the assessment at Key Stage 4, though still called GCSE, will change to reflect the curricular changes. The first of these National Curriculum GCSEs is scheduled to be administered in 1994 in mathematics and the sciences; English; and music and physical education. Technology follows in 1995, history and geography in 1996; and modern languages in 1997.

6. At present the traditional GCE A-level, along with the new AS-level, are used for assessment after the additional two years of schooling and should continue to be evaluated as in the past. The schools in England and Wales are having to cope with a curricular methodological gap between the GCSE and the GCE A- and AS-levels. Many schools are introducing additional classwork in all examination subjects at the beginning of the Sixth Form course to overcome this. In reviewing transcripts of students who do not complete the A-or AS- levels, exercise care in interpreting such coursework as A-level standard as it is designed to help the student who has taken GCSE exams prepare for the A- and AS-level curriculum.

7. Advanced standing credit should not be awarded for both an AS- and an A-level result in the same subject.

8. Placement decisions based on GCE A- and AS-level examination results should be made only after careful review of the syllabus for the specific examination board as there is some variation among the examining boards. The AS- level is so new that it is especially critical to review the syllabus.

9. Given the high level of interest and concern in England and Wales about the lack of articulation between the CGSE and the A-levels, some changes are likely to be made. The forthcoming report of the SEAC sub-committee charged with assessing the situation should be studied. An extension of the National Curriculum to the 16-19 age group is under consideration and could change both the syllabuses and assessment at the GCE A- and AS-level.

10. The universities are considering how their degree courses can be modified to fit better with the GCSE and the National Curriculum. The first degree courses in England and Wales are highly specialized and narrow in focus. Such a move inevitably would change the character of the GCE A- and AS- level, which itself is one of the most specialized secondary school curriculums in the world.

11. The introduction of criterion-referenced grading has presented problems for the examiners of the GCSE-level examinations. Indications are that, except for the classwork assessments, grading is still norm-referenced.

12. The Records of Achievement which schools are required to maintain for each student, are similar to report cards, but should not be accepted as official documents although they may be useful in providing information.

13. While the standard route to the GCE A- and AS-level is the GCE O-level or GCSE, there are other routes such as BTEC courses. Many A-level examinations require no prerequisites.

14. The term "further education" in the placement recommendations is used in the U.S. context, not the British.

Table 2.1. A Comparison of GCE O-Level and GCSE Syllabuses

GCE O-Level Common Core	GCSE A	GCSE B
Arithmetic		
Number and place value	x	x
Real number line	x	x
Units of mass, measurement, money, 24 hour clock	x	x
Vulgar and decimal fractions	x	x
Ratio-percentage	x	x
Financial transactions, profit and loss, simple interest	x	x
Averages, mean, median, mode	x	x
Expression of numbers	x	
Use of common logarithms, square roots, reciprocals	x	sq roots
Approximation and estimates	x	x
Positive integers-bases to 10 add, subtract, multiply	x	x
Algebra		
Idea, notation of a set, finite or infinite		
Venn diagrams		
Arithmetical generalization in formula	x	x
Interpretation, evaluation, manipulation of formula	x	x
Integral and fractional indices	x	x
Algebraic fractions	x	x
Solution of simple equations, quadratic equations	x	x
2D rectangular coordinates		
Linear and quadratic functions and their Cartesian graphs	x	x
Vector as displacement-addition, multiplication	x	x
Matrices-addition and multiplication	x	x
Algebra of 2 x 2 matrices including identity, zero, inverse matrices	x	x

GCE O-Level	GCSE-A	GCSE-B
Geometry		
Properties of angles at a point	x	x
Angle properties of polygons, rotational point-line symmetry in 2D	x	x
Congruency and similarity of triangles	x	x
Relationships between areas of similar triangles and between volumes of similar solids	x	x
Properties of chords and angle, properties of circle	x	x
Mensuration and geometric properties of a circle	x	x
Mensuration and geometric properties of triangle, rectangle, parallelogram and trapezium	x	x
Mensuration of circle	x	x
Volume and surface area of simple solids, including cube, cuboid, prism and cylinder	x	x
Pythagoras theorem-applications	x	x
Sine, cosine and tangent of an acute angle	x	x
Solutions of right angled triangles	x	x

Arithmetic and Mensuration	A paper-	B paper-	GCSE-A	GCSE-B
Problems-cube, cuboid pyramid, tetrahedron, prism, cylinder, cone, sphere		cone and sphere	x	x
Radian measure				
Compound interest and stocks	x		x	x
Rates and taxes	x		x	x
Problems on foreign exchange	x		x	x

GCE O-Level (Common Core)	GCSE A	GCSE B
Algebra		
A paper-	**B paper-**	
Formula to express functional relation, variation	x	
Solution of quadratic equations	x	x	x
Simultaneous equations in two unknowns—one linear-one quadratic	x	x	x
Simple theory-indices			
Graphs from statistical or experimental data	x	x	x
Determination of linear law	x		
Trigonometry **A paper-**	**B paper-**	
Sine and cosine of angles 0-360 degrees	x	x	x
Sine rule for triangles Cosine rule for triangles	x	x	x
3D-right angled triangles		x	x
Height, distance, bearings	x	x	x
Geometry **A paper-**	**B paper-**	
Properties of tangents	x		
Intersecting chord theorem	x	x	x
Simple loci-extend to 3D		x	

GCE O-Level (Common Core)	GCSE A	GCSE B
Direct and transverse common tangents to two circles		
Following constructions: **A paper-**	**B paper-**	
Bisection of angles and straight lines	x		
Perpendiculars to given line and of angle equal to given angle	x		
Triangles, quadrilaterals, circles from simple data	x		
Triangle equal in area to quadrilateral	x		
Square equal in area to given rectangle	x		
Segment of circle containing given angle	x		
Calculus- **A paper**	**B paper-**	
Differentiation and integration if integral powers of	x		
Application to rates of change, gradient, maximal and minimal areas			

Source: Prepared with assistance from the University of London.

Note: The major difference between GCSE syllabus A and GCSE Syllabus B is in the percentage of teacher-assessed coursework. Two written examinations account for 80% of the marks, teacher assessment for 20% for Syllabus A, whereas Syllabus B has 50% assessment by two written examinations and 50% teacher-assessed coursework.

*Integrated mathematics–includes some calculus.

**Traditional math–no calculus.

Table 2.2. A Comparison of U.S. First-Year Calculus, GCE A-Level, AS-Level, IB and College Board AP Syllabuses

U.S. Calculus	GCE A	GCE AS	IB	AP (AB and BC)
Functions, limits continuity	x	x	x	x
Differentiation		x		
definition of derivative	x	x	x	x
power sum, product and quotient rules	x	x	x	x
chain rule	x		x	x
differentiation of trigonometric functions	x	x	x	x
implicit differentiation	x		x	x
higher order derivatives	x	x	x	x
Newton's method	x		x	
mean value theorem	x	x	x	x
Application of derivative	x		x	
graph sketching	x	x	x	x
related rate problems	x	x	x	x
maximum and minimum	x	x	x	x
problems	x	x	x	x
linear and quadratic approximations	x	x	x	
differentials	x	x	x	
The definite integral				
definition	x	x	x	x
the fundamental theorem	x	x	x	x
evaluation of integrals	x	x	x	
Applications of the definite integral				
plane areas	x	x	x	
volumes (slicing, washers, shells)	x	x	x	x
arc length			x	
surface area			x	x
work	x		x	
mass, moments, centers of mass	x			
fluid pressure				
L'Hopitals rule and indeterminate form				x
Transcendental functions				
inverse trigonometric functions	x		x	
natural log	x		x	
exponential	x	x	x	
definition, differential and integration	x	x	x	
Further techniques of integration			x	
parts	x		x	
trigonometric integrals	x	x	x	
trigonometric substitutions				
partial fractions	x		x	
improper integrals	x			
Infinite series				
definition of convergence of series		x		

U.S. Calculus	GCE A	GCE AS	IB	AP (AB and BC)
convergence testsd			x	x
absolute convergence			x	x
power series			x	x
Taylor polynomials			x	x
Taylor series		x	x	x
Plane analytic geometry				
conic sections				
translation and rotation of axes				
Polar coordinates				
graphs of polar equations				
lines tangent to polar curves				
arc length				
surface area				
Three dimensional analytic geometry				
Cartesian coordinates	x			
quadric surfaces sketching			x	
vectors	x	x		
dot product	x			
cross product				
planes	x			
lines	x			
vector valued fraction	x			

Source: Prepared with assistance from the University of London.

Guide to the Understanding
of Placement Recommendations

The National Council on the Evaluation of Foreign Educational Credentials (referred to as "the Council") has approved the placement recommendations published in this PIER report in consultation with the workshop directors and editors. For detailed information on the Council and its membership, see page v.

Over the years, certain phrases used repeatedly in the recommendations have acquired specific meanings within Council usage. To assist the reader in understanding the intent of these phrases, the Council has prepared the following "Guide to the Understanding of Placement Recommendations." It provides an index to the meanings of the placement recommendations that appear specifically in this workshop report.

Questions or comments about Council placement recommendations should be sent to this address: Chair, National Council on the Evaluation of Foreign Educational Credentials, c/o AACRAO, One Dupont Circle, NW, Suite 330, Washington, DC 20036-1171.

Secondary

May be placed in grade....

This recommendation is used if freshman admission cannot be recommended, but specific secondary school placement is suggested by the total years of primary and secondary school studies represented by the credential.

Primarily a vocational qualification.

This statement is used for credentials awarded for secondary nonacademic training programs in specific job-related fields (e.g., apprenticeships). Admission does not usually require a specific background. The credentials do not give access to higher education.

May be considered for freshman admission.

This statement is for graduates of academic, university-preparatory secondary school programs and other programs that can be considered for freshman admission without reservations or qualifiers. (For the U.K. workshop report, special qualifiers were added to this placement recommendation.)

An academic enrichment program at the upper secondary level.

By utilizing this statement, the Council is providing descriptive information only, not a placement recommendation. Evaluators should follow the practice employed at their institutions for similar programs.

Undergraduate Admission

May be considered for undergraduate admission with up to ... year(s) of transfer credit, determined through a course-by-course analysis.

This recommendation sets the maximum amount of credit, depending on the length of study, for a university program. The phrasing "course-by-course analysis" asks the evaluator to look carefully at course contents, such as course descriptions from catalogs, in order to determine the appropriateness of transfer credit. For this U.K. workshop report, special qualifiers were added to this placement recommendation.

Graduate or Advanced Professional Admission

May be considered for graduate admission.

This recommendation is used if the program of study is considered to provide adequate preparation for graduate study, without reservation or qualifiers. Normally such a program represents a total of 16 years of education and gives access to graduate education within the foreign system. This recommendation may be used for programs requiring more than 16 years of study if no graduate transfer credit is recommended.

May be considered for [graduate admission and] graduate transfer credit, determined through a course-by-course analysis.

This recommendation provides guidance regarding the allowance of graduate transfer credit for the credential. The phrasing "course-by-course analysis" asks the evaluator to look carefully at course contents, such as course descriptions from catalogs, in order to determine the appropriateness of graduate transfer credit.

May be considered comparable to a U.S. master's degree.

This recommendation is used if the program of study is considered comparable to that of a U.S. master's program. This recommendation is usually not used for first degrees that may represent a level of academic attainment comparable to that of a master's degree but that are different in program structure.

May be considered comparable to an earned U.S. doctorate.

This recommendation is used if the program of study is considered comparable to a U.S. doctoral program. There may be differences in the structure and requirements of the program, but the credential represents advanced research and dissertation work of a sufficient-ly high level to recommend doctoral comparability.

A first professional degree in . . . [medicine, dentistry, veterinary medicine, architecture]. May be considered for graduate admission.

This statement is used to point out the first professional degrees awarded in a particular field. No graduate transfer credit is awarded. While preparation for the profession occurs at the graduate level in the U.S., it occurs at the undergraduate level in many foreign educational systems.

A professional qualification. May be considered for academic placement on the basis of other credentials.

This recommendation is used for credentials that represent advanced training, primarily nonacademic in nature, and that are not appropriate for placement determination.

Represents completion of undergraduate teacher education courses.

By utilizing this statement, the Council is providing descriptive information only, not a placement recommendation. Evaluators should follow the practice employed at their institutions for similar undergraduate teacher education courses.

Placement Recommendations

Credential	Entrance Requirement	Length of Program	Gives Access in United Kingdom to	Placement Recommendation
1. General Certificate of Education Ordinary Level [GCE O] (1951-1987*) (p. 24; see also Fisher, pp. 38-39, 32-47)	Completion of 3 years of secondary education	2 years (total 11 years primary and secondary)	Further study; employment	May be considered for freshman admission with a minimum of 5 O-level passes in different subjects, including English and math, with grades A-C.
2. Certificate of Secondary Education [CSE] (p. 24; see also Fisher, pp. 23-24, 30)	Completion of 3 years of secondary education	2 years (total 11 years primary and secondary)	Further study; employment	May be considered for freshman admission with a minimum of 5 passes in different subjects, including English and math, with grade of 1.
3. General Certificate of Secondary Education [GCSE] (Since 1987) pp. 30-31	Completion of primary education	5 years (total 11 years primary and secondary)	Further study; employment	May be considered for freshman admission with a minimum of 5 passes in different subjects, including English and math, with grades A-C.
4. General Certificate of Education Advanced Level [GCE A] (p. 33; see also Fisher, pp. 39-40)	GCE O-level or GCSE	2 years (total 13 years primary and secondary)	Further study	May be considered for undergraduate admission if anterior qualifications are considered appropriate preparation; may be considered for up to 1 year of advanced standing credit in each subject corresponding to an A-level pass.
5. General Certificate of Education Advanced Supplementary Level [GCE AS] (Since 1988) (p. 35)	GCE O-level or GCSE	2 years (total 13 years primary and secondary)	Further study	May be considered for undergraduate admission if anterior qualifications are considered appropriate preparation; may be considered for up to 1/2 year of advanced standing credit in each subject corresponding to an AS-level pass after a review of the syllabus.

* GCE O-level available for overseas students only after 1987.

III. HIGHER EDUCATION IN THE U.K.

Polytechnics, Colleges and Institutes of Higher Education

Introduction

In England, Wales, and Northern Ireland higher education generally means education beyond the standard represented by the General Certificate of Education Advanced Level (A-level) examinations. Institutions providing higher education are universities and, since 1965, the polytechnics, colleges and institutes of higher education.

There are 42 self-governing universities in England, Wales, and Northern Ireland empowered by Royal Charter to award degrees. Their source of funding, with one exception, comes mainly from the government through the Universities Funding Council (UFC). The University of Buckingham in England is the only private institution and is supported by students' fees.

There are 30 polytechnics, all in England and Wales, which together with the colleges and institutes of higher education provide most of the advanced fulltime programs similar to those offered at universities. The polytechnics, colleges and institutes of higher education are publicly funded, receiving their funding through the Polytechnics and Colleges Funding Council (PCFC).

Both universities and polytechnics offer programs leading to undergraduate degrees to which admission may be gained on the basis of appropriate school-leaving qualifications, and to higher research degrees which require a first degree for admission. Original research, traditionally an important function of universities, also is undertaken at polytechnics where the emphasis is mainly on "applied" research. Many programs are offered at both universities and polytechnics, but there are often differences in structures and teaching methods. Polytechnics in particular provide a wide range of professionally oriented programs and have a significant commitment to nondegree and part-time studies. In addition to their own degree programs, polytechnics offer programs leading to certificates, diplomas, first and higher research degrees awarded by the Council for National Academic Awards (CNAA), which is an independent body with its own Royal Charter.

The colleges and institutes of higher education vary greatly in size and in the range of courses they offer. They provide certificate, diploma and degree programs validated by the CNAA, as well as various kinds of nondegree programs. The certificates, diplomas, degrees and other academic distinctions awarded by the CNAA in accordance with the statutes of its Royal Charter are consistent and comparable in standard with awards conferred throughout higher education in the United Kingdom including the universities.

A few of the programs in the polytechnics and some of those in the colleges and institutes of higher education, and almost all in the field of teacher education are "validated" (approved) by and lead to degrees from a local university.

The polytechnics, colleges and institutes of higher education also provide instruction which prepares students for the Higher National Certificate/Diploma (HNC/HND) and the National Certificate/Diploma (NC/ND), both awarded by the Business and Technician Education Council (BTEC). Other programs are offered at the colleges of further education (see the chapter on secondary education for more information).

Institutions of Higher Education

Polytechnics

The polytechnics were formed in the late 1960s to expand the higher education system in order to offer greater opportunities for people to obtain academic credentials. Thirty institutions were established through an amalgamation of a number of existing colleges of commerce specializing in business and accounting and other institutions emphasizing teaching in the social sciences and humanities, science and engineering, art and design and teacher education. This grouping of previously existing institutions accounts for multiple-campus sites and sometimes confusing address listings.

In addition to providing courses of study leading to the awards of the CNAA and BTEC, the polytechnics provide courses of study set by numerous professional bodies. They offer an applied or practical approach to learning, stressing the development of skills transferable to the work environment. Polytechnic education, therefore, often is professionally oriented and is designed to meet the needs of business and industry as well as the professions including law, engineering, accountancy and social services. In addition to providing programs leading to CNAA certificates, diplomas and first (bachelor's) degrees, the polytechnics also offer programs leading to CNAA postgraduate certificates and diplomas as well as to graduate awards such as master's degrees by coursework, master's degrees by research, the doctor of philosophy (PhD or DPhil), and also what are called "higher doctorates," which are degrees with titles such as doctor of letters (DLit) or doctor of science (DSc).

Since the polytechnics are expected to work closely with business and industry, many programs of study are offered through a modular structure or through various nontraditional types of attendance patterns. The degree programs which operate on a modular scheme consist of self-contained courses at various levels. Students are examined on each course as they complete it rather than just at the end of the year. Modular programs offer considerable flexibility and choice and enable students to take a course in an area outside their main subjects to fulfill a personal interest.

The number of modules required for a degree may vary from institution to institution and, therefore, the number required per year also may vary. The sample modular scheme shown below is offered by Oxford Polytechnic.

Stage I. Certificate of Higher Education [CertHE]

Pass at least 10 basic modules including those compulsory for one Double Field or two Single Fields (one year fulltime, up to two years part-time). Single field refers to the study of a single subject like history or psychology. Double field emphasizes a subject area such as languages for business, human biology or applied geology.

Stage II.

Pass at least 8+ modules	Pass at least 16+ modules	Pass at least 18+ modules	Pass at least 27+ modules
DipHE	DipHE	DipHE	DipHE
	BA/BSc Degree	BA/BSc Hons Degree	
			BEd Hons BA Hons Nursing Midwifery

Normal length of fulltime program

2 years	3 years	3 years	4 years

The above sample modular scheme is not meant to imply that each year of study consists of eight modules. For example, at the West London Institute of Higher Education, six modules are taken per year, with 18 modules required for a three-year bachelor's program and 24 modules for a four-year bachelor's program (BEd [Hons]). At Coventry Polytechnic, an eight module annual scheme is adopted, while at Hatfield Polytechnic the Master of Engineering (MEng) program indicates 10 modules as a "fulltime" academic year.

Responding to the needs of mature students–those 21 years or older–the polytechnics have developed flexible admissions policies and programs such as the Higher Introductory Technology and Engineering Conversion Course [HITECC], which is a form of access course. It is a nationally recognized one-year program of study designed to prepare students without A-levels in physics and mathematics to enter a Higher National Diploma or degree program in engineering or technology.

Another example of an access course is the one-year fulltime "foundation" program of study designed to prepare students to enter professions such as accounting or art and design and to enable students to enter an appropriate first degree or other award programs. Appendix A, Sample 1 lists the courses for the foundation program in Accountancy at Coventry Polytechnic. See also document 3.1. The Associate Student Scheme is a program which permits mature students to attend regular course offerings to determine whether they are capable of or are interested in further study. Students may choose whether they wish to be graded in the course which, if graded, could be applied toward a degree program.

In addition, a number of institutions participate in the Credit Accumulation and Transfer Scheme (CATS) allowing students greater movement between institutions. Currently, mature students make up from 25%-60% of polytechnic enrollments. Because of these responses to the needs of both students and employers, the polytechnics are recognized as being accessible and innovative, characteristics that have particular relevance to the 1990s. Appendix B contains a list of the polytechnics in England and Wales.

Colleges and Institutes of Higher Education

The difference between the polytechnics and the colleges and institutes of higher education is largely historical. Discussion in the early 1970s focused on a number of problems associated with teacher education. The 1972 government White Paper, *Education: A Framework for Expansion,* suggested that colleges of education were too narrowly focused on the training of teachers and that, due to an oversupply of teachers and a projected decline in student enrollment in the 1970s, these colleges should be incorporated into the public sector and merged with colleges of further education and other institutions to form what are now called colleges and institutes of higher education.

Beginning in 1974, 64 of these major institutions were formed to offer a wider variety of courses, at degree level and below, than previously was available in the colleges of education. They prepared students for careers in teaching, business, technology and the professions. These institutions, according to the 1972 White Paper, "will not be easily distinguishable by function from a polytechnic or other further education colleges."

Currently, the difference seems to be one of size. The colleges and institutes of higher education tend to have smaller enrollments than the polytechnics, with a narrower range of programs. Since these institutions offer programs leading to many of the academic awards offered by the CNAA through the polytechnics, the admission requirements and the types of programs are the same as those described for the polytechnics. There-fore, there is no difference in the quality of programs between these institutions. See Appendix C for a list of colleges of further education and colleges and institutes of higher education.

Colleges of Education (Teacher Education)

The three-year colleges of education, which prior to 1960 were two-year institutions, provided programs leading to the Certificate in Education. By the mid 1970s, the colleges of education and the three-year certificate programs were phased out, replaced by degree programs provided at the colleges and institutes of higher education, polytechnics and universities.

Following the 1972 White Paper, *Education: A Framework for Expansion,* the Diploma of Higher Education was created and the colleges of education were reorganized. The curriculum for the Diploma of Higher Education is designed to be equivalent to the first two years of a four-year Honours Bachelor of Education degree. Teacher education today is conducted at university departments of education, many polytechnics and colleges and institutes of higher education.

Before the reorganization of teacher education, the three-year Certificate in Education course was comprised of general education and professional training pursued concurrently. Currently, the teacher education qualifications are:

1. a three-year program leading to the Bachelor of Education (BEd) degree;

2. a four-year program leading to the Bachelor of Education (BEd) Honours degree;

3. a one-year program of study leading to the Certificate in Education, taken concurrently with the Bachelor of Arts or Bachelor of Science programs whereby the bachelor's degree and certificate are awarded concurrently at the end of four years, or a one-year postgraduate program of professional training leading to the Post-Graduate Certificate in Education (PGCE) following a three- or four-year degree (i.e., the Bachelor of Arts or Bachelor of Science).

In 1983 the government established the National Council for the Accreditation of Teacher Education to validate the professional content of all courses in initial

DIPLOMA

in

ACCOUNTANCY
(FOUNDATION COURSE)

awarded to

The following subjects have been studied

Financial Accountancy
Principles of Management Accounting·
Principles of Law
Economics
Data Processing and Systems Design
Quantitative Techniques
Business Management and Environment

THE AWARD IS MADE AT PASS LEVEL

date   12 September 1989   signed *Sue Hsefre*   Academic Registrar

COVENTRY
POLYTECHNIC

Document 3.1a. Diploma in Accounting (Foundation Course) with Notification of Examination Results

NOTIFICATION OF EXAMINATION RESULTS 1988/89
(REFERRED/DEFERRED UPDATE)

Ref:

Date 19/ 9/89

Name:
Course: Polytechnic Diploma in Accountancy (Foundation Course)   Overall Result: Pass
Stage: 1

BMS150 Accounting   ac1 56 ac2 46 tot 102
BMS154 Data Processing & Systems Design   cw   62
BMS155 Business Management and Economic History   ex   49
EC914 Economics   ex   46
LS910 Principles of English Law   ex   54
SO915 Quantitative Techniques   ex   66 **

** Referred Results

Pass, awarded a Polytechnic Diploma in Accountancy.

Academic Registrar

COVENTRY
POLYTECHNIC

Document 3.1b. page 2

teacher training programs provided by university departments of education, polytechnics, colleges and institutes of higher education.

Students who completed the initial teacher training programs with one further year of study to earn the Post-Graduate Certificate in Education (PGCE) are able to upgrade their credential. A two-year PGCE is available for those whose first degree is not in the subject they wish to teach on the secondary level. In-service coursework leads to the award of the Diploma of Professional Studies in Education (DipPSE). This program of study is designed to enable practicing professionals to study different aspects of their profession and contains significant elements of research. This post-experience education is also called "INSET," which refers to training available for individuals already working in the field.

Today, there are a number of different routes by which students may become qualified to teach in schools. The principal routes to obtain Qualified Teacher Status (QTS) are:

a. a four-year fulltime program of study leading either to the Bachelor of Education (BEd) with Honours or to the Bachelor of Science (BSc) or Bachelor of Arts (BA) with Honours and the Certificate in Education (CertEd);

b. a three-year degree course in a subject appropriate to the school curriculum followed by a program of study leading to the award of the Post-Graduate Certificate in Education (PGCE);

c. for entrants with the equivalent of one year's successful fulltime undergraduate study in an appropriate subject area, a two-year fulltime program of study leading to the award of the BEd;

d. satisfactory completion of a period of service as "licensed" or "articled" teacher.

To address the teacher shortage in some areas, the government introduced two new ways to gain QTS: licensed teacher in 1989, and articled teacher in 1990.

The licensed teacher credential is experience-based (on-the-job) and obtained through the Local Education Authority (LEA) while the articled teacher credential is similar to the PGCE but offered at the school of employment. These courses are overseen by the local partnerships of education authorities and the respective colleges and not the National Council for the Accreditation of Teachers.

Validating and Credential Awarding Bodies

The Council for National Academic Awards

The Council for National Academic Awards (CNAA) is an autonomous organization established by Royal Charter in 1964. It is empowered to award degrees, diplomas, certificates and other academic awards and distinctions to students who have pursued programs of study or research approved by the CNAA at polytechnics, colleges and institutes of higher education in the United Kingdom including the Scottish central institutions.

The CNAA is the largest single degree-awarding body in the United Kingdom. More than a third of all students who are studying for a degree in the U.K. attend CNAA-approved programs. As of 1989, there were over 120 institutions offering nearly 2,300 undergraduate and sub-degree level programs approved by the CNAA with close to 190,000 registered students.

By the terms of its Charter and Statutes, CNAA awards are considered comparable in standard to those conferred by universities in the United Kingdom. They are recognized as such by professional institutes, employers and universities for professional membership and employment and for entry to higher degree programs.

Until 1987 the CNAA validated syllabuses developed by the polytechnic or college staff. Validation is the process by which the CNAA determines that a program meets the requirements for a CNAA award. This procedure then is followed by the approval process which is the formal confirmation by CNAA of the program's acceptability. Subsequent to approval, the program is reviewed at intervals of not more than seven years to insure that it continues to meet standards.

In 1987 the CNAA introduced radical changes which altered its future relationships with polytechnics and colleges. A system of accreditation was introduced, under which the CNAA licensed institutions to take full responsibility for the approval and review of their own programs. The term "accredited institution" is used to describe the relationship of many polytechnics and some colleges and institutes of higher education with the

CNAA. Today, all 30 polytechnics and a number of the colleges and institutes of higher education have received CNAA accreditation. Institutions which have not yet received accreditation continue to have their programs validated, approved and reviewed by the CNAA. These institutions commonly are referred to as associated institutions and are eligible to apply to the CNAA for accreditation.

To qualify for accreditation, an institution must demonstrate that it is able to adopt procedures required for the initial validation, approval, periodic review and revision and modification of all programs which lead to CNAA awards. Institutions accredited by the CNAA have the authority under the Council's charter and statutes, to validate, monitor, review and approve new programs and to modify existing ones on CNAA's behalf. Accreditation signifies that an institution has satisfied the Council that it has suitable experience in and an appropriate organization for maintaining academic standards. Presently, those institutions having CNAA accreditation are permitted to issue their own certificates, diplomas and degrees but they still are CNAA awards; all documents note that the qualification has been awarded under the Royal Charter of the CNAA.

The CNAA reserves the right to withdraw its accreditation should an institution fail to maintain standards. Every five to seven years, the Council reviews accredited institutions to determine if it should continue its accreditation.

As of July 1983, the Council validates shorter programs subject to the following conditions: the program is within a scheme leading to a CNAA award and is comprised of separate, self-contained courses; a program which does not fulfill the above condition must be at the same level as a CNAA award; the program is at least one term long (fulltime) or its part-time equivalent.

The CNAA also encourages and supports open learning, defined as the opportunity extended to students to develop greater control over their program of study than is provided by traditional curriculums. The forms of open learning currently in effect are flexible admission policies providing easier access; flexible attendance patterns in terms of time or mode of study and location including distance learning, a scheme whereby students may carry out their study away from the physical location of instruction; and resource-based learning whereby students devise their own learning strategies to attain specific course objectives.

As of 1990 the programs providing open learning include the Diploma of Higher Education (DipHE) and the BA/BSc Honours by independent study at North East London Polytechnic, the Master of Science (MSc) in Applied Statistics at Sheffield Polytechnic and the Diploma in Educational Technology at Dundee College of Education.

Admission Criteria for CNAA Awards

Pre-Degree and First Degree Programs

Generally, there are three routes toward acceptance for CNAA pre- and first degree programs:

a. The standard qualification is two GCE A-level passes and three subject passes at GCE O-level/GCSE Grade C or better/CSE Grade 1. The A-level passes must be in different subjects from the O-level/GCSE/CSE subjects. With the recent addition of an Advanced Supplementary (AS) level pass, two AS-level subject passes may substitute for one A-level result;

b. Vocational awards such as the Ordinary National Certificate or Diploma (ONC/OND) or the Business and Technician Education Council (BTEC) National Certificate or National Diploma (NC/ND);

c. Students from nontraditional backgrounds, lacking the specific credentials listed above, may take preparation or access courses to qualify for entry. These courses involve a minimum of one year of fulltime study and generally prepare a student for a degree program at a specific institution. Open University credits and the European and International Baccalaureate secondary school diplomas also are acceptable admissions credentials. Mature students without formal qualification also may be eligible for admission. Students without formal educational qualifications must demonstrate that they have the motivation and experience to enter higher education directly. This generally is determined through a personal interview with an admission tutor.

Postgraduate (Including Post-Experience) and Graduate Programs

Admission to a postgraduate program requires a bachelor's (first) degree or higher or, in the case of "post-experience" programs, other appropriate qualifications and/or experience. The polytechnics, colleges and institutes of higher education do not publish formal statements about all the non-U.K. degrees or other qualifications they recognize for the purpose of entry. No degree or other qualification, whether obtained in Great Britain or elsewhere, automatically secures a place for its holder. An applicant's suitability is individually assessed by each institution to which he or she applies.

In many institutions graduates of first degree programs must first register for a master's degree before going on to do research for the degree of Doctor of Philosophy (PhD or DPhil). Students who then decide to leave after one or two years can do so with a recognized qualification while those who do well and wish to continue their studies can apply to change their registration to PhD/DPhil candidacy.

Postgraduate programs are intended to enhance or to develop special aspects of the academic and professional competence of those who, although not necessarily graduates, have obtained an initial qualification in their chosen field and have subsequently had several years of relevant practical experience. There are programs of this kind in many higher education institutions, leading to a variety of degrees, diplomas or certificates. Many of them are part-time, to enable participants to continue in their jobs while they study; but there are many fulltime post-experience programs as well, especially in education, business administration/management and engineering/technology. In these subject areas, particularly, there may be no very clearcut distinction between "postgraduate" and "post-experience" programs. Many programs intended mainly for graduates are open also to suitably qualified nongraduates, and may require a period of relevant practical experience, even if a degree normally is necessary.

Awards

Pre-Degree Level

Certificate (Cert): Admission requires five subject passes at GCE O-level/GCSE grade C or better/CSE grade 1. This award, which has not been given since April 1988, required one year of fulltime academic study in a specialized field of study and served as a substitute for and was accepted in lieu of the Advanced Levels. Holders of this award were eligible to enter into the first year of a higher award or bachelor's degree program. The Certificate was regarded as a qualification available in a limited number of programs in arts, social science or social studies and was approved with the

needs of mature students in mind so as to give them access to degree programs.

Certificate of Higher Education [CertHE]: Admission requires two A-levels and three subject passes at GCE O-level/GCSE grade C or better/CSE grade 1 or the BTEC NC/ND. The A-level passes must be in subjects different from O-level/GCSE/CSE passes. This award was introduced in April 1988 to upgrade and replace the Certificate mentioned above. It requires one year of fulltime academic study and is equivalent to the first year of a bachelor's (honours) degree. Holders of this award are eligible to enter into the second year of a higher award or bachelor's degree program. See Appendix A, Sample 2.

Certificate in Education [CertEd]: Admission requires two A-levels and three subject passes at GCE O-level/GCSE grade C or better/CSE grade 1 (including English and mathematics), or the BTEC NC/ND. The A-level passes must be in subjects different from O-level/GCSE/CSE passes. At least one year of fulltime study in the theory and practice of teaching is required. Practical competence in teaching must also be demonstrated. It is at A-level equivalent to the first year of an Honours degree. This award is part of the one-year component of the combined BA/BSc degree program.

Certificate in Education (Further Education) [CertEd-FE]: Admission requires two A-levels and three subject passes at GCE O-level/GCSE grade C or better/CSE grade 1 or the BTEC NC/ND. The A-level passes must be in subjects different from O-level/GCSE/CSE passes. This award requires one year of fulltime academic study in the theory and practice of teaching. Practical competence in teaching must also be demonstrated. It is at a level equivalent to the first year of an Honours degree. The award is designed for those who wish to teach at a college of further education and can be earned concurrently with either a BA or BSc with Honours. The combined program is four years of fulltime study.

Diploma of Higher Education [DipHE]: Admission requires two A-levels and three subject passes at GCE O-level/GCSE grade C or better/CSE grade 1 or the BTEC NC/ND. The A-level passes must be in subjects different from O-level/GCSE/CSE passes. This award requires two years of fulltime academic study. It is at a level equivalent to the first two years of an Honours degree. This Diploma plus experience assessed through the Credit Accumulation and Transfer Scheme can lead to admission to graduate study. This is a feature unique to this particular award.

First Degrees

Bachelor of Arts [BA] and Bachelor of Science [BSc] (Unclassified/Ordinary or Honours): The Bachelor of Arts [BA] and Bachelor of Science [BSc] are awards which may be pursued as Unclassified/Ordinary or Honours. The BA traditionally is given in art and design, the arts and humanities, combined studies in the arts and in social or business studies. The BSc is offered in science or mathematics, whether applied or pure.

Admission to the Bachelor's degree (Unclassified/Ordinary or Honours) requires two A-levels and three subject passes at GCE 0-level/GCSE grade C or better/CSE grade 1 or the BTEC NC/ND. The A-level passes must be in subjects different from the O-level/GCSE/CSE passes. The program requires three years of fulltime undergraduate study.

Three circumstances may lead to a bachelor's unclassified/ordinary degree:

1. the program of study is designed to lead only to the unclassified/ordinary degree;

2. the student fails to achieve an Honours degree;

3. the student, usually one studying part-time, has made a prior decision to opt for the unclassified/ordinary degree, rather than for the Honours degree which also is offered.

Holders of the Bachelor's Unclassified/Ordinary degree may pursue a postgraduate certificate or diploma and sometimes with additional qualifications, such as a Post-Graduate Certificate in Education or Diploma in Professional Studies, a graduate (master's) degree.

In addition to demonstrating a higher quality of performance than is necessary for the unclassified/ordinary degree, students pursuing a Bachelor's Honours degree must also complete one or two additional modules and exhibit a higher level of independent study. This degree is usually required to be admitted for study at the master's (graduate) degree level. See Appendix A, Sample 4.

Information as to whether a bachelor's degree was pursued as honours is specified on educational records (transcript and diploma). See sample documents 3.2 and 3.3. Some institutions may indicate on the documents that a bachelor's degree was pursued as Unclassified/Ordinary, some make no mention. See sample document 3.4.

Bachelor of Education [BEd]: Admission requires two A-levels and three subject passes at GCE O-level/GCSE grade C or better/CSE grade 1 or the BTEC NC/ND. The A-level passes must be in subjects different from O-level/GCSE/CSE passes.

The title of BEd is reserved for teacher education programs. The normal length of time for a BEd program is four years of fulltime study with the third year reserved solely for a practice teaching experience. Holders of a BTEC Higher National Diploma (HND) or its equivalent may complete the Unclassified/Ordinary degree with two years of study. Depending on the field of study and institution, additional courses are required for the Honours degree.

The in-service BEd is designed for students who already are qualified and experienced teachers holding a Certificate of Education or equivalent qualification. The minimum length of the program is one calendar year of fulltime study or the part-time equivalent. See Appendix A, Sample 5.

Bachelor of Engineering [BEng Honours/BEng]: Admission requires two A-levels and three subject passes at GCE O-level/GCSE grade C or better/CSE grade 1 or the BTEC NC/ND. One A-level pass must be in a mathematical subject and one in physics or engineering science. Depending on the institution and program of study, other requirements may be necessary. The title of BEng rather than BSc is reserved for a three-year fulltime program of study involving a technologically broad education with an emphasis on engineering applications. The degree may lead to registration with the Engineering Council subject to the other conditions set by the Council. The Honours degree is required for graduate study. See Appendix A. Samples 3 and 6.

Bachelor of Laws [LLB]: Admission requires two A-levels and three subject passes at GCE O-level/GCSE grade C or better/CSE grade 1 or the BTEC NC/ND. A pass in English may be required. The A-level passes must be in subjects different from O-level/GCSE/CSE passes. This award involves three years of specialized study in law. A BA or BSc may be awarded where legal and other studies are combined. Since the degree itself does not qualify for the practice of law, holders of this degree must have a minimum period of professional training and pass additional examinations. (For further information refer to the World Education Series volume, *United Kingdom*, 1976, by Stephen Fisher, pp. 201-202.)

Council for National Academic Awards

of BRISTOL POLYTECHNIC

has been awarded the degree of
BACHELOR OF EDUCATION
with SECOND CLASS HONOURS (2nd Division)
having followed an approved programme

03 July 1986

Director
Bristol Polytechnic

Chairman

Chief Officer

COUNCIL FOR NATIONAL ACADEMIC AWARDS

Document 3.2a. Bachelor of Education Degree Awarded by CNAA for Studies Completed at Bristol Polytechnic

b Bristol Polytechnic

FACULTY OF EDUCATION

CNAA B.ED. DEGREE TRANSCRIPT

NAME: ....   DATES ATTENDED: 1982 - 1986.

AS SUBJECT: History   PS PROGRAMME: 3-12 / XXXXXXXXXXXXXXX

UNIT PLACING		SECTOR*	UNIT NO.	TITLE	GRADE AWARDED
YEAR 1	1	AS	701	Role of Evidence in Historical Study	C
	2	ES	101	Foundation:Teachers & Schools Children Learning	C
	3	PS	201	Introduction to Roles & Functions of a Primary Teacher	C
	4	AS	702	Renaissance,Reconnaissance & Reformation	B
	5	ES	102	Foundation:Teachers & Schools Children Learning	B
	6	PS	202	Curriculum Perspectives Basic Skills	C
YEAR 2	7	AS	703	17th Century Western Europe:England & the United Provinces	
	8	ES	106	Childhood & Culture	A
	9	PS	203	Curriculum Perspectives	C
	10	PS	204	Teaching Practice Primary ESN(S)	P
	11	PS	248	Physical Education in the Primary School	B
	12	ES	111	The Curriculum	B
YEAR 3	13	PS	205	Curriculum Perspectives	B
	14	AS	704	Historiography and Depth Study	B
	15/16	PS	206	Teaching Practice Primary	P
	17	PS	260	Teaching Children with Learning Difficulties	D
	18	AS	706	19th Century Liberalism,Nationalism,Socialism in Europe	C

YEAR 4 (HONOURS)

SECTORS STUDIED:

HONOURS CLASSIFICATION: BEd Hons 2-2.

Key: AS   = Academic Studies
      ES   = Education Studies
      PS   = Professional Studies   CNAA B.Ed. Course Director
      Grades   = A - D = Pass; E = Fail
      TP Units : P = Pass; D = Distinction

NB This is a transcript of results, not a certificate, diploma or degree.

Document 3.2b. Transcript for BEd Honours Degree from Bristol Polytechnic

Council for National Academic Awards

of PORTSMOUTH POLYTECHNIC

has been awarded the degree of

BACHELOR OF SCIENCE

with SECOND CLASS HONOURS (1st Division)

having followed an approved sandwich programme in

MECHANICAL ENGINEERING

2nd July 1987

President

PORTSMOUTH POLYTECHNIC

Chairman

Chief Officer

Document 3.3a. BSc (Honours) Degree in Engineering (Sandwich Program), Awarded by CNAA for
Completion of Studies at Portsmouth Polytechnic

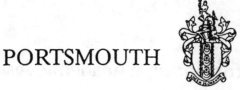

PORTSMOUTH POLYTECHNIC

Department of Mechanical Engineering
Anglesea Building, Anglesea Road, Portsmouth PO1 3DJ
Telephone Portsmouth (0705) 827681

9 March, 1989

NAME:

DATE OF BIRTH:

COURSE: BSc (Hons) Mechanical Engineering

Transcript of Studies

Subject	Year/Grade 1	2	3	4
Mathematics	2	1	3	
Thermofluid Mechanics	2	3	2	
Mechanics of Solids	1	3	3	
Engineering Production	2	2	1	2
Science of Materials	2	3	3	
Engineering Design	3	2	1	3
Electrical Engineering	4	2	-	
Complementary Studies	1	1	1	
Control			2	
Mechanics of Fluids				2
Dynamics and Control				1
Naval Architecture				2
Management Studies				2
Engineering Project				1

AWARD: Upper Second Class Honours

DATE OF AWARD: July 1987

Signed ..P.A.George.....
        Mr. P.A. George
        Director of Studies

KEY TO GRADES:

% Mark	Grade
70+	1
60-69	2
50-59	3
40-49	4

Document 3.3b. page 2

Council for National Academic Awards

of PORTSMOUTH POLYTECHNIC

has been awarded the degree of
BACHELOR OF SCIENCE
having completed a course in
CIVIL ENGINEERING

11 July 1980

President
Portsmouth Polytechnic

Chairman

Chief Officer

COUNCIL FOR NATIONAL ACADEMIC AWARDS

Document 3.4a. BSc (Unclassified/Ordinary) Degree Awarded by CNAA for Studies Completed at
Portsmouth Polytechnic

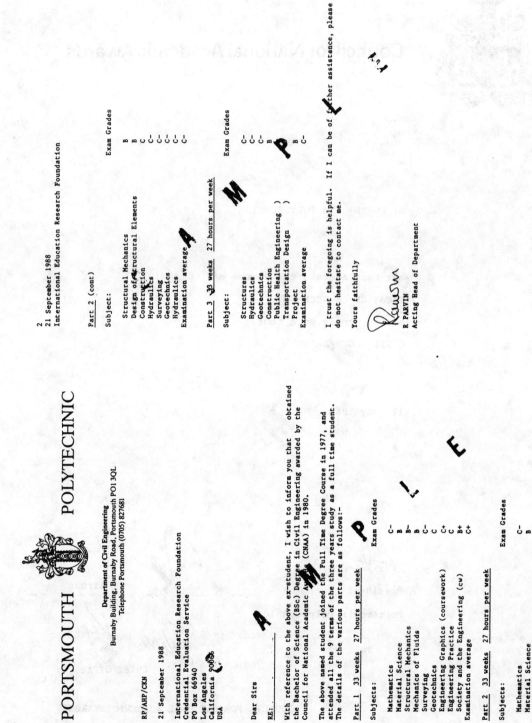

PORTSMOUTH POLYTECHNIC

Department of Civil Engineering
Burnaby Building, Burnaby Road, Portsmouth PO1 3QL
Telephone Portsmouth (0705) 827681

RP/AHP/CKN

21 September 1988

International Education Research Foundation
Credential Evaluation Service
PO Box 66940
Los Angeles
California 90066
USA

Dear Sirs

RE:

With reference to the above ex-student, I wish to inform you that obtained the Bachelor of Science (BSc) Degree in Civil Engineering awarded by the Council for National Academic Award (CNAA) in 1980.

The above named student joined the Full Time Degree Course in 1977, and attended all the 9 terms of the three years study as a full time student. The details of the various parts are as follows:-

Part 1   33 weeks   27 hours per week

Subjects:	Exam Grades
Mathematics	C-
Material Science	B-
Structural Mechanics	B-
Mechanics of Fluids	B-
Surveying	C-
Geotechnics	C+
Engineering Graphics (coursework)	C+
Engineering Practice	C
Society and the Engineering (cw)	B+
Examination average	C+

Part 2   33 weeks   27 hours per week

Subjects:	Exam Grades
Mathematics	C-
Material Science	B

2
21 September 1988
International Education Research Foundation

Part 2 (cont)

Subject:	Exam Grades
Structural Mechanics	B
Design of Structural Elements	B
Construction	C-
Hydraulics	C-
Surveying	C-
Geotechnics	C-
Hydraulics	C-
Examination average	C-

Part 3   33 weeks   27 hours per week

Subject:	Exam Grades
Structures	C-
Hydraulics	C-
Geotechnics	B-
Construction	B
Public Health Engineering)	
Transportation Design)	
Project	
Examination average	C-

I trust the foregoing is helpful. If I can be of further assistance, please do not hesitate to contact me.

Yours faithfully

R PARVIN
Acting Head of Department

Cont/....

Document 3.4b. page 2

Bachelor of Town Planning [BTP]: Admission requires a first degree or professional qualification in an appropriate field. The length of the program will be not less than one academic year or the equivalent. The award is available only as an unclassified degree and is comparable to a second bachelor's degree, if the holder previously has earned a first degree. If not, it is regarded as a first degree.

Graduate Diploma in Music [Grad Dip Mus]: Admission requires one A-level and three subject passes at GCE O-level/GCSE grade C or better/CSE grade 1 and two practical studies in music (at least one of which must be at the Grade VIII level of the Associate Board of the Royal Schools of Music). The A-level passes must be in subjects different from O-level/GCSE/CSE passes. This award requires three years of fulltime academic study and demonstrated competence in music performance and is offered only at specialized institutions. While considered at first degree level, it is a performance-oriented program and lacks the theoretical content and scope of a BA degree in music.

Master of Engineering [MEng]: Admission requires two A-levels and three subject passes at GCE O-level/GCSE grade C or better/CSE grade 1 or the BTEC NC/ND. The A-level passes must be in mathematics and either in physics or engineering science. The A-level passes must be in subjects different from O-level/GCSE/CSE passes. This first degree award requires a four-year program of study in Engineering, including three years of fulltime study at the Honours degree level and one additional year of fulltime study beyond that required for the award of the BEng with Honours. The degree is designed for BEng Honours students with a fourth or extra year allowing for the study of the broader aspects of Engineering including courses in international business and management studies. Selection into this program generally is made at the end of the first year or beginning of the second year of a BEng Honours program and is based on a strong academic performance in written examinations, acceptable performance in tests assessing motivation and personality, followed by an interview with a team from industry and academia. Broader in scope than a BEng Honours program, it is considered an enriched or extended bachelor's degree and not a graduate level "master's" degree.

Post-Experience and Postgraduate Awards

Diploma in Professional Studies [DipPS]: Admission requires professional qualification and ex-

perience in one of the following areas: education, health visiting, midwifery, nursing and sports coaching. The program of study is designed to enable practicing professionals to study different aspects of their profession and contains significant elements of practical research. The length of study is one academic year, fulltime, at Honours degree standard. See Appendix A, Sample 7.

Post-Graduate Certificate in Education [PGCE]: Admission requires a recent bachelor's degree. This award requires one year of fulltime study in the theory and practice of teaching with demonstrated teaching competence. This program is designed for those who wish to teach but whose undergraduate bachelor's degree program did not cover the required courses in education. See Appendix A, Sample 8 and document 3.5.

Post-Graduate Diploma [PGDip]: Admission requires a recent bachelor's degree. A minimum of 25 weeks of fulltime study is required in the subject (area of concentration) studied at first degree level, but in a more advanced and intensive fashion.

Diploma in Management Studies [DMS]: Admission requires a bachelor's degree or the BTEC HNC/HND with appropriate experience. Mature students over the age of 25 without a degree or diploma may be accepted if they have at least four years of managerial experience. This program leads to a post-experience, postgraduate diploma that is general, rather than specialized, and is not built on prior coursework. It is designed to help students develop and improve their managerial skills through an understanding of management processes in the business environment. It is a two stage program, taken over a two-year period on a part-time basis. See Appendix A, Sample 9.

Master's degree (Master of Arts [MA] or Master of Science [MSc]) (earned by coursework): Admission requires a bachelor's honours degree. The master's degree earned through coursework requires a minimum of one year of fulltime study in a field in which the student has an appropriate prior background. This is more intensive and advanced than a bachelor's degree and requires an element of advanced independent work.

The MA degree generally is awarded in the arts and humanities, art and communications design and other areas of study where specialized titles are not appropriate (e.g., MA in Performance Arts or MA in Fine Arts). The degree of MSc is granted in pure and applied science or mathematics. Titles of the programs of study leading to the MA or MSc generally will reflect or give

Council for National Academic Awards

of LEEDS POLYTECHNIC

has been awarded the

POSTGRADUATE CERTIFICATE IN EDUCATION

having followed an approved programme in

CHILDREN WITH SEVERE LEARNING DIFFICULTIES

19th June 1987

Director
Leeds Polytechnic

Chairman

Chief Office

COUNCIL FOR NATIONAL ACADEMIC AWARD

Document 3.5a. Post-Graduate Certificate in Education Awarded by CNAA for Studies Completed at Leeds Polytechnic

Leeds
POLYTECHNIC

Faculty of Educational and Leisure Studies
Dean: D W Pyle BSc BA MSc DoEd ABPS
Department of Education
Acting Head: E Miller BA MA DoEd MAEd

Beckett Park
Leeds
LS6 3QS

Leeds (0532) 759061

AF/BJC

17th June 1988.

TO WHOM IT MAY CONCERN

The above student was enrolled on the course P.G.C.E. Children with
Severe Learning Difficulties, at Leeds Polytechnic from 1986 to 1987.
was awarded a Pass in all assessed work.

Details of the course are as follows:

Course Title: Post Graduate Certificate in Education (Children with
Severe Learning Difficulties)

Course Length: 36 weeks

Course Elements:

(a) Teaching Experience – Primary School   7 weeks

Special School   9 weeks

(b) Foundation Studies – Growing & Learning

Atypical Child Development

Handicapped in Society   110 hours

(c) Subject Studies   – Social Skills   12 hours

Movement   30 hours

Creative Studies   30 hours

Maths   30 hours

Science   18 hours

In addition to the above all students complete 2 weeks placement with a
professional working in a field related to Special Education.

Yours sincerely,

A. R. Freeman
(Course Director)

a specific indication of the field studied (e.g., MSc in Water Pollution Control or MA in Criminology). The CNAA distinguishes between master's degree programs involving coursework (MA, MSc, MBA or MEd) and those which are research degrees (MPhil) by the title of the master's degree.

Master of Business Administration [MBA]: Admission requires a BA or BSc Honours; degree equivalent professional qualification; Diploma in Management Studies (DMS); or over 23 years of age with appropriate practical experience. The program focuses on the general principles and functions of management and the development of management skills. The program requires 2-3 years of part-time study.

Master of Education [MEd]: Admission requires a BEd Honours Degree; an Honours Degree with a substantial studies component and successful completion of a professional teacher training program; a Diploma in Professional Studies in Education [DipPSE]; or a BEd degree in which the Honours award was not offered. All applicants should have at least three years of teaching experience.

The program of study focuses on curriculum, teaching and management, staff and policy development and research evaluation. It is designed for those interested in educational administration and not in further teaching credentials. It is a master's degree earned by coursework that can be completed in one year on a fulltime basis or two years on a part-time basis.

Master of Philosophy [MPhil]: Admission requires a bachelor's honours degree. The MPhil consists of supervised scholarly research followed by a written thesis. The program of research must involve 18 to 36 months of fulltime study (or 30 to 48 months of part-time study) and must be defended by oral examination.

Doctor of Philosophy (PhD or DPhil): Admission requires a bachelor's honours degree or a master's ((MA/MSc or MPhil) degree in a discipline consistent with the proposed area of research. The master's degree must include training in the preparation of a research project.

The PhD is a research degree requiring an independent and critical evaluation of an appropriate topic and requires no formal coursework. A thesis demonstrating a significant and original contribution to knowledge is required. It must be defended by oral examination. The minimum period required for research

via transfer from the MPhil registration is 33 to 60 months for a fulltime student and 45 to 72 months for a part-time student. Should a student enter the PhD program directly after completing an honours bachelor's degree, 24 to 60 months of fulltime study and 36 to 72 months of part-time study is required. According to the CNAA guidelines, fulltime students are expected to spend 35 hours per week in their research and part-time students 12 hours per week.

In many institutions, holders of a bachelor's honours degree must first register for a master's degree before continuing on to do the research for the degree of doctor of philosophy. Thus, students who leave after one or two years can do so with a recognized qualification. Students who wish to continue their studies may apply to change their registration to PhD or DPhil candidature. If they are judged suitable for transfer to PhD registration, the period for which they have already been studying counts towards the requirements for the doctorate. The duration of studies for students entering with a bachelor's honours degree is five years and two years for those with the MPhil.

Higher Doctorates (Doctor of Letter [DLitt], Doctor of Science [DSc], Doctor of Technology [DTech]): A candidate for the DLitt, DSc, or DTech must be a leading authority in the field of study and a bachelor's degree holder of seven years' standing or a higher degree holder of four years' standing. The qualifying applicant must have made an original and substantial contribution to the advancement or application of knowledge in that field.

Classifications of Degrees

The bachelor's degree with honours is classified or graded as First Class, Upper Second Class, Lower Second Class and Third Class. There is also a provision for a Pass award should studies not meet with other classifications.

Classification of honours bachelor's degrees are as follow: First Class, Upper Second Class, Lower Second Class, Third Class, and Pass.

The bachelor's unclassified degree, may receive the following notations: Distinction, Honours, and Pass.

As noted earlier, the distinction between an honours degree and an unclassified or ordinary degree is that the honours degree program is more concentrated and demands more of the student. The unclassified or ordinary degree "with honours" is a measure of quality performance for one who has achieved a high standard of performance in the examinations.

Credit Accumulation and Transfer Scheme

The CNAA Credit Accumulation and Transfer Scheme (CATS) was established in 1985 and funded for an initial five-year period. The CAT Scheme primarily is designed to encourage and support nontraditional entrants to higher education. The Scheme provides a hierarchy of qualifications leading to an award based broadly on one year of fulltime study or its equivalent taken part-time or in some nontraditional way.

The CAT Scheme provides for the award of certificates of higher education, diplomas of higher education, degrees, honours degrees, postgraduate diplomas and master's degrees to individual students through the accumulation of academic credit points from programs of study composed of individual courses. A student's program of study is negotiated individually and may be taken through full- or part-time study, by distance learning or by a combination of these modes and may incorporate credit for the successful completion of employment-based training. When CATS "negotiates" a program, the CNAA alone awards the degree.

Credits per course are assigned on the basis of the number of courses required and not on the number which must be passed. The total value of successful completion of one year of work is 120 credits. Therefore, a student passing only four courses could transfer no more than 60 credits.

Credit transfer operates in several ways, regardless of whether a student completes the work for an award in one continuous period of study or with interruption. The student may transfer to an institution with the credit obtained from another one or from one program to another within an institution; register with an institution but also attend and obtain credit for courses taken elsewhere; or register centrally with the CNAA CAT Scheme to study for an award based on several types of learning experience or on study in several institutions.

The CNAA will be responsible directly for negotiating and approving the program of study of a centrally registered student.

The credit ratings allocated by the CAT Scheme to CNAA registered individual courses are advisory to other institutions, as each institution may apply other

values. Accumulated credits must form an acceptable program under the CNAA's general educational requirements before an award is made. A student will not be awarded a degree for an unrelated collection of credit points.

Awards at various levels are available from the CNAA under the CAT Scheme. Levels relate to standards of work and not necessarily to the year in which the course is taken during a program of studies. A level is assigned to a course by considering the award to which the student's program of study is leading and the prior knowledge or experience needed by the student. The level defines the position that the course occupies in the curriculum. This process may be likened to the course numbering system used in the United States, where 100, 200, 300, 400 level undergraduate courses form a hierarchy.

Level 1: the first year of a fulltime three-year degree unclassified/ordinary or honours;

Level 2: a standard normally encountered in the second year of a fulltime three-year degree, unclassified/ordinary or honours;

Level 3: a standard normally encountered in the final year of a fulltime three-year degree, unclassified/ordinary or honours.

Level M: a standard comparable to graduate level. Research degrees such as the MPhil and PhD are not part of the CAT Scheme.

The following are examples of the rating and credit value of several CNAA awards:

CHE	120 credits at Level 1
DipHE	120 credits at Level 1 and 120 credits at Level 2
Unclassified/ Ordinary Degree	360 credits, including at least 60 at Level 3 and no more than 120 at Level 1
Honours Degree	360 credits including at least 120 at Level 3 and no more than 120 at Level 1
Post-Graduate Diploma	70 credits at Level M
Master's Degree	120 credits at Level M

The CNAA also considers the BTEC awards such as the Higher National Certificate (HNC) and the Higher National Diploma (HND) for credit rating through the

CAT Scheme. These awards are granted 80 to 120 points, respectively, at Levels 1 and 2. An HND program may be judged to lead into the third year of a closely related degree program as it represents 120 additional points beyond the HNC. If this occurs, the total credit points may rise to 240.

The address of CNAA is 244-54 Gray's Inn Road, London WCIX 8BP, England.

Business and Technician Education Council

The Business and Technician Education Council (BTEC) was formed in 1983 by the merger of the Business Education Council (BEC) and the Technician Education Council (TEC). Like its predecessors, BTEC is an independent council established by the Secretary of State for Education and Science.

BTEC offers a range of nationally recognized non-degree qualifications in a variety of areas of study such as agriculture; business and finance; caring services; computing and information systems; construction; design; distribution; engineering; home economics; horticulture; hotel and catering; information technology; leisure services; public administration and science. In addition, it offers foundation programs designed for those aged 14 to 16 and provides pre-vocational programs leading to the Certificate of Pre-Vocational Education (CPVE) for those 16 and over. The CPVE programs are offered in conjunction with the City and Guilds of London Institute.

Programs leading to BTEC qualifications are run in colleges and polytechnics and, in the case of pre-vocational programs, secondary schools throughout England, Wales and Northern Ireland. Some continuing education programs are carried out by companies and may be studied using different modes–fulltime, day release, evening study, block release, sandwich, and open and distance learning. The content of programs will vary somewhat between institutions to reflect local and regional needs. However, all programs leading to the various BTEC awards are constructed as follows:

1. Core - Studies which are compulsory for all students taking courses leading to a specific qualification;

2. Options - A package of courses which, together with the core element and its related courses, provides a complete program of study.

The BTEC certificate programs are part-time and the diploma programs are fulltime. Students enrolled in diploma programs complete more courses (referred to as "units" by BTEC) taken from the optional component of the program. BTEC and the institutions offering these studies maintain that part-time students in the certificate programs compensate for this deficiency in coursework through their work experience such that the education acquired is comparable to the level of preparation and knowledge of the fulltime diploma programs. Work experience is not a required component of the certificate program as students enrolled in the program already are in the workforce.

Award Levels

BTEC offers four main levels of qualifications: First, National, Higher National and Continuing Education. Students who complete individual courses or short study programs receive a Certificate of Achievement, which on its own should not be considered as the basis for admission since it represents a partially completed program. Courses required for individual awards usually are studied consecutively so that possession of a National Certificate/Diploma (NC/ND) is a prerequisite for entry to a Higher National Certificate/Diploma program of study.

In England, Wales and Northern Ireland the Ordinary National Certificates and Diplomas (ONC/OND) have been replaced by BTEC awards and in Scotland by the Scottish Vocational Education Council (SCOT-VEC) awards.

Entry Requirements and Length of Programs

BTEC Continuing Education Certificate/Diploma: The programs and courses at this level are designed for adults normally at least 21 years old. Entry requirements and length of programs vary according to individual needs. Students tend to be admitted on the basis of suitable prior experience and ability rather than formal academic qualifications.

BTEC First Certificate/Diploma: Students must be at least 16 years of age. No formal qualifications are required. The certificate program requires one year of part-time study while the diploma program requires one year of fulltime or two years of part-time study.

BTEC National Certificate/Diploma [NC/ND]: Students must be at least 16 years old, and for most programs have for admission a BTEC First Certificate/Diploma, or four passes at GCE O-level/GCSE grade C or better/CSE Grade 1 or a Certificate of Pre-Vocational Education (CPVE). The certificate program requires two years part-time and the diploma is two years' fulltime or three years part-time/sandwich study. See documents 3.6, 3.7 and 3.8.

BTEC Higher National Certificate/Diploma [HNC/HND]: Students must be at least 18 years old and hold an appropriate BTEC National award or suitable GCE A-level passes. The certificate is two years of part-time study and the diploma is two years' fulltime or three years' part-time/sandwich study. See documents 3.6, 3.7 and 3.8.

Pre-Vocational Programs

The CPVE is awarded jointly by BTEC and the City and Guilds of London Institute and is designed for those students age 16 who wish to stay on at school or college after their period of compulsory education and who do not have clear academic and vocational objectives. No formal qualifications are required for entry. The CPVE is one year in duration, prepares young people for work and includes work experience. Students are exposed to a number of vocational choices whereby they can explore an option more deeply. The CPVE structure consists of three components: the core, vocational studies and additional studies. The core is made up of 10 essential areas: communication, numeracy, personal and career development, industrial, social and environmental studies, science and technology, information technology, creative development, practical skills and problem solving.

Assessment and Grading

The general framework for grades by BTEC is: **Distinction** - outstanding performance in all major areas of a course; **Merit** - outstanding performance in some areas of the course; **Pass** - satisfactory performance in all major areas of the course; **Fail.**

Sample Curriculum Leading to BTEC Awards

1. BTEC First Certificate/Diploma: Business And Finance

Core Subjects Only

A. Customer/Consumer
B. Profit and Profitability
C. People in Distribution
D. The Distributive Theory
E. Distributive Organization
F. Stock
G. Marketing

2. BTEC National Certificate/Diploma: Business and Finance

Core Subjects
Year I
A. Business-related Skills
B. People in Organizations
C. The Organization in Its Environment
D. Finance

Year II
E. Business-Related Skills
F. People in Organization II
G. The Organization Its Environment II

Standard Option Courses
Accounting
Advertising
Business Law Human Resource Management
Business Location and the Environment I
Business Location and the Environment II
Business Policy and Performance
Business Statistics
Elements of Banking I
Elements of Banking II
Elements of Building Society Practice
Employment, Industry and Change
Employment Practices/Industrial Relations
Information Processing I
Information Processing II
Insurance of the Person
International Trade
Law and Public Administration
Library and Information Work Marketing
People, Technology and Work Principles
   and Practices of Insurance

Higher National Certificate

IN ENGINEERING

IS AWARDED TO

WHO HAS SATISFACTORILY COMPLETED A BTEC-APPROVED COURSE AT
LIVERPOOL POLYTECHNIC

DATE OF AWARD: DECEMBER 1986

H.N. Raine.
Chairman

[signature]
Chief Executive

T217545.135007/79/41.135007.F015908.M.000000/0387

Document 3.6a. Higher National Certificate Awarded by BTEC for Studies Completed at Liverpool Polytechnic

Registered office Central House Upper Woburn Place London WC1H 0HH England

Notification of Performance on a BTEC approved course

DECEMBER 1986

Student   Student
registration   name
number

F015908
LIVERPOOL POLYTECHNIC

(135007)

UNIT	UNIT VALUE	LEVEL	GRADE
* THE USE OF COMPUTERS	0.5	II	PASS
MATHEMATICS	1.0	III	PASS
MECHANICAL SCIENCE	1.0	III	PASS
MANUFACTURING TECHNOLOGY	1.0	III	PASS
ENGINEERING DRAWING AND DESIGN	1.0	III	PASS
* APPLIED HEAT	1.0	III	PASS
* PROPERTIES OF MATERIALS	1.0	III	PASS
* ENGINEERING COMPUTATION	0.5	III	PASS
MATHEMATICS	1.0	IV	PASS
MECHANICAL SCIENCE	1.0	IV	PASS
MANUFACTURING TECHNOLOGY (A)	1.0	IV	PASS
* PROPERTIES OF MATERIALS	1.0	IV	PASS
* THERMODYNAMICS AND FLUIDS	1.0	IV	PASS
ENGINEERING INSTRUMENTATION AND CONTROL	1.0	IV	PASS
GENERAL STUDIES AND COMMUNICATION (A)	1.0	-	PASS
MECHANICAL SCIENCE	1.0	V	PASS

--TOTAL LISTED GRADES: 16

THE STUDENT HAS FULFILLED BTEC'S REQUIREMENT FOR PRACTICAL EXPERIENCE

THIS STUDENT HAS QUALIFIED FOR THE COUNCIL'S HIGHER NATIONAL CERTIFICATE IN
ENGINEERING
PROGRAMME NUMBER: 135007/79/41
ITEMS PREFIXED BY AN ASTERISK ARE SUPPLEMENTARY TO THE AWARD

Document 3.6b. page 2

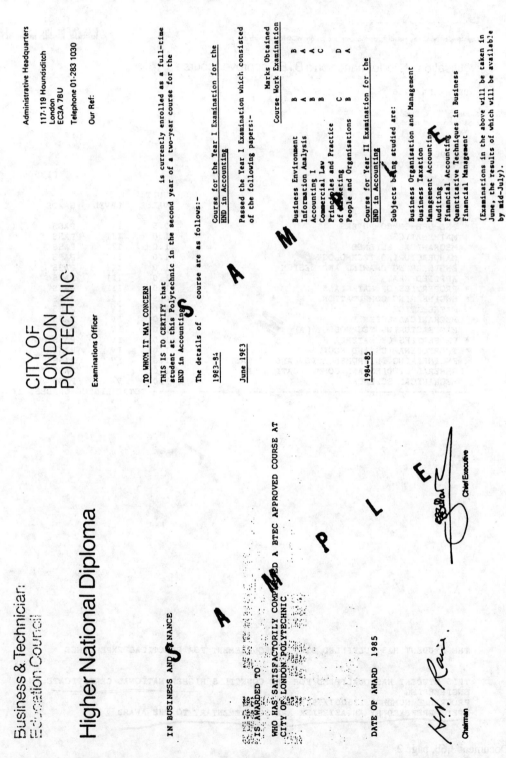

CITY OF
LONDON
POLYTECHNIC

Administrative Headquarters
117-119 Houndsditch
London
EC3A 7BU
Telephone 01-283 1030

Our Ref:

Examinations Officer

TO WHOM IT MAY CONCERN

THIS IS TO CERTIFY that   is currently enrolled as a full-time
student at this Polytechnic in the second year of a two-year course for the
HND in Accounting.

The details of course are as follows:-

1983-84

Course for the Year I Examination for the
HND in Accounting

Passed the Year I Examination which consisted
of the following papers:-

June 1983

	Marks Obtained	
	Course Work	Examination
Business Environment	B	B
Information Analysis	A	A
Accounting I	B	A
Commercial Law	B	C
Principles and Practice of Marketing	C	D
People and Organisations	B	A

1984-85

Course for Year II Examination for the
HND in Accounting

Subjects being studied are:

Business Organisation and Management
Business Taxation
Management Accounting
Auditing
Financial Accounting
Quantitative Techniques in Business
Financial Management

(Examinations in the above will be taken in
June, the results of which will be available
by mid-July).

SAMPLE

Business & Technician
Education Council

Higher National Diploma

IN BUSINESS AND FINANCE

IS AWARDED TO

WHO HAS SATISFACTORILY COMPLETED A BTEC APPROVED COURSE AT
CITY OF LONDON POLYTECHNIC

DATE OF AWARD 1985

SAMPLE

Chairman

Chief Executive

0721303943:144100:3D100:F74422

Document 3.7a. Higher National Diploma Awarded by BTEC for Studies Completed at City of London
Polytechnic

Business & Technician Education Council

Registered office Central House Upper Woburn Place London WC1H0HH England

Notification of Performance on a BTEC approved course
IN CALENDAR YEAR 1985

Student registration number	Student name		Course level
			HIGHER NATIONAL

MODULE CODE	MODULE NAME	IN COURSE GRADE	EXAM GRADE
Q046	ACCOUNTING II	A	A
Q060	BUSINESS ORGANISATION AND MANAGEMENT	B	B
V033	BUSINESS TAXATION	C	B
V048	FINANCIAL MANAGEMENT	A	C
V069	AUDITING	A	B
V540	QUANTITATIVE TECHNIQUES IN BUSINESS	B	C

CROSS MODULAR ASSESSMENT B
THIS STUDENT HAS QUALIFIED FOR THE COUNCIL'S HIGHER NATIONAL DIPLOMA
IN BUSINESS AND FINANCE WHICH WILL FOLLOW
****

KEY   A-EXCELLENT PASS   C-GOOD PASS   E-FAIL   S-ABSENT
      B-VERY GOOD PASS   D-PASS   F-FAIL   P-PROCEED

144100   CITY OF LONDON POLYTECHNIC

1/1
30100
20/08/85   4952

Document 3.7b. *continued*

Business & Technician Education Council

Registered office Central House Upper Woburn Place London WC1 0HH England

Notification of Performance on a BTEC approved course
IN CALENDAR YEAR 1984

Course level   **HIGHER NATIONAL**

MODULE CODE	MODULE NAME	IN COURSE GRADE	EXAM GRADE
Q030	THE BUSINESS ENVIRONMENT	B	B
Q036	INFORMATION ANALYSIS	A	A
Q040	PEOPLE AND ORGANISATION	B	A
Q045	ACCOUNTING I	B	A
V353	COMMERCIAL LAW	B	C
V390	PRINCIPLES AND PRACTICE OF MARKETING	C	D

CROSS MODULAR ASSESSMENT   B

THIS STUDENT IS QUALIFIED TO PROCEED TO YEAR 2
OF THE COUNCIL'S HIGHER NATIONAL DIPLOMA COURSE IN BUSINESS STUDIES
****

KEY	A-EXCELLENT PASS	C-GOOD PASS	E-FAIL	S-ABSENT	1/1
	B-VERY GOOD PASS	D-PASS	F-FAIL	P-PROCEED	3D100

144100   CITY OF LONDON POLYTECHNIC   21/08/84   4541

Document 3.7c. HNC Notification of Performance *continued*

LIVERPOOL POLYTECHNIC

Rector John McKenzie BSc(Eng). MPhil

Department of Mechanical, Marine and Production Engineering

Byrom Street. Liverpool
L3 3AF
051-207 3581 ext

Head of Department:
Professor W B Prove BSc PhD DSc CEng FIMechE FIProdE

22nd October 1985

AB/AB

Dear ...

Further to your telephone conversation of 16th October 1985 in which you requested confirmation of the units passed to date on the BTEC Higher Diploma Course in Mechanical and Production Engineering. I would confirm the following units have successfully been completed.

No.	Unit	Title	Level	Notes
WS	WS	Workshop Practice	None	Pre-requisite.
ES	ES	Engineering Science	III	Pre-requisite.
1	02	Mathematics	III	
2	03	Mechanical Science	III	
3	04	Manufacturing Technology	III	Credited with pass as a result of passing Unit 44 for which Unit 04 is the pre-requisite.
4	05	Engineering Drawing and Design	III	
5	07	Applied Heat	III	
6	08	Properties of Materials	III	
7	09	Use of Computers	II	Half Unit.
8	10	Mathematics	IV	
9	11	Mechanical Science	IV	
10	12	Manufacturing Technology A	IV	
11	13	Properties of Materials	IV	
12	16	Thermodynamics/Fluid Mechanics	IV	
13	17	Engineering Instrumentation & Control	IV	
14	18	Engineering Design	IV	

/continued .....

- 2 -

15	35	Mechanical Science	V	
16	43	Engineering Computation	III	
17	44	Manufacturing Technologh B	IV	
18	52A	General Studies & Communication	A1 & A2	
19	54	Management & Communication Studies	IV	Half Unit.

Yours sincerely,

Dr. A. Boyle
Deputy Head of Department

Document 3.8a. Statement of Partial Completion of a Prescribed BTEC Higher National Diploma Course at Liverpool Polytechnic, Validated by BTEC's Examination. Because the program is incomplete, the HNC has not been conferred.

Business & Technician
Education Council

Record of Success

IS AWARDED TO ...

WHO SUCCESSFULLY COMPLETED THE FOLLOWING

UNIT	UNIT VALUE	LEVEL	GRADE
THE USE OF COMPUTERS	0.5	II	PASS
ENGINEERING COMPUTATION	0.5	III	PASS

AT LIVERPOOL POLYTECHNIC

DATE OF AWARD: MARCH 1987

Chairman   Chief Executive

Central House Upper Woburn Place London WC1H 0HH England

Business & Technician
Education Council

Record of Success

IS AWARDED TO ...

WHO SUCCESSFULLY COMPLETED THE FOLLOWING

UNIT	UNIT VALUE	LEVEL	GRADE
GENERAL STUDIES AND COMMUNICATION (A)	1.0	-	PASS
ENGINEERING DESIGN	1.0	IV	PASS
MANUFACTURING TECHNOLOGY (B)	1.0	IV	PASS
MANAGEMENT AND COMMUNICATION STUDIES	1.0	IV	PASS

AT LIVERPOOL POLYTECHNIC

DATE OF AWARD: MARCH 1987

Chairman   Chief Executive

R221456.135007.L004925.M.000000/0587

Central House Upper Woburn Place London WC1H 0HH England

Document 3.8b. *continued*

Property and Pecuniary Insurance
Sales Function and Selling Methods

3. BTEC Higher National Certificate/
Diploma: Business and Finance

Core Subjects Only

Year I
A. Work Organizations
B. The External Environment and Operations

C. Operational Techniques

Year II.
D. Organizational Structures
E. Financial Planning and Procedures Control
F. Environment and Enterprise

The address of BTEC is Central House, Upper Woburn Place, London WXIH OHH, England.

Future Plans and Priorities of the Polytechnics, Colleges and Institutes of Higher Education

As of the late 1980s, a third of a million students are registered in courses offered through the polytechnics, colleges and institutes of higher education. This figure now exceeds university enrollment, a circumstance unforeseen 20 years ago when a second higher education system, separate from the universities, was first introduced. This trend toward higher enrollment in the polytechnics and colleges is due in part to the increasing admission of students to CNAA or BTEC-approved programs in science, technology, business and management. In addition, there has been an increase in the admission of mature and nontraditional students, including those studying in part-time and sandwich modes. Generally, the polytechnics and colleges are more likely to enroll these students than the universities.

This trend toward larger enrollment has resulted in significant cost to the polytechnics and colleges. Strained by a 47% increase in student enrollment in the past 10 years and a 20% reduction in budget allocations

that puts their per capita expenditure on students at 50%, the universities, the polytechnics, colleges and institutes of higher education are considering a number of changes in the next few years. These may involve some restructuring of academic programs and staff and the possible merging of some of the smaller colleges with other institutions and universities. Due to new funding formulas which require more efficiency and greater accountability, institutions will need to find ways of generating outside income, including consultancy, that is, making resources such as faculty and the expertise of the institution available to the business and industry with an increasing emphasis on the preparation of continuing education or short courses tailored to the individual needs of corporate employees.

Historically, the polytechnics and colleges and institutes of higher education have been controlled locally and the universities centrally, creating obstacles to any possible unification of the two sectors. However, a number of these obstacles have been removed and the 1990s may see an end to the division between the polytechnic and university sectors. The Education Reform Act of 1988 ended the Local Education Authority (LEA) control of the polytechnics. The Polytechnics and Colleges Funding Council (PCFC) was established in the early 1980s to create a more centralized funding system. The Polytechnics Central Admissions Systems (PCAS) now coordinates the application process for the polytechnics and colleges, paralleling the centralized system used at the universities.

The polytechnics and colleges and institutions of higher education also have been granted the authority to monitor and modify existing degree programs and approve new ones, a responsibility formerly held only by the CNAA. A number of organizations including the Committee of Directors of Polytechnics (CDP) and the PCFC want to grant even greater autonomy to the polytechnics and colleges and institutes of higher education by providing them with the authority to award their own degrees. By removing this responsibility from the CNAA, the CNAA will eventually play an advisory role in higher education, similar to the regional accrediting agencies in the United States.

Regardless of whether the division between the polytechnic and university sectors disappears entirely, a number of other priorities and concerns exist for the polytechnics and colleges in the 1990s. These include encouraging greater diversity by increasing the number of mature and nontraditional students in higher education; developing further the credit transfer, or CAT, system to facilitate greater movement between institutions; continuing to strengthen links between higher education and business and industry; and creating greater flexibility within the system by encouraging open and distance learning and innovative modular program schemes.

Since Great Britain's future economic development lies within the European Economic Community (EEC), there is considerable concern in the polytechnics and colleges as to whether their graduates will be ready to compete effectively abroad after all trade barriers have been lifted in 1992. To prepare for these developments, there has been a trend toward internationalizing or Europeanizing various degree programs particularly in business, technology and engineering. Courses have been introduced stressing the culture and customs of other countries; language components also are included in a number of programs; and academic and work exchange programs have become increasingly popular.

Advice for Admissions Officers

1. The polytechnics, colleges and institutes of higher education are increasingly issuing documents comparable to American transcripts, that is, individual subjects with final examination grades. In some cases, information such as the lecture and laboratory hours of instruction or credits is reported. The grades reported for each individual subject should not take precedence over the classifications of the final degree awards. If information on grading scales is not provided, it may be obtained through the institution. It should be noted that many courses completed in these institutions lead to external examinations/awards offered by bodies such as the Business and Technicians Education Council, the City and Guilds of London Institute and Pitman Examinations Institute. Records of these reports must be obtained through the appropriate external examining board.

2. Access programs oftentimes serve as substitutes for and are accepted in lieu of the A-levels for higher education admissions purposes.

3. The BTEC National Certificate and Diploma (NC/ND) and Higher National Certificate and Diploma (HNC/HND) vary in content in that some programs are highly vocationally oriented as compared to others which may not have a vocational content.

Placement Recommendations

Note: See "Guide to the Understanding of Placement Recommendations," page 47 and the statement on the role of the National Council on the Evaluation of Foreign Educational Credentials in developing these placement recommendations on page v. Students who have completed some coursework for any of the programs listed below may be considered for undergraduate admission with up to one year of transfer credit, determined through a course-by-course analysis. If length of study is cited, it refers to the standard length of the program when pursued fulltime. The actual period of attendance may be longer.

Credential	Entrance Requirement	Length of Program	Gives Access in United Kingdom to	Placement Recommendation
1. Certificate of Pre-Vocational Education [CPVE] (p. 70)	16 years of age	1 year fulltime	Employment; BTEC First Certificate/Diploma or further study	A vocational qualification.
2. BTEC First Certificate (pp. 70-71)	16 years of age	1 year part-time	BTEC National Certificate	A vocational credential.
3. BTEC First Diploma (pp. 70-71)	16 years of age	1 year fulltime or 2 years part-time	BTEC National Diploma	A vocational credential.
4. BTEC National Certificate [NC] (p. 71)	16 years of age and BTEC First Certificate; or 4 subject passes at GCE O-level, CSE grade 1, or GCSE grades A-C	2 years part-time	Employment; BTEC Higher National Certificate	May be considered for freshman admission if a vocational program is appropriate preparation.
5. BTEC National Diploma [ND] (p. 71)	16 years of age and BTEC First Diploma; or Certificate of Pre-vocational Education; or 4 subject passes at GCE O-level, CSE grade 1, or GCSE grades A-C	2 years fulltim or 3 years part-time or Sandwich	Employment; BTEC Higher National Diploma	May be considered for freshman admission if a vocational program is appropriate preparation.

	Credential	Entrance Requirements	Duration	Purpose	U.S. Equivalency
6.	BTEC Higher National Certificate [HNC] (p. 71)	1 A-level and 3 subject passes at GCE O-level, CSE grade 1, or GCSE grades A-C; or 18 years of age and BTEC National Certificate	2 years part-time	Employment; further study	May be considered for undergraduate admission with up to 1 year of transfer credit, determined through a course-by-course analysis.
7.	BTEC Higher National Diploma [HND] (p. 71)	1 A-level and 3 subject passes at GCE O-level, CSE grade 1, or GCSE grades A-C; or 18 years of age and BTEC National Diploma	2 years fulltime or 3 years Sandwich	Employment; further study	May be considered for undergraduate admission with up to 1 1/2 years of transfer credit, determined through a course-by-course analysis.
8.	CNAA Certificate (pre-April 1988) (p. 57)	5 subject passes at GCE O-level, CSE grade 1, or GCSE grades A-C	1 year fulltime	Further study	May be considered for up to 1 semester of undergraduate transfer credit, determined through a course-by-course analysis.
9.	Certificate of Higher Education [CertHE] (p. 57)	2 A-level and 3 subject passes at GCE O-level, CSE grade 1, or GCSE grades A-C; BTEC National Certificate; or BTEC National Diploma	1 year fulltime	Further study	May be considered for up to 1 year of undergraduate transfer credit, determined through a course-by-course analysis.
10.	Certificate in Education [CertEd] (p. 57)	Concurrent enrollment in a Bachelor of Arts or Bachelor of Science degree program	1 year fulltime	Employment; further study	Represents completion of undergraduate teacher education courses.

11. Certificate in Education (Further Education) [CertEd-FE] (p. 57)	2 A-level and 3 subject passes at CGE O-level or CSE grade 1, or GCSE grades A-C; BTEC National Certificate; or BTEC National Diploma	1 year fulltime	Further study	May be considered for up to 1 year of undergraduate transfer credit, determined through a course-by-course analysis.
12. Diploma of Higher Education [DipHE] (p. 57)	2 A-level and 3 subject passes at CGE O-level or CSE grade 1, or GCSE grades A-C; BTEC National Certificate; or BTEC National Diploma	2 years fulltime	Further study	May be considered for up to 2 years of undergraduate transfer credit, determined through a course-by-course analysis.
13. Bachelor of Arts/Bachelor of Science (Unclassified/ Ordinary) [BA/BSc] (p. 57)	2 A-level and 3 subject passes at CGE O-level or CSE grade 1, or GCSE grades A-C; BTEC National Certificate; or BTEC National Diploma	3 years fulltime	Further study	May be considered for graduate admission if the program followed is appropriate preparation.
14. Bachelor of Arts/Bachelor of Science (Honours) [BA/BSc (Hons)] (p. 58)	2 A-level and 3 subject passes at CGE O-level or CSE grade 1, or GCSE grades A-C; BTEC National Certificate; or BTEC National Diploma	3 years fulltime	Graduate study	May be considered for graduate admission.
15. Bachelor of Education (Unclassified) [BEd] (p. 58)	2 A-level and 3 subject passes at CGE O-level or CSE grade 1, or GCSE grades A-C; BTEC National Certificate; or BTEC National Diploma	4 years fulltime	Further study	May be considered for graduate admission if the program followed is appropriate preparation.

Program	Entrance Requirements	Length	Leads to	Notes
16. Bachelor of Education (Honours) [BEd (Hons)] (p. 58)	2 A-level and 3 subject passes at CGE O-level or CSE grade 1, or GCSE grades A–C; BTEC National Certificate; or BTEC National Diploma	4 years fulltime	Graduate study	May be considered for graduate admission.
17. Bachelor of Engineering (Unclassified/Ordinary) [BEng] (p. 58)	2 A-level and 3 subject passes at CGE O-level or CSE grade 1, or GCSE grades A–C; BTEC National Certificate; or BTEC National Diploma	3 years fulltime	Further study	May be considered for graduate admission if the program followed is appropriate preparation.
18. Bachelor of Engineering (Honours) [BEng (Hons)] (p. 58)	2 A-level and 3 subject passes at CGE O-level or CSE grade 1, or GCSE grades A–C; BTEC National Certificate; or BTEC National Diploma	3 years fulltime	Graduate study	May be considered for graduate admission.
19. Master of Engineering [MEng] (p. 65)	Enrollment in a Bachelor of Engineering (Honours) program	2 years fulltime	Graduate study	A first degree; may be considered for graduate admission.
20. Bachelor of Laws [LLB] (p. 58)	2 A-level and 3 subject passes at CGE O-level or CSE grades 1, or GCSE grades A–C; BTEC National Certificate; or BTEC National Diploma	3 years fulltime	Professional certifying examinations in law and/or graduate study	May be considered for graduate admission.

21. Bachelor of Town Planning (Unclassified) [BTP] (p. 65)	Bachelor's degree or professional qualification in an appropriate field	1 year fulltime	Employment	May be considered for up to 1 year of undergraduate transfer credit, determined through a course-by-course analysis.
22. Graduate Diploma in Music [Grad Dip Mus] (p. 65)	1 A-level and 3 subject passes at CGE O-level or CSE grade 1, or GCSE grades A-C and 2 practical studies in Music at least at Grade VIII	3 years fulltime	Further study	May be considered for graduate admission as are graduates of U.S. schools of music.
23. Diploma in Professional Studies [DipPS], in Post-Experience and Postgraduate Awards in a Subject Area (for Diplomas in health-related fields, see placement recommendations under Nursing) (p. 65)	Bachelor's degree in education or professional qualification and experience	1 year fulltime or 2 years part-time	Further study	May be considered for up to 1 year of undergraduate transfer credit, determined through a course-by-course analysis.
24. Post-Graduate Certificate in Education [PGCE] (p. 65)	Bachelor's degree other than the Bachelor of Education	1 year fulltime	Employment	May be considered comparable to a 1-year undergraduate teacher training program.
25. Post-Graduate Diploma [PGDip] (p. 65)	Bachelor's degree (unclassified/ordinary)	25 weeks fulltime	Graduate study	May be considered for graduate admission.
26. Diploma in Management Studies [DMS] (p. 65)	Bachelor's degree; or BTEC Higher National Certificate or BTEC Higher National Diploma and appropriate experience; or 25 years of age and 4 years of managerial experience	2 years part-time	Employment; further study	May be considered for up to 1 year of undergraduate transfer credit, determined through a course-by-course analysis.

	Entry requirement	Duration	Purpose	Comparability
27. Master of Business Administration [MBA] (p. 68)	Bachelor's honours degree; or a degree-equivalent professional qualification; or Diploma in Management Studies	2-3 years part-time	Employment	May be considered comparable to a U.S. master's degree.
28. Master of Education [MEd] (p. 68)	3 years teaching experience and Bachelor of Education honours degree or honours degree with a concentration in Education studies or Diploma of Professional Studies in Education or Bachelor of Education degree in which the honours award is not offered	1 year fulltime or 2 years part-time	Employment	May be considered comparable to a U.S. master's degree.
29. Master of Arts/Master of Science [MA/MSc] (Note: The Master of Arts degrees from Oxford and Cambridge Universities are not earned degrees.) (pp. 65, 68)	Bachelor's honours degree	40 weeks fulltime	Further study	May be considered comparable to a U.S. master's degree.
30. Master of Philosophy [MPhil] (p. 68)	Bachelor's honours degree	18-36 months fulltime	Further study	May be considered comparable to a U.S. master's degree.

31. Doctor of Philosophy [PhD] (p. 68)	Bachelor's honours degree or master's in a related field	24-60 months fulltime or 36-72 months part-time after bachelor's honours degree (research only) or 33-60 months fulltime or 45-72 months part-time after MPhil	Employment	May be considered comparable to a U.S. earned doctorate.
32. Doctor of Letters [DLitt] Doctor of Sciences [DSc] Doctor of Technology [DTech] (p. 68)	Requires a first degree held 7 or more years; or a higher degree held 4 or more years	—	—	Awarded for substantial and original contribution to the field.

IV. SCOTLAND

Background to Scottish Education

Scotland, if one includes the nearly 800 islands that surround it, contains but 30,414 square miles of land and a population of some five million people. Its northernmost point, in the Shetlands, is parallel in latitude to Anchorage, Alaska. The mainland can be divided into three distinct geographical areas: the Highlands in the north which includes over half the land mass but with a small, scattered population; the Southern Uplands that borders the north of England which are mainly agricultural, and the Central Lowlands. In the latter, which contains the bulk of the population, lies the industrial city of Glasgow and its satellite towns, on the banks of the Clyde River; and to the east, on the Firth of Forth, Edinburgh, the capital of Scotland.

Much of Scotland's history is concerned with its often troubled relationship with England. In its early days, a desire to remain independent prompted Scotland to seek alliances with Holland, Scandinavia and France. Even today more similarities are said to exist between Scottish institutions and their European counterparts than between Scotland and England. Centuries of border conflict were reduced if not ended by the accession to the English throne of the Scottish King James VI and I, in 1603, and in 1707, by the Act of Union between the two countries. This Act made it possible to maintain a separate system of education and protect both Scottish law, church and education. Also kept were the so-called ancient universities, Aberdeen, Edinburgh, St. Andrews, and later Glasgow, providing the impetus for Scottish control of its own education. The result has been a homogeneous educational system, not without its many vocal critics, but with institutions close to the community they serve.

Scotland also claims to have had a long and democratic history of providing a general education to its young. Reference to support this claim often is made to the First Book of Discipline, influenced by John Knox, the great Calvinist reformer of Scotland and published in 1560. "The children of the poor must be supported and sustained on the charge of the kirk . . . If they be found apt to learning and letters, then may they not . . . be permitted to reject learning, but must be charged to continue their study, so that the commonwealth may have some comfort in them."

In later years the so-called "Lad o' Pairts," the clever son of a poor family whom the parish supported financially to attend school, sitting beside the son of the laird, and going with him to university, was long held to be a truth and contributed to the belief in England that Scottish education was the superior. Nevertheless, Scotland has been able to maintain a distinctive educational system that in recent years has proven to be both capable of change and responsive to Scottish needs. Of importance in achieving this goal was the move from London to Edinburgh in 1939 of the Scottish Education Department (SED).

The Scottish Education Department

The Scottish Education Department (SED), along with the Departments of Agriculture and Fisheries, Home and Health, Development, and Industry, form the Scottish Office. Each Department has a Secretary who reports to the Permanent Secretary; both they and the Permanent Secretary are Civil Servants. The Permanent Secretary, in turn, reports to the Secretary of State for Scotland, who is an elected member of Parliament and a member of the Cabinet. Among the Permanent Secretary's wide range of responsibilities is the supervision and development of educational services in Scotland. Only the Scottish universities are not within the Permanent Secretary's direct purview. During the 1980s successive Permanent Secretaries and the Secretaries of State were strong advocates of change in Scottish education.

Public education in Scotland has been described as being an uneasy partnership between central and local governments, acting on the advice of various educational committees and the pressure of interest groups. Conflicting priorities in the social goals of central and local authorities and industrial action, such as the lengthy teacher's strike of the late 1980s, have delayed or altered the paths of change. Nevertheless, significant developments have occurred and still are occurring; consensus has been achieved, and the Secretary of State, through the SED, has acted to effect them.

Among the responsibilities of the SED to all sectors of the educational system, except the universities, is guidance in matters of curriculum and pedagogy, control of the cost and quality of educational building, educational research, the training and supply of teachers (with the General Teaching Council), and financing the

Scotland

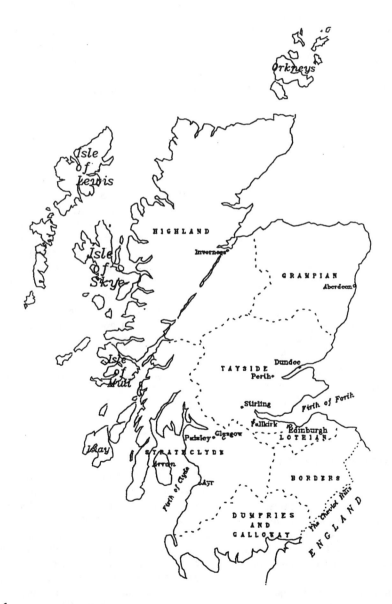

Figure 4.1.

five colleges of education and 12 of the 15 central institutions (CIs). The three CI colleges of agriculture are funded by their own Scottish Office Department. In 1990 they were merged into one Scottish Agricultural College with three campuses.

The nine regional and three island Local Education Authorities (LEAs) have legal responsibility for the curriculum taught in their schools as well as for staff, equipment and the maintenance and construction of buildings and raising of money from local taxes to pay their costs. The LEAs also fund the 49 further education (FE) colleges within their respective areas of jurisdiction. Several other educational committees and bodies both advise and make reports to the SED and to the Secretaries. These include the Scottish Consultative Council on the Curriculum, The Scottish Examination Board and The Inspectorate.

Scottish Consultative Council on the Curriculum.

The Scottish Consultative Council on the Curriculum (SCCC) describes its mandate as being "—the principal advisory body to the Secretary of State for Scotland in all matters relating to the curriculum for 3-18 year olds." In 1988 the SCCC was "privatized" and now charges fees for services. It incorporates the former Consultative Committee on the Curriculum and the Scottish Curriculum Development Service. It consists of a Chairman and 30 other Council members appointed from a "...wide range of appropriate parental, industrial and professional bodies." Although, of necessity, the SCCC still must work closely with the Scottish teaching profession, "privatization" and the make-up of the Council reflect the SED's goal both for broadening and making more occupationally relevant what is being taught in the schools.

The Scottish Examination Board

The Scottish Examination Board (SEB) sets, proctors and marks all examinations taken by students in S4 (Secondary 4), both standard and "O" Grade; in S5 for Higher Grade; and in S6 for the Certificate of Sixth Year Studies (CSYS). Changes in the School System, especially those in S3 and S4 which result in Standard Grade examinations at up to three different performance/curriculum levels per subject, have increased the demands placed upon its resources, as well as increased the num-

ber of students writing SEB examinations. In 1988 the SEB employed some 4,000 teachers to help set 355 different subject and subject level papers, to proctor the 149,901 students who wrote one or more of its examinations and to mark a total of 658,878 papers.

The SEB issues the Scottish Certificate of Education (SCE) which includes the results of all S4 and S5 examinations taken in the annual May-June examinations and the separate CSYS for examinations taken for S6 courses. These Certificates are not cumulative; thus, students will possess separate certificates for examinations taken in different years. These alone are their official statements of achievement; there are no separate diplomas issued by the schools. The SEB has a chairman and 37 other members coming from the universities, the central institutions, the colleges of education, the educational advisors, the further education institutions and from industry.

The Inspectorate

Responsibility for monitoring and evaluating the quality of education is that of Her Majesty's Inspectorate whose mandate is to inspect all nonuniversity educational institutions to ensure that the curriculum being taught or the training provided and the standards applied, as well as all matters of school building, equipment and finance, meet approved requirements. They are the principal advisors in these matters to the Secretary of State for Scotland and provide their reports to the SED, other governmental Departments and the institutions affected.

Primary and Secondary Education

Education to 1980

Children began their formal schooling at age 5 in Primary 1 (P1) and remained there until age 12 in Primary 7 (P7). Prior to P1, some 30% of 3- to 5-year-olds attended locally supported nursery schools. Subsequently they entered secondary school (S1 to S4) for four years of compulsory education at the end of which they wrote examinations for the Scottish Examination Board and, if successful, received the Scottish Certificate of Education Ordinary (O) grade. At age 16, whether or not they reached S4 or were successful in the "0" grade examinations, the majority of students left school. Some entered trades or skill training programs, many sponsored by SCOTBEC (Scottish Business Education Council) or SCOTEC (Scottish Technical Education Council), both of which sponsored courses, set examinations, and issued certificates in their own names. In 1985 these two bodies joined together as SCOTVEC (Scottish Vocational Educational Council).

Some students who passed the O-grade examinations entered a fifth year of secondary education (S5) to prepare for the SCE Higher (H) grade examinations at age 17. These are known as "the Highers." Success led to admission on a selective basis to the universities, colleges of education, central institutions and training programs in various professions, such as Chartered Accountancy. See chart 4.1 for the educational system of Scotland. Some students remained in school one more year (S6) and wrote examinations for the Certificate of Sixth Year Studies (CSYS).

The following paragraph, from a letter written by a teacher to the editor of the *Times Educational Supplement* (Scotland) in 1980, illustrates the concern that many educators and parents had with the curriculum then in place. "Surely it is a shocking indictment of Scottish education that in the 1980s when most children have to attend secondary school for four years (S1-S4) the only national certificate showing what they have achieved during those years is basically designed for the top 30% of the school population, many of whom will in any case go on to obtain Higher passes in their fifth or sixth years. For many fourth year school leavers, secondary education ends with a certificate showing two or three O-level passes often at D or E, and some do not have even this, far less a nationally acceptable 'leavers' statement' of the qualities they have shown and the standards reached in all the subjects they have studied."

Earlier in this letter the writer argued that the irrelevancy of the curriculum destroyed student enthusiasm for learning in S3 and S4 and left a "vast silent majority" marking time until they reached school leaving age, feeling themselves to be second-class citizens. Other educators complained that the narrow curriculum did nothing to challenge the more able students.

Changes to School Education After 1980

The first substantial proposals to effect changes in the Scottish school system occurred in 1977, with the release of two separate enquiry reports sponsored by the SED, named after their respective chairpersons. The Munn Report recommended the restructuring of S3 and S4 to meet the needs and abilities of all 14- to 15-year-olds by making both teaching and learning more responsive to modern needs and allowing learning to cross the traditional subject boundaries by modularizing the curriculum. The Dunning Report more radically proposed that all students be given the opportunity to take instruction leading to a broadly based Certificate of Education awarded at the completion of S4. In addition, it recommended the use of teacher assessment as well as formal examinations, the report of student progress in a meaningful way, and, of greatest significance, the evaluation of all students only on the basis of their positive achievements.

Further impetus for change to the curriculum came from the Manpower Services Commission (MSC) through its Technical and Vocational Educational Initiatives (TVEI) program. This was a result of a general concern in the United Kingdom about the large number of untrained, unemployed, youth leaving school each year. It was intended to be a catalyst for change in school curriculum. The MSC offered each of the 116 education authorities in the United Kingdom seed money of up to £2 million per year for five years to introduce TVEI into the curriculum of 14- to 18-year-olds. Of this funding, 25% was for new buildings, 15% for administration and 60% for additional teaching staff. Not surprisingly this massive influx of money was well received by the education authorities, including those in Scotland, and the inclusion of vocational and technical courses for this age group became a significant part of school curriculum. For Scotland, TVEI offered a practical application of the Munn and Dunning proposals, especially those related to modularizing the curriculum. ". . . to reflect the more active, practical styles of learning and leading to nationally recognized vocational qualifications . . . ."

Primary Through Secondary Four

All these proposals, developed by the various educational bodies in Scotland, led in 1986 to the introduction of a new broadly based and flexible curriculum. Included in it were modules of learning, cross-disciplinary instruction, technical and vocational subjects, assessment for positive results only, and new Standard Grade examinations at S4.

Primary school students (P1-P7) now follow instruction in five modes of learning, which become eight modes in Secondary School (S1-S4) (see Chart 4.2). Minimum and maximum percentages of time are man-

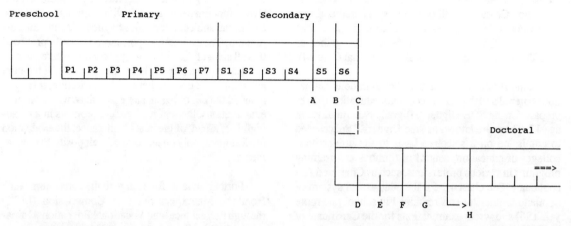

Key to alphabetic codes: Codes denote minimum year in which respective qualifications may be awarded:
they are not indicated for each succeeding level.

A   SCE Standard (or '0') Levels
B   SCE Highers
C   Certificate of Sixth Year Studies
D   Higher National Certificate (Scotvec)
E   Higher National Diploma (Scotvec)
F   Three Year Ordinary Degree
G   Four Year Honours Degree
H   Masters Degree or Post-Graduate Diploma
      (One or Two Years)

Chart 4.1. The Educational System of Scotland, 1990

---

dated for instruction in each mode. Within each, teachers instruct students, as far as possible, in relation to individual abilities and interests. All instruction prior to S3 stresses the process of learning, rather than prescribed content. Less flexibility exists in S3 and little in S4, as students begin their preparation for Standard or Ordinary level exams. Streaming of students according to their various abilities now occurs as they prepare for Standard Grade examinations which test for achievement at four different levels: Credit, General, Foundation and Completed Course. All students pass at one of these levels; no student who attends classes receives a result of less than Completed Course. There are no failing grades.

Some students include within their studies SEB short course modules, akin to SCOTVEC modules elsewhere described. Completion of these modules appears on the sample Scottish Certificate of Education as electronic systems (1/2 module), electronics in society (1/2 module), electronics and music (full module) and health and exercise (full module). These are alternative and/or enriching short courses of 20 (1/2) or 40 (full)

hours each. Completed modules are recorded without a grade; incomplete modules are not recorded.

The new Standard Grade examinations have been introduced as follows with the corresponding O-Grade phased out one year later:

1986	English, general science, mathematics, social and vocational studies
1988	Art and design, computer studies, contemporary social studies, craft design, French, home economics, Latin
1990	Biology, chemistry, Gaelic (native speakers), Gaelic (learners), geography, German, history, Italian, modern studies, music, office and information studies, physical education, physics, Russian, Spanish, technical studies
1991	Economics, Greek, religious studies
1992	Accounting and finance
1993	Classical studies, drama, technical drawing

Note that biology, chemistry and physics are not offered at foundation level.

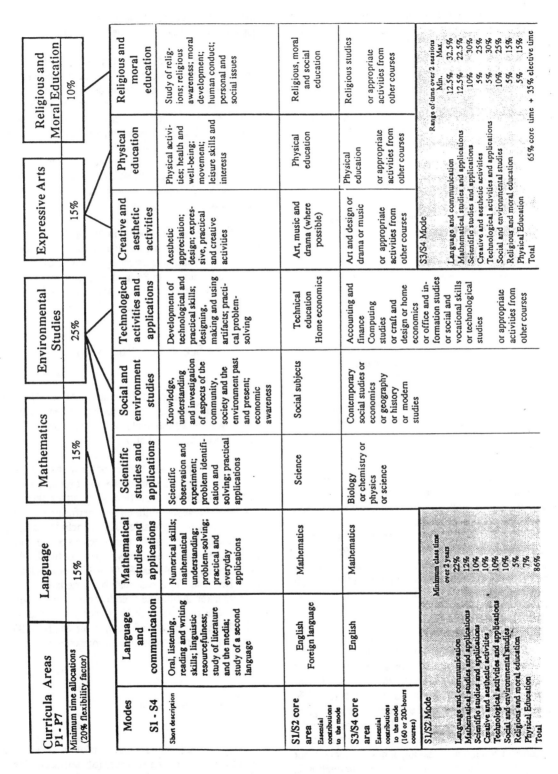

Curricula Areas P1-P7 — Minimum time allocations (20% flexibility factor)

Area	%
Language	15%
Mathematics	15%
Environmental Studies	25%
Expressive Arts	15%
Religious and Moral Education	10%

Modes S1 - S4	Language and communication	Mathematical studies and applications	Scientific studies and applications	Social and environment studies	Technological activities and applications	Creative and aesthetic activities	Physical education	Religious and moral education
Short description	Oral, listening, reading and writing skills; linguistic resourcefulness; study of literature and the media; study of a second language	Numerical skills; mathematical understanding; problem-solving; practical and everyday applications	Scientific observation and experiment; problem identification and solving; practical applications	Knowledge, understanding and investigation of aspects of the community, society and the environment past and present; economic awareness	Development of technological and practical skills; designing, making and using artifacts; practical problem-solving	Aesthetic appreciation; design; expressive, practical and creative activities	Physical activities; health and well-being; movement; leisure skills and interests	Study of religions; religious awareness; moral development; human conduct; personal and social issues
S1/S2 core area — Essential contributions to the mode	English Foreign language	Mathematics	Science	Social subjects	Technical education Home economics	Art, music and drama (where possible)	Physical education	Religious, moral and social education
S3/S4 core area — Essential contributions to the mode (160 or 200-hours courses)	English — or appropriate activities from other courses	Mathematics	Biology or chemistry or physics or science	Contemporary social studies or economics or geography or history or modern studies	Accounting and finance Computing studies or craft and design or home economics or office and information studies or social and vocational skills or technological studies — or appropriate activities from other courses	Art and design or drama or music — or appropriate activities from other courses	Physical education — or appropriate activities from other courses	Religious studies — or appropriate activities from other courses

S1/S2 Mode

	Minimum class time over 2 years
Language and communication	22%
Mathematical studies and applications	12%
Scientific studies and applications	10%
Creative and aesthetic activities	10%
Technological activities and applications	10%
Social and environmental studies	10%
Religious and moral education	5%
Physical Education	7%
Total	86%

S3/S4 Mode

	Range of time over 2 sessions Min.	Max.
Language and communication	12.5%	32.5%
Mathematical studies and applications	12.5%	22.5%
Scientific studies and applications	10%	30%
Creative and aesthetic activities	5%	25%
Technological activities and applications	5%	30%
Social and environmental studies	10%	25%
Religious and moral education	5%	15%
Physical Education	5%	15%
Total	65% core time + 35% elective time	

Chart 4.2   Scottish Curricular Areas, Primary and Secondary

Some important differences between examinations for the SCE O-Grade and for Standard Grade, as given in SED publications, are as follows.

The SCE Ordinary marking systems:

	Scaled Mark		Scaled Mark
Grade	% until 1985	Grade	% since 1985
A	70-100	1	77-100
B	60-69	2	65-76
C	50-59	3	50-64
D	not recorded	4	40-49
E	not recorded	5	30-39

The SCE Standard Grade Marking System since 1986:

Subject level	Award	Equivalence to former SCE O-Level results
	1	higher than A
Credit	2	A/B
	3	C
General	4	near pass
	5	low level - some achievement
Foundation	6	minimum passing grade
Completed Course	7	completed course but failed examination

No negative marks or comments now appear on SEB Certificates.

Examinations begin in May and last until early June. Each is about one hour in length. All students write between six and eight subject papers at two different levels, for a total of 12 to 16 examinations in all. They are advised by teachers as to whether they should attempt Credit and General or General and Foundation examinations in each subject. Only the most positive result at the highest award level appears on the Scottish Certificate of Education. A student who does not appear for a given examination receives no record of the course on the Certificate.

Another difference from O-Grade is that each Standard Grade result includes a teacher-assigned profile of performance that constitutes 33% of the final award made; the examination itself constitutes 67%. Each element of the profile for a given course is assigned a value from 1 to 5 by the teacher. French, for example, (see document 4.1) bears values for the elements of Reading, Listening and Speaking. If any element has not been given a value by the teacher, the examination is incomplete, and no result appears on the Certificate. (See also Science, document 4.1). A subsequent submis-

sion for the missing element will produce a revised result and the reissuance of the Certificate.

Finally, it should be noted that the Scottish Certificate of Education is a record of a student's performance in a given year; it is not a cumulative document. Complete documentation, then, would consist of all yearly certificates. Increasingly, with the flexibility now encouraged in Scottish education, students will possess Certificates for two or more years showing mixtures of Standard Grade, Higher Grade and SEB Short courses. They also may have Certificates issued in the same years by SCOTVEC. Together they constitute the only "high school transcripts" available.

Thus admission officers in North America, when evaluating applications, should request separate certificates issued to students for each year of school they have completed, from S4 to S6, and should expect mixtures of academic levels in the courses reported on each certificate.

After Secondary Four (S4)

Attendance at school from ages 5 to 16 (P1 to S4) is both compulsory and progressive. Students advance year by year, and all students must write Standard Grade examinations at the end of S4.

Subsequent to S4, changes occur in that, while all persons less than 18 years of age must remain in some form of recognized education, alternatives related to individual interests, abilities and performance in the examinations are available. These included employment, in which the employer provides inspected on-the-job training; employment, in which day or block release is required so that relevant SCOTVEC modules leading to the National Certificate may be earned; SCOTVEC modules taken in fulltime attendance at a further education college or school; SCE Higher courses and examinations; Certificate of Sixth Year Study (CSYS) courses and examinations; or some reasonable combination of the above.

SCE Higher Grade

Higher Grade courses can be taken by students in one year (S5) or over two years (S5-S6) according to their academic ability. Those who complete five or more Standard Grade examinations in one year at the Credit

Scottish Certificate of Education

SPECIMEN   *The Scottish Examination Board hereby certifies that*

SPECIMEN   *presented for the Scottish Certificate of Education in* 1989 *by* STIRLINGBRIDGE ACADEMY

gained the following award(s):

Subject	Grade	Award	Profile of Performance (Standard Grade Only)	
ART AND DESIGN	Ordinary	4 *		
FRENCH	Standard	2	Reading	3
			Listening	3
			Speaking	2
			Writing	2
SCIENCE	Standard	#	Knowledge and Understanding	5
			Problem Solving	4
SECRETARIAL STUDIES	Ordinary	3		
SHORTHAND 60 WPM	-	-		
SOCIAL AND VOCATIONAL SKILLS	Standard	3	Communicative Abilities	3
			Practical Abilities	4
GERMAN	Higher	C		
MUSIC PARTS I, II AND IV	Higher	A		
MUSIC - PRACTICAL HARMONY	-	-		

Short Course	*Short Course*	*Short Course*
ELECTRONIC SYSTEMS (X 1/2)	ELECTRONICS IN SOCIETY (X 1/2)	ELECTRONICS AND MUSIC
HEALTH AND EXERCISE		

X Special provision has been made for the candidate to an extent requiring endorsement of the certificate. Details of the provisions made are available from the board on request.

 # The candidate has been graded only in the element(s) shown in the Profile of Performance because one or more of the element grades required for an overall award is missing.

1/1234567-01234   SPECIMEN SPECIMEN SPECIMEN SPECIMEN SPECIMEN SPECIMEN SPECIMEN

Director

Document 4.1. Scottish Certificate of Education

level are expected to complete five Higher courses and Examinations in one year. Students less successful in S4 may take two years or more to complete their "Highers," taken after 12 years of sequential education. Highers represent the basic requirements for entry to Scottish universities, colleges and professions.

The Higher Grade marking system is as follows: A = 70-100%; B = 60-69%; C = 50-59%; and D = 40-49%. Only results in bands A, B and C are designated as passes. Student performance on the Higher Grade below that required for a D is not entered on the Certificate of Education. Published results are of positive achievement only.

Results at the Higher level are based solely upon success in the examinations, and students are prepared for them using traditional teaching methods. They are reported on the Scottish Certificate of Education, along with the results of SEB O-Grade or Standard Grade examinations or SEB modules, completed in the same school year. Those students who complete their Highers in one academic year (S5), typically with a minimum of three Higher classes, two with minimum B grades and one with minimum C grade, and who have two Standard or O-level passes in other subjects, enter tertiary education. Other students who do not meet these requirements or who do meet them but choose to enrich their education, may remain in school for a sixth year to take further Highers or CSYS courses.

Higher courses and examinations are available in the following subjects:

Accounting	Greek
Agricultural Science	Hebrew
Anatomy, Physiology	History (Traditional)
and Health	History (Alternative)
Art and Design	Home Economics
Biology	(Revised)
Chemistry	Home Economics
Computing Studies	(Fabrics and Fashion)
Craft and Design	Home Economics (Food
Economic History	and Nutrition)
Economics	Horticultural Science
Engineering	Italian
English	Latin
English (Revised)	Latin (Revised)
French	Mathematics
French (Revised)	Mathematics (Revised)
Gaelic (Learners)	Metalwork
Gaelic (Native Speakers)	Modern Studies
Geography	Music
Geology	Navigation
German	Norwegian

Physics	Secretarial Studies
Portuguese	Spanish
Religious Studies	Swedish
Russian	Technical Drawing

Certificate of Sixth Year Studies

Those students, who remain in school after S5, have completed the prerequisite Higher courses and examinations and have not reached the school-leaving age of 18, may take from one to three courses in S6 that lead to inclusion on a Certificate of Sixth Year Studies (CSYS; see document 4.2). Its purpose has been described as follows:

Of the pupils who remain in school for a sixth year (some 6,000), 34% study for the Certificate of Sixth Year Studies, which, though it contains elements of work at a more advanced standard than Highers, is intended to introduce pupils to new methods of study rather than to improve their qualifications for entry to higher education. The rest will be aiming to improve their qualifications at Higher Grade.

CSYS courses may be taught partly in the classroom, if enrollment and staff so warrant, or be on a tutorial basis. In either case, there are new expectations that the student can study on a relatively independent basis and in most subjects, can prepare and submit an independent project or paper to the appropriate SEB examination committee for evaluation.

The CSYS marking system is as follows: A, B, C, D, and E whereby E is the lowest possible passing result. Performances at lower than E are not recorded on the CSYS. The final result represents a variable combination of formal examination and papers or projects submitted earlier for evaluation by the examiners, as well as oral examination. Courses available for the CSYS and their methods of evaluation are as follows:

Art	No exam, 100% panel evaluation of oral/ written presentations.
Biology	Two exams (20% + 50%), Lab 20%, Project 30%.
Chemistry	Two exams (45% + 22%), Lab 33%.
Economics	Two exams (42% + 25%), Dissertation 33%.
Engineering	Two exams (20% + 20%), Project 50%, Industrial Visit 10%.

Certificate of Sixth Year Studies

The Scottish Examination Board hereby certifies that

presented for the Certificate of Sixth Year Studi

IN 1989 BY GRYFFE HIGH SCHOOL HOUSTON

was in that year awarded the Certificate in the following subject(s) with the Ranking(s) shown:—

Subject	Ranking
CHEMISTRY	B
MATHEMATICS – PAPER I	E
PAPER II	E
PHYSICS	C

1/006952-03732

J. H. Warner
Director

Document 4.2   Certificate of Sixth Year Studies

English	Two exams (33% + 33%), Dissertation 33%.
Geography	One exam 20%, Dissertation or Folio 40%, Field Study 40%.
History	Two exams (20% + 20%), Dissertation 50%.
Mathematics	One to five papers in various topics and variable assessment.
Modern Languages (French, German, Italian, Russian and Spanish)	Now being revised.
Modern Studies	Two exams (20% + 30%), Dissertation 50%.
Physics	Examination 50%, Project 50%.
Secretarial Studies	Exam 27%, Practical 33%, Dissertation 40%.

Examinations and courses are available also in Gaelic, Greek and Latin. Full descriptions of these courses are provided in the SEB publication *Certificate of Sixth Year Studies.*

A review of Sixth Year Studies is anticipated, possibly in conjunction with a review of the Highers. Such a review might result in the abolition of the CSYS, its becoming the required level for admission to tertiary education, or, at a minimum, the Highers and CSYS both being part of a better articulated sequence of instruction and examination from S4 to S6. Note that document 4.3 provides an analysis of the content of the various levels of mathematics required at Standard Grade, Higher Grade and CSYS and offers a comparison with the content of mathematics courses taught in secondary and university courses in Nova Scotia, Canada.

Vocational Education and SCOTVEC

The 1980s was a period of change in Scottish vocational education. The changes probably were greatest at the levels of Non-Advanced (S4 or below) and Advanced level courses. Modules offered flexibility in time, and place of offering, in completion times as well as relevance and applicability for those taking the modules, whatever the age, and whether for career development or general interest (see chart 4.3).

Thus, in 1983 the government introduced its "Action Plan" to overhaul throughly education and training for young people aged 16 to 18. In 1985 this led to the consolidation of the two existing vocational examining bodies—the Scottish Technician Education Council (SCOTEC) and the Scottish Business Education Council (SCOTBEC)—into one body, the Scottish Vocational Education Council (SCOTVEC) and the introduction of the new National Certificate which is attractive to a broader market than just the 16- to 18-year-olds originally targeted.

SCOTVEC is the major body responsible for developing, accrediting and awarding vocational qualifications in Scotland. It works in partnership with industry and commerce, trade unions, professional bodies and educational institutions to assure the quality, relevance and flexibility of vocational education offerings. SCOTVEC now is the principal examining body for business and technical programs below degree level in Scotland, although students may also sit examinations for the various British examining boards. In 1989 SCOTVEC had some 2,500 courses, called modules, available at the National Certificate level. Since 1987 SCOTVEC has been working actively to revise the programs at the Advanced level in collaboration with educational institutions and employers. These new programs will be phased in over a three-year period, 1990-93, and are being taught in further education colleges.

Qualifications

SCOTVEC's current educational awards are given at three levels:

1. The National Certificate, awarded for programs at non-advanced level, with instruction provided in the schools or in the further education (FE) colleges;
2. The Higher National Certificate (HNC) and the Higher National Diploma (HND), both advanced level, post-S4 and taught primarily in the FE colleges and sometimes in the central institutions (CI);
3. Postgraduate/post-experience diplomas offered in both the FEs and the CIs.

In addition to the National Certificate, the HNC/HND and Diplomas, SCOTVEC has introduced a number of educational initiatives which will take effect in the early 1990s. All are based on the module system. These new developments include Scottish Vocational Qualifications (SVQs); Accreditation of Prior Learning (APL); Work-Place Assessed Units; and Open learning as part of study for the National Certificate. Chart 4.4

SCE - MATHEMATICS

THE STANDARD GRADE

FOUNDATION LEVEL: The student interprets and communicates mathematics in familiar everyday contexts.

CONTENT: Some of the topics covered at this level are:
-numbers: +,-,x,÷ of whole numbers and decimals; percentages and fractions
-money:simple interest, budgets, profit and loss
-direct proportion
-units of measurement
-geometry: rectilinear figures and right angled triangles, radius and diameter of circles
-symmetry about a line
-straightforward graphs and tables

GENERAL LEVEL: Much of the content is the same as in the foundation level but the student now operates in a more mathematical context.

CONTENT: The topics covered at the foundation level are extended. For example:
-number : + and - of integers; +,-,x of fractions, whole number exponents
-inverse proportion
-geometry : perimeter and area of circles are included, more properties of parallelograms, volumes of cylinders and triangular prisms, Pythagoras' theorem
-rotational symmetry
-graphs and charts are more sophisticated including misleading scales, pie charts
-Cartesian coordinate system
Some new topics introduced at this level are:
-right angled trigonometry
-algebra: collecting like terms, monomial factors,simple linear equations and inequalities

CREDIT LEVEL: Mathematics is communicated and interpreted in more theoretical contexts.

CONTENT: Again the topics overlap but are extended. For example:
-number : x and ÷ of integers; division of fractions; simplification of radicals
-money: compound interest
-inverse variation,
-geometry: length of the arc of circle and area of a sector, more on properties of chords and tangents to circles
-trigonometry: laws of sines and cosines, elementary trig identities, graphs of the sine, cosine and tangent functions
-trigonometric equations
-algebra : quadratic equations, fractional equations
-functions: notation, linear and quadratic functions

THE HIGHER GRADE

TOPICS: those that would be covered in a precalculus course (*functions, intermediate algebra, analytic geometry and trigonometry*)
Some additional topics are sequences and series, matrices, transformational geometry and the matrix representation of transformations, vectors, and some calculus.
LEVEL: Students doing well in the Higher grade should be well prepared for first year university mathematics courses.

SIXTH YEAR STUDIES

PAPER I ALGEBRA AND NUMBER SYSTEMS

TOPICS: Sets, relations ,mappings, induction, elementary number theory, complex numbers, matrices and algebraic structures
LEVEL: This course is beyond a high school level course. It might well be offered at the first year level as a 3-hour credit course. It would prepare students for a first course in Abstract Algebra offered at the 2nd or 3rd year level.

PAPER II GEOMETRY AND CALCULUS

TOPICS: Selected topics from geometry (vectors, 3-space, conic sections), differential and integral calculus.
LEVEL: For a student whose mathematics requirement is a course in business calculus or who is majoring in economics, a pass in this course should satisfy their calculus requirement. For a student majoring in mathematics, or requiring a course in advanced calculus, a theoretically based calculus course should be taken.

PAPER III PROBABILITY AND STATISTICS

TOPICS: those covered in a standard precalculus probability and statistics course (*tree diagrams, Venn diagrams, axioms for computing probability, Bayes' Rule, Random Variables, Expected Value, Variance, binomial distribution, hypergeometric distribution, Poisson distribution, Estimation, Central Limit Theorem, Hypothesis Testing, Chi-Square tests of fit*)
LEVEL : This course might be given as a 6-hour "service" course at the first year level to non- science students or other students who will not be taking calculus.

PAPER IV NUMERICAL ANALYSIS AND COMPUTER PROGRAMMING

TOPICS : The numerical Analysis portion covers topics that would normally be in a 2nd year Numerical Methods course in a North American University.
LEVEL: This might well be given as a 3-hour credit course.

The computer programming portion probably falls short of what is expected of a 1st year University course in programming, but is much more than most high schools would cover.

PAPER V MATHEMATICAL TOPICS IN MECHANICS

In a North American University, these topics would constitute a 3 hour credit in Physics or possibly an engineering mechanics course. Few mathematics departments would cover this material. However it is university level work.

Document 4.3   SCE Mathematics, Standard and Higher Grades

summarizes the entry requirements and length of each qualification.

National Certificate

SCOTVEC modules which lead to a National Certificate are offered in some 500 educational institutions, ranging from colleges of further education to secondary-level schools and through the various vocational training schemes. By allowing students to select individual modules, or courses, to fill gaps in their previous education, the National Certificate makes it possible for those who may not qualify otherwise to proceed to higher study. Applicants to HNC/HND or university study now often offer National Certificate modules, in addition to Higher and Standard and/or Ordinary grades, with their application to provide a stronger case for admission.

Equivalencies have been established in some cases between National Certificate modules and courses of other examinations boards, such as the City and Guilds of London Institute (CGLI) and the former SCOTBEC and SCOTEC. The CGLI equivalencies generally are in the area of craft studies. Thus, a student who successfully completes an agreed program of National Certificate modules may have his or her National Certificate endorsed, directly on the Certificate, as equivalent to a specific City and Guilds craft certificate. In the early years of the National Certificate, the advantage of this endorsement was that the CGLI certificate, which had been in existence for years and was a known entity, was more readily accepted by U.K. employers and colleges. The equivalency agreements took effect April 25, 1985 for a minimum of five years.

Admission

Study toward the National Certificate is open to anyone over the age of 16. It may be undertaken at the secondary level alongside SCE Standard or Ordinary and Higher grades but generally is undertaken after completion of secondary school.

Certificate Structure

The National Certificate is awarded for the completion of one or several modules or on completion of a set of modules (Group Award) which are combined to further the student's career interest or to qualify the student for entry into a higher program. For instance, to receive the SCOTVEC National Certificate in Business Studies, students complete the following modules:

Business Studies - SCOTVEC
(Equivalent to former SCOTBEC HNC in Business Studies B930.)

	Hours
Communication 4	80
Financial Record Keeping I	40
Mathematics: Statistics I	40
Introduction to Economics	40
Contemporary Economic Issues	40
Electives	240
TOTAL	480

From 1985 to 1990 SCOTVEC awarded the National Certificate, which listed all the modules completed. From 1990, in addition to the National Certificate, students will also receive a Record of Education and Training (RET) which is a cumulative record listing the individual modules completed as well as all Group Awards. For instance, the Preliminary Certificate in Agriculture as a Group Award is indicated in the RET. With the RET, SCOTVEC also includes a course outline detailing the contents of the module in a "Statement of Module Learning Outcome Details." Examples of these are provided in documents 4.4 to 4.9.

The standard length of study for a National Certificate module is 40 hours, but the length is flexible, ranging from 20 to 140 hours. SCOTVEC credit values are measured in increments of 20 hours.

Module length (Hours)	SCOTVEC Credit Value
20	.5
40	1.0
60	1.5
80	2.0
100	2.5
120	3.0
140	3.5

More modules are being produced by SCOTVEC or by FE colleges in response to specific local needs. All modules must be validated by SCOTVEC and be assigned a SCOTVEC code before they can be offered to students. It should be noted, however, that the FE colleges are entitled to offer courses validated by bodies other than SCOTVEC. (See sample course offerings of Perth College of Further Education below.) Each approved module is described in a five- to seven-page document which covers its purpose, preferred entry level, learning outcomes intended, content, suggested learning and teaching approaches, assessment proce-

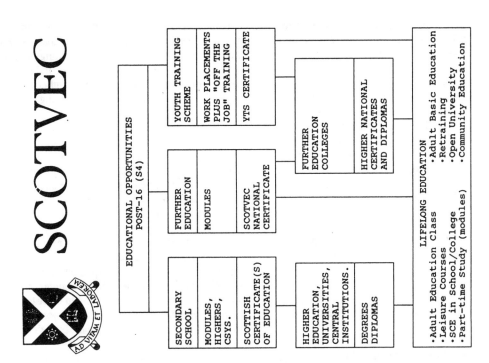

Chart 4.3. SCOTVEC Chart of Educational Opportunities, Adapted from SCOTVEC Diagram

Course	Entry Requirements	Length of Training
Apprenticeship Scheme for Agriculture with National Certificate Modules	General Education	2/3 years incl. day or block release
SCOTVEC National Certificate (Modular)	Dependent on modules selected	
SCOTVEC Higher National Diploma in Agriculture	2 SCE 'H' grade passes including Mathematics or Science 3 SCE 'O' grade passes at band A,B or C, the whole to include Mathematics, Chemistry and English (or GCE/GCSE equivalent) plus adequate practical experience	3 years sandwich
SCOTVEC Higher National Diploma in Engineering	SCE 'H' grade passes in Mathematics and Engineering Science or Physics plus 3 other SCE 'O' grade passes at band A,B or C including English (or GCE/ GCSE equivalent)	3 years sandwich
Degree in Agriculture - BSc (Agric)	University entrance requirements - usually 3/4 SCE 'H' grade passes plus 'O' grade passes (or GCE/GCSE	3/4 years
Post-diploma courses	equivalent) Higher National Diploma or exceptionally National Diploma	1 year
Post-graduate courses: Master of Science - MSc Master of Philosophy - MPhil Doctor of Philosophy - PhD	Honours degree	1/3 years

Chart 4.4. Courses in Scotland–Summary of Entry Requirements and Duration

dures and descriptions of the material to be covered for each outcome. A SCOTVEC module typically requires that five to seven learning outcomes be achieved.

The grading system for the National Certificate is competence-based and criterion-referenced. Thus there are no grades attached to the modules. The student's Certificate or Record of Education and Training will list achievement in individual modules and learning outcomes. The absence of marks explains why the universities have been reluctant to consider the National Certificate. They would like to see a grading system similar to that of the SCE Highers.

Higher National Certificate/Diploma and Postgraduate/Post-Experience Studies

In 1989 SCOTVEC offered business courses at the Advanced level in colleges of further education and central institutions as follows:

Higher National Certificate (HNC) in accounting; accounting technician studies; business studies; business studies (travel and tourism); distribution studies; management services; management studies; secretarial studies, legal studies, public administration.

Higher National Diploma (HND) in accounting; business studies; business studies and languages; business studies (office management); business studies (small business enterprise); business studies (travel and tourism); business studies (transport); hotel, catering and institutional management; secretarial studies; secretarial studies (with languages), communication studies, legal studies, information studies.

Postgraduate/Post-Experience Studies: Diplomas in industrial administration, public administration, graduate secretaries, personnel management.

Curriculums

Between 1985 and 1990 SCOTVEC's HNC/HND courses had not yet become modular and the structure of the awards was similar to that of the former SCOTBEC awards. SCOTVEC's new modular system of Advanced Courses for the HNC and the HND are being phased in over a three-year period, starting in September 1990. New courses have been introduced each academic year so that by 1993 all students will be enrolled in the new programs. These courses have been developed cooperatively by SCOTVEC, the colleges, employers and the professional bodies. In September 1990, new business courses in computing, accounting, hospitality services and management (Diploma in Industrial Administration) were introduced. In September 1991, business studies and secretarial studies are being introduced.

The revised modular courses are called Higher National Units with a credit load ranging from 1 credit (40 hours of study) to 3.5 credits (140 hours of study). Units have a length which is a full or half multiple of 40 hours. A minimum of 12 credits is required for an HNC and 30 credits for an HND. The HNC constitutes the first year, or 40%, of the HND.

An example of the structure of a new HNC/HND award in accounting is that of Dundee Institute of Technology which requires the completion of 15 credits for the HNC and 30 for the HND. Students who have completed 15 credits for the HNC can enter the second year of the HND. It is possible for the Diploma graduates to seek admission to Year Three of the bachelor's degree course in accounting:

HNC in Accounting
Dundee Institute of Technology

Year I - 33 weeks

Subject	Credits	Contact hours	Weekly hours
Financial accounting	3	120	3.5
Management accounting systems	3	120	3.5
Domestic economic environment	2	80	2.5
Business law	2	80	2.5
Quantitative methods	3	120	3.5
Organization and management theories	1	40	1.25
Information technology applications	1	40	1.25
TOTAL	15	600	18.0

Year II - 33 weeks

Advanced financial accounting statements	2	80	2.5
Management accounting or control and appraisal	2	80	2.5
Auditing	2	80	2.5
Income tax	2	80	2.5
(7 optional credits)	7	280	8.5
TOTAL	15	600	18.5

SCOTTISH VOCATIONAL EDUCATION COUNCIL

THE STORY OF ELIZABETH POLLY

To explain how the Record of Education and Training (RET) will operate we have chosen to illustrate its potential by outlining a short fictional "case study". (See Elizabeth Polly's RET). It demonstrates clearly the way in which a fairly individualised pattern of training can be accurately documented so that potential employers can see at a glance what has been achieved. Since all the information is held centrally in SCOTVEC's database it can be readily authenticated.

Elizabeth lives in rural Scotland and attended a local secondary school. As she was uncertain about her future career she decided to take advantage of the opportunity to broaden her knowledge of different vocational areas by undertaking some SCOTVEC modules, alongside her other studies. She successfully completed modules in Typing, German and Financial Record Keeping (see items 1 to 3 on the RET).

Although she enjoyed the modular programme she did not want to pursue a full time career as a secretary or in accounting. After she left school she talked to her local careers officer and he suggested she might go on a Youth Training Scheme (YTS) programme with a local employer who ran a market garden and a garden centre. This would give her a variety of experience such as running a small office and practical horticultural work. For her off-the-job training she undertook a programme of National Certificate modules (see items 4-9 on the RET). Elizabeth spent a year on YTS and enjoyed it, but realised that what she really wanted to do was to become involved in the agricultural industry, possibly eventually as a farm manager. After visiting her local agricultural college she decided to take a course of National Certificate modules leading to the Preliminary Certificate in Agriculture, which could lead to an HND and possibly eventually to a degree.

As she had already been successful in the computing and first aid modules required for the Certificate, Elizabeth was able to substitute alternative units which would be useful in her future career as a farm manager. She opted to study Higher National Units in Staff Management and Market Management as these would be useful either in general or more specialised agricultural management. She passed both of these in June 1990 (items 19 and 20). She also decided to enhance her German and undertook this in her own time using the college flexi-study facilities (see item 16).

Elizabeth was successful and achieved the Preliminary Certificate in Agriculture. Her RET also lists all the modules and units that she achieved and also shows the Scottish vocational qualifications which she gained. Its recognition by the Lead Body for industry, the Agricultural Training Board, is also shown on the RET.

Elizabeth has been offered a place on an HND course. If she accepts this, then her RET will be updated at the appropriate time to indicate the HN Units she achieves and will also be endorsed to show that she has been awarded the HND. Elizabeth's RET is a highly individual one, but even although it may be unique it is still easy to understand. A potential employer will be able to tell at a glance that not only has she achieved a vocational qualification in agriculture but also that she can type, has some basic knowledge of computers, German and accountancy and possesses significant horticultural skills. If the employer requires additional information about the exact competences she possesses he can obtain this from SCOTVEC or the college.

Document 4.4. Scottish Vocational Education Council Explanation of RET

SPECIMEN

SCOTVEC

SCOTTISH VOCATIONAL
EDUCATION COUNCIL

RECORD OF
EDUCATION AND TRAINING

This is to certify that

ELIZABETH POLLY

has been successful in achieving the following:

National Certificate Modules

Code	Module	Completed	Item
72108	Typewriting 2	January 1988	1
62250	Financial Record Keeping 1	January 1988	2
61402	Modern Languages 1: German	June 1988	3
78005	Green Plant (1/2)	November 1988	4
78181	Plant Identification: Introduction (1/2)	November 1988	5
81091	Introduction to Computers	December 1988	6
61179	Accident Prevention and First Aid (1/2)	December 1988	7
78134	Tree & Shrub Planting (1/2)	March 1989	8
68035	Home and Allotment Gardening	June 1989	9
78080	Tractor Operation 1	December 1989	10
78023	Introduction to Estate Maintenance (1/2)	December 1989	11
78003	An introduction to Crops and Soils (1/2)	February 1990	12
88097	Basic Livestock Care: Mammals	February 1990	13
98051	Fertilisers Quantity and Application	February 1990	14
68061	Tractor Operation 2	June 1990	15
91375	Language 2: German	June 1990	16
78028	Introduction to Farm Building Maintenance (1/2)	June 1990	17
68102	Livestock Health and Hygiene	June 1990	18

Higher National Units

Code	Unit	Completed	Grade	Item
6502579	Staff Management	June 1990	Pass	19
6502589	Market Management	June 1990	Pass	20

Group Award

The following Group Award has been gained and separately certificated as a result of the above achievements:

Preliminary Certificate in Agriculture   June 1990
(Items 6,7,10,11,12,13,14,15,17,18)

Date 2 August 1990   Reference 892345678   Chief Executive

Document 4.5   SCOTVEC Record of Education and Training

SPECIMEN

SCOTVEC
SCOTTISH VOCATIONAL
EDUCATION COUNCIL

RECORD OF EDUCATION AND TRAINING

ENDORSEMENTS

ELIZABETH POLLY

The Preliminary Certificate in Agriculture incorporates the occupational standards identified by the Agricultural Training Board at Level 1 and is recognised as a Scottish Vocational Qualification

Date 2 August 1990   Reference 892345678

Chief Executive

Document 4.6   SCOTVEC RET Endorsements

SCOTTISH VOCATIONAL QUALIFICATION

This is to certify that

has achieved the award of SAMPLE

PRELIMINARY CERTIFICATE

IN

AGRICULTURE

Results in the individual components which are required for this award are listed on the candidate's Record of Education and Training.

The Preliminary Certificate in Agriculture incorporates the Level 1 occupational standards identified by the Agricultural Training Board and is recognised as a Scottish Vocational Qualification.

Chief Executive
Scottish Vocational
Education Council

Director
Agricultural Training
Board

Document 4.7   SCOTVEC Scottish Vocational Qualification

SCOTTISH VOCATIONAL EDUCATION COUNCIL

NATIONAL CERTIFICATE

THIS IS TO CERTIFY THAT

MISS DANIELLE POLLY

has successfully completed the modules detailed below

Module Title	Date of Completion
64917 Hand Tools and Machinery: Brass Instruments	4 December 1987
71620 Music Making: Solo 1 (Strings1)	1 July 1988

The learning outcomes relating to the above modules have been detailed to the student on separate documentation

SPECIMEN

Date 25 May 1989   Reference 843456789   Chief Executive

Document 4.8   SCOTVEC National Certificate

SCOTTISH VOCATIONAL EDUCATION COUNCIL   PAGE   1

STATEMENT OF MODULE LEARNING OUTCOME DETAILS GAINED BY

MISS DANIELLE POLLY   843456789

Module 64916 Hand Tools and Machinery: Stringed Instruments
Studied At Anytown College
Learning Outcomes Completed on 4 December 1987

    1 know hand tools and machinery used in the repair and making
      of stringed instruments;

    2 know why particular materials are used in the manufacture of
      tools and machinery;

    3 use and maintain tools correctly;

    5 work safely.

Module 64917 Hand Tools and Machinery: Brass Instruments
Studied At Anytown College
Learning Outcomes Completed on 4 December 1987

    1 know hand tools and machinery used in the repair and
      manufacture of brass instruments;

    2 know why particular materials are used in the manufacture of
      tools and machinery;

    3 use and maintain tools correctly;

    4 make simple tools;

    5 work safely.

Module 64918 Woodwind Instruments: Dismantling and
               Reassembling 1 (Flutes and Clarinets)
Studied At Anytown College
Learning Outcomes Completed on 4 December 1987

    1 know the sound and the main features of flutes and
      clarinets;

    2 know the names, function and operation of keywork components
      and socket and tenon joints;

    3 plan a dismantling procedure;

SPECIMEN

Module 71620 Music Making: Solo 1 (Strings1)
Studied At Anytown College
Learning Outcomes Completed on 1 July 1988

    1 perform music which uses the most accessible notes and
      techniques appropriate to the chosen instrument/voice;

    2 operate an effective work routine, including where
      appropriate, the implementation of instructions.

************************************** E N D **************************************

Document 4.9. SCOTVEC Statement of Module Learning Outcome

Grading

Grading at SCOTVEC Advanced level (prior to 1990) was as follows:

Grade 1	80-100%
Grade 2	70-79%
Grade 3	65-69%
Grade 4	60-64%
Grade 5	55-59%
Grade 6	50-54%
Grade 7	45-49%
Grade 8	40-44%
Grade 9	30-39%
Grade 10	0-29%

Grade 1-6 are passes.

Grading, from 1990, has two awards: PASS or MERIT. There are no failing grades; incomplete modules are not reported. The grading, as in all SCOTVEC modules, is criterion-referenced and competence-based. It is basically PASS/FAIL grading in U.S. terminology, although demonstration of superior performance can be awarded a MERIT qualification. The Certificate indicates whether the student has achieved MERIT performance in each unit and also lists all units achieved.

Both the National Certificate Catalogue of Module Descriptors and individual module descriptors (the full module course outlines) are available from SCOTVEC. Also available is a *Guide to Equivalences Between SCOTVEC and City and Guilds*. Address: SCOTVEC, Hanover House, 24 Douglas Street, Glasgow, G27 NQ.

Sample SCOTVEC Awards

Business Programs Below Degree Level Prior to 1985

Since SCOTVEC has only been in existence since 1985, it is important to look at the structure of business qualifications prior to its formation since a majority of credentials submitted in the U.S. for years will be from the former examinations bodies. Before 1973, the examinations body was the Scottish Council for Commercial, Administrative and Professional Education (SCCAPE). From 1973 to 1985, the major examination body in business education in Scotland was the Scottish Business Education Council (SCOTBEC). The levels

and standards of the examinations of these two associations were fairly similar.

SCCAPE

Junior Awards	No formal entrance requirements
Intermediate Awards	Junior Awards or SCE ordinary passes required for admission
Advanced Awards	Intermediate awards or SCE Higher passes required for admission
Specialized Awards	University graduates or, on an exceptional basis, professional experience required for admission

SCOTBEC

Stage I/Junior "O" Awards	No formal entrance requirements)
Stage II or Intermediate Awards	Junior Awards or SCE ordinary level passes required for admission
Stage III/Advanced Awards	Intermediate Awards or SCE higher passes required for admission
Stage IV/Specialized Awards	University graduates or exceptionally-appropriate professional experience

These certificates and diplomas were offered in business studies, accounting, management services, business administration, European marketing and languages, office studies, business machine operations, hotel receptionist, secretarial studies, computer studies, public administration and police studies. These national awards were compared generally to the ordinary and higher certificates as follows:

Stage I	below Ordinary level
Stage II	at Ordinary National Certificate/Diploma level
Stage III	at Higher National Certificate/Diploma level
Stage IV	postgraduate diplomas for university graduates or holders of equivalent qualifications

Agriculture

Agricultural education in Scotland is offered in 22 institutions. It follows a typical Scottish pattern in that different levels of instruction are offered at different types of institutions, although the lines of demarcation are not rigid. Cooperation among the offering institutions is frequent. Included among these 22 institutions are four universities; three agricultural colleges, which are also listed as central institutions; some specialized agricultural colleges including the Scottish School of Forestry at Inverness; and several colleges of further education. In 1990 the three CI agricultural colleges were merged into one Scottish Agricultural College with three campuses.

Since 1984 all certificate and diploma courses have been comprised of groups of 40-hour modules of instruction validated by SCOTVEC. The record of achievement is the nonspecific SCOTVEC Record of Training and Achievement, which lists all modules completed by a student and separately identifies which of these modules have been offered towards a specific Group Award. An example is document 4.5 the Preliminary Certificate in Agriculture awarded to "Elizabeth Polly" for 10 of the 20 40-hour modules completed.

Examples of qualifications offered in agricultural subjects follow:

1. Colleges of Further Education -
    Motherwell College

City and Guilds - Horticulture	Day release
SCOTVEC Certificate in Agriculture	Block or Day release
SCOTVEC Certificate in Horticulture	Block or Day release

2. Specialized Agricultural Colleges -
    Oatridge Agricultural College

Degree in Agriculture (with East of Scotland College of Agriculture)	3 years
Certificate in General Agriculture	1 year, FT
Certificate in Agricultural Engineering (with West Lothian Further Education College)	Block release or 1 year, FT
Certificate in Horse Management	1 year, FT
Certificate in Horticulture	1 year, FT

Certificate in Sports Turf Maintenance and Management	1 year, FT
Certificates in Agriculture-various topics	Block release
Certificate in Amenity Horticulture	Day release
Certificate in Greenkeeping and Groundmanship	Day or block release
Youth Training Scheme in Agriculture	Block release
Youth Training Scheme in Agricultural Engineering	Block release
Youth Training Scheme in Greenkeeping, and Groundmanship, Horticulture and Horse Care	Block release

Further Education Colleges

There are 49 further education (FE) colleges in Scotland. The largest has an enrollment of 11,000 students, and the average per college is 4,000. The total number of students easily outnumbers that in all other tertiary level institutions combined. These colleges provide vocational and technical education to both school leavers and adults, the course level falling generally between that of the National Certificate after S4 and the Higher National Diplomas of the central institutions. They offer courses relevant to the community they serve, including courses of cultural or general interest. They also contract to offer special courses for local business or industry. Many FE courses are taught on a day or block release basis, and most are modular. Their principal validating body is SCOTVEC.

Since the FE colleges were intended to serve local or regional rather than national needs, they have been funded directly by their local education authority. Until 1989 each college, through its council membership, reflected the goals of its respective authority. In that year the Self-Governing Schools (Scotland) Act was enacted to require ". . . college councils to give more weight to business interest," thus providing them with more independence and flexibility. To ensure this, the Act established the maximum size of college councils at 20 and required that 50% be from industry, commerce, or the professions.

The brochure "Fast Forward with Further Education," available from the SED, 43 Jeffrey St., Edinburgh, Scotland, EH1 1DN, provides brief and useful descriptions of each FE college.

A sample of some of the many and varied courses offered at one of the larger FE colleges follows.

PERTH COLLEGE OF FURTHER EDUCATION
Crieff Rd, Perth, Scotland, PH1 2NX;
Tel. 0738-21171
Enrollment: FT 750; PT 6750
Teaching Staff: FT 130; PT 46 FT equiv.
Academic Year: 3 terms (about 33 weeks total)

Perth College of Further Education offers a wide range of programs from SCOTVEC modules for the secondary schools to Higher National Diplomas, as well as short-course and training programs for regional industry and commerce. It has an annual budget of £4,200,000, of which £700,000 comes from income-bearing courses, the remainder coming from the LEA. The majority of its students take courses on a part-time or sandwich basis. It acts as a Resource Center for the Open College and has an Academic Division that prepares post-S4 students for SCE Standard, O- or Higher Grade examinations. Other programs are offered in six divisions of the College.

Division	Examples of Programs Available (validated by)
1. Construction	Advanced craft in brickwork (City and Guilds); train as a plumber (Youth Training Scheme)
2. Commercial	Word processing 1 (Royal Society of Arts); HND in secretarial studies with languages (SCOTVEC)
3. Electronic Applications	HND in computing; media studies; theater skills (all SCOTVEC)
4. General Engineering	Certificate of basic training (Engineering Industry Training Board); abrasive wheel regulations (Perth College)
5. Motor Vehicle and Land Based Industries	Train in agriculture (Youth Training Scheme); HNC in motor vehicle engineering (SCOTVEC)
6. Hospitality, Caring	Nursery nursing (National Nursing Education and Social Studies Board); Certificate in Social Care (SCOTVEC); Junior Catering Management Certificate (Hotel Catering

and Institutional Management Association)

The names and addresses of Further Education Colleges in Scotland follow. An asterisk (*) indicates those FE colleges offering programs in business subjects, a # those FE colleges offering programs in agriculture subjects.

Aberdeen College of Commerce, Ruthrieston Center, Holburn St., Aberdeen, Scotland AB9 2YT; Tel. (0224) 572811 *

Aberdeen Technical College, Gallowgate, Aberdeen, Scotland AB9 1DN; Tel. (0224) 640366

Angus College, Keptie Rd., Arbroath, Angus, Scotland DD11 3EA; Tel. (0241) 72056 # *

Anniesland College, Hatfield Dr., Glasgow, Scotland G12 0YE; Tel. (041) 357 3969

Ayr College, Dam Park, Ayr, Scotland KA8 0EU; Tel. (0292) 265184 *

Banff and Buchan College of Further Education, Henderson Rd., Fraserburgh, Scotland AB4 5RF; Tel. (0346) 25777/8/9 *

Barmulloch College, 186 Rye Rd., Barmulloch, Glasgow, Scotland H21 3JY; Tel. (041) 558 9071

Barony Agricultural College, Parkgate, Dumfries, Scotland DG1 3NE; Tel. (038 786) 251/677/655 #

Bell College of Technology, Almada St., Hamilton, Scotland ML3 0JB; Tel. (0698) 283100 *

Borders College, Thorniedean, Melrose Rd., Galashiels, Scotland TD12 2AF; Tel. (0896) 57755 #

Cambuslang College, Glasgow Rd., Cambuslang, Glasgow, Scotland G72 7BS; Tel. (041) 641 619/8 *

Cardonald College, 690 Mosspark Dr., Glasgow, Scotland G52 3AY; Tel. (041) 883 6151-4/1119 *

Central College of Commerce, 300 Cathedral St., Glasgow, Scotland H1 2TA; Tel. (041) 552 3941 *

Clackmannan College, Branshill Rd., Alloa, Scotland FK10 3BT; Tel. (0259) 215121 *

Clinterty Agricultural College, Kinellar, Aberdeen, Scotland AB5 0TN; Tel. (0224) 790393 #

Clydebank College, Kilbowie Rd., Clydebank, Scotland G81 2AA; Tel. (041) 952 7771 *

Coatbridge College, Kildonan St., Coatbridge, Scotland ML5 3LS; Tel. (0236) 22316-8/21599/34935 *

Cumbernauld College, Tryst Rd., Cumbernauld, Glasgow, Scotland G67 1HU; Tel. (0236) 731811 *

Dumfries and Galloway College of Technology, Heathhall, Dumfries, Scotland DG1 3QZ; Tel. (0387) 61261 *

Dundee College, 30 Constitution Rd., Dundee, Scotland DD3 6TB; Tel. (0382) 29151 # *

Elmwood Agricultural and Technical College, Carslogi Rd., Cupar, Scotland KY15 4JB; Tel. (0334) 52781 # *

Falkirk College of Technology, Grangemouth Rd. Falkirk, Stirlingshire, Scotland FK2 9AD; Tel. (0324) 24981 # *

Fife College of Technology, St. Brycedale Ave., Kirkcaldy, Scotland KY1 1EX; Tel. (0592) 268591 *

Glasgow College of Building and Printing, 60 North Hanover Street, Glasgow, Scotland G1 2BP; Tel. (041) 332 9669

Glasgow College of Food Technology, 230 Cathedral St., Glasgow, Scotland G1 2TG; Tel. (041) 552 3751

Glasgow College of Nautical Studies, 21 Thistle St., Glasgow, Scotland G5 9XB; Tel. (041) 429 3201

Glenrothes College, Stenton Rd., Glenrothes, Scotland KY6 2RA; Tel. (0592) 772233 *

Inverness College of Further and Higher Education, 3 Longman Rd., Longman South, Inverness, Scotland IV1 1SA; Tel. (0463) 236681 *

James Watt College, Finnart St., Greenock, Scotland PA16 8HF; Tel. (0475) 24433 *

Jewel and Esk Valley College, Esbank Center, Newbattle Rd., Dalkeith, Scotland EH22 3AE; Tel. (031) 663 1951 *

John Wheatley College, 1346 Shettleston Rd., Shettleston, Glasgow, Scotland G32 9AT; Tel. (041) 778 2426

Kilmarnock College, Holehouse Rd., Kilmarnock, Scotland KA3 7AT; Tel. (0563) 23501 # *

Kirkwall Further Education Center, Kirkwall, Orkney, Scotland KW15 1QN; Tel. (0856) 2102 or 2839 #

Langside College, 50 Prospecthill Rd., Glasgow, Scotland G42 9LB; Tel. (041) 649 4991 #

Lauder College, North Fod, Halbeath, Dunfermline, Scotland KY1 5DY; Tel. (03820) 72601

Lews Castle College, Stornoway, Isle of Lewis, Scotland PA86 0XR; Tel. (0851) 3311 *

Moray College of Further Education, Hay St., Elgin, Scotland IV30 1NQ; Tel. (0343) 543425 *

Motherwell College, Dalzell Dr., Motherwell, Scotland ML1 2DD; Tel. (0698) 59641 # *

Oatridge Agricultural College, Ecclesmachan, Broxburn, West Lothian, Scotland EH52 6NH; Tel. (0506) 854387 #

Perth College, Brahan Estate, Crieff Rd., Perth, Scotland PH1 2NX; Tel. (0738) 21171 # *

Reid Kerr College, Renfrew Rd., Paisley, Scotland PA3 4DR; Tel. (041) 889 4225/8870/9993 *

Shetland College, Gressy Loan, Lerwick, Scotland ZE1 0BB; Tel. (0595) 5514 #

Springburn College, 110 Flemington St., Glasgow, Scotland G21 4BX; Tel. (041) 558 9001 *

Stevenson College, Bankhead Ave., Sighthill, Edinburgh, Scotland EH11 4DE; Tel. (031) 453 6161 *

Stow College, 43 Shamrock St., Glasgow, Scotland G4 9LD; Tel. (041) 332 1786 *

Telford College, Crewe Toll, Edinburgh, Scotland EH4 2NZ; Tel.(031) 332 2491*

Thurso Technical College, Ormlie Rd., Thurso, Caithness, Scotland KW14 7EE; Tel. (0847) 66161 # *

West Lothian College, Marjoribanks St., Bathgate, Scotland EH48 1QJ; Tel. (0506) 634300 *

Tertiary Level Institutions

The Central Institutions

In Scotland, education leading to degrees is offered in three distinctive types of tertiary level institutions: universities, teachers colleges and central institutions. Until 1990, there were 15 central institutions or CIs, including the three colleges of agriculture. They can be grouped by the major types of programs each offers:

1. Art, Design and Architecture	Duncan of Jordanstone College of Art
	Edinburgh College of Art
	Glasgow School of Art
2. Business, Engineering and Technical	Robert Gordon's Institute of Technology
	Dundee Institute of Technology
	Glasgow College
	Napier Polytechnic of Edinburgh
	Paisley College
	Scottish College of Textiles
3. Health and Hospitality	Queen Margaret College
	Queen's College
4. Music and Drama	Royal Scottish College of Music and Drama
5. Agriculture	East of Scotland College of Agriculture
	North of Scotland College of Agriculture
	West of Scotland College of Agriculture

Programs

Programs offered at the central institutions include those leading to the Higher National Diploma (HND), bachelors' degrees with or without honours, and a limited number of specialized masters' degrees and postgraduate diplomas. Some of the central institutions provide facilities for candidates to undertake research leading to CNAA doctorates. Also offered are short and/or specialized courses for the professions and industry.

Most programs leading to undergraduate degrees are sandwich, either "thick" (one full year of work experience) or "thin" (several short periods alternating with academic work). The CIs may not offer programs leading to qualifications in the liberal arts, social sciences or teacher education. They alone are authorized to offer programs in subjects such as architecture, applied arts and the health sciences. In subjects such as engineering, their mandate overlaps that of the universities. In architecture, full cooperation occurs in that most central institution Faculties or Schools of Architecture have become one and the same as those of a neighboring university: Duncan of Jordanstone with Dundee University, Edinburgh College of Art with Edinburgh and Heriot-Watt Universities, and Glasgow School of Art with Glasgow University.

Each central institution is managed by a governing body that includes representatives from industry, commerce, the professions and educational groups. Until 1988, the Secretary of State appointed these members. The CIs always have received their financial support from the SED, and, in consequence, have been responsive to governmental direction and national priorities. The comparatively close relationship of the CIs with the government did not, however, prevent their funding from becoming performance-related in 1987 with the "less efficient" receiving lower increases in financial support. In this respect, they are now treated in the same manner as are the universities.

In recent years there has been considerable growth in the number of degree courses offered at the CIs. However, since the institutions themselves do not possess degree granting rights, most programs are validated by the Council for National Academic Awards (CNAA). The CNAA has delegated to some of its member institutions the right to validate their own degree programs using CNAA criteria and methods. Robert Gordon's Institute of Technology, Dundee Institute of Technology and Napier Polytechnic do this. Other CIs have made agreements for some of their degree programs to be validated by a Scottish University. A different arrangement in 1945 enabled the Edinburgh College of Art and Edinburgh University to offer jointly a program that led to the Master of Arts with Honours in Fine Arts (an undergraduate qualification).

More recent changes include the amalgamation of the three Agriculture Colleges into a single Scottish College of Agriculture with three campuses (1990) and the development of close ties between Duncan of Jordanstone and the University of Dundee (1989) and between the Scottish College of Textiles and Heriot-Watt in 1990. In the latter cases, the universities accept the college's faculty as those of the university, welcome the students to their own Student Union and provide full access to library facilities. The North of Scotland College of Agriculture shares its facilities and staff with the Department of Agriculture of the University of Aberdeen forming the School of Agriculture - Aberdeen. Similar relations exist between the West of Scotland Agricultural College (Ayr) and Strathclyde University as well as between the East of Scotland College of Agriculture and Edinburgh University. These arrangements foster cooperation in research and the offering of degree programs.

Examples of qualifications offered at the North of Scotland College of Agriculture:

Higher National Diploma in Agriculture	3 years FT
Diploma in Agriculture	2 years
Post-Graduate Diploma in Farm Business, Organization and Management	1 year
Diploma in Rural Business Management	Day or Block release

It seems likely in the future that more arrangements such as these, and those between Duncan of Jordanstone and Dundee, will be made. Alternatively, the larger CIs may seek degree-granting status as universities.

All degrees awarded by the central institutions, whether validated by CNAA or a cooperating university, or self-validated using CNAA criteria, bear the approval of both the offering and the validating bodies.

A traditional BA (Ordinary) in Accounting is offered at the Dundee Institute of Technology:

Year I (33 weeks)	Total hours
Accounting I (financial/managerial)	187
Economics I	66
Law I	78

Behavioral science	66
Quantitative methods I	66
Information technology I	66
TOTAL	529 hours

Year II (33 weeks)	Total hours
Accounting II (financial/managerial)	165
Economics II	66
Law II	66
Business management	66
Quantitative methods II	66
Information technology II	66
TOTAL	495 hours

Year III (33 weeks)	Total hours
Advanced financial accounting	66
Advanced management accounting	66
Taxation	66
Financial management	66
Two optional subjects	99
Integrative coursework	32
TOTAL	395 hours

Admission

The standard minimum basis for admission to CIs, as to the universities, is three Higher level passes in prescribed subjects and two other subjects at Ordinary or Standard grade. Admission to many programs is limited, as applications greatly outnumber places available. These CIs long have accepted students with non-traditional qualifications.

CI programs are providing career and professionally oriented education, increasing mobility, providing progression through the various levels of education available to Scots, and offering opportunities for them to broaden their educational base. Efforts are being made in cooperation with the CNAA, SCOTVEC and professional bodies for the better integration of programs and the transferability of credit. With respect to the latter, the HNC may lead to admission into a degree program with credit for the first year or it may lead to the HND with credit for the first two years.

The single most complete guide to the CIs and their programs is the *Scottish Central Institutions Handbook*, published annually by the Centrally Funded Colleges, Room 54, Moray House College, Holyrood Road, Edinburgh EH8 8AG, Scotland.

An example of one of the many and varied courses offered at the central institutions, taken on a sandwich basis, follows:

Electrical and Electronic Engineering
Paisley College of Technology

BEng (4 Years' Sandwich)
BEng Hons (5 Years' Sandwich)

Year I

Two Terms	Network analysis (AC/DC networks, capacitors, inductors)
	Electronics
	Engineering science (waves, optics, atomic physics and mechanics)
	Mathematics (algebra and analysis)
	Computers and programming
One Term	Engineering applications (basic workshop practice)

Year II

Two Terms	Network analysis (fields and waves)
	Electronics (digital techniques)
	Mathematics (statistics and analysis)
	Engineering science (kinetics, thermodynamics)
	Business management
One Term	Industrial training

Year III

Two Terms	Mathematics
	Business management
	Electronics digital techniques (micro-processors and power systems)
	Materials devices (electrical and magnetic properties)
	Marketing
One Term	Industrial training

Year IV (BEngOrd)

Three Terms	Project
	Product engineering
	Three of: power plant; power systems engineering; analog electronics; communications; systems engineering; micro-electronic engineering and systems

Year IV (BEngHons)

Two Terms	Mathematics
	Control and product engineering
	Four of: power plant; power systems engineering; analog electronics; communications; systems engineering; micro-electronic engineering and digital systems; waves and application
One Term	Industrial training

Year V (BEngHons)

Three Terms	Major project
	Advanced studies in four subjects listed above, plus digital signal processing; and microwaves and optics

Graduates who obtain a second class or higher Honours degree and who complete four years of work experience, including one year taken within the degree, meet the requirements for membership in the Institution of Electrical Engineers.

Institutional Profiles

The calendar for all central institutions is three terms lasting 33-34 weeks. The length for each qualification presumes fulltime enrollment.

DUNCAN OF JORDANSTONE COLLEGE OF ART
Perth Rd., Dundee, Scotland DD1 4HT; Tel. 0382-23261

Founded in 1911 as part of the Dundee Institute of Art and Technology, the College received its present name in 1975 when the Institute became the Dundee College of Technology and Duncan of Jordanstone College of Art. In 1989 Duncan of Jordanstone become the College of Art of the University of Dundee though remaining a central institution and retaining its name. Until 1989 all programs except architecture and regional planning (Dundee) were validated by CNAA. Since 1989 all programs are validated by the University.

Qualifications	*Years*	*Programs*
HND (until 1990)	3	Home economics (food and nutrition or home and community studies); hotel catering and institutional management
MA (after 1990)	3	Food and welfare studies (undergraduate)
BA(Hons) Fine Art	4	Painting; sculpture; printmaking; video
BA(Hons) Design	4	Graphics; illustration; printed textiles; constructed textiles; jewelery and metal-smithing; ceramics; interior and environmental design
BSc	4	Town and regional planning
BSc/BArch(Hons)	3+2	Architecture
Post-Graduate Diploma	3	Electronic imaging
MA/MPhil	4 terms	Public art and design (postgraduate)

DUNDEE INSTITUTE OF TECHNOLOGY
Bell St., Dundee Scotland, DD1 1HG; Tel. 0382-27225

The Dundee Technical Institute was founded in the late nineteenth century and became a central institution in 1902. Its name changed to the Dundee Technical College and School of Art (1911), the Dundee Institute of Art and Technology (1933), the Dundee College of Technology (1975) and to its present name in 1988. The College offers programs in three faculties: Engineering and Construction, Management, and Sciences. Its degree programs are self-validated in accordance with CNAA criteria; HNC and HND programs by SCOTVEC.

Qualifications	*Years*	*Programs*
HND	2	Accounting; biological sciences; building; chemistry with business; civil engineering; computing; electronic systems; engineering; medical sciences
BA	3	Accounting
BA/BA (Hons)	3/4	Business studies; commerce; applied economics
BSc	3	Electronic systems; quantity surveying
BSc/BSc (Hons)	3/4	Biotechnology; chemistry with business; applicable mathematics; biology; chemistry; computing; mathematics; micro-systems; physics
BSc (Hons)	4	Nursing
BEng/BEng(Hons)	3/4	Civil and mechanical engineering
BEng (Hons)	4	Electrical and electronic engineering
Post-Graduate Diplomas	1	Computer-based electronic systems; information technology; management studies; manufacturing systems engineering; software engineering
MSc	4 terms	Electrical power engineering and management (with Dundee University)

EDINBURGH COLLEGE OF ART
Lauriston Place, Edinburgh, Scotland EH3 9DF;
Tel. 031-229 9311

The Edinburgh College of Art was established as a central institution in 1909. In 1945 the college and the University of Edinburgh agreed to offer a joint MA (Hons) in Fine Arts. In subsequent years, its other programs were offered with Heriot-Watt University. Since 1985, all programs offered by the College, with the exception of the MA(Hons) in Fine Arts, have led to degrees validated by Heriot-Watt. Instruction is provided through the Faculty of Arts and Design or in the Faculty of Environmental Design.

Qualifications	Years	Programs
BA, BA(Hons)	4	Design; sculpture; painting; landscape architecture (Hons only)
BArch(Hons)	4	Architecture
BSc(Hons)	4	Town planning
MA(Hons)	5	Fine arts (validated Edinburgh)
Post-Graduate Certificate	1	Housing
Post-Graduate Diplomas	1	Architecture; architectural conservation; design; fine art; housing; painting; printmaking; planning studies (developing countries); sculpture; urban design
MArch	1	Architecture
MDes	15 mos	Design; painting; printmaking; sculpture
MFA	2	Design; painting; printmaking; sculpture
MSc	1	Architectural conservation
	2	Urban design and regional planning
PhD	-	Research

GLASGOW COLLEGE
70 Cowcaddens Rd., Glasgow, Scotland G4 0BA;
Tel. 041-332 7090

Glasgow College was founded in 1971 and became a central institution in 1985. The College offers programs in three Faculties: Business and Administrative Studies; Life and Social Sciences; and Science, Engineering and Construction. Degree courses are validated by CNAA; certificate and diploma programs by SCOTVEC.

Qualifications	Years	Programs
HNC	1	Accounting; chemistry; medical sciences; police studies; public administration
HND	2	Accountancy; applied physics with electronics; legal studies; secretarial studies; public administration
HND	3	Civil engineering; electrical and electronic engineering; endorsement in chemistry; mechanical engineering
BA	3	Accountancy; communication studies; public administration; risk management; social sciences
BA	4	Commerce; nursing studies
BA(Hons)	4	Social sciences
BSc	3	Applied biology; building; chemistry with information technology and instrumentation; computer information systems; quantity surveying
BSc	4	Mathematics for business analysis; ophthalmic optics
BSc(Hons)	4	Applied biology; chemistry with information technology and instrumentation; mathematics for business analysis; ophthalmic optics
BEng/BEng(Hons)	3/4	Micro-electronics; manufacture with micro-electronics; mechanical electronic systems
Post-Graduate Diploma	1	Management studies; public administration and management (developing countries); systems analysis and design; personnel management
MSc/PhD	-	Research

GLASGOW SCHOOL OF ART
167 Renfrew St., Glasgow, Scotland G3 6RQ;
Tel. 041-232 9797

The Glasgow School of Art grew from the Government School of Design, founded in the 1840s. It offers programs in three schools: Fine Art; Design; and the Mackintosh School of Architecture. The latter is also part of the University of Glasgow which validates the degrees. Other degrees are validated by CNAA.

Qualifications	Years	Programs
BA/BA(Hons)	4	Fine Art (drawing and painting; environmental art; photography; printmaking; sculpture; design (ceramics;

		embroidered and woven textiles; graphic design; industrial/interior design; printed textiles); silver-smithing (jewelery)
BEng		Product design engineering (University of Glasgow)
BArchitectural Studies	3	Architecture (University of Glasgow)
BArchitectural Studies(Hons)	4	Architecture (University of Glasgow)
Post-Graduate Diplomas	1	Fine Art; design
	2	Architecture
MArch	1	Architecture (research or courses)
MA (postgraduate)	4 terms	Design
	2	Fine Art
		institutional management; printing (administration and production)
BA	3	Accounting; applied economics; publishing; photographic studies; export studies and languages
BA	4	Interior design
BA/BA(Hons)	4/4	Business studies; commerce
BA(Hons)	4	Hospitality management
BEd/BEd(Hons)	4/4	Technology (with Moray House College of Education)
BEng/BEng(Hons)	4	Engineering with management
BEng/BEng(Hons)	4/5	Electronic and communication; energy; transportation
BSc	3	Quantity surveying; applied physics with microelectronics; building; electronic and electrical engineering
BSc/BSc(Hons)	3/4	Applied chemistry (with Scottish College of Textiles) (until 1990); biological sciences; computing; mathematics with engineering technology; science with industrial studies; life sciences
BSc/BSc(Hons)	4/4	Industrial design (technology)
Post-Graduate Diplomas	1	Administrative and information management; advanced electronic systems; business administration; careers guidance; European marketing and languages; information technology; personnel management; secretarial studies; systems analysis and design; transportation planning in developing countries
MSc	1	Biology of water resource management; information technology
PhD	-	Research

NAPIER POLYTECHNIC OF EDINBURGH
219 Colinton Rd., Edinburgh, Scotland EH14 1DJ; Tel. 031-444 2266

Napier College of Science and Technology opened in 1964 and merged with the Edinburgh College of Commerce in 1974 to form Napier College of Commerce and Technology. In 1988 it obtained its present name. Napier offers programs in four faculties: Humanities, Professional Studies, Science and Technology. Its degree programs are self-validated in accordance with CNAA criteria; its HND and HNC programs are validated by SCOTVEC.

Qualifications	Years	Programs
HNC	1	Accounting; business studies; life sciences; photography, audio-visual technology
Diploma	2	Diploma in Applied Music (validated by Napier).
HND	2	Accounting; biological sciences; business studies; chemistry; communication studies; computing; electronic and electrical engineering; industrial physics with micro-computing; journalism studies; legal studies; mathematics, operational research and statistics; office studies; office studies with languages; software engineering
HND	3	Business studies and languages; civil engineering; engineering; hotel catering and

PAISLEY COLLEGE OF TECHNOLOGY
High St., Paisley, Scotland PA1 2BE; Tel. 041-848 3000

Paisley College was founded in 1897 as the Paisley Technical College and School of Art. It obtained its present name in 1950, when it became a central institution. Paisley offers programs in three schools: Engineering; Information, Social and Management Sciences; and Science and Technology. Its degree programs are validated by the CNAA.

Qualifications	Years	Programs
BSc	3	General science
BA/BA(Hons)	3/4	Applied social studies with social administration or with technology and society; business economics with marketing, with personnel management or with finance; business information technology
BA/BA(Hons)	4/5	Applied social studies with Certificate of Qualification in Social Work
BSc/BSc(Hons)	3/4	Computing science; computing science, statistics and operational research; land economics; biology; chemistry; mathematical sciences; physical science for micro-electronics; physics
BSc(Hons)	4	Computing science with digital control; industrial chemistry
BEng/BEng(Hons)	3/4	Electrical and electronic, electronic product; industrial; mechanical engineering
BEng(Hons)	4	Civil; chemical engineering
Post-Graduate Diplomas	1	Engineering design of buildings; computer aided engineering; quality engineering; computing; alcohol studies; careers guidance; information technology; marketing
Post-Professional Diplomas	1	Health visiting (validated by National Board for Nursing, Midwifery, and Health Visiting for Scotland)
MSc	1	Engineering design of buildings; pressure vessel design
MPhil, PhD	-	Research

QUEEN MARGARET COLLEGE
Clerwood Terrace, Edinburgh, Scotland EH22 8TS; Tel. 031-339 8111

The College was founded in 1875 as the Edinburgh School of Cookery, became a central institution in 1909, was renamed the Edinburgh College of Domestic Science in 1930, and given its present name in 1971. Courses are offered in three broad categories: health care, business management and information, and theater arts. Degree programs are validated by the CNAA and diploma programs by SCOTVEC or by the health professions.

Qualifications	Years	Programs
Diploma	1	Advanced nursing; community mental health care; district nursing and health visiting; primary health care (validated by the National Board for Nursing, Midwifery, and Health Visiting for Scotland)
HND	2	Information studies; hotel, catering and institutional management
Diploma	3	Podiatric medicine (validated by Council for Professions Supplementary to Medicine); drama: acting or stage management (validated by the Conference of Drama Schools)
BA	3	Communication studies; hospitality enterprise with tourism; applied consumer studies
BA	4	Nursing studies
BSc	3	Food studies; occupational therapy; physiotherapy
BSc	4	Dietetics
BSc/BSc(Hons)	3/4	Speech pathology and therapy
Post-Graduate Diploma	1	Hospitality management
Post-Graduate BSc(Hons)	2	Health studies
MBA	1	Health services management (validated by Heriot-Watt)
MPhil, PhD	-	Research

THE QUEEN'S COLLEGE, GLASGOW
1 Park Drive, Glasgow, Scotland G3 6LP; Tel. 041-334 8141

The Queen's College, Glasgow was founded in 1875 and became a central institution in 1972. Programs are offered in two faculties: Health Studies and Management Studies. Degree programs are validated by CNAA; HND programs by SCOTVEC. Other programs are validated by the College itself or by professional health professions.

Qualifications	Years	Programs
Certificate	1	Health education (validated by Queen's)
HND	2	Beauty therapy; consumer and marketing studies

Qualifications	Years	Programs
HND	3	Hotel, catering and marketing studies
Diplomas	3	Occupational therapy (validated by College of Occupational Therapists); orthoptics (validated by British Orthoptics Society); podiatric medicine (validated by Society of Chiropodists); radiography (validated by College of Radiographers); social work (validated by CCETSW)
BA	3	Consumer and management studies; hotel catering management
BSc	3	Physiotherapy
	3/4	Human nutrition and dietetics
BSc(Hons)	4	Health studies
Post-Graduate Certificate	1	Qualification in social work
Post-Graduate Diplomas	1	Dietetics; hotel, catering and accommodation management

ROBERT GORDON'S INSTITUTE OF TECHNOLOGY
Schoolhill, Aberdeen, Scotland AB9 1FR;
Tel. 0224-633611

RGIT traces its origins to 1750 as Robert Gordon's Hospital. In 1881 the Hospital became Robert Gordon's College, and in 1884 it incorporated the Aberdeen Mechanic's Institute and the Gray's School of Science and Art. In 1903 it was renamed Robert Gordon's Technical College and became a central institution. In 1967 the Institute obtained its present title. Programs are offered in four Faculties: Design (which includes Gray's School of Art and the Scott Sutherland School of Architecture); Health and Food Science; Management; and Science and Technology. All degree programs are self-validated using CNAA guidelines and criteria. Other programs are validated by SCOTVEC.

Qualifications	Years	Programs
HND	2	Applied physics with micro-processor instrumentation; chemistry; computing; electronic and electrical engineering
HND/BA	2/3	Hotel catering and institutional administration
BA	3	Commerce
BA	4	Applied social studies
BA/BA(Hons)	3/4	Business studies, librarianship and information studies
BA/BA(Hons)	4	Public administration; fine art; design and craft
BSc	3	Quantity surveying; food, textiles and consumer studies; electronic and electrical engineering; mechanical engineering
BSc/BSc(Hons)	3/4	Nutrition and dietetics; applied chemistry; applied physics; materials and analytical science; mathematical sciences with computing; computer science
BSC(Hons)	4	Architecture; pharmacy; human nutrition
BEng/BEng(Hons)	3/4	Electronics and electrical engineering; electronic and information engineering; engineering technology
Post-Graduate Diplomas	1	Advanced architectural studies; art and design; management studies; personnel administration; librarianship and information studies; computing; information engineering; computer applications in engineering; off-shore engineering; off-shore materials and corrosion engineering (with Newcastle-upon-Tyne Polytechnic); design and development; rural and regional resources planning
MLitt	1-2	Historical studies (awarded by University of Aberdeen)
MSc	1-2	Design and development; rural and regional resources planning; off-shore engineering; off-shore materials and corrosion engineering (with Newcastle-upon-Tyne)
PhD	-	Research

ROYAL SCOTTISH ACADEMY OF MUSIC AND DRAMA
100 Renfrew St., Glasgow, Scotland G2 3DB;
Tel. 041-332 4104

The RSAMD began as the Glasgow Athenaeum, founded in 1847 to provide adult education in Commerce, Science and the Arts. By 1928 most of the Athenaeum's activities had been transferred to other institutions, and its School of Music had become the Scottish National Academy of Music with formal links to the University of Glasgow. In 1939 it became a central institution. Since 1947 it has been part of the Associated Board of the Royal Schools of Music, an examining body. In 1950 the College of Dramatic Art was added.

Qualifications	Years	Programs
Diploma	2	Stage management studies (validated by National

		Council for Drama Training)
	3	Dramatic art (validated by National Council for Drama Training), teaching
	4	Performance
BA	3	Musical studies (validated by CNAA), dramatic studies (validated by University of Glasgow)
BA(Hons)	4	Musical studies (validated by the University of Glasgow)
BEd	4	Music (CNAA and General Teaching Council for Scotland) (with St. Andrew's Bearsden and Jordanhill)
Certificates in Post-Graduate Studies	-	Music (validated by RSAMD), various instruments

SCOTTISH COLLEGE OF TEXTILES

Netherdale, Galashiels, Scotland TD1 3HF; Tel. 0896 3351

The Scottish College of Textiles was founded in 1883 with a mandate for programs related to the textile and clothing industry, both technical and management. Degree programs are validated by CNAA, certificate and diploma programs by SCOTVEC. The College validated its own Associateship in Clothing Studies. Degree programs in polymer sciences were taught cooperatively with Napier Polytechnic. In 1990 the Scottish College of Textiles became the Faculty of Textiles of Heriot-Watt University, though remaining a central institution.

Qualifications	Years	Programs
HNC	1	Textiles
HND	2	Accounting; business studies (language option); computing; information management; secretarial studies (with language option)
Associateship in	3	Textiles and clothing studies (last admissions Clothing 1989/90)
BA(Hons)	4	Industrial design (textiles)
BSc/BSc (Hons)	3/4	Applied chemistry (polymer and colour science); textiles with clothing studies (last entry 1989/90)
BSc/BSc(Hons)	4/4	Applied chemistry (colour science and technology or materials chemistry); clothing; textiles with clothing studies (first entry 1990/91)
Post-Graduate Diplomas	1	Clothing studies; computer studies; design; industrial administration (personnel or marketing)
MPhil, PhD	-	Research

Colleges of Education

For information on colleges of education and teacher training programs, see "Teacher Training" later in this chapter.

Universities

Scotland has eight universities: Aberdeen, Dundee, Edinburgh, Glasgow, Heriot-Watt (in Edinburgh), St. Andrews, Stirling and Strathclyde (in Glasgow). Each is a center for research and teaching. A total of 48,400 students enrolled at these institutions in 1987; 85% were studying for first degrees and just over 70% claimed Scottish domicile. In addition to the eight universities named above, Britain's Open University enrolled over 8,400 students from Scotland in 1989.

The most frequently earned first degree in Scotland is the four-year honours degree, which begins with more breadth in the early years than corresponding programs in England. Degrees in medicine, dentistry and veterinary science require five to six years. Advanced degrees take anywhere from one to three years on a fulltime basis.

University Finance in Scotland

Scottish universities have received their government funds through the University Grants Committee (UGC) and its successor since 1988, the Universities Funding Council (UFC). Whereas the UGC dealt primarily with funding and served as a buffer between government and the universities, the UFC is concerned explicitly with political strategy and university management. It has no advisory role in determining what resources the universities need, nor does it give block grants which the institutions can spend as they see fit. When it was created in 1988, the UFC was given a statutory Scottish committee designed to look out for Scottish interests. This step plainly fell short of the demand in some quarters for "devolution," or total Scottish control of its universities (a demand not pressed, in the end, by the universities' vice-chancellors and principals).

The Scottish universities were subject to the same major cuts in funding and in "home-grown" enrollments that affected other British universities after 1980. It was thought in 1982 that £21 million and 3,000 students would be removed from the university system in Scotland between 1980 and 1984. Of the eight universities,

Stirling was conceded to be the hardest hit. By 1982 the reductions in staff at the four most affected institutions were notable: Aberdeen, 112 academic posts, 200 nonacademic; St. Andrews, 50 academic, 70 nonacademic; Stirling, 34 academic; and Dundee, 33 academic. The universities' financial straits during the decade led to talk of possible merger of institutions or, in the case of St. Andrews and Dundee, reunion. Stirling explored possible merger with Paisley College of Technology as a way to rebound from the substantial funding cuts it experienced in 1981. Neither of these proposals came to pass, however.

Even where economies could be achieved by cuts or transfers, the changes in the Scottish university landscape were striking. Heriot-Watt, though in something of a favored position as a technological institution, cut two degree programs in 1981 and then had to close its pharmacy department at mid-decade. In 1987 Dundee proposed the transfer of some of its departments to St. Andrews as an economy measure that would permit its continued existence as an independent institution. It forecast that a considerable share of its teaching duties would devolve to St. Andrews under the plan. The proposal involved transfer of geology and geography; joint teaching of foreign languages and mathematical sciences; and major reductions in size in chemistry and physics.

During the same period, Dundee had to respond to a UGC proposal that its dental school be closed. In 1987 Aberdeen proposed to the UGC a plan to drop music, classics, Russian, social work, history and philosophy of science, and linguistics. The university's principal announced that in light of the cuts Aberdeen was "now trimmed to the bone." In 1988 Edinburgh University projected a deficit of £3 million and announced that over three years it would have to reduce academic jobs by 170 instead of the 60 originally planned. The proposed reductions represented 12% of Edinburgh's academic and related staff and included the only lecturer in Turkish in Scotland.

As UGC funding in the mid-1980s focused increasingly on evaluations of research productivity, the Scottish universities were recipients of both good and bad news. In 1986 Edinburgh and Glasgow received the highest rankings for strength of research activity; Stirling and Dundee received lower marks. Aberdeen, St. Andrews, Heriot-Watt and Strathclyde were rated in the middle. Interestingly, the money did not flow solely to the top of the rankings: the three overall funding increases granted that year went to Glasgow, Heriot-Watt and Strathclyde. Edinburgh was "rewarded" with a smaller budget reduction than might otherwise have been assessed (*Times Education Supplement*, May 30, 1986; May 1, 1987; June 24, 1988).

By the start of the 1990s there were signs that budgets were becoming stable if not improving. Aberdeen reported in December, 1989, that it was on target to balance its books and therefore likely to make the transition to the even lower funding and staffing levels mandated for 1992-93. Stirling recorded balanced finances by late 1989 and could claim over half of its income from sources other than the UFC (*Times Higher Education Supplement*, November 3, 1989; December 8, 1989).

Structure of First Degree Courses

The structure of first degrees in Scotland generally is different from what is found in the rest of the United Kingdom. Some of the distinguishing features are curricular flexibility in many areas of study; broadly based studies, especially in the first two years; a pattern of three-year ordinary (or general) degrees parallel to four-year honours degrees; and the use of the term "Master" to designate certain first degrees.

Except for professional programs such as medicine, law, engineering, divinity and some in business subjects, where the curriculum is fairly fixed, Scottish university students have wide options in choice of subjects. Only Heriot-Watt and Strathclyde universities admit students directly to a particular course of study. Stirling admits its students to the university as a whole.

At other institutions and in the BA programs and some science programs at Strathclyde, students are admitted to a faculty rather than to a degree program or department. The "faculty" includes a broad group of related subjects (e.g., social sciences) within which a candidate's major field will fall. The entry requirements for all applicants to a particular faculty will be the same, or nearly so, and any special subject requirements stipulated by departments are kept to a minimum. In the arts and sciences, the requirement that students choose three or even four separate subjects in the first year virtually demands breadth in the early stages. This insistence upon broad exploration (at least outside the professional disciplines) before settling on a degree goal is a characteristic of Scottish university education. And while the professional programs are relatively fixed by comparison, there are exceptions; at some universities engineering students may wait a year or even two years before deciding upon their specialty.

The breadth of first degree programs, especially in the first year, is rooted in the way these programs articulate with the Scottish secondary system. First degree programs are designed for holders of Scottish Certificate of Education qualifications, normally obtained at the age of 17 or after. Even though most Scottish entrants remain at school for an additional year after sitting for Highers, teaching at Scottish universities assumes prior instruction to SCE Higher grade only.

Because Scottish university entrants are younger than their English and Welsh counterparts and because Scottish secondary education is itself more broadly based in the final years, the level of first year university work tends to be less advanced than south of the border. As the authors of *British Qualifications* note, "the wider spread of subjects and the rather less specialized character of many of the courses mean that the level of the Scottish four-year honours courses reaches a standard about the same as that of the English and Welsh three-year honours degree course."

Ordinary and Honours Degrees

The three-year ordinary (or general) degree in arts or sciences is designed to provide a broad, general education and has no equivalent in England and Wales. A designated degree (e.g., "BSc Des. in Chemistry") is an ordinary degree that provides an element of specialization within a three-year program. Although fewer students now elect these three-year options than in the past—one recent estimate put the portion at about a third of first degrees granted—it is important to note the Scottish insistence that the ordinary degree is not an inferior substitute for an honours degree, nor merely a "failed" honours program. It should be noted that some universities do grant four-year ordinary degrees when the fourth-year dissertation or project is incomplete or inadequate. Still, the common pattern is for undergraduates to demonstrate in the first two years their fitness to continue to the more typical honours degree (four years total) by taking a variety of subjects.

The choice of specialization may be delayed until the end of the second year and sometimes even the start of the third. This Scottish tradition has been called "common start and late differentiation," in contrast to the English tendency to separate honours and ordinary from the beginning.

Deciding on honours or ordinary is of course only one aspect of the student's choice. At Edinburgh students can select from over 200 separate first degree subjects. While there are many variations in the names of degrees, a basic distinction exists between single honours and joint honours. For example, at St. Andrews a candidate for Honours in Biochemistry will devote the last two years of study to the appropriate sequence of courses in that subject. In the same vein, a candidate for Honours in Biochemistry with Microbiology will devote two years to the course, taking some units in common with the "straight" Biochemistry student and others focused on special topics in Microbiology. However, a candidate for Joint Honours in Biochemistry and Chemistry will devote one Honours year to Biochemistry and the other Honours year to Chemistry and might do the subjects in either order. The charts on (Dundee and Edinburgh) show how different subjects may be combined at honours level (See charts 4.5 to 4.8.)

At the four ancient universities (Aberdeen, Edinburgh, Glasgow, St. Andrews) and at Dundee, the MA, whether ordinary or honours, is a first degree. St. Andrews grants an MTheol which is similarly a first degree and must be distinguished from the MTh, a master's-level degree taught at other institutions. At the above institutions the degrees of MA and MTheol are no more advanced than BSc or BD.

For all their flexibility, the amount of choice possible in Scottish first degree programs has come under pressure because of government funding policies. Stirling, for instance, now requires students to spend at least a year in the main field of study requested at the time of entry (though subsidiary areas still are freely chosen). Science students at Edinburgh are less free to move between broad areas of the curriculum (e.g., biological vs. physical science) than was formerly the case. Dundee and St. Andrews also have "channelled" entry to the sciences a bit more, though transfer between areas is possible.

In engineering, Glasgow and Dundee find themselves somewhere between the faculty-entry approach and the scheme of direct admission to departments which is characteristic of Heriot-Watt and Strathclyde. Compromises also are emerging outside the science and technical fields. Popular programs such as psychology now may require a higher "going rate" than others in the same faculty, despite the efforts of faculty-entry institutions to have uniform entry requirements regardless of major field.

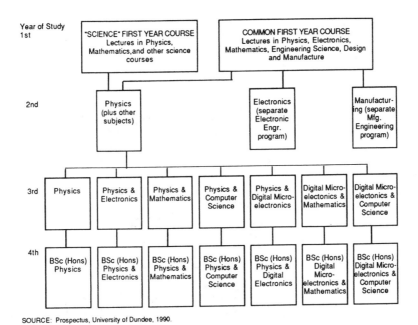

SOURCE: Prospectus, University of Dundee, 1990.

Chart 4.5. BSc (Hons) Options in Physics, University of Dundee

Type of Degree	Level 1	Level 2	Level 3	Level 4
Ordinary (three years)	4 or 5 Units	a further 6 or 5 Units to make 10 in total		
Designated (three years)	4 or 5 Units	4 or 3 Units	at least 3 units in Designated subject with other units to make 12 in total	
Honours (four years)	4 or 5 Units 8 Units in subjects which lay the foundation for Honours choice at levels 3 and 4	4 or 3 Units	4 Units in Honours subject or subjects	4 further Units in Honours subject or subjects

NOTE: Each course is assigned a unit value (1, 2, 3 or 4) according to the amount of time and work involved. One unit is defined as one-quarter of the normal yearly work load.

SOURCE: Adapted from University of Aberdeen Undergraduate Prospectus. Entry 1990.

Chart 4.6. BSc (Pure Science) Degree Structure, University of Aberdeen

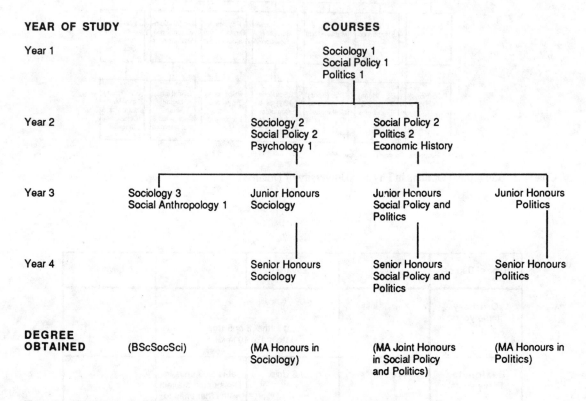

**SAMPLE CURRICULA, FACULTY OF SOCIAL SCIENCES
UNIVERSITY OF EDINBURGH**
Illustrating four alternative routes to a degree starting from a common first-year curriculum.

YEAR OF STUDY	COURSES			
Year 1		Sociology 1 Social Policy 1 Politics 1		
Year 2		Sociology 2 Social Policy 2 Psychology 1	Social Policy 2 Politics 2 Economic History	
Year 3	Sociology 3 Social Anthropology 1	Junior Honours Sociology	Junior Honours Social Policy and Politics	Junior Honours Politics
Year 4		Senior Honours Sociology	Senior Honours Social Policy and Politics	Senior Honours Politics
DEGREE OBTAINED	(BScSocSci)	(MA Honours in Sociology)	(MA Joint Honours in Social Policy and Politics)	(MA Honours in Politics)

This table illustrates only a few of the ways a single first-year curriculum could develop.

SOURCE: Adapted from University of Edinburgh Undergraduate Prospectus, 1990.

Chart 4.7. Specimen Curricula, Faculty of Social Sciences, University of Edinburgh

Possible Arrangements for First-Year Courses
St. Andrews MA (Ordinary)

	Year One	*Year Two*	*Year Three*
(i)	3 First Arts classes	2 First Arts classes and 1 Second Arts class	2 Second Arts classes
(ii)	3 First Arts classes	2 First Arts classes and 1 Second Arts class	1 Second Arts class and 1 Third Arts class
(iii)	3 First Arts classes	1 First Arts class and 2 Second Arts classes	2 Third Arts classes

Adapted from <u>Prospectus, 1990 Entry</u>, University of St. Andrews.

Arts Degree Structure
St. Andrews University

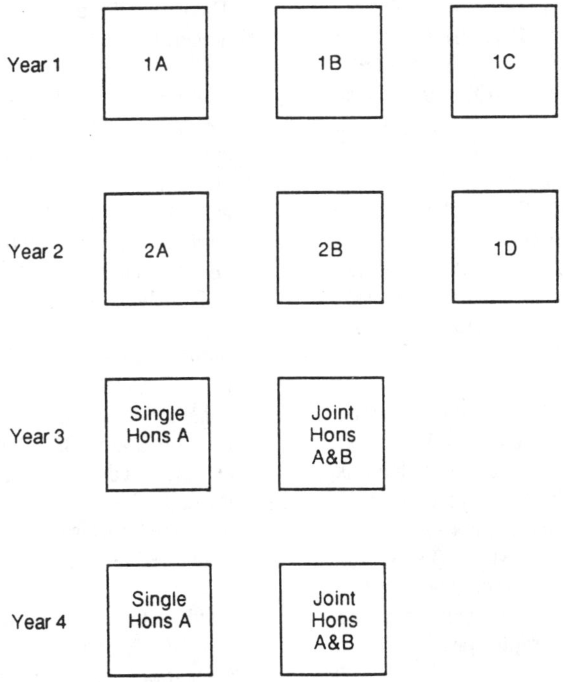

Year 1	1A	1B	1C
Year 2	2A	2B	1D
Year 3	Single Hons A	Joint Hons A&B	
Year 4	Single Hons A	Joint Hons A&B	

(A, B, C, D represent names of different subjects)

Adapted from <u>Prospectus, 1990 Entry</u>, University of St. Andrews.

Chart 4.8. St. Andrews University Course Structure

Advanced Standing

Advanced standing upon entry from school is possible in some fields of study and may exempt a student from as much as the entire first year of a four-year honours degree. The basis for such advanced standing usually is high grades on GCE A-levels or the Certificate of Sixth Year Studies. In science and engineering, Higher National Certificates and Diplomas may bring entry directly to the second or even the third year. The universities caution school leavers that direct entry to second year means less opportunity to change the program of study after an exploratory period. Each university sets its own policies with respect to these exemptions, but, in general, advanced entry is widely available in science, sometimes available in arts and social sciences, and only rarely in medicine, law or divinity.

Grading

Although the methods used to evaluate students' performance are more varied than in the past, end-of-year (or "end-of-session") examinations still provide the main evidence regarding a student's progress toward a degree (see also Advice to Admissions Officers). These degree examinations often are marked according to the usual British scale of 0 to 100. But the scheme of marks usually will be tied to a scheme of grades as well (examples are grades of A through G; High Distinction, Distinction, Pass, Fail; and First Class, Second Class, Pass, Fail). In Honours degree examinations the results are commonly graded according to the university's overall pattern for classifying degrees themselves (First Class, Upper and Lower Second Class, etc.).

It is common now for the universities to issue documents summarizing results obtained in degree examinations or units of study. In fact, these credentials often bear the title of "transcript," and in their most complete form give courses, exam results and an explanatory key to the grading system. Marks (i.e., points awarded on the 0 to 100 scale) may or may not appear, but this will not be important except in cases where the grade on the academic record is simply "pass."

Admission Requirements

Applicants to first degree programs must meet two types of entrance requirements: (1) general entrance requirements, specifying broad educational background; and (2) additional requirements set by particular faculties or degree programs. Even when general and special requirements have been met, however, admission to a program is not assured. Selection may depend on attainment of a higher level of performance than is represented by the stated requirements. (On the other hand, some programs have no requirements beyond those for general entrance.) Scottish applicants whose Higher grade records do not meet a stated admission standard may be accepted on the basis of a Certificate of Sixth Year Studies (CSYS). For school-leavers, the "referee's report" (a school evaluation or recommendation) may be reviewed to assess personal motivation or identify cases meriting special consideration. Since 1985, applicants to all Scottish universities have applied directly to the Universities Central Council on Admission (UCCA). Prior to 1985 candidates applied directly to Glasgow and Strathclyde and to UCCA for the other six universities.

General Entrance Requirements

Through 1990 the Scottish universities announced their general entrance requirements as follows:

1. *Scottish Certificate of Education (SCE); General Certificate of Education (GCE).* Passes in five approved subjects, including English, of which either three are on SCE Higher grade or two are at GCE Advanced level; *or* passes in four approved subjects, including English, of which either all are on SCE Higher grade or three are at GCE Advanced level.

   Subjects are not counted at more than one grade or level. Grades of A, B or C on SCE Higher grade are considered as Higher grade passes. Grades of A through E at GCE Advanced level are considered as Advanced level passes. Two passes (grades A through E) at GCE Advanced Supplementary (AS) level are "provisionally accepted" as equal to one Advanced level pass.

   Grades of A, B and C at GCE Ordinary level or on the GCSE (General Certificate of Secondary Education) are regarded as Ordinary level passes. SCE awards accepted as Ordinary grade passes include the following:

   Ordinary grade   Grades 1, 2, 3
                                      (previously bands
                                      A, B, C)

Standard grade
  (certain subjects)   Grades 1, 2, 3
Higher grade   Band D

Note: Acceptance of grades 1, 2 and 3 at SCE Standard grade began in the mid-1980s and is not yet complete or uniform. The following subjects either have "substantive approval" or "provisional approval" for present examinations through 1993: art and design, biology, chemistry, computing studies, economics, English, French, Gaelic, geography, German, Greek, history, Italian, Latin, mathematics, modern studies, music, physics, religious studies, Russian, Spanish.

2. *Certificates and Diplomas in Technical and Business Education.* An approved certificate or diploma, at a standard deemed acceptable by the individual university, supplemented by a pass in English (as defined above). See appendices for a partial list of approved qualifications.

3. *Other U.K. Qualifications.* Among these are university degrees, including those earned at the Open University, and teaching diplomas from Scottish Colleges of Education. Also, Open University credits may be accepted in complete or partial satisfaction of general entrance requirements under certain conditions.

The recent publication of the Scottish Universities Council on Entrance (SUCE), aimed at those who will enter in 1991, gives the general entrance requirements in more general terms, presumably because of the increased emphasis on broadened access. The universities state that candidates under age 21 "normally" will be expected to have three SCE Higher grade passes, or two GCE Advanced level passes, or one GCE A-level plus two AS-level passes, or four GCE AS-level passes and a pass in English in an acceptable exam (usually a pass of at least SCE O/S, GCE O, or GCSE, but SCOTVEC National Certificate communication module 91003 also is acceptable).

The entrance guide for 1991 notes: "Applicants may also offer some appropriate mixture of SCE Higher grade and GCE passes or SCE Higher grade and SCOT-VEC National Certificate modules." Although this language reflects the accommodations being made to nontraditional qualifications, it does not imply that SUCE has established equivalencies between the SCOTVEC modules and SCE/GCE qualifications. Each university is responsible for determining its own criteria for acceptance of these credentials.

Faculty and Course Requirements

The full range of requirements which must be satisfied, in addition to the general requirements listed above, are varied and detailed. In general, these requirements are specified in terms of passes in a first sitting of SCE or GCE examinations. In some cases they also include specifications for the Certificate of Sixth Year Studies where this is an appropriate qualification. The so-called "going rate" is set according to anticipated demand for places and the faculty's or program's definition of suitable preparation for that field.

Full details of faculty and course admission requirements may be found in *University Entrance: The Official Guide* (available from Sheed & Ward Ltd., 2 Creechurch Lane, London EC3 5AQ or *Scottish Universities Entrance Guide* (available from the Secretary, Scottish Universities Council on Entrance, 12 The Links, St. Andrews, Fife, KY16 9JB). An abbreviated version of faculty and course requirements appears each year in *Commonwealth Universities Yearbook.*

Certificate of Sixth Year Studies

Because the sixth year of secondary school is peculiar to Scotland, a U.S. observer might assume there is a clear-cut articulation between the Certificate of Sixth Year Studies and university admission. This is not the case. The Scottish universities always have expressed their primary entrance requirements in terms of performance on Higher grades, even if sixth year results are taken into account. The Scottish Universities Council on Entrance (SUCE) writes:

In the case of Scottish applicants, factors which will be taken into account include range and standards of Higher grade passes and evidence of successful study in the sixth year. In the case of a candidate who has failed narrowly to meet the admission standard expressed in terms of Higher grade passes, a university faculty or department may be prepared to accept a Certificate of Sixth Year Studies grading of specified quality in lieu of an improved band of pass on the Higher grade.

Heriot-Watt's schools liaison officer answers the question of whether a Scottish student with the necessary "going rate" should complete a sixth year before coming to the university, as follows: "...you can, of course, come straight to the University after your fifth year. You may, however, prefer to take sixth year studies in appropriate subjects. Although first year courses at the university start assuming knowledge of the Highers' syllabuses only, the transition to a university course is much smoother if you have done some sixth year studies . . . there will be an overlap . . . to give you an easier settling in period." (*Scottish Universities Entrance Guide*, 1990, p. 2; *Guide for Applicants for Entry in October 1990*, p. 21)

Thus, actual admissions practice with regard to sixth year studies varies among the universities and within the faculties of the same university. To differing extents the Scottish universities encourage otherwise-qualified students to complete a sixth year in order to gain maturity or get some experience with project-oriented studies. Students appear to heed the advice. The trend has been toward increased sixth year attendance, even for those who do not need to improve their qualifications. But the universities' support for a sixth year (traditionally stronger in any case in the east of Scotland than in the west) may be waning as they compete with others for enough well-qualified students in some fields of study. Then too, some admissions officers express doubt about the wisdom of urging a sixth year when the student's school may be unable to offer a curriculum of sufficient strength to justify the time invested. On the other hand, the project-oriented curriculum of the sixth year seems especially suited to some university disciplines such as engineering where there appears to be a trend toward offering students direct entry to the second year, based on a strong CSYS record.

Mature/Wider Access

Except in the most highly selective programs, mature applicants, those aged 21 or over, may be admitted to university on the basis of a wide range of attainments other than traditional school qualifications. The individual universities set their own requirements and often take interviews into account. Provision for special access programs is developing rapidly.

The Scottish Wider Access Program (SWAP) is aimed at improving entry to all higher education, including the universities; each Scottish university participates and will guarantee admission to students who succeed in appropriate access courses. Such courses are usually

one year fulltime, sometimes longer, and are offered by the universities or the colleges of further education. Typically, no formal qualifications are required for admission. The curriculum covers traditional academic school subjects but may devote attention to study skills or word processing. The courses are suitable for any mature student and are targeted above all at the unemployed, women, single parents, ethnic minorities, and all socially and economically disadvantaged groups.

The intersection of access programs and SCOTVEC qualifications (see Vocational Education and SCOTVEC) is an especially interesting recent development. It now is possible to complete a series of modules for a SCOTVEC National Certificate and be guaranteed admission to a number of degree programs. NORSWAP, the region of SWAP which includes the University of Aberdeen, has designed one-year access programs that, if successfully completed, assure admission to pure science or engineering at the university. Glasgow also may accept SCOTVEC modules for students interested in science or engineering. A plan for two of the NORSWAP schemes, showing the number of modules and their titles, is given in chart 4.9.

Although there is no established equivalency between SCOTVEC modules and SEB Higher grades, it is clear that SCOTVEC qualifications are gaining increased acceptance with universities. For instance, the SCOTVEC module "Communications 3" now is recognized universally as meeting the English component of the general entrance requirements.

Special access routes still are small contributors to university enrollments. The following figures from Heriot-Watt University for the class entering in 1988 indicate the main routes to university entrance and suggest, for one institution at least, the relative importance of each.

	From Secondary School	From Further Education
Scottish	53%	5%
Other U.K.	23%	4%
Other EC	2%	1%
Non-EC Overseas	7%	4%
	85%	14.7%

From Another University .3%

Total students in class   1,026
   (including 214 mature entrants)

Scottish Credentials in England

Scottish secondary credentials are accepted by other British universities but not in a consistent fashion. Every university in the United Kingdom accepts Scottish qualifications, though the Universities of London, Exeter and Warwick did not do so until fairly recently. The Certificate of Sixth Year Studies is in some cases accepted by some universities that will not accept the Higher grades. This means that a Scottish student applying to English universities may find that the most direct route consists of continuing through the sixth year rather than switching to a GCE A-level course after Higher Grade exams.

Graduate Study

Graduate programs in Scotland do not differ greatly from corresponding programs in England. It may be important, however, to be able to understand the implications of phrases such as, "MSc Degree: by research and thesis or by examination and dissertation." The following information is taken largely from the postgraduate prospectus of the University of Dundee, but the general framework applies to the other universities as well.

Research Degrees

Candidates for a research degree follow a research plan for a period which varies according to the degree sought and sometimes the classification and content of the student's first degree. Part-time study normally is possible. Applicants for research degrees ordinarily hold an honours degree, except when they have graduated in a discipline where honours is not awarded (e.g., medicine).

Non-honours graduates usually must take preparatory courses before being accepted. In some subjects, such as economics and engineering, a postgraduate diploma course (see below) may serve as the appropriate preliminary study.

The PhD usually requires three years (nine terms) to complete on a fulltime basis. Usually research degrees at master's level are MLitt and MPhil, though the latter also may be a "taught" degree.

The master's degree typically takes one year fulltime (four terms, summer included). Master's candidates whose research topics are promising and whose work is strong may transfer to a PhD program. Presentation of a thesis culminates the student's research.

Postgraduate Degree Programs

Postgraduate degree "courses," as opposed to research degrees, involve formal study through coursework. A "taught" master's degree program normally takes at least a year of fulltime study, concluded by written examinations. Sometimes preliminary coursework is required of applicants whose preparation is insufficient. The examinations, which may consist of essays or reports in lieu of conventional exam papers, normally take place during summer term and can be sat only once. The fourth, or summer, term of a master's course often is devoted to the preparation of a dissertation. Students sometimes apply to transfer to a research degree part-way through a coursework-based program.

Special Higher Degrees

The program listings in the profiles adopt Stephen Fisher's term of "special degrees" for degrees such as DLitt, DSc, LLD (Fisher 1976). These generally are granted only to an university's own graduates who submit their published scholarship or research for review by the academic senate or a faculty committee appointed by the senate. The work submitted must be judged to constitute "an original and substantial contribution" to the candidate's field of study. Degrees of this type are awarded only after an interval of five to seven years after graduation.

Postgraduate Diplomas

Diploma programs normally last for one academic year, with examinations at the end of the year. Some diploma programs take longer, depending on the background and experience of the applicant. Social work, for instance, may take as many as seven terms; a diploma in architecture typically takes one or two years of academic study, depending on the length and content of the student's first architecture degree. Although postgraduate diplomas are most often undergraduate in content, at some universities diploma coursework may be used to gain exemption from the first year of a

SCOTVEC NATIONAL CERTIFICATE COMPONENTS
GUARANTEEING ADMISSION TO UNIVERSITY OF ABERDEEN
(one year full-time, colleges of further education)

Degree Program	Modules			
	Communications	Mathematics	Core Technology	Optional Technology
Engineering	Cmu. 3 1.0 Cmu. 4 2.0 Learn/Study Skills 0.5 One Other 1.0	Maths Gr. 3 2.0 Anal/Alg. 1 1.0 Anal/Alg 2 1.0 Anal/Alg 3 or 1.0 Computing 1 Calculus 1A 0.5 Calculus 1B 0.5	Fund. of Tech: 1.0 Mechanical Fund. of Tech: 1.0 Electrical	Additional technology modules to make a total of at least 20
Pure Science	Cmu. 3 1.0 Cmu. 4 2.0 Learn/Study Skills 0.5	**Mathematics/Science** Analysis/Algebra 1 1.0 Physics 1 or Chem. 1 1.0 Two of the following four groups: Anal/Alg 2 1.0 Inorg. Chem. 0.5 Calculus 1A 0.5 Organic Chem 0.5 Calculus 1B 0.5 Phys. Chem. 0.5 Biology 1.0 Phys: Heat 0.5 Cell Str/Bioch. 1.0 Phys: Mech. 0.5 Metabol.Path- 1.0 Phys: Waves 0.5 ways/Physiolo- Phys: Electr.1 0.5 gical Processes DC Circuits		**Additional Science** Additional science modules to make a total of at least 17

SOURCE: Letter from the Registry, Academic Section, University of Aberdeen, March 1990.

Chart 4.9. SCOTVEC National Certificate Components, University of Aberdeen

two-year taught master's degree program. This means that such diplomas cannot be categorized as graduate or undergraduate in North American terms. The level depends on whether the diploma builds upon the student's first degree or simply broadens it.

Programs of Study

The following sections discuss broad areas of study available at Scottish universities, with the exception of education which is treated in a separate section. First degrees receive primary attention. No attempt has been made to discuss all programs with professional or vocational characteristics, especially when the resulting degree is a Bachelor of Science which, even though specialized, follows the usual structure for science degrees (e.g., "BSc in Brewing and Distilling" at Heriot-Watt).

Arts, Sciences, Social Sciences

Hundreds of programs are offered in the humanities, social sciences and natural sciences. Most degrees follow the general pattern of three years for ordinary (or general or designated or pass) and four years for honours, as described above under First Degrees. Degrees include BA, MA, BSc and also the Bachelor of Music (BMus) degree granted by Edinburgh and Glasgow.

The following are exceptional patterns: An MA (a first degree) in a modern foreign language may requires five years for honours because in some languages students spend a year, usually the third, living in a country where the language is spoken. Glasgow grants a BSc in Speech Pathology and Therapeutics which is four years' ordinary, five years' honours; however, instruction for this degree is given at Jordanhill College of Education.

Charts 4.5 to 4.8 show the range of choices open to students in constructing a degree in single or multiple subjects at selected universities, and will suggest how credentials may be analyzed when assigning credits to portions of a degree. Detailed information may be obtained from the student or from the university.

Agriculture/Natural Resources

Most specialized degree programs in natural resource fields (agriculture, aquaculture, forestry, etc.)

result in Bachelor of Science degrees and follow the usual ordinary (or designated) and honours pattern. These degrees may carry special designations such as BSc Agr or BSc For. In addition, Aberdeen offers two related degrees: a three-year BTech in Agricultural Business Management taught at the North of Scotland College of Agriculture and aimed at students in agribusiness and a Bachelor of Land Economy (BLE). The BLE is a three-year ordinary or four-year honours degree focusing on issues of land use, land management and investment, and conservation. The curriculum integrates law, economics, quantitative studies and resource management. Most graduates plan to qualify as members of the Royal Institute of Chartered Surveyors. The ordinary BLE may be awarded with distinction or commendation. The DipLE is a one-year vocational course for graduates who wish to prepare for careers in surveying and have first degrees in law or economics.

Lists of sample university programs in agriculture follow:

University of Aberdeen
   Bachelor of Science (Agriculture) - designated (3 years)
   Bachelor of Science (Agriculture) - Honours (Agriculture, Agricultural Sciences, Agricultural Economics, Forest Science) (4 years)
   Master of Arts - Honours (Economics and Agriculture) (an undergraduate degree) (4 years)
   Master of Science (Agricultural Engineering, Agricultural Economics) (1 year)
   Post-Graduate Diplomas (Agricultural Economics and Animal Nutrition, Forestry, Modern Botanical Methods Soil Science) (1 year)
   Doctor of Philosophy (3 years)

University of Edinburgh
   Bachelor of Science with Honours in Agriculture (4 years)
   Bachelor of Science with Honours in Animal Science, Crop and Soil Science, or Agricultural Microbiology (4 years)
   Bachelor of Science with Honours in Agricultural Economics (4 years)
   Bachelor of Science with Honours in Forest Science (4 years)
   Master of Science or Post-Graduate Diplomas in Tropical Animal Production and Health, Resource Management, Rural Science, Animal Breeding, and Seed Technology (1 year)

Master of Philosophy (2 years)
Doctor of Philosophy (3 years)
Bachelor of Science (Veterinary Science) (5 years)
Master of Science in Veterinary Science (1 year)
Master of Philosophy in Veterinary Science (2 years)
Doctor of Philosophy in Veterinary Science (3 years)

University of Glasgow
Bachelor of Science (Honours) in Agricultural Sciences (Agricultural Botany, Agricultural Food, and Sciences [with the West of Scotland College of Agriculture], Agricultural Botany, Agricultural Food, Environmental Chemistry) (4 years)
Bachelor of Science (Honours) in Agricultural Economics (4 years)
Master of Science or Post-Graduate Diplomas in Poultry Science, Applied Entomology, and Ruminant Science (1 year)
Master of Science (By research) (1 year)
Doctor of Philosophy (3 years)
Bachelor of Veterinary Medical Science (5 years)

University of Strathclyde
Bachelor of Science (Honours) in Horticulture (4 years)

Architecture and Planning

The pattern of architecture studies taught at institutions of higher education, mostly in concert with a university, can be confusing because of the variety of degrees leading toward the same professional certification. The overall length of an academic program in architecture is five years, organized in a 4+1 or 3+2 pattern (see chart 4.10). A period of professional training (not less than two additional years) leads to the Professional Practice Exams (Royal Institute of British Architects [RIBA] Part III) and possible registration as an architect. Students may take one year of professional training after exemption from Part I and the other year after Part II; or they may take both years of professional training after Part II.

Chart 4.10 summarizes the names of degrees which may be earned in progressing toward professional certification. There are two benchmarks that generally can be relied on: after three years of academic study students may earn a qualification that will exempt them from Part I of the RIBA examinations; and after five years of

academic study they may earn another qualification giving exemption from Part II of RIBA exams. Note that the "BArch" designation may signify anywhere from three to five years of academic study, depending on the institution. At Strathclyde University and at Dundee, the BArch degree parallels other institutions' postgraduate diplomas with respect to exemption from professional examinations. The candidate for the two-year BArch(Hons) at Duncan of Jordanstone/Dundee University must hold the Ordinary BSc in architecture, or an equivalent qualification for entry; the candidate for BArch (unclassified) at Strathclyde must have an Honours degree or equivalent in architecture. For these two "advanced degrees" and for the various architecture diplomas, it is normally expected that a year of professional training has been finished before entry.

The Association of Scottish Schools of Architecture will provide details about any degree program. Inquiries should be directed to the Head of one of the six member schools.

Related Degrees: Planning degrees (Town & Regional, Town & Country, etc.) typically are four-year honours degrees, BA or BSc (four-year ordinary also is possible at Heriot-Watt). Heriot-Watt also grants a three-year ordinary degree, a BSc in Planning Studies. In similar fashion, this university's BA in Landscape Architecture may be earned in four years, ordinary or honours; those finishing three years who are not accepted into the honours year may be granted a BA in Landscape Studies. All these programs are given in cooperation with a central institution.

Business

The first and postgraduate business degrees offered in Scottish universities are varied in their nomenclature and in the length of study (see profiles of universities) but are generally the same as those offered in other fields of study. The field of business is currently a dynamic one with many new programs being introduced, such as the Doctor of Business Administration (DBA) at the University of Strathclyde Business School; and new varieties of MBA programs including distance learning (Heriot-Watt and Strathclyde); as well as new modular courses and part-time study. The introduction of modular courses and credits will provide U.S. evaluators with a more precise measurement of studies than was previously available. Important in the area of business also are the qualifications offered by the three professional business associations in Scotland: the Faculty of Actuaries, the Institute of Bankers in Scot-

DEGREE PROGRAMS IN ARCHITECTURE AT SCOTTISH INSTITUTIONS OF HIGHER EDUCATION

	Duncan of Jordanstone Coll. of Art with Dundee University	Edinburgh Coll. of Art with Heriot-Watt University	Edinburgh University	Glasgow School of Art with Glasgow Univ.	Robert Gordon's Institute of Tech. (Aberdeen)	Strathclyde University
Years 1–3	BSc (Arch)*	BA in Arch Studies*	BSc (SocSc)*	BArch (Ord)*		BSc in Arch Studies*
(Year 4)	PROFESSIONAL TRAINING 1§					BSc in Arch Studies*
Year 5	BArch (Hons)†	BArch (Ord or Hons)	MA (Hons) in Arch	BArch (Hons)	BSc(Hons) in Arch	BSc(Hons) Arch Studies
Year 6	Dip Arch†	Dip Arch†	Dip Arch†	Dip Arch†	Dip Adv. Arch Studies†	PROF. TRAIN. 1
(Year 7)	PROFESSIONAL TRAINING 2 / Sit for Professional Practice Exams (RIBA Part III)					BArch†

* Earliest exemption from Part I of RIBA Professional Examinations

§ Sometimes done as "Year 5," i.e., after completing a four-year first degree

† Exemption from Part II of RIBA Professional Examinations

SOURCES: Prospectuses and calendars of the universities and RGIT; information from Mr. Michael Munday, Association of Scottish Schools of Architecture

Chart 4.10. Degree Programs in Architecture at Scottish Institutions of Higher Education

land and the Institute of Chartered Accountants of Scotland.

Grading varies from institution to institution. The following example is taken from the University of Aberdeen, Department of Accountancy.

70% and above	First class honours
60-69%	Second class honours, upper division
50-59%	Second class honours, lower division
40-49%	Third class honours

Strathclyde University's Business School, which is the largest university business school in Scotland, enrolling some 40% of all Scottish business degree students and 10% of all business degree students in the United Kingdom, offers three-year ordinary/four-year honours degrees in business. It works on a credit-based modular system. The total lecture hours are standardized as multiples of the basic unit of 20 hours which result in greater flexibility and a wider range of subjects. The BA pass degree requires a minimum of 33 credits over three years with two main, or principal, subjects or one principal and one specialist subject. The specialist subjects are finance and tourism. The degree structure at Strathclyde follows:

BA Ordinary degree
Year I	10-12 credits (five subjects)
Year II	12 credits (two or three subjects)
Year III	12 credits (two or three subjects)

To proceed from year I to year II, students must have passed a minimum of eight credits; to proceed from the second to third year students must have completed 18 credits by the end of the second year. A more traditional BA in Accounting is offered at Dundee Institute of Technology (see Central Institutions).

As is true for the undergraduate degrees, a variety of business specializations are available at the postgraduate level. Postgraduate qualifications are the Master of Arts/Master of Science, MBA, Master of Accountancy, new DBA and a variety of postgraduate diplomas (see university list). Also available are research degrees such as the MPhil and the PhD.

An example of a Scottish MBA program is the degree at Strathclyde. It was restructured in 1988 and now is credit-based, the MBA consisting of 50 credits, the first 20 of which form the Diploma in Business award, taken as an integral part of the degree. To be admitted, applicants must hold a good honours degree or the equivalent and have three years of business experience, or an Ordinary degree with five years of business experience and have completed the Diploma in Business. The fulltime program requires 12 months, but students may also attend part-time and through open learning.

Each credit consists of 12 class hours including two hours of case study presentation. The degree structure for the MBA from Strathclyde follows:

MBA	Credits
Diploma in Business (Compulsory):	
General and strategic management	3
Computing and business applications	1
Accounting	2
Business economics	2
Data management	2
Human resources	2
Finance	2
Marketing	2
Operations	2
Integrative business situations	2
SUBTOTAL	20 credits
Functional management options (3)	6
SUBTOTAL	6
Integrative studies (Compulsory)	
Strategic management	2
Managerial skills	2
Integrative cases	2
Information systems	1
Legal environment	1
Electives (4)	8
Project (or additional courses)	8
SUBTOTAL	24 credits
TOTAL	50 credits

The degree structure for the Doctor of Business Administration (Strathclyde) requires three years of fulltime study and research following the BA (Hons):

Year I	Study for one of the 15 master's degree programs at Strathclyde Business School. These programs are described in the chapter on Scottish universities.
Year II	Study research methods and prepare research proposal
Year III	Complete research and thesis

The degree is awarded on the basis of the thesis. Progression requires successfully passing all examinations and reports.

Divinity/Theology

Studies in divinity are available at the four ancient universities. The Bachelor of Divinity is four years at either ordinary or honours, with greater concentration on one or two subjects toward the end of the honours curriculum. University graduates can complete the BD in three years, again at either ordinary or honours level. Only St. Andrews offers theological studies in a degree structure similar to the Scottish MA; this is the undergraduate Master of Theology (three years for ordinary, four for honours). The MTheol permits specialization in two theological areas rather than the five specified by the BD. Although ordination is the goal of most divinity students, those aiming at the ministry for Church of Scotland are urged to complete an ordinary Arts degree and then take the three-year BD.

Aberdeen offers a three-year Bachelor of Theology (BTh) which can be studied part-time in five years. The four ancient universities provide a three-year Licenciate (or Licence) in Theology (LTh) aimed at older applicants preparing for ordination. The syllabus is similar to that of the degree programs but the quality of work required of students is not as high and the qualification does not have degree status. Postgraduate programs include Master of Theology (MTh; not to be confused with St. Andrews' undergraduate MTheol), MPhil, PhD, and certificate and diploma programs.

Engineering

Several different first degrees may be earned at the six institutions which offer programs. The BEng (Hons) and BEng (Ord or Pass) both require four years. Where both classifications are possible the honours designation signifies completion of a research project with dissertation. Some joint honours degrees, for example, the BEng Joint Honours in Engineering and Business Management, take five years to complete.

Depending on the university, students may enter a specific program from the start or may study a common curriculum for a year before specializing. Aberdeen alone permits deferment of specialization until after the second year.

Some universities have retained the BSc in Engineering (Ord) or (Hons), granted after three years or four years, respectively; but the national Engineering

Council has pressed for expansion of the BEng, and the stronger students will aim toward this enhanced and more demanding option. The BEng is the qualification which leads most directly to corporate membership in the engineering institutions and, after appropriate experience, to qualification as a Chartered Engineer.

The MEng degree is a five-year first degree for which highly able students are typically selected after the third year. The additional year of study involves an industrially-based project, usually drawing on the university's links with local companies. An exception is Heriot-Watt's MEng in petroleum engineering which is a one-year second degree designed as a "conversion course" for engineers needing specific training in this field.

Glasgow offers a four-year BTech Ed (Ord or Hons) for teachers who will teach technological subjects in Scottish schools. Graduates receive an introduction to several areas of engineering and are qualified to teach at secondary level in Scotland. The BTech at Strathclyde is a three-year ordinary degree taught jointly with Bell College of Technology. Strong performance allows students to transfer to Strathclyde's BEng program and to complete the degree after one additional year of study. (See charts 4.11 and 4.12.)

Health Fields

Medicine: Medicine is taught as a first degree in Scotland. The so-called "conjoint" degree of Bachelor of Medicine and Bachelor of Surgery (MB, ChB) requires five years. Dundee and Edinburgh offer a premedical year for outstanding students who nevertheless lack the appropriate science background; such students need six years to finish the degree.

Medical programs with two phases are divided between pre-clinical and clinical studies; those with three phases designate a middle period as a bridge between the two. St. Andrews offers only the pre-clinical phase of medical study; its BSc (Medical Science) degree graduates are assured of a place at the University of Manchester for three more years of clinical studies to earn the MB, ChB. They also are free to apply to the clinical phase of other medical schools.

Dentistry: The Bachelor of Dental Surgery (BDS), a first professional degree, requires five years at Edinburgh and Glasgow and five and one half years at

Year 1	Year 2	Year 3	Year 4

STRUCTURES

WATER ENGINEERING

SURVEYING | GEOTECHNICS

COMPUTER-AIDED ANALYSIS | TRANSPORT

O P T I O N S

CIVIL ENGINEERING

ENGINEERING DESIGN

MATERIALS

MATHEMATICS

PHYSICS | MANAGEMENT

P R O J E C T

The first three years are common with the course for the degree of MEng in Civil Engineering.

SOURCE: Heriot-Watt University Prospectus, 1989.

Chart 4.11. BEng in Civil Engineering, Heriot-Watt University

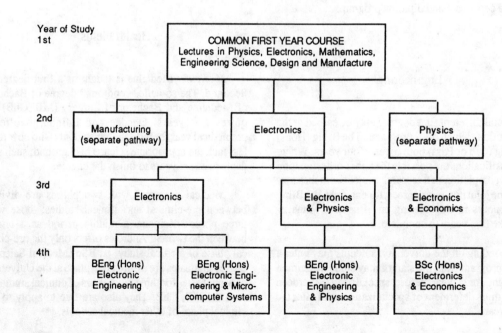

Year of Study
1st

COMMON FIRST YEAR COURSE
Lectures in Physics, Electronics, Mathematics, Engineering Science, Design and Manufacture

2nd

Manufacturing (separate pathway) — Electronics — Physics (separate pathway)

3rd

Electronics — Electronics & Physics — Electronics & Economics

4th

BEng (Hons) Electronic Engineering — BEng (Hons) Electronic Engineering & Microcomputer Systems — BEng (Hons) Electronic Engineering & Physics — BSc (Hons) Electronics & Economics

SOURCE: Adapted from University of Dundee Prospectus, 1990 entry.

Chart 4.12. Electronic Engineering, University of Dundee

Dundee. Programs are divided into pre-clinical and clinical phases: two and three years, respectively, with variations or "bridging" periods. Edinburgh and Dundee call the first year, covering chiefly science subjects, "pre-dental," and will admit students with strong preparation in secondary school (for instance, five Higher grades at AAABB, including chemistry and two from physics, biology and mathematics) directly to the second year. Scottish dental curriculums currently are under review. Dundee, for example, is considering extending its curriculum by two terms.

Veterinary Medicine: This program is taught at Glasgow and Edinburgh; admission is highly competitive. The Bachelor of Veterinary Medicine and Surgery (BVMS) requires five years. The first two years, designated pre-clinical, develop a working knowledge of normal, healthy domestic animals. The third year, the para-clinical phase, focuses on animal diseases. The final two years are substantially clinical, with increasing emphasis on diagnosis and treatment.

Nursing and Pharmacy: Nursing is not primarily a university program and is described fully elsewhere in this publication. Glasgow offers a Bachelor of Nursing degree (BN), one of the few in Britain awarded by a university medical faculty. The strongest graduates may be awarded the degree with honours or commendation. The four-year program leads to the professional qualification of Registered General Nurse. Edinburgh's four-year BSc in Nursing Studies, either general or honours, also leads to registration. Both programs integrate academic and clinical learning from the second or even the first year of study with increasing clinical responsibilities in later years. See chapter V for more information on nursing programs.

Strathclyde is the only Scottish university still offering pharmacy. (It is also offered at Robert Gordon's Institute of Technology). The degree is a four-year honours degree, after which students complete a year of postgraduate preregistration training before obtaining full registration with the Pharmaceutical Society of Great Britain. The final year allows for specialization in pharmaceutical chemistry, pharmaceutics or pharmacology and involves students in clinical pharmacy.

In medicine, dentistry and veterinary medicine, especially able students may be invited to interrupt their professional studies for a year to complete a bachelor's degree with honours in medical science. (At Glasgow the intercalated program requires one year for an ordinary degree or two years for honours.) These so-called "intercalated degrees" (BSc, BMSc, BMedBiol, BSc Medical Sciences, BSc Dental Sciences, BSc Veterinary

Sciences) provide extra depth, typically at honours level, in one or two academic subjects, e.g., anatomy, biochemistry, genetics, pathology, or pharmacology. Normally the student must resume the professional curriculum immediately after finishing the intercalated year(s).

The intercalated degree is begun after a minimum of two (sometimes three) years in the professional program, but in some cases may be done after finishing the entire professional curriculum. The point of interruption does not in itself affect the course of study in the intercalated year. The intercalated degree is conferred separately from the professional degree as soon as all course, exam, and thesis requirements are satisfied.

At Edinburgh and Glasgow the total years of study required for the intercalated degree correspond to the normal first-degree pattern of three years for ordinary, four years for honours. (This is true at Edinburgh even if the intercalated honours year is inserted after the second professional year, since the student must return to complete the third professional year before the intercalated degree is granted.) At two other universities (Aberdeen and Dundee) the intercalated year, taken after the second year of professional study, may result in an honours degree after a total of only three years of study. Since admission to medical, dental, and veterinary programs is highly competitive to begin with, and since only selected students are invited to take an intercalated degree, the likelihood of encountering a three-year honours degree without its companion professional degree must be small.

Law

The Bachelor of Laws (LLB) is taken primarily by students who intend to be lawyers, but is taken also by a significant number who go on to other careers. Three-year ordinary and four-year honours degrees are offered. Either ordinary or honours may be structured to include the courses needed to practice law, but neither degree requires inclusion of the professional courses. The structure of the first and second year curriculums depends partly on whether the student wants to keep open the options of professional preparation, honours, or both, in years three and four. Honours degrees typically emphasize small-group discussion and require an extended essay.

Those holding other first degrees normally can complete an LLB (Ord) in two years. A good honours degree (perhaps a First or Upper Second) or "meritorious performance" in an ordinary degree usually is needed for admission.

Scottish LLB programs train for practice in Scotland. Dundee, however, offers courses that permit students to earn qualifications comparable to those granted at an English university. Its graduates can obtain the same exemptions from professional requirements to become a solicitor or barrister as can be obtained in an English law program.

The one-year Diploma in Legal Practice is offered at all universities granting the LLB and is required for those entering the legal profession in Scotland. Permission to continue to the DipLP is automatic at some universities but involves a selective admissions process at others.

Themes and Developments in Scottish University Education

A "Distinctive" University System?

To appreciate current issues of higher education in Scotland, it helps to understand the Scottish observation that their system is more Scottish than British. Scots often argue that many proposals for educational change in Britain fail to take account of special circumstances in Scotland. Some of the distinctive features of Scottish education already have been mentioned. They can be more fully summarized as follows:

1. A secondary school system characterized by a broad curriculum and absence of early specialization;

2. A broadly based examination system which provides the basic qualification for higher education after the fifth year;

3. As a result, a tendency for students to enter higher education at the age of 17 or 18;

4. Consistent with this early entry, a four-year honours degree course in most subjects;

5. Broadly based three-year ordinary degree programs existing beside honours programs;

6. By international standards, high participation rates in higher education;

7. Universities which admit large numbers of students from outside Scotland. About 15% of the students in Britain attend Scottish universities. This figure would be only 9.4% if enrollments

were directly in line with the Scottish population. (See chart 4.13.)

With the exception of Stirling, Scottish universities are "community institutions" rather than campus universities on the English model. In 1988 the rector of Aberdeen University called for the return of financial control to Scotland on the grounds that institutions so closely allied to their community roots ought to have a maximum of local control. (Pickard 1988)

Some Scottish educators have worried that government funding policies could create a tier of universities without important research activities, that this trend would be harmful especially to Scotland because the country's "unique educational system carries an inherent obligation to ensure that qualified school leavers have access to as comprehensive a range of degree courses as is found in any developed country." (Williams October 17, 1986)

Proposals for Credit Transfer

If the goal of the recently developed access programs has been to maximize opportunities for entry to higher education, the goal of streamlined credit transfer has been to maximize "exit" from the system; that is, to ensure with limited financial resources as many graduates as possible. Transfer of credit from one British institution to another has occurred for some years on a case-by-case basis. (To note a dramatic example, it is now possible to enter the final year of certain first-degree programs at Glasgow upon completion of a suitable pattern of studies elsewhere.)

Today, however, several forces are promoting easier credit transfer within British higher education, among them the governmentally mandated goal of educational efficiency and the European Community's commitment to student mobility through ERASMUS. Scottish universities are notably active in this effort, partly because the country's educational structure is of a manageable size and partly because Scottish educators see natural links between their system and those on the Continent.

The universities may possibly embrace CNAA's Credit Accumulation and Transfer Scheme (CATS) as their mechanism for facilitating transfer among themselves and with the central institutions. At the same time, however, work is proceeding on a different approach that would mirror the European Community Course Credit Transfer Scheme. This Scottish ECTS would

SCOTTISH UNIVERSITIES: FACTS AND FIGURES

University (date of foundation)	Aberdeen (1495)	Dundee (1967)	Edinburgh (1573)	Glasgow (1451)	Heriot-Watt (1966)	St Andrews (1410)	Stirling (1967)	Strathclyde (1964)
Total Undergraduates	5300	3400	8800	10,700	3400	3600	2600	6200
Postgraduates (FT)	290	190	560	540	210	100	200	630
Ratio Male/Female	1.1:1	1.3:1	1:1	1.3:1	2.1:1	1:1	1:1	1.6:1
Scottish Domicile (Undergrads)	71%	57%	56%	85%	65%	35%	52%	87%
Reside at University at Home or Other	50% 50%	47% 53%	40% 60%	23% 77%	19% 81%	61% 39%	70% 30%	28% 72%
Library (approximate) volumes periodicals	1,000,000 4500	460,000 3800	2,000,000 12,000	1,500,000 7000	125,000 2000	750,000 4000	400,000 2400	400,000 4075
Calendar	Two half-year terms (eff. 1990)	Three terms	Three terms	Three terms	Three terms	Three terms	15-week Semesters	12-week semesters + 4-week block in Jan

SOURCES: Scottish Universities Entrance Guide, 1991; SED Statistical Bulletin, April 1989; Commonwealth Universities Yearbook, 1989.

Chart 4.13. Scottish Universities, Facts and Figures

focus chiefly on defining equivalencies between academic programs. These equivalencies, expressed in terms of units of study, would be established without requiring institutions to adopt credit-based (or "modularized") curriculums for their programs; the SECTS unit system would exist independently of each university's or CI's own course scheme. A uniform transcript showing courses and prearranged transfer credits is an essential part of the system in the judgment of its planners. A pilot SECTS program in engineering, chemistry, economics/business administration, and possibly computer science may be launched in the near future if funding and broad-based support from the various institutions are forthcoming.

The central institutions, already committed to CATS as a matter of policy, understandably express reservations about a new transfer scheme which would require more funding and might conceivably encourage their best students to transfer to universities rather than complete their CI degrees.

INSTITUTIONAL PROFILES

UNIVERSITY OF ABERDEEN
Aberdeen, Scotland AB9 1FX; Tel. 0224-272000; FAX 0224-487048

Aberdeen follows the Scottish pattern of admission to an area of study rather than a particular department (the exceptions are agriculture, divinity, forestry, land economy, law and medicine). However, the university's academic structure is such that "admission to a faculty" would be a misnomer; "admission to a degree course" is the Aberdeen equivalent and may not imply departmental admission. Arts and Social Sciences, Science and Engineering admit to a "degree course" and permit later selection of specialties. All programs except Medicine provide ordinary and honours degrees, and Science offers a three-year designated degree.

In October 1990 Aberdeen launched a "modular" academic calendar with two half-year terms and a system of credits for full-year and half-year courses.

Classification of Honours Degrees: First Class, Second
   Class (Upper), Second Class (Lower), Third Class.
First Degrees: three years' Ordinary or (in science)
   Designated, four years' Honours; except BD (four
   years, three for degree holders); BEng Ord or Hons
   (four); MB,ChB (five). Also intercalated medical
   degrees (BMed Biol, Ord or Hons); see Health Fields.
Higher Degrees: LLM, MLE, MLitt, MMedSci, MMus,
   MPhil, MSc, MTh, PhD

Higher Special Degrees: LLD, DLitt, DMus, DSc
Higher Medical Degrees: MD, ChM
Specialized Postgraduate Diplomas: agricultural
   economics, animal nutrition, applied artificial
   intelligence, clinical pharmacology, engineering
   (biomedical, civil, electrical power), environmental
   remote sensing, forestry, industrial physics,
   information technology, land economy, legal practice,
   marine and fisheries science, medical physics, modern
   botanical methods, pastoral studies, psychotherapy,
   rural and regional resources planning, social
   gerontology, soil science, technological and vocational
   studies
Licence: LTh, three years.

UNIVERSITY OF DUNDEE
Dundee, Scotland DD1 4HN; Tel. 0382-23181; FAX 0392-201604

The University of Dundee has offered university education in various disciplines and professional studies since 1882, but it has existed as a wholly separate institution only since 1967. Founded as University College in 1881, it had no power to grant its own degrees; like the other so-called "civic" universities, its teaching was directed toward the external degrees offered by the University of London. After 1897 it was affiliated with the University of St. Andrews and offered medicine jointly with that university. It was called Queen's College until it achieved independent university status in 1967.

Dundee is organized into departments within five faculties: Medicine and Dentistry; Science and Engineering; Law, Arts and Social Sciences; Environmental Studies (in conjunction with Duncan of Jordanstone College of Art). It follows the usual pattern of three-year ordinary and four-year honours degrees with typical exceptions for some longer professional programs (medicine, dentistry, architecture). The university describes itself as having a "vocational bias" characterized by its specialist degree and diploma programs available at postgraduate level in medicine, dentistry, pure science, law, engineering, education and social science.

Classification of Honours Degrees: First Class, Second
   Class (Upper), Second Class (Lower), Third Class.
   LLB and MA Ord may be awarded with distinction;
   MB,ChB and BDS with honours or commendation.
First Degrees: three years' Ordinary, four years' Honours;
   BEng (four); BDS (four and one half, five and one half
   with pre-dental year) MB,ChB (five). Also intercalated
   medical degrees; see Health Fields.
Advanced Degree: BArch(Hons)(two years beyond
   three-year BSc Arch)
Higher Degrees: LLM, MPhil, MPH, MSc, MMSc, MSSc,
   MDSc, PhD
Higher Special Degrees: DLitt, DSc, LLD
Higher Medical Degrees: MD, ChM, DDSc
Specialized Postgraduate Diplomas: digital
   mapping/remote sensing, engineering (civil, electrical,
   electronic/microcomputer systems, mechanical,

structural), legal practice, medical education, mineral law, odontology, petroleum law, social work

UNIVERSITY OF EDINBURGH
Old College, South Bridge, Edinburgh, Scotland EH8 9YL; Tel. 031-667-1011

The University of Edinburgh claims 250 degree programs in all. It is the sixth oldest British university and one of the largest. Each of the nine faculties offers three-year ordinary (or general) degrees and four-year honours degrees. Professional/vocational degrees are offered in divinity, law, medicine including dentistry, music, veterinary medicine, architecture, and applied science. Other degrees are offered in arts, divinity, social sciences and science. The general degrees are MA (General), BSc (SocSc) and BSc Honours degrees are MA (Hons) in arts and in social sciences, and BSc (Hons) in science. The MA (General Honours) is an honours degree with broad content and flexible construction.

Normally courses in three subjects are taken in the first year, followed by second courses in at least two of the subjects in the second year. After this foundation a student chooses two or three subjects to follow to degree level. Joint Honours degrees are usually within the same faculty, but some, e.g., BCom in Business Studies and Law, span two.

Classification of Honours Degrees: First Class, Second
    Class (Upper), Second Class (Lower), Third Class
First Degrees: three years' Ordinary or General, four years'
    Honours, except BD Gen or Hons (four years, three
    years for degree holders); BA in Religious Studies
    (three), MA in Religious Studies (four); BEng Pass and
    Hons (four); MA (Hons in Arch.); MB,ChB (five or
    six); BDS, BVMS (five). Also intercalated medical
    degrees (BSc in a science; BSc [Medical Sciences];
    BSc [Dental Sciences]; BSc [Veterinary Sciences]).
    See Health Fields.
Higher Degrees: LLM, MLA (21 months), MLitt, MMus,
    MPhil, MSc, MTh, PhD
Higher Special Degrees: DD, DLitt, DMus, DSc, LLD
Higher Medical Degrees: MD, ChM, DDS, DVMS
Specialized Postgraduate Diplomas: advanced legal studies,
    advanced social work studies, advanced studies in
    nursing and education, animal breeding, animal health,
    architecture, astronomical technology, Christian
    education, clinical oncology, cognitive science/natural
    language, community dental health, community
    education, community health, cultural resource
    management, environmental chemistry, fire
    engineering, geographical information systems, health
    promotion/health education, information technology,
    landscape studies, legal practice, medical
    radiodiagnosis, ministry, neuroscience, nursing,
    psychiatry, public health, remote sensing and image
    processing technology, resource management, rural
    science, seed technology, theology and development,
    tropical veterinary medicine, tropical veterinary science
Licenciate: LTh, three years

UNIVERSITY OF GLASGOW
Glasgow, Scotland G12 8QQ; Tel. 041-339-8855

The University of Glasgow is one of the oldest and largest universities in the U.K. It has the oldest University School of Engineering in Britain. A total of 22 different first degrees is available in arts, social sciences, divinity, engineering, law and financial studies, medicine, science and veterinary medicine. Exceptions to the usual ordinary/honours system are the MEng and MA (SocSci) with Qualification in Social Work degrees, both five years and designated as neither ordinary nor honours. Medical, nursing, dentistry and veterinary students follow a fixed curriculum of five years (four for nursing). Glasgow cooperates with Jordanhill College of Education to offer a BEd degree and a new degree in technical education (BTechEd) designed to produce new teachers of technology.

Glasgow appears to be in the forefront of efforts to increase access for nontraditional students. It has agreed to accept SCOTVEC modules from two colleges of further education and also works closely with local educational authorities to encourage entrants from schools that send few students to universities.

Classification of Honours Degrees: First Class, Second
    Class (Upper), Second Class (Lower), Third Class
First Degrees: three years' Ordinary, four years' Honours,
    except MA in Modern Languages (five); BScEng Ord
    (three or four); BEng (four); BD Ord or Hons (four
    years, three for degree holders); BN (four); BSc in
    Speech Pathology (four Ord, five Hons); BArch Ord
    (three); BArch Hons (four); MEng, MA with Qual. in
    Social Work, MB,ChB, BDS, BVMS (all five). Also
    intercalated medical degrees (BSc); see Health Fields.
Higher Degrees: LLM, MAppSci, MArch, MCC, MLitt,
    MMus, MPhil, MPH, MSc, MSc(MedSci),
    MSc(VetSci), MTh, MUnivAdmin, MVM, PhD
Higher Special Degrees: DEng, DLitt, DSc, LLD
Higher Medical Degrees: MD, DDS, DVM, DVS
Specialized Postgraduate Diplomas: applied entomology,
    architecture (one year), cartography, decorative arts,
    development policy, digital mapping, divinity (six
    months), engineering (aeronautical, civil, desalination
    technology, electronics and electrical, mechanical,
    membrane technology, naval architecture and ocean,
    optoelectronic devices/systems), experimental
    parasitology, financial studies, forensic toxicology,
    information technology, photogrammetry/remote
    sensing, poultry science, Roman law, ruminant science,
    surveying, veterinary medicine
Licenciate: LTh, three years

HERIOT-WATT UNIVERSITY
Riccarton Campus, Edinburgh, Scotland EH14 4AS; Tel. 031-449-5111; FAX 031-449-5153

Heriot-Watt University traces its origins to the Edinburgh School of Arts, founded in 1821 as the first technical institute in the United Kingdom. By 1885 it bore the name Heriot-Watt College and obtained the status of central institution in 1902.

In 1908 its art department was established as a separate central institution (the Edinburgh College of Art), and both schools' awards at diploma-level gained acceptance as degree standard qualifications. Heriot-Watt became a university in 1966 and promptly reaffirmed its strong ties with Edinburgh College of Arts, so that by the mid-1980s a number of college units were also departments of the university.

Heriot-Watt gives priority to studies "of direct industrial, commercial and social relevance" and takes pride in its strong links with business and industry, including a scientific and industrial Research Park integrated into the campus. Its faculties include Science, Engineering, Economic and Social Studies, Environmental Studies and Art and Design (the last two in collaboration with ECA).

Heriot-Watt's high percentage of Scottish students reflects its strong local attachments. A special modular MSc course is available to part-time candidates in industry who complete one or two modules at a time (six are needed for the degree).

Classification of Honours Degrees: First Class, Second
　　Class (Upper), Second Class (Lower), Third Class
First Degrees: three years' Ordinary or General, four years'
　　Honours; but BEng, BA in Languages (Interpreting
　　and Translating), BArch and some other four-year BA
　　and BSc degrees may be awarded as Ord as well as
　　Hons. BA Arch Studies, BA Landscape Studies, BSc
　　Planning Studies, all three years. MEng, five years.
Higher Degrees: MArch, MDes, MEng (higher degree only
　　in Petroleum Engr), MFA, MPhil, MSc, M Urban and
　　Regional Planning, PhD
Higher Special Degrees: DEng, DSc, DLitt
Specialized Postgraduate Diplomas: acoustics, vibration
　　and noise control, actuarial science, Arabic-English
　　translation/interpretation, architectural conservation,
　　architecture, biotechnology, brewing and distilling,
　　building and project management, building service
　　engineering/management, construction management,
　　design, digital techniques, engineering (structural,
　　hydraulic, highway, electrical power, subsea),
　　housing/housing studies, marine resource
　　development/protection/management, marine resource
　　management, medical physics, optoelectronics,
　　planning studies, soil mechanics, town and country
　　planning, urban design

THE OPEN UNIVERSITY (SCOTLAND)
Region 11 Office: 60 Melville St., Edinburgh, Scotland
EH3 7HF; Tel. 031-226-3851

The Open University is a British rather than a Scottish institution. Scotland is Region 11 of The Open University, administered from offices in Edinburgh and Glasgow. Approximately 7,600 students were registered in undergraduate courses in 1989, with more than 800 more enrolled as "associate students" in continuing education or diploma programs. The Open University is Scotland's chief provider of part-time first degrees.

OU students take advantage of 35 study centers in most of the principal centers of population; in addition, local counselors are available in a number of smaller communities. For a variety of reasons, most notably the relative remoteness of parts of Scotland, particular emphasis is put upon special teaching techniques, including instruction by telephone (conference calls, etc.) and videotape facilities.

School teachers always have constituted a substantial portion of the Open University's enrollment, a development thought by some to be at odds with the goal of reaching a "nontraditional" student population. In Scotland, however, teachers constitute a smaller portion of registrants than in Britain in general. This may be because Scotland traditionally has had more degree-holding teachers than elsewhere in the U.K.

The Open University has agreements on credit transfer with a number of Scottish institutions—St. Andrews, Heriot-Watt, Stirling, Strathclyde and the Faculty of Arts at Edinburgh. Three colleges of education, Jordanhill, Notre Dame and Dundee, offer courses that may be credited toward the OU's Diploma in Reading Development. The Scottish Education Department gives the same recognition for salary purposes to the OU honours degree as to degrees from other universities.

UNIVERSITY OF ST. ANDREWS
St. Andrews, Fife, Scotland KY16 9AJ; Tel. 0334-76161

St. Andrews is the oldest university in Scotland and the third oldest in Britain after Oxford and Cambridge. For a time it was closely integrated with Queen's College of Dundee, until that institution became the University of Dundee in 1967. St. Andrews' 4,000 students are distributed in three faculties: Arts, Science (including Medical Science) and Divinity. In addition to the first degrees of MA, BSc, BD and MTheol, St. Andrews offers higher degrees in all faculties and departments.

Most first degrees follow the usual pattern of three years for ordinary and four years for honours. Those graduating with a BSc (Medical Science) are assured of a place at the University of Manchester where they can graduate as MB, ChB (Bachelor of Medicine, Bachelor of Surgery) after three years of clinical studies. In certain fields, chiefly at honours level, St. Andrews' students may cross-register at the University of Dundee and apply work completed there toward their degree programs.

Classification of Honours Degrees: First Class, Second
　　Class (Upper), Second Class (Lower), Third Class
First Degrees: three years' Ordinary, four years' Honours,
　　including BSc (Med Sci), which leads to MB, ChB
　　after three years of clinical studies at University of
　　Manchester. BD Ord or Hons (four years, three for
　　degree holders).
Higher Degrees: MLitt, MPhil, MSc, PhD
Higher Special Degrees: DLitt, DSc

Specialized Postgraduate Diplomas: divinity, pastoral
theology, ministry (six months), medical science (two
years)
Licenciate: LTh, three years

UNIVERSITY OF STIRLING
Stirling, Scotland FK9 4LA; Tel. 0786-73171;
FAX 0786-63000

From its founding in 1967, Stirling has offered an innovative approach within the British university system. The Stirling
first degrees (BA, BSc and BAcc, all granted as either general
or honours) retain the characteristic breadth of Scottish
degrees but broaden them still further through interdisciplinary
study. It is the only Scottish university that admits students to
the university as a whole rather than to a program or a faculty.

Stirling's distinctive features are a semester system, with
half-year courses in contrast to the typical year-long courses;
division of degree programs into two parts (Part I, a broad,
three-semester introductory segment, and Part II, an additional
three semesters for a general degree and five semesters for a
single- or combined-subject honours degree); and assessment
through periodic exams and assignments as well as through
final examinations.

Part I includes at least eight semester units ("courses" in
American terms) with at least one major and one subsidiary
course. A *major course* consists of three semester units, usually one in each semester of Part I. A *subsidiary course* comprises two semester units. A *minor* is a course lasting one
semester.

For Part II, the general degree requires at least 15 semester
units to include a general degree major course (six semester
units in one subject); a general degree subsidiary course (four
semester units in a second subject); a total of seven semester
units outside the major course (which may include units in the
subsidiary course).

Admission to the honours degree, either in a single subject or combination of subjects, depends on a student's performance in Part I studies. A great number of combinations is
possible.

Classification of Honours Degrees: First Class, Second
Class (Upper), Second Class (Lower), Third Class.
General degree may be granted with distinction. Units
of study graded A (v. good), B (good), C (satisfactory),
D ("compensatable" fail [may be balanced by higher
grades in other units]), E (fail)
First Degrees: three years' General, four years' Honours
Higher Degrees: MLitt, MPhil, MSc, PhD
Higher Special Degrees: DLitt, DSc
Specialized Postgraduate Diplomas: aquaculture, aquatic
pathobiology, aquatic veterinary studies,
entrepreneurial studies, environmental management,
housing administration, industrial relations,
information systems management, information
technology, public relations, publishing studies,

applied social research, social work, technological
economics, technology management

UNIVERSITY OF STRATHCLYDE
Glasgow, Scotland, G1 1XQ; Tel. 041-552-4400-9;
FAX 041-522-0775

Strathclyde was Britain's first technological university,
tracing its roots to the late eighteenth century. The principles
on which it was founded by John Anderson include attention
to "useful learning" and studies applicable to trade and
manufacture; accessibility to those historically denied admission to the established universities, including women. Strathclyde today enrolls a quarter of its students from families
holding manual or semiskilled employment as compared to the
U.K. average of about 5%. Governance is through trustees
drawn from the local community, corresponding to today's
"lay members" of the University Court. The University continues to emphasize its links with industry and commerce,
ranking fifth in 1986 among British universities in income
from industrial research contracts.

Strathclyde is the third largest university in Scotland and
has a high proportion of postgraduates (nearly 25%) and
mature students, those over 21. Although focused on science
and engineering, with large departments in computer science
and electronic engineering, some 40% of its students study
humanities or social sciences. Its four faculties are Arts and
Social Studies, Engineering, Science and Business. The business school is one of the largest in Europe.

Strathclyde has begun a modular system of instruction
with credits assigned to both compulsory and elective classes.
Students must obtain a certain minimum of credits to proceed
from one year of study to the next. Effective Autumn 1990,
Strathclyde has two twelve-week terms of study separated by
a four-week period in January devoted to mid-session examinations.

Classification of Honours Degrees: First Class, Second
Class (Upper), Second Class (Lower), Third Class
First Degrees: three years' Pass, four years' Honours; BA
in Modern Languages (five); MEng Hons (five).
Advanced Degree: BArch (one year after BSc in Arch.
Studies [Hons])
Higher Degrees: LLM, MArch, MLitt, MPhil, MSc, PhD
Higher Special Degrees: DLitt, DSc
Specialized Postgraduate Diplomas: In engineering—
bioengineering, biomechanics, computer-aided
building design, construction, electrical power,
fabrication of materials, facilities management,
geotechnical, highway, information technical systems,
marine technology, mechanical, optical electronics,
petroleum, process engineering, production
engineering and management, production/processing,
properties/applications of engineering, materials,
public health and environmental, ship production
technology, soil/water management, structural, surface
mining/land reclamation, urban design, water. *In other
fields of study—*industrial mathematics, instrumental
methods of analysis, food composition/processing.

Teacher Training

Teacher education in Scotland has a long history, built on the work of early teacher training pioneers, such as David Stow. In 1837 he opened the Glasgow Normal School, said to be the first institution in Britain designed specifically for the training of teachers. This early institution was the beginning of the present Jordanhill College of Education. Moray House College of Education traces its roots to an even earlier institution, the Edinburgh Sessional School, started in 1813.

As early as 1906 major regulations established a format for Scottish teacher training, which was not unlike the present structure. The 1906 Regulations introduced three types of teacher training certificates: the Teacher's General Certificate (for primary school teachers); the Teacher's Higher Certificate (for secondary school teachers); and the Teacher's Special Certificate (which pertained to specialist subjects and eventually became the Teacher's Technical Certificate).

Primary teachers could be trained through a two-year postsecondary college course; a three-year college course, which incorporated university attendance; or a one-year fulltime postgraduate course following a degree. The latter was a unique program compared with those of most other European countries, which usually offered their primary teacher training at the secondary school level. Although this format of training primary teachers—a general degree followed by a one-year teacher training program—has been much debated over the years, with detractors stating that a one-year period is not sufficient to train a good primary school teacher, it was maintained and, in fact, was strongly endorsed when the Secretary of State for Scotland revised teacher training programs in 1984. It then was estimated that 45% of new graduate primary teachers after 1988 would hold a first university degree, followed by the one-year Post-Graduate Certificate in Education, while 55% would have a four-year BEd in Primary Education.

The traditional Scottish Ordinary degree consisted of five subjects: two studied for two years and three for one year, including a foreign language, a course in philosophy and a course in science. It was felt the degree fulfilled the requirements of a broad-based academic education for primary teachers. It is not clear how well these requirements will be met within the curriculum of the many new bachelor's degrees offered by U.K. universities, the CNAA or the Open University. However, a working party established in 1990 by the General Teaching Council for Scotland at the invitation of the

Secretary of State, is looking into the possibility of revising the one-year certificate, beginning in 1992, possibly by extending coursework into the probationary teaching period.

For secondary teacher training, the 1906 regulations outlined a format that also has proved durable: secondary school teachers were expected to hold a degree in the teaching subject (in general, Scottish secondary teachers have been, and still are, limited to one or two teaching subjects except in the case of languages or science), followed by a one-year fulltime teacher training course. This also is the current format of training. The 1906 entrance requirements were more stringent than today's, requiring applicants to hold a first or second class honours degree; third class degrees were not accepted until a 1959 amendment to the 1931 regulations.

The 1906 regulations also introduced another enduring feature unique to Scottish teacher education. Within their one-year teacher training the prospective secondary school teachers also could train for primary school teaching and generally receive some practice teaching during their period of study. The four-year BEd degrees introduced in 1965 also included this double training. This practice continued until December 1980 when the Scottish Education Department prohibited holders of the Teaching Qualification (Secondary Education) from teaching general subjects in primary schools. However, secondary school teachers still can teach specialist subjects—art, music, home economics, physical education and a modern foreign language, (a pilot program in 1990)—in primary schools.

A major development occurred in 1958 when the two-year teacher General Certificate course and the three-year nongraduate courses were extended to a three-year diploma of a college of education, which was seen as enhancing the status of the colleges of education. This extension of their programs prepared the colleges for the next development: expansion into degree programs.

The 1963 Robbins Report recommended that students in colleges of education be allowed to work toward a four-year Bachelor of Education degree, awarded by a neighboring university. Aberdeen College of Education introduced the first such degree which was awarded by Aberdeen University in 1965. Jordanhill and Moray House Colleges of Education started their four-year BEd degrees in 1966 (these were awarded by Glasgow University and Edinburgh University, respectively). Dundee College of Education established its BEd in 1968 (awarded by the University of Dundee). All of these colleges except Dundee required separate admission for the BEd and the diploma program. Dundee admitted students to the BEd following satisfactory performance in their first two years in the diploma program. Dundee's pattern was later followed by the other colleges of education as they introduced their own BEd degrees. This pattern allowed graduates to achieve Teaching Qualifications in both primary and secondary education although they could opt to study only primary education. Notre Dame was the first college to offer an Education degree validated by CNAA.

Over the years the study period for the original two-year teacher qualification has been extended to three years, and a four-year BEd has been introduced in primary teacher education. However, since the requirement for qualified teacher status was the three-year diploma, the BEd was taken by a minority of teachers. In 1983, however, this debate was won by those advocating an all-graduate profession when the Secretary of State for Scotland proposed that a four-year BEd be mandatory for primary education teachers, starting with the academic year 1984-85. Similarly, the Department of Education and Science had mandated that all new primary teachers in England had to be graduates as of the 1984 academic year.

Among other changes taking effect in 1984 was the abolition of the existing BEd degrees for both primary and secondary teachers. The last admission of secondary teachers for the four-year BEd was in 1982, except for secondary teachers in music education, physical education and technology who still continue to study for a "concurrent" four-year BEd degree—that is, a degree program in which both the academic and education courses are taught within the BEd degree, similar to a U.S. bachelor's degree program in education.

In all other subjects, secondary teachers are educated in the traditional pattern: a subject matter degree followed by a one-year Post-Graduate Certificate in Education. Expected teacher shortages in the 1990s may lead to changes in the educational programs by prompting more flexible forms of entry into teacher training. The General Teaching Council for Scotland will ensure such changes do not result in any lowering of professional standards.

Role of the Scottish Education Department

The Secretary of State for Scotland is responsible for the overall supervision and development of teacher education in Scotland through the Scottish Education Department. The SED funds the teacher training colleges, issues guidance on curriculum and admission to teacher training and together with the General Teaching Council oversees teacher training and supply. By setting targets for the number of teachers in the various subject areas and by issuing its Memorandum on Entry to Courses for Teacher Training in Scotland, the SED affects enrollments and program developments in the colleges of education.

Through Her Majesty's Inspectorate, the SED inspects and evaluates the colleges of education. The Inspectorate also has input in all committees and working parties concerned with teacher education and thus is able to give advice for the continuing development of teacher education. The SED also issues guidance regarding the in-service and staff development needs of teachers, which then is delineated further by the Scottish Committee for Staff Development in Education (SCOSDE) in cooperation with the colleges of education.

The address for the Scottish Education Department is New St. Andrews House, St. James Centre, Edinburgh, Scotland EH1 3SX.

Role of the General Teaching Council for Scotland

The General Teaching Council for Scotland, established as a statutory body by the Teaching Council (Scotland) Act of 1965, amended by the Amendment of Constitution of Council Order 1970, is *inter alia* responsible for the registration of teachers and the professional accreditation of pre-service courses.

The Council reviews standards of education, training and fitness to teach that are appropriate to new teachers; considers and makes recommendations to the Secretary of State for Scotland relating to the supply of teachers; keeps informed about the instruction in colleges of education; establishes and keeps a register of individuals who are entitled to be registered; determines whether registration should be refused or withdrawn (see document 4.10).

The address for the General Teaching Council for Scotland is 5 Royal Terrace, Edinburgh, Scotland EH7 5AF.

The General Teaching Council for Scotland
ESTABLISHED BY THE TEACHING COUNCIL (SCOTLAND) ACT 1965

SAMPLE

CERTIFICATE OF FULL REGISTRATION

THIS IS TO CERTIFY THAT   REGISTRATION NUMBER

HAS FULFILLED THE CONDITIONS FOR PROVISIONALLY REGISTERED TEACHERS AS

DESCRIBED IN THE TEACHERS' REGISTRATION (SCOTLAND) RULES AND IS NOW A

FULLY REGISTERED TEACHER IN RESPECT OF A TEACHING QUALIFICATION

5 Royal Terrace   Certificate Issued
Edinburgh EH7 5AF   Registrar

Document 4.10. The General Teaching Council of Scotland Certificate of Full Registration

Validation

All programs in the colleges of education leading to a Teaching Qualification must conform to mandatory conditions established by the Secretary of State for Scotland in consultation with the General Teaching Council. All courses are professionally accredited by the General Teaching Council and are validated externally either by a university, the Council for National Academic Awards (CNAA) or the Scottish Council for the Validation of Courses for Teachers (SCOVACT) to ensure their academic rigor. In-service courses are accredited by SCOSDE and validated by an appropriate agency.

Admission

Admissions requirements are set out and revised annually in the *Memorandum on Entry to Courses for Teacher Training in Scotland*, by the Scottish Education Department in consultation with the General Teaching Council and the Colleges.

Admission to a four-year primary teacher training course leading to the BEd in Primary Education requires:

1. SCE Higher Grade passes in at least three subjects (one must be English) and passes at Ordinary or Standard Grade in two other subjects. A pass in mathematics (either grade) must be included; or

2. two GCE passes at Advanced Level and four at Ordinary Level, in different subjects. Passes at either level in mathematics and both English language and English literature are required; or

3. successful completion of the Primary Education course in one of the Scottish Wider Access Programs.

Admission to a one-year course leading to the Post-Graduate Certificate in Education requires:

1. a degree from a U.K. university, the CNAA or the Open University; and

2. an SCE pass on the Higher Grade in English (for degree courses begun after January 31, 1987); and

3. an SCE pass on the Ordinary or Standard Grade in mathematics.

Admission to secondary teacher training leading to the Post-Graduate Certificate in Education requires a degree from a U.K. university, the CNAA or the Open University, with specialization in the subject(s) to be taught. Admission to a BEd (Secondary) degree program on or after January 31, 1987 requires an SCE pass at the Higher Grade in English. Additional requirements appropriate to the specialization are set by the colleges for the BEd (Secondary) degree in physical education, music or technology.

Admission to further education teacher training (at Jordanhill College of Education) requires that applicants be employed currently in the further education sector and hold one of the following qualifications:

1. a relevant degree from a U.K. university, the CNAA or the Open University;

2. a relevant associateship or diploma of a central institution or college of education;

3. a relevant Higher Diploma or Higher Certificate of SCOTVEC;

4. Part III, Full Technological Certificate or Licentiateship of the City and Guilds of London Institute;

5. other qualifications in certain areas which are the equivalent standard for that area to those listed above.

In addition, applicants should have an SCE Higher Grade in English and an SCE Ordinary or Standard Grade in mathematics. Starting in the Fall 1989, students may, but are not required to, apply to all five colleges of education through a single agency, the Teacher Education Admissions Clearing House (TEACH).

Grading

The marks awarded in the colleges of education are A-E with A-D passing or 1-5 with 1-4 passing. St. Andrews gives no individual grades for the first year of the program but requires students to receive a grade of satisfactory (s) in all subjects. The University of Stirling uses grades A-E, with A-C passing.

Pre-Service Qualifications

In 1990 the five teacher training colleges as well as the University of Stirling offered the initial, or pre-ser-

vice, course as well as in-service training for qualified teachers. In addition, the universities offered postgraduate academic programs leading to advanced diplomas, certificates and degrees such as the MEd, MPhil, MLitt and PhD.

Scottish teacher education terminology distinguishes between pre-service education, that is, the initial programs (BEd and the Post-Graduate Certificate in Education) leading to the Teaching Qualification for those who have not yet registered with the General Teaching Council, and in-service teacher training programs, offered to teachers already registered with the General Teaching Council, who are seeking additional qualifications.

Graduates of the pre-service teacher training programs are awarded both the academic qualification (either the BEd, the Post-Graduate Certificate in Education or, at the University of Stirling, the BA/BSc degree with a Diploma in Education) and the Teaching Qualification. The following academic qualifications are available:

1. four-year Bachelor of Education (BEd) in Primary Education (see curriculum below) was introduced as the basic degree leading to the Teaching Qualification (Primary Education) in 1984. Although the degree varies somewhat from college to college, the basic structure consists of one-third compulsory subjects (language, mathematics, environmental studies, art, music, drama, physical education and religious and moral education); one-third the primary school curriculum as a whole; and one-third optional courses. Some 24 weeks of the four-year program are dedicated to student teaching.

2. Post-Graduate Certificate in Education (Primary). This is offered to those already holding a degree and generally requires 36 weeks which includes 18 weeks of student teaching (see curriculum below).

3. Post-Graduate Certificate in Education (Secondary). This one-year course is for prospective secondary school teachers who already hold a first degree and includes 18 weeks of student teaching.

PGCE (Secondary), Moray House College of Education

Subjects	Hours
Theory and practice of learning and teaching	

BEd (Primary), Moray House College of Education

Subjects	Year 1	Year 2	Year 3	Year 4	Total
Main course components:		(Hours per year)			
Theory/practice of teaching	81	81	110	105	377
Language	81	81	-	-	162
Mathematics	81	81	-	-	162
Physical environment	81	81	-	-	162
Social environment	81	81	-	-	162
Expressive arts and Physical education	81	81	-	-	162
Thematic studies	-	-	66	63	129
Option A (language or mathematics or environmental studies)	-	-	66	63	129
Option B (Visual arts, Drama or music or physical education)	-	-	66	63	129
Religious education	-	-	22	21	43
Professional project (year 4)					
TOTAL	486	486	330	315	1617
Student teaching days:	25	30	50	45	150

PGCE (Primary), Moray House College of Education

Subjects	Hours
Theory and practice of teaching (including resources and introduction to microcomputers)	99
Language arts	48
Primary mathematics	48
Environmental studies	48
Expressive arts and physical education	96
Health education	10.5
Religious education	13

Student teaching	Term 1	Term 2	Term 3	Total
weeks	7	7	4	18

BEd Technology, Moray House College of Education

Subjects	Year 1	Year 2	Year 3	Year 4	Hons
Technological resource elements					
Craft, design and communication:					
–Materials and manufacturing	40				
–Realization skills	170	60			
–Design and communication	40	51	46		
–Mathematics	80	44	-		
–Computing and control	40	44			
–Engineering technology	100	100	90		
–Engineering systems	-	-	78		
Advanced manufacturing technology	96				
Computer-aided engineering	60				
Systems and control	60				
Technological activity	90	110	210	80	160
					80
Theory and practice of education	60	90	120	90	120
School experience	100	80	96	172	172
Industrial placement		100			

1. Subject study
   a. first teaching subject   92
   b. second teaching subject or
      supplementary study   92
   2. Professional studies   108
   3. Health education   11
   Student teaching: 18.5 weeks

4. BEd (Technology)This program qualifies graduates to teach craft and design, technological studies and a range of the new (SCOTVEC) modules.

In-Service Qualifications

Until in-service training for teachers underwent a number of changes during the 1980s the colleges of education had offered a variety of in-service certificates, diplomas and associateships. The new structure of in-service training is tied to a system of staff development, delineated and supervised by the Scottish Committee for Staff Development in Education (SCOSDE).

Established by the Secretary of State for Scotland in 1987, under the guidance of the Scottish Education Department, SCOSDE publishes an annual program of national staff development priorities, which then are taken into account when regional staff development programs are planned. These range from short seminars to "Award-Bearing Courses," that is, courses that lead to a three-tier structure of qualifications as follows (only levels 1 and 2 were developed by 1990):

	Hours
Level 1	
Certificate (equivalent to one term of fulltime study)	120
Diploma (equivalent to one year of fulltime study)	360
Level 2	
BEd degree (equivalent to 4 terms of fulltime study)	480
Level 3	
MEd degree (equivalent to 4 terms of fulltime study)	480

The coursework for these credentials is offered by the colleges of education through full- or part-time attendance, distance learning and other modes of learning. Much of the study is modular and credit-based.

The in-service BEd, which is designed to upgrade the skills of practicing primary school teachers who hold the former three-year Diploma in Education, differs from the pre-service BEd both in structure and content. Also other in-service qualifications at the certificate and diploma levels are offered. The subject depends on regional or subject area needs.

1. The in-service BEd program at Craigie College of Education admits qualified teachers with two years of teaching experience and lasts three years part-time. Holders of the one-year former qualifications, the Associateship in Upper Primary Education or the Associateship in Early Primary Education, may be eligible for exemptions from parts of the program. The program is modular, with most modules requiring 20 hours, and consists of the following areas: professional concerns (120 hours), curricular concerns (180 hours), option study (90 hours), applied educational studies (90 hours) for a total of 480 hours.

2. The Certificate in Primary Science from Northern College, validated by CNAA, is offered mainly through distance learning and consists of study modules with some college attendance. Admission requires the Teaching Qualification (Primary Education) and three years of teaching experience. The course is comprised of science, environmental studies in primary education (20 hours), progression and differences of key ideas in science (20 hours), using resources flexibly (20 hours), management of language development through environmental studies (20 hours), management skills in planning for science (20 hours), evaluating an effective curriculum (20 hours) for a total of 120 hours.

3. The Diploma in Professional Studies in Education: Special Educational Needs from Northern College requires 19 weeks of college attendance and 14 weeks of school experience in a school different from the usual teaching school. Admission requires the Teaching Qualification. The one-year program consists of the following: consultancy (90 hours), learning and teaching (90 hours), the curriculum (90 hours), and school experience (90 hours), for a total of 360 hours.

Colleges of Education

In the early 1980s, with the decline in pupil numbers and consequent decreasing need for teachers the Scottish Education Department closed or merged five of the existing 10 Colleges of Education. As a result Scotland had five Colleges of Education in 1990: Craigie, Jordanhill, Moray House, Northern and St. Andrew's (see college profiles). St. Andrew's College is the only denominational College of Education and offers a wide range of secondary school subjects in order to provide for the requirements of Catholic schools.

The colleges of education in 1980 are listed below:

Aberdeen College of Education (in 1987, joined with Dundee College of Education, becoming the Northern College of Education)

Callendar Park College of Education (in 1982, joined with Moray House College of Education)

Craigie College of Education

Craiglockhart College of Education (in 1981, joined with Notre Dame to form St. Andrew's College)

Dundee College of Education (in 1987, joined with Aberdeen College of Education to form Northern College of Education)

Dunfermline College of Physical Education (in 1987, incorporated Moray House College of Education as the Scottish Centre for Physical Education, Movement and Leisure Studies)

Hamilton College of Education (in 1981, was merged with Jordanhill College of Education)

Jordanhill College of Education

Moray House College of Education

Notre Dame College of Education (in 1981, joined with Craiglockhart College of Education to form St. Andrews College of Education)

Profiles of the Colleges of Education and the programs they offer (1990) follow.

CRAIGIE COLLEGE OF EDUCATION
Ayr, Scotland KA8 OSR; Tel. 0292-260321-4
Calendar: 3 terms (10 weeks)

The College was established in 1964 and until 1978 provided only a three-year diploma and a one-year Post-Graduate Certificate in Education for teachers in primary education. At that point, a four-year BEd course was introduced, taught jointly with the University of Strathclyde. In 1984 the current BEd (Primary Education) was adopted, replacing the previously jointly taught degree and the three-

year diploma. From 1991 Craigie will expand into secondary teacher training and will provide a PGCE in Secondary Education. The BEd course was revised in 1990 and now offers a BEd degree with honours.

Validation: The BEd (fulltime and in-service) and the Post-Graduate Certificate of Education (Primary) are awarded in the name of the University of Strathclyde and validated by the Scottish Council for the Validation of Courses for Teachers (SCOVACT). In-service qualifications are awarded in the name of Craigie College of Education.

BEd - Bachelor of Education (Primary Education)	4 years
Post-Graduate Certificate in Primary Education	36 weeks

In-Service Courses:

BEd (Primary Education) In-Service degree	3 years PT
Associateship in Early Education (to 1990)	1 year
Special Qualification in Nursery Education	1 term
Special Qualification in Infant Education	1 year PT
Post-Initial Qualification in Infant and Nursery Education (to 1990)	1 year
Associateship in Upper Primary Education (to 1990)	2 years PT
Advanced Certificate in Religious Education (Secondary Education) (to 1990)	2 years PT
Post-Graduate Certificate in Religious Studies (not for secondary teachers) (to 1990)	2 years PT
In-Service Course in Social Care	1 year PT
Certificate in Educational Computing	1 year PT
Certificate in the Management of Learning Support	1 year PT
Certificate in Primary Environmental Studies	1 year PT

JORDANHILL COLLEGE OF EDUCATION
76 Southbrae Drive, Glasgow, Scotland G13 1PP;
Tel. 041-959-1232
Calendar: 3 terms (10 weeks)

The origins of Jordanhill College of Education lie in the work of David Stow, one of the world's pioneers of teacher training. In 1828 he opened a school for teacher training in the Drygate and in 1837 opened the Glasgow Normal School, the first institute in Britain built specifically for training teachers. In 1921 a new Glasgow Provincial Committee established Jordanhill College incorporating the Glasgow Normal School and a Free Church equivalent, which also had been established based on Stow's ideas. The College trained both primary and secondary school teachers. From the 1960s it has trained social workers, youth leaders and speech therapists. It includes also the School of Further Education, established in 1963, which is the sole training agency for further education teachers in Scotland. The Scottish School of Physical Education, which had been located on campus, was phased out in the period

1986-88. In 1981 the college absorbed Hamilton College, which was closed by the Government. Hamilton College, established in 1964, offered the Diploma in Education (Primary) and also had a sizeable in-service program.

Validation: The degrees are awarded either by the University of Glasgow or the CNAA and validated either by SCOVACT or by CNAA. In-service certificates and diplomas are awarded by Jordanhill and validated by SCOVACT or CNAA.

Bachelor of Education Honours (Primary Education)	4 years
Bachelor of Education (Post-School Education)	
In-Service Courses:	3 years PT
Bachelor of Education (Music) in conjunction with the Royal Scottish Academy of Music and Drama	4 years
Bachelor of Technological Education (in conjunction with the University of Glasgow)	4 years
BSc in Speech Pathology	4 years
Bachelor of Arts (sport in the community/outdoor education in the community/community arts - CNAA)	3 years
MEd (Glasgow University)	3 years PT
MEd (CNAA)	1 year PT
MPhil (University of Glasgow)	2 years PT
MPhil (CNAA)	3 years PT
MLitt (University of Glasgow)	3 years PT
Diploma in Community Education (youth and community work)	3 years
Certificate in Post-School Education Studies	1 term equivalent
Diploma in Post-School Education Studies	1 years equivalent
Certificate in Education (Further Education)	5 terms PT
Post-Graduate Certificate in Education (Primary Education) (CNAA)	1 year/36 weeks
Post-Graduate Certificate in Education (Secondary Education) (CNAA)	1 year/36 weeks
Post-Graduate Certificate in Education (Further Education)	1 1/2 years PT
Post-Graduate Certificate in Community Education (youth and community work)	
	1 year

MORAY HOUSE COLLEGE OF EDUCATION
Holyrood Road, Edinburgh, Scotland EH8 8AQ;
Tel. 031-556-8455; FAX 031-557-3458
Calendar: 3 terms (10 weeks)

The College was established when the Free Church started a training center for teachers in Old Moray House in 1846 with the first session starting in 1848. However, the beginnings of the training of teachers in Edinburgh started even earlier with the establishment of the Edinburgh Sessional School in 1813. Moray House is directly descended from this early school.

In recent years Moray House has undergone a number of changes: in 1982 it took over the former Callendar Park College of Education in Falkirk, and in April 1987 it merged with Dunfermline College of Physical Education. The latter now is incorporated as the Scottish Centre for Physical Education, Movement and Leisure Studies within Moray House. Dunfermline College of Physical Education was founded in October 1905 as a training college for women in physical education. From 1950 to 1966, when the College moved to Cramond, Edinburgh, the College was located in Aberdeen. Callendar Park College of Education, founded in 1964, concentrated on primary teaching. It had a small enrollment and its numbers dwindled so that by 1981 it had only 200 students. It was annexed by Moray House and closed a year later.

Validation: The undergraduate degrees taught by Moray House are validated by the CNAA; master's degrees by the cooperating university.

BEd (Primary Education) and Honours degree	4 years
BEd (Physical Education) and Honours degree	4 years
BEd (Technology) (in conjunction with Napier Polytechnic) and Honours degree	4 years
Bachelor of Arts (recreation) and Honours degree	4 years
MSc in Educational Psychology (Joint degree, awarded by Edinburgh University)	1 year
MEd in Special Educational Needs (with Stirling University)	2 years PT
Diploma in Community Education	2/3 years
Certificate in Community Education	2 years PT
Diploma in Professional Studies in Education (DPSE): Sports Coaching	1 year
Diploma in Outdoor Education	1 year
Diploma in Social Work	3 years
Post-Graduate Certificate in Education (Primary)	1 year
Post-Graduate Certificate in Education (Secondary)	1 year
Post-Graduate/MA Diploma in Recreation and Leisure Policy	1 year
Post-Graduate Certificate in Community Education	1 year
In-Service Courses:	
Diploma in Guidance	2 years, 5 PT
DPSE: Special Educational Needs (recorded pupils)	1 year PT
DPSE: Special Educational Needs (nonrecorded secondary pupils)	1 year PT
DPSE: Special Educational Needs (nonrecorded primary pupils)	1 year PT
DPSE for teachers of visually impaired children (recorded and nonrecorded)	1 year PT
DPSE for teachers of hearing impaired children (recorded and nonrecorded)	1 year PT
DPSE: Computing	2 years PT

DPSE: Early Education   2 years PT

Moray House also offers a number of Overseas Education courses.

NORTHERN COLLEGE OF EDUCATION

Aberdeen Campus: Hilton Place, Aberdeen, Scotland AB9 1FA; Tel. 0224-283500
Dundee Campus: Gardyne Road, Broughty Ferry, Dundee, Scotland DD5 1NY; Tel. 0382-453433
Calendar: 3 terms (33 weeks)

The present College was established in 1987 through the merger of Aberdeen College of Education and Dundee College of Education. Dundee College of Education, founded in 1905, established the Dundee Training College for Kings' Scholars, which admitted its first students in 1906. Until 1959 when the name was changed to Dundee College of Education, it was known either as Dundee Training College or the St. Andrews and Dundee Training College. Aberdeen College of Education, which received its current name in 1958, dates to a college of teacher education, established in 1893 by the Church of Scotland. A year later the Free Church of Scotland set up its own teachers college. These two colleges were brought together in 1907 to form a training center which became Aberdeen College of Education.

Validation: Degrees, diplomas and certificates are validated by the CNAA.

Diploma in Community Education - Dundee	2-3 years
Diploma in Social Work - Aberdeen/Dundee	2 years
Certificate in Social Service (modular form)	3-5 years PT
Certificate in Social Care	PT (short-term)
BEd (Primary Education) - Dundee/Aberdeen	4 years
BEd (Music) - Aberdeen	4 years
Post-Graduate Certificate in Education (Primary) - Aberdeen/Dundee	36 weeks
Post-Graduate Certificate in Education (Secondary) - Aberdeen	36 weeks
Post-Graduate Certificate in Community Education - Dundee	1 year
In-service training for teachers, social workers and community education workers (Aberdeen/Dundee)	

ST. ANDREWS COLLEGE

Bearsden, Glasgow, Scotland G61 4QA; Tel. 041-943-1424
Calendar: 3 terms (33 weeks)

The College was established as Scotland's only denominational college of education in September 1981 when the two existing Scottish Catholic colleges of education, Notre Dame (Glasgow) and Craiglockhart (Edinburgh), were merged to become St. Andrew's College. Notre Dame was founded in 1881 as Notre Dame Training College by the Sisters of Notre Dame for the training of female teachers, and Craiglockhart, in 1918, as Craiglockhart Training College under the auspices of the Society of Sacred Heart, to train female teachers. They were designated colleges of education in 1958. Male students were admitted to Notre Dame in 1967 and to Craiglockhart in 1962. St. Andrew's now trains both primary and secondary teachers for the Catholic schools. The pre-service programs are offered at the Bearsden Campus in Glasgow; in-service programs are given at Bearsden and at sites in Edinburgh and Dundee.

Validation: Degrees, diplomas and certificates are validated by the CNAA.

BEd (Primary Education)	4 years
BEd in Music Education Hons (with Jordanhill College and Royal Scottish Academy of Music and Drama.)	36 weeks
Post-Graduate Certificate in Education (Primary Education)	
Post-Graduate Certificate in Education (Secondary Education)	36 weeks

In-Service Programs:

BEd (Primary Education) - In-Service	3 years P/T
- Post-initial Certificate in Nursery and Infant Education	1 year
- Special Qualification in Nursery Education	1-2 terms P/T
- Special Qualification in Infant Education	2 years P/T
- Associateship in Early Education	1 year
- Diploma in Special Education	1 year
- Specialist Qualification (Secondary) in Religious Education	2 years P/T
- College Certificate in Guidance	1 year P/T

Additional in-service programs change according to need.

UNIVERSITY OF STIRLING

Stirling, Scotland FK9 4LA; Tel. 0786-73171;
FAX 0786-63000
Calendar: two semesters (15 weeks each)

Founded in 1967, the University of Stirling is the only Scottish university to offer pre-service or initial teacher training. Some 50 students graduate each year with the BSc/BA degree and with the Diploma in Education. Stirling's Teaching Qualification is an anomaly in that it operates outside the control of the SED.

Validation: Stirling validates its own degrees.

BA in Educational Studies (In-service)	3 years PT
BA/BSc (Ord./Hons) and Diploma in Education	3 1/2; 4 1/2 years
Bachelor of Educational Studies (Overseas)	18 months
MEd	1 year/2 PT

Universities

Over the years Scottish universities have participated in teacher training. They have awarded the qualifications of the colleges of education or offered jointly taught degrees. An example of the former is the BEd of Craigie College of Education which is awarded by the University of Strathclyde, and an example of the latter is the MSc degree in Psychology offered jointly by Moray House College of Education and the University of Edinburgh and awarded by the university. Since initial teacher training is the province of the colleges of education, the universities, with the exception of the University of Stirling, only offer postgraduate diplomas and graduate degrees. The University of Stirling is the only university to offer the initial teaching qualification, which differs from those of the colleges of education in that it consists of a BA/BSc degree together with a Diploma in Education and lasts three and a half years for the ordinary degree and four and a half years for the honours degree.

University postgraduate programs in education are offered at Aberdeen, Dundee, Edinburgh, Glasgow, Stirling and Strathclyde which validates the programs of Craigie College of Education. These programs include the Diploma in Education and the MEd, both of which are taught programs requiring course attendance, and the basically research degrees, MPhil, MLitt and PhD.

University Admission

Admission follows the standard university requirements and, for master's and higher degrees, includes an appropriate first degree or equivalent qualification. Generally, admission to the Diploma in Education and the MEd requires a Teaching Qualification.

University Curriculums

The curriculums for the taught Diploma in Education and the MEd degrees vary among institutions. Typical of these programs are the Diploma in Education and MEd degree from the University of Aberdeen.

The DipEd is open to all qualified teachers and others in educational work. The usual entrance requirement is a degree or professional qualification with a good level of achievement. The program requires six courses which can be completed in one year fulltime or over a maximum period of four years' part-time: one core course (current issues in education) and five courses (assessment in education, educational guidance, educational technology, home and school, philosophy of education) selected from available offerings. Each course is given once a week for two hours (24 hours each) during two terms for a total of 144 contact hours. The third term in the academic year is free for individual research. The diploma qualifies for admission to the MEd degree. Qualified teachers may be admitted to the MEd after completing three courses.

The MEd degree is offered with specialization in either educational studies or higher education and requires one year fulltime or up to four years' part-time. Admission is based on the Diploma in Education or a similar qualification such as a BEd degree or postgraduate diploma or associateship. Six courses are required as well as a thesis, which has the weight of two courses. The courses and hours are educational research methods (required) for 24 hours, curriculum theory (24 hours), comparative education (24 hours), educational administration and management I and II (48 hours), instructional design (24 hours), and thesis (48 hours), for a total of 192 hours.

Teaching Qualifications

Registration with the General Teaching Council is mandatory for employment as a primary or secondary school teacher in an education authority school. Graduates who have completed an initial/pre-service program at one of the five colleges of education or the University of Stirling and who have earned a Teaching Qualification are entitled to be registered as probationary teachers. On successful completion of two years of probationary service, the General Teaching Council awards a Certificate of Registration which fully registers the teacher to teach in State schools. (See document 4.10.)

The Teaching Qualifications are:

1. Teaching Qualification (Primary Education) - granted on completion of a four-year BEd (Primary Education) or the Post-Graduate Certificate in Education (Primary), following a degree from a U.K. university, the CNAA or the Open University.

2. Teaching Qualification (Secondary Education) - granted on completion of a one year

Post-Graduate Certificate in Education (Secondary) following a degree from a U.K. university, the CNAA or the Open University; or completion of a concurrent BEd in physical education, music or technology; or the concurrent BSc/BA with the Diploma in Education from the University of Stirling.

3. Teaching Qualification (Further Education) - granted on completion of a part-time program at Jordanhill College of Education following a degree or other acceptable qualification.

Advice to Admissions Officers

1. Like all British universities, Scottish institutions traditionally have given great weight to degree (end-of-year or end-of-session) examinations. North American evaluators should be able to obtain these results from students in virtually all cases, but there are variations in the universities' procedures which may spell confusion for the unwary.

   At Heriot-Watt students receive continuous assessment based on written work throughout the term, and in some, but not all, cases may earn exemption from end-of-session exams. In subsequent years even first term exams are rare, and students may take year-end exams only. At St. Andrews, success in class exams in December and March earns Class Certificates which admit the student to the end-of-year degree examinations. Strong results throughout the year are recognized by a "Rank Certificate" which may exempt a student from the first year degree exams, except in some science areas.

   At Edinburgh assessment is by class exam each term and a degree exam at the end of the year; increasingly, however, class work during the term also is taken into account. Strathclyde states: "Degree examinations provide the main evidence for decisions regarding progress." Yet a few classes are graded on assignments only, and in most cases internal and external assessment are combined in measuring the student's progress. With regard to assessment Strathclyde appears increasingly to resemble Stirling, whose evaluation system is noteworthy for the attention it gives to continuous assessment and end-of-semester examinations.

2. Regulations on second sittings of failed examinations vary. Usually the university specifies a maximum number of exams which may be taken again. In some cases a final honours examination may be attempted only once.

3. A typical first-year schedule at a Scottish university will include at least four lecture courses. Each consists of two lecture hours and one tutorial hour per week (50-minute hour). In science or engineering, some subjects have labs of three hours per week. This means that contact hours will total between 12 and 18 in the first year. The expectation is that each contact hour is matched by an hour outside class. This means, since in the U.S. institutions often use two out-of-class hours for each one in class, that somewhat less is expected of the Scottish student than of the U.S. student.

4. When considering diplomas for graduate credit, it is good practice to obtain a statement from the source university as to whether the credential provides exemption from studies toward a higher degree.

5. Each year the Scottish Universities Council on Entrance publishes the *Scottish Universities' Entrance Guide*, which gives entrance requirements for the universities in terms of Scottish and other examinations. The *Guide* and the separate *Supplement* give a comprehensive list of acceptable exams and syllabuses. Both are available from SUCE, 12 The Links, St. Andrews, Fife KY16 9JB (£2 each outside the UK).

   All Scottish universities publish annual prospectuses for undergraduate and postgraduate study. These publications can be obtained by writing to the address given for each institution. Requests should be directed to The Secretary or Admissions Officer.

Placement Recommendations

Note: See "Guide to the Understanding of Placement Recommendations," page 47 and the statement on the role of the National Council on the Evaluation of Foreign Educational Credentials in developing these placement recommendations on page v. Students who have completed some coursework for any of the programs listed below may be considered for undergraduate admission with up to one year of transfer credit, determined through a course-by-course analysis. If length of study is cited, it refers to the standard length of the program when pursued fulltime. The actual period of attendance may be longer.

Credential	Entrance Requirement	Length of Program	Gives Access in United Kingdom to	Placement Recommendation
1. Scottish Certificate of Education Ordinary or Standard Grade (pp. 90-92, 94)	Completion of Primary 7	4 years (total 11 years primary and secondary)	Secondary 5	May be placed in U.S. grade 12.
2. National Certificate (pp. 100-102)	16 years of age	Variable	Employment; further study	A vocational qualification.
3. Scottish Certificate of Education Higher Grade (pp. 94, 96)	Ordinary or Standard Grade	1 year (total of 12 years primary and secondary)	Further study; Certificate of Sixth Year Study	May be considered for freshman admission with a minimum of 2 Highers plus 3 academic Ordinary or Standard Grade subjects in different areas.
4. Certificate of Sixth Year Studies [CSYS] (pp. 96-98)	Scottish Certificate of Education Higher Grade	1 year	Further study	An academic enrichment program at the upper secondary level.
5. Higher National Certificate [HNC] (pp. 102, 109)	2-3 Higher Grade subjects; or appropriate National Certificate modules	1 year fulltime; 2 years part-time	Employment; further study	May be considered for up to 1 year of undergraduate transfer credit, determined through a course-by-course analysis.
6. Higher National Diploma [HND] (pp. 102, 109)	Higher National Certificate	1 year fulltime	Employment; further study	May be considered for up to 1 year of undergraduate transfer credit, determined through a course-by-course analysis.

or	2-3 SCE Higher Grade and 3 Ordinary or Standard Grade subjects	Employment; further study	May be considered for up to 2 years of undergraduate transfer credit, determined through a course-by-course analysis.
7. Three-Year First Degree, Ordinary, General, or Designated (MA, BA, BSc, BAcc, LLB, BLE, BMus, MTheol, BTh, BScArch, BArch, BA Arch Studies, BScArch Stud, BScEng, BEng, BCom) (pp. 113-14, 122, 126-28)	4 SCE Higher Grade subjects; or 3 SCE Higher Grade and 2 Ordinary or Standard Grade subjects	Further study; employment	May be considered for undergraduate admission with up to 3 years of undergraduate transfer credits, determined through a course-by-course analysis.
8A. Four-Year First Degree (MA Hons, BA Hons, BSc Hons, BAcc Hons, BMus Hons, MTheol Hons, BCom Hons, BScEng Hons, BD Ord or Hons, MA [Religious Studies]) (pp. 114-15, 122, 126-28)	4 SCE Higher Grade subjects; or 3 SCE Higher Grade and 2 Ordinary or Standard Grade subjects	Graduate study	May be considered for graduate admission.
8B. Four-Year First Degree (LLB Hons, BLE Hons, BN, BSc or BSc Hons [Nursing], BA [Nursing Studies], BSc Ord [Speech Pathology], BSc or BSc Hons [Pharmacy], BEng Pass or Hons) (pp. 135, 137)	4 SCE Higher Grade subjects; or 3 SCE Higher Grade and 2 Ordinary or Standard Grade subjects	Graduate study	May be considered for graduate admission.
9. Bachelor of Engineering (Honours) [BEng (Hons)] (p. 135)	Bachelor of Engineering Ordinary	Graduate study	May be considered for graduate admission.
or	4 SCE Higher Grade subjects; or 3 SCE Higher Grade and 2 Ordinary or Standard Grade subjects	Graduate study; professional qualification	May be considered for graduate admission.

	Degree	Entrance Requirements	Length	Leads to	Notes
10.	Bachelor of Technology Education (Ordinary) or (Honours) [BTechEd (Ord)] [BTechEd (Hons)] (p. 135)	4 SCE Higher Grade subjects; or 3 SCE Higher Grade and 2 Ordinary or Standard Grade subjects	4 years fulltime	Employment; further study	May be considered for graduate admission.
11.	Bachelor of Divinity (Honours) [BD (Hons)] (p. 135)	4 SCE Higher Grade subjects; or 3 SCE Higher Grade and 2 Ordinary or Standard Grade subjects	5 years fulltime	Further study; employment	May be considered for graduate admission
		or			
		First degree	3 years fulltime	Further study; employment	May be considered for graduate admission.
12.	Bachelor of Science (Speech Pathology) (Honours) (p. 131)	4 SCE Higher Grade subjects; or 3 SCE Higher Grade and 2 Ordinary or Standard Grade subjects	5 years fulltime	Further study; employment	May be considered for graduate admission.
13.	Bachelor of Veterinary Medicine and Surgery [BVMS] (p. 137)	4 SCE Higher Grade subjects; or 3 SCE Higher Grade and 2 Ordinary or Standard Grade subjects	5 years fulltime	Further study; employment	A first professional degree in veterinary medicine; may be considered for graduate admission.
14.	Bachelor of Medicine [MB] Bachelor of Surgery [ChB] (p. 135)	4 SCE Higher Grade subjects; or 3 SCE Higher Grade and 2 Ordinary or Standard Grade subjects	5 years fulltime	Registration examination; further study	A first professional degree in medicine; may be considered for graduate admission.
15.	Bachelor of Dental Surgery [BDS] (pp. 135, 137)	4 SCE Higher Grade subjects; or 3 SCE Higher Grade and 2 Ordinary or Standard Grade subjects	4 1/2 years fulltime	Registration examination; further study	A first professional degree in dentistry; may be considered for graduate admission.

16. Master of Engineering [MEng] (p. 135)	Completion of 3 years of Bachelor of Engineering program	2 years fulltime	Further study; employment	May be considered for graduate admission.
17. Bachelor of Architecture (Ordinary) or (Honours)–Edinburgh College of Art with Heriot-Watt Univ. [BArch(Ord)] [BArch(Hons)], Master of Arts (Honours) in Architecture-Edinburgh Univ. [MA(Hons)Arch], Bachelor of Architecture (Honours)–Glasgow Univ [BArch(Hons)], Bachelor of Science (Honours) in Architecture-Robert Gordon's [BSc(Hons)Arch], Bachelor of Science in Architectural Studies (Honours)–Strathclyde Univ. [BScArchStudies(Hons)] (pp. 132, 133)	4 SCE Higher Grade subjects; or 3 SCE Higher Grade and 2 Ordinary or Standard Grade subjects	4 years fulltime	Further study	May be considered for graduate admission.
18a. Bachelor of Architecture (Honours)–Duncan of Jordanstone with Dundee Univ. [BArch(Hons)] (pp. 132, 133)	BSc in Architecture-Dundee, plus one year of professional training (normally), or equivalent qualification	2 years fulltime	Graduate study; employment	A professional degree in architecture; may be considered for graduate admission.
18b. Bachelor of Architecture-Strathclyde Univ. [BArch] (pp. 132, 133)	BSc Arch. Studies (Hons)-Strathclyde, plus one year of professional training, or equivalent qualification	1 year fulltime	Graduate study; employment	A professional degree in architecture; may be considered for graduate admission.

Credential	Admission requirement	Length of program	Gives access to	Placement recommendation
18c. Diploma in Advanced Architectural Studies-Robert Gordon's [Dip Adv. Arch. Studies], Diploma in Architecture-Edinburgh, Architecture-Edinburgh, Glasgow, Heriot-Watt [DipArch] (pp. 132, 133)	A four-year degree in architecture [BSc(Hons) in Arch, MA(Hons) in Arch, BArch(Hons), BArch (Ord or Hons)], plus one year professional training; or a three-year degree in architecture [BSc in Arch, BSc(SocSci), BArch(Ord), BA in Arch. Studies], plus one year of professional training	1 year fulltime after four-year degree; 2 years fulltime after three-year degree	Employment	A professional qualification in architecture; may be considered for graduate admission.
19. Post-Graduate Diploma (pp. 129, 131)	3-year first degree	1 or 2 years	Graduate study; employment	May be considered for graduate admission.
20. Post-Graduate Diploma (pp. 129, 131)	4-year first degree	1 or 2 years	Graduate study; employment	May be considered for graduate transfer credit, determined through a course-by-course analysis.
21. MLE, MMus, MUnivAdmin, MTh, MMedSci, MAppSci, MVM, LLM, MArch, MPH, MCom, MAcc, MBAcc (pp. 140, 141, 142, 143)	Honours degree	1 year	Further study; employment	May be considered comparable to a U.S. master's degree.
22. Master of Business Administration [MBA] (pp. 132, 134)	Honours degree	12 months fulltime; 2-3 years part-time	Further study; employment	May be considered comparable to a U.S. master's degree.
23. Master of Science [MSc] (p. 129)	Ordinary degree	Minimum of 7 terms fulltime	Further study; employment	May be considered comparable to a U.S. master's degree.
or	Honours degree	Minimum of 1 year fulltime	Further study; employment	May be considered comparable to a U.S. master's degree.

	Entrance requirement	Length of program	Gives access to	Placement recommendation
23. Master of Science (Urban/Regional Planning) [MSc] Master of Applied Science (Clinical Psychology) [MAppSci] (pp. 129, 141)	Honours degree	2 years fulltime	Further study; employment	May be considered comparable to a U.S. master's degree.
24. Master of Landscape Architecture [MLA] (p. 141)	Honours degree	21 months fulltime	Further study; employment	May be considered comparable to a U.S. master's degree.
25. Master of Literature [MLitt] Master of Philosophy [MPhil] (p. 129)	Honours degree	Variable	Further study; employment	May be considered comparable to a U.S. master's degree.
26. Master of Architecture [MArch] (p. 133)	Honours degree	4 terms fulltime	Employment	May be considered comparable to a U.S. master's degree.
27. Doctor of Philosophy [PhD] Doctor of Business Administration [DBA] (pp. 129, 132, 134)	Honours degree	2 years after master's; 3 years after honours bachelor's	Employment	May be considered comparable to an earned U.S. doctorate degree.
28. Diploma in Education [DipEd] (prior to 1984) (p. 144)	4 SCE Higher Grade subjects; or 3 SCE Higher Grade and 2 Ordinary or Standard Grade subjects	3 years	Employment; further study	May be considered for up to 3 years of undergraduate transfer credit, determined through a course-by-course analysis.
29. Bachelor of Education (Ordinary) (Honours) [BEd] (pp. 144-45, 146, 147)	4 SCE Higher Grade subjects; or 3 SCE Higher Grade and 2 Ordinary or Standard Grade subjects	4 years	Employment; further study	May be considered for graduate admission.
30. Diploma in Education (Stirling University) [DipEd] (p. 153)	Concurrent enrollment in a Bachelor of Arts or Bachelor of Science degree program	3 1/2 years (Ordinary) or 4 1/2 years (Honours)	Employment	Represents completion of undergraduate teacher education courses.

31. Post-Graduate Certificate in Education [PGCE] (pp. 146–47, 148)	Bachelor of Arts or Bachelor of Science	1 year fulltime	Employment; further study	May be considered for graduate admission.
32. Diploma in Education [DipEd] (p. 153)	Bachelor's degree and teaching qualification	1 year fulltime	Further study; employment	May be considered for graduate admission and transfer credit, determined through a course-by-course analysis.
33. Master of Education [MEd] (pp. 149, 153)	A first degree and teaching qualification or Diploma in Education	1 year fulltime; 2-4 years part-time	Further study; employment	May be considered comparable to a U.S. master's degree.

In-Service

34. Certificate in _____ (Subject Area) (p. 149)	A first degree and teaching qualification; or 3-year (pre-1984) Diploma in Education and 3 years of teaching experience	Equivalent to 1 term of fulltime study	Further study; employment	Represents completion of undergraduate teacher education courses.
35. Diploma in _____ (Subject Area) (p. 149)	A first degree and teaching qualification; or 3-year (pre-1984) Diploma in Education and 3 years of teaching experience	Equivalent to 1 year of fulltime study	Further study; employment	Represents completion of undergraduate teacher education courses.
36. Bachelor of Education [BEd] (p. 149)	3-year (pre-1984) Diploma in Education and 2 years' teaching experience	3 years part-time	Further study; employment	May be considered for graduate admission.

V. BRITISH PROFESSIONAL QUALIFICATIONS

Introduction

The area of the British educational system generally referred to as professional qualifications is often the source of confusion for U.S. admission officers and credential evaluators. As noted in the 1976 World Education Series volume on the United Kingdom,

> There is [sic] a multitude of ways in which people obtain recognized qualifications for all kinds of trades and professions. In some cases, the licensing of practitioners is governed by law and there are statutory boards that determine qualifications. In others, the practitioners are governed by relatively independent associations or societies that maintain standards and accredit professionals, generally through granting them membership. In still others, the governance is not in the hands of boards or societies: individual employers and government agencies recognize awards from independent examining organizations, such as the City and Guilds of London Institute. In almost all cases, though, regardless of the method of establishing professional qualifications, the basis is examination, whether an association's own exams or in the recognition of equivalent exams, (e.g., those for university awards). (Fisher 1976, 173)

This chapter is designed to provide a general guide to the great variety of qualifying associations and institutes that exist in the U.K. It is not a comprehensive review of all qualifying bodies. In fact, the three Scottish professional business associations are not included (see Appendix D). The description of the structure and functioning of the qualifying bodies selected for this report as well as the models presented later in this chapter, are intended to help admissions officers and credential evaluators develop a better understanding of this confusing aspect of professional education in the United Kingdom.

Four professions are presented: accountancy, engineering, management and nursing. With the exception of nursing, only selected qualifying bodies are discussed within each area as a complete review of all of the associations that fall under each profession is not possible. The review of accountancy (accounting) is limited to two professional accounting bodies and two associations providing qualifications in support of accounting. Engineering is limited to the main bodies in the field of electrical engineering. Information on the Engineering Council also is provided. Management, unlike the other qualifications, is problematic because it is not an easily defined field. The associations reviewed under management do not necessarily define the field and should not be viewed as representing the entirety of management education and training in the United Kingdom.

The following factors were considered when selecting the associations for review: credentials from the particular association are seen frequently in the United States; the association's structure represents a general pattern for professional organizations; or the size and reputation of the association require consideration.

With the exception of nursing, no placement recommendations are offered as membership in an association in and of itself may not represent an academic qualification or translate into an academic framework. Also, many qualifying bodies offer exemptions to educational requirements or qualifying examinations for membership based on previous education, work experience or membership in another association. As a result, placement recommendations would be extremely complex since various exemptions and alternate routes to membership must be considered. In addition, most associations build their entry and membership requirements on education that is part of the mainstream of British education. Those academic qualifications and credentials are dealt with elsewhere.

Historical Perspective

In the introduction to *British Higher Education,* Tony Becher suggests that, like many other aspects of British life, higher education in the United Kingdom has been the "product of tradition and pragmatism rather than of logic and the rigorous application of principles. Almost every generalization that can be made about it is subject to one or more qualification." (Becher 1987, 2) Becher's observations may serve as well to describe aspects of British professional associations. Modern professional associations have evolved from uniquely British traditions, some dating as far back as the Middle Ages.

The modern professional association appears to mirror some of the traditions of the medieval guilds. While a claim for direct descendance from the Middle Ages may not be possible, a "spiritual" kinship is suggested in the medieval guild principles of hierarchy and the system of apprenticeship. Guild members were organized by grades or levels, to ensure members of the same grade had identical rights. The lowest or beginning grade was the apprentice who could progress through various grades to the highest level, that of master. The apprentice learned by watching the master. In time, it was hoped the apprentice would be able to duplicate the master's work and in the process absorb a sense of the master's standards and ethics.

This kinship with the Middle Ages is also suggested in George Renard's definition of the Medieval guild as "a voluntary association of (individuals) carrying on the same trade...and pledging themselves...to defend their common interest. It demanded...proofs of capability, morality, orthodoxy, political loyalty, and often the regular payment of a contribution." (Renard 1968, 27) Contained in this definition is the principle of self-governance: practitioners governing their own profession.

The professions and professional associations in the United Kingdom have developed from practitioners forming organizations for their mutual benefit–the admission, training, practice and, to varying degrees, the status of their profession. However, as pointed out by Michael Burrage, unlike the development of professions in other countries, the United Kingdom has been unique in that the precept of self governance has never been seriously challenged, "either by the state, by the universities, from within the professions themselves or by the public at large." (Goodlad 1985, 35-36) In his comparison of the history of professions in France, the United Kingdom and the United States, Burrage suggests several reasons for the unique characteristics of the British professions.

...as the English professions have come to admit that universities...have a part to play in the education of their members, and that university degrees might indeed augment their status, they have sought to limit the universities to a preliminary or part-time role...[and] as a result no doubt of apprenticeship training, they appear to have succeeded in recruiting a higher proportion of practitioners as members of professional associations....One may therefore reasonably suggest that the English have a higher sense of professional solidarity than their counter-

parts (elsewhere), and correspondingly also, though it would be extremely difficult to test, that they are more inclined to accept and conform to their profession's rules of etiquette and ethics. There is, at least, no English parallel to the French and American experience of large sectors of the professions developing for long periods without any form of professional regulation. (Goodlad 1985, 35-36)

Categories of Qualifications

Burrage's hypotheses help establish a context for the particular characteristics of British professional qualifications. However, to understand better this unique feature of the British educational system, it is useful to establish categories of qualifications.

Regulated Professional Qualifications

Regulated professional qualifications are those that are regulated in the U.K. by statute or common law. Regulation in this context means that the practicing of a profession is limited to those who have an appropriate educational qualification and a "license" to practice.

Professional associations for regulated professions do not play a significant role in the licensing procedures for their professions. They function primarily as learned societies. Regulated professions in this category are similar to licensed professions in the United States in which professional associations are learned societies with licensing under the control of each state. However, unlike what exists in the United States and many other countries, there are relatively few regulated professions in the United Kingdom.

According to a recent Department of Trade and Industry publication on the European Single Market, the following professions and occupations in the United Kingdom are regulated: medicine, dentistry, nursing, midwifery, veterinary medicine, pharmacy, actuary (certain activities only), auditor, solicitor, barrister (in England, Wales and Northern Ireland), advocate (in Scotland), patent agent, chemist (analyst), marine engineer, ophthalmic optician, teacher (in publicly funded schools), and mine manager (certain posts). Nursing is the only qualification presented in this report that falls under the category of a regulated professional qualification.

Professional Qualifications

Professional qualifications are those for which "permission" to practice is controlled to a very large extent by the respective professional association. Most professional associations in this category have dual roles and should be described as professional qualifying associations or bodies. They function both as learned societies and as the bodies that determine the requirements for practicing. As a result, membership in a professional qualifying body is the route to practice. Professional associations control access to their professions almost entirely, free from any outside regulation, influence or guidance. Most of the chartered associations may be placed in this category.

Some professions in this category have greater control over the access to practice than others. The factor governing the degree of control is the history and reputation of the particular professional qualifying association. Associations with strong reputations tend to exert stronger control over access to practice, and, as a result, function in a manner similar to the regulated professions. Associations that are less well known tend to have weaker control over access to practice. For example, the Institute of Chartered Accountants in England and Wales (ICAEW) is widely recognized; therefore, it is virtually impossible for an individual with appropriate education in accounting to get a job as a chartered accountant without also obtaining the qualifications of the Institute. This kind of control is very similar to the licensing control that states have over Certified Public Accountants in the United States.

On the other hand, engineering does not display the same control over its profession. An individual with a degree in electrical engineering may obtain employment as an electrical engineer without being a member of the Institution of Electrical Engineers. Membership in a professional qualifying association in and of itself must not be viewed as a license to practice. In fact, many individuals with educational qualifications in engineering choose not to become members of a professional association, but nevertheless are practicing engineers.

Other Professions

There are other qualifications that do not fit the descriptions of regulated profession qualifications or professional qualifications. These are more vocational or para-professional in nature than professional. Many of these are auxiliary to professions. For example, the Association of Accounting Technicians offers qualifications for those working in the accounting profession, but not as accountants. The qualifications in this last category may have little currency beyond a very narrow segment of the business world.

Structure of Qualifying Associations

Regardless of the category in which an association is placed, there is a similarity in the organizational structure of the various associations. Usually there are several levels of membership, ranging from student to full, with higher honorary levels granted after a designated period of full membership or, in some instances, additional education. In most cases, individuals who have satisfied educational requirements and completed a period of practical training or employment are eligible to apply for full membership.

Generally, the educational requirements consist of two components:

1. the completion of an educational program and

2. the passing of the association's own qualifying examinations.

Educational requirements may be satisfied in a number of acceptable ways. In addition, exemptions may be granted from all or part of the educational requirements, as well as the association's qualifying examinations, based on an academic qualification or membership in another qualifying body. Receiving exemptions and satisfying an association's requirements in a variety of ways are often sources of confusion to U.S. admissions officers and credential evaluators.

Royal Charters and Chartered Bodies

An organization hoping to obtain a Royal Charter petitions Her Majesty's Privy Council. Upon receiving a petition, the Council determines whether or not the petitioning body is an appropriate body to receive a charter. To accomplish this, the Council seeks the opinion of interested individuals and organizations whose opinions might have bearing on the Council's decision.

In the case of a professional association seeking a charter, the Privy Council satisfies itself that the objectives of the association are in the public interest, as well as those of the association's members and its particular profession or discipline. The Council also evaluates whether the association's goals are being achieved and whether, for the association's particular discipline, high professional standards have been established through education and training. In this context, the association must require that its members have professional qualifications and experience and promulgate a code of professional conduct. The Council also reviews whether the association has established itself with government, academia, industry, commerce and the public as the dominant body in the given professional area or discipline.

The granting of a Royal Charter confers upon a professional body a status that sets it apart from other qualifying bodies. In effect, the granting of a Royal Charter approximates regulating or "licensing" for the particular profession by virtue of the status that is attached to chartered bodies.

The designation and use of the term "Chartered" for full members of a chartered body is usually considered separately from the granting of a charter. At an appropriate time, the association decides if the use of the title "Chartered" by its members will be meaningful to the general public. For example, members of the Chartered Institute of Bankers do not call themselves Chartered Bankers. Regardless of whether chartered associations choose to use the term Chartered for their full members, professional associations granted Royal Charters are perceived as requiring high professional standing of their members who must meet stringent educational requirements and satisfy rigorous codes of conduct, practice and discipline. In general, this perception is accurate.

Notes to Admissions Officers and Credential Evaluators

It is important to understand that the category of membership in any professional association cannot be used to determine an academic level either in U.K. or U.S. terms, as there are alternate routes to gaining membership, some of which are not accomplished through formal education. Thus, admission to a U.S.

institution and/or possible transfer credits must be determined through a review of the means used to obtain membership–academic or not–which will lead to an analysis of the academic programs pursued to attain a membership level.

The following provides the reader with a structure for analyzing all professional qualifications, not only those presented in this report.

1. Qualifications are expressed as levels or grades of membership. For example, **Member** or **Associate** of the Institute of Chartered Accountants.

2. Qualifying bodies set their own membership requirements.

3. Most qualifying bodies award membership on the satisfaction of some combination of educational, examination and training/experience requirements.

4. Graduateship, a level below full membership, generally is an indication that the educational and examination requirements have been satisfied, but not the training or experience component.

5. Frequently, the educational requirements are stated in terms of academic qualifications, for which placement recommendations appear elsewhere.

6. Generally, only registered students may sit for examinations. This designation is an indication that an individual has met, at minimum, the entry requirements and intends to work towards full membership. Often, entry requirements are stated in terms of academic qualifications; however, they vary and may include a specific period of relevant experience or the payment of a fee in addition to or in substitution for the academic qualification.

7. Exemptions from some or all examinations may be granted, based on prior academic qualifications or membership in other associations.

8. Requirements for membership always are available from the professional body and usually will appear in summary form in the publication *British Qualifications.*

9. Lower levels of membership are more likely to have academic qualifications as entry requirements.

10. Academic entry requirements for each membership level usually represent only a part of the overall requirement for entry at that level, as membership is based on a level of attainment which includes proficiency in the professional field as well as academic accomplishment. There

is often a sliding scale, where professional achievement may substitute for portions of academic qualifications. Both formal training and experience (some of which may be supervised by the professional body), play roles in acceptance into membership levels. While these usually are separate from the academic qualifications, they may serve as substitutes which are noted often as "exemptions."

11. A level of membership may be based wholly on the results of examinations which are not tied directly to academic qualifications. Generally, these examinations are set by the professional body and may be based on a synthesis of academic and professional knowledge.

12. Time frames may be set specifically for minimum years of experience.

13. There is a hierarchy of membership levels within an association.

14. On occasion, levels of membership, often based on proficiency examinations, may give access to a level of formal education in the U.K. more advanced than anterior qualifications would seem to permit. This "quantum leap" is based upon a review of the "professionalism" of the person as seen through the level of membership.

15. Four points should be considered in reviewing documents: the qualifying body itself; the level of membership or the completion of an examination represented by the document; the requirements for the level of membership or examination stated on the document (information available directly from the association); and how the individual obtained the level of membership (whether by correspondence course, exemption based on an academic qualification, completion of a college of further education preparation course, etc.).

The following models, based upon membership levels of associations dealt with in the text, are presented to clarify the above notes.

Document 5.1. Certificate of Membership, The Institute of Chartered Accountants in England and Wales

1. Document 5.1, dated March 1, 1988, identifies the name of the qualifying body and the level of mem-

bership. It states that the individual has attained **Membership** in the **Institute of Chartered Accountants in England and Wales (ICAEW)**.

2. The best source of information on the requirements for levels of membership is the Institute itself. Most qualifying bodies will comply readily to your requests.

Information supplied by the ICAEW indicates that there are three stages to satisfying the requirements for Membership: completion of acceptable accounting education; completion of approved accountancy practical training; passing the Institute's examinations. The educational component of the membership will be of greatest interest; however, the Certificate of Membership does not reveal how the educational components were satisfied.

3. As educational requirements may be satisfied in a number of ways, the individual will have to supply this information as well as the required academic documentation.

Document 5.2. Certificate of Membership, The Institute of Financial Accountants

1. Document 5.2, dated June 10, 1988, identifies the qualifying body and the level of membership. It states that the individual was admitted to the **Institute of Financial Accountants (IFA)** in 1983 and was elected to **Fellowship** on May 6, 1988.

2. The IFA defines eligibility for Fellowship as having been an Associate with five years' experience in a senior post as an accountant or lecturer in accountancy.

3. As Fellowship is based on Associateship, the requirements for this latter level need to be determined. Individuals must complete the IFA Levels 1-4 examinations, as well as three years of approved practical training to be eligible for Associateship. As an intermediate step, individuals completing Levels 1 and 2 examinations and having two years of IFA-approved practical training, attain Licentiateship. The base requirements for sitting the examinations is holding the status of Registered Student which, in turn, requires four GCSE passes (English, mathematics or a math-related subject, and two other academic subjects or a BTEC First Certificate or Diploma in Business and Finance).

THE INSTITUTE
OF CHARTERED ACCOUNTANTS
IN ENGLAND AND WALES

INCORPORATED BY ROYAL CHARTER 11TH MAY 1880

CERTIFICATE
OF MEMBERSHIP

THIS IS TO CERTIFY THAT

HAS THIS DAY BEEN ADMITTED TO
MEMBERSHIP OF THE INSTITUTE,
GIVEN UNDER THE COMMON SEAL OF
THE INSTITUTE OF CHARTERED ACCOUNTANTS
IN ENGLAND AND WALES

MEMBERS OF THE COUNCIL

SECRETARY

MEMBERSHIP NUMBER

DATED THIS FIRST DAY OF MARCH 1988

Document 5.1. Certificate of Membership, The Institute of Chartered Accountants in England and Wales

4. As there are a number of ways of becoming an Associate, the individual must state the route taken and supply the needed documentation:

a. Become a Registered Student.

b. Prepare for the examinations either by 1) studying business subjects in a college of further education, or 2) for the Levels 1 and 2 exams, following the curriculum for a BTEC National Certificate/Diploma in Business and Finance with an accounting specialization, or 3) for the Levels 3 and 4 exams, following the curriculum for a BTEC Higher National Certificate/Diploma in Business and Finance with an accounting specialization.

After determining how Associateship is obtained, the educational components of all academic programs must be assessed. U.S. institutional policy will determine whether to evaluate for credit the "educational experiences" that are not included in academic programs.

Document 5.3. Certificate and Diploma Examination Results Notification, The Chartered Institute of Marketing

1. Document 5.3, dated August 7, 1990, identifies the name of the qualifying body and the qualification earned. It shows the results of four examinations for the **Certificate** of the **Chartered Institute of Marketing (CIM)**.

2. Information supplied by CIM indicates several options for admission to the Certificate examinations: four GCSE passes, plus one GCE A-level pass; or a BTEC or SCOTVEC National Certificate/Diploma in Business Studies; or five GCSE and at least one year of fulltime marketing experience; or three years' approved fulltime experience and the approval of an employer and/or marketing tutor.

3. The individual must provide documentation on how the entry requirements were met (see #2 above).

4. The individual must provide documentation on how preparation for the examinations was pursued: whether it was through attendance at a college of further education, a college of higher education, a polytechnic, or through a correspondence course.

U.S. institutional policy will determine whether to evaluate for credit the "educational experiences" which are not included in academic programs.

Qualifying Bodies

The descriptions of the various qualifying bodies selected for this report appear in the following order: Engineering, Accountancy and Management. A brief review of the history of each association is presented, followed by discussions of the various levels of membership; the educational, training and experience requirements; and, where appropriate, methods of study and training. Nursing has been given its own section. Nursing is considered a regulated profession and is organized in a different manner from other qualifying bodies. Placement recommendations have been placed at the end of the complete section on British Professional Qualifications.

ENGINEERING

THE ENGINEERING COUNCIL AND BOARD FOR ENGINEERS' REGISTRATION

The Engineering Council

Established by Royal Charter in 1981, the Engineering Council replaced the Council of Engineering Institutions (CEI). The Council is fully independent, receiving no money from the government. It works with various engineering institutions to establish criteria for qualification standards and procedures.

The Engineering Council has the following goals and concerns: the advancement of education in and promotion of the science and practice of engineering; the promotion of an awareness that the registered engineer is a central figure in the expansion of British industry and commerce; and that engineers must be "technically competent, market conscious, commercially adept, environmentally sensitive and responsive to human needs." (The Engineering Council 1985, 1)

Incorporated 1916

THE INSTITUTE OF FINANCIAL ACCOUNTANTS

Certificate of Membership

THIS IS TO CERTIFY THAT

_____

ADMITTED AN

ASSOCIATE IN 19 83 WAS ELECTED A

Fellow

ON THE **6th** DAY OF **May** 19 **88**

GIVEN UNDER THE COMMON SEAL OF
THE INSTITUTE OF
FINANCIAL ACCOUNTANTS

THIS **1oth** DAY OF **June** 19 **88**

MEMBERS OF THE COUNCIL

SECRETARY
REGISTERED NO.

—

N.B. This Certificate remains the property of the Institute and must be returned immediately on termination of Membership.

Document 5.2. Certificate of Membership, The Institute of Financial Accountants

Patron HRH The Prince Philip Duke of Edinburgh KG KT

Registered Office:
Moor Hall, Cookham, Maidenhead, Berkshire, SL6 9QH.
Telephone: Bourne End (062 85) 24922
Telex No. 849462 TELFAC G   Fax 06285 31382

The Chartered Institute of Marketing  **Marketing Education**

Marketing means Business

CERTIFICATE AND DIPLOMA
EXAMINATIONS

RESULTS NOTIFICATION

Registration Number   Date   7th August   1990

You have been awarded the following grades for the examinations of:-
June 1990

Examination:	Subject:	Grade:
CERT	FUNDAMENTALS OF MARKETING	C
	ECONOMICS FOR MARKETING	C
	PRINCIPLES AND PRACTICE OF SELLING	C
	QUANTITATIVE STUDIES	C

Total subjects   4

KEY TO RESULTS: A - Distinction   B - Good Pass   C - Pass
                  D - Marginal Failure   E - Failure   F - Poor Failure

In all cases the decision of the examiners must be accepted as final
and correspondence cannot be entered into under any circumstances.
Grade D (Marginal Failure) awards are subject to additional scrutiny
before the results are published.

Certificates and Diplomas will be issued to successful students in May
and November each year.

B D North BA MCIM
Education Administration Manager

Document 5.3. Certificate and Diploma Examination Results Notification, The Chartered Institute of Marketing

To this end, the Council has established a system of Nominated Bodies made up of professional engineering institutions that have agreed to conform to the Council's standards. As a result, Nominated Bodies are able to certify that individuals seeking admission to the Council's Register have met the standards of the Council. There are currently 46 institutions with Nominated status. Each is entitled to representation on one of the Council's five Executive Group Committees.

Engineering is not a regulated profession in the U.K. As a result, registration with the Engineering Council is not a license to practice but an indication that the standards of education, training and experience of the Engineering Council and the Board for Engineers' Registration have been met.

The Board for Engineers' Registration and the Register

The Board for Engineers' Registration (BER) is the Engineering Council's designated authority for registration. Working closely with the 46 professional engineering institutions, the main task of the BER is the establishment of guidelines for Engineering Council registration. Using its standards as guidelines, the BER also approves (accredits) and monitors relevant programs at universities, polytechnics and technical colleges, as well as approves programs of training and experience.

The goal of the BER and the Register is to provide a recognized guide to the competence and qualification of an engineer. The BER also is concerned that the engineering qualifying bodies maintain high levels of professional conduct, but it does not have regulatory powers. The BER is concerned with maintaining and raising standards but not with the detailed arrangements within the various sectors of the system, or how those standards are reached, nor how individual universities, polytechnics or college conduct their affairs to give students maximum opportunities (The Engineering Council 1990, E4).

There are three sections of the Engineering Council's Register: Professional Engineer, Incorporated Engineer, and Engineering Technician. Within each section, there are three stages: education, training, and experience, respectively.

The *Engineering Technician* section requires the following:

Stage 1 - Minimally, a BTEC or SCOTVEC National Certificate. The education requirement may also be satisfied with a City Guilds of London Institute's (CGLI) Advanced Craft Part II Certificate, combined with subsequent training, such as Industrial Training Board modules and CGLI career extension work to the CGLI level of Master or Licentiate or a combined Stage 1 and Stage 2 assessment when an individual has a CGLI Craft Part II Certificate supplemented by a variety of other learning experiences. The sum of Stages 1, 2 and 3 of the Engineering Technician section is assessed through a professional review.

Stage 2 - Not less than two years on a structured approved program, longer if the training is informal.

Stage 3 - Not less than two years during which education and training are applied at an appropriate responsible level.

Upon satisfying Stage 3, an individual may be entered on the Register as an Engineering Technician and is entitled to use the designation, "EngTech." An Engineering Technician may work through the stages and sections to become an Incorporated Engineer or Professional Engineer.

The *Incorporated Engineer* section requires the following:

Stage 1 - Minimally, an Engineering Council-approved Business and Technician Education Council (BTEC) or Scottish Vocational Education Council (SCOTVEC) Higher National Certificate. However, several engineering qualifying bodies have minimum education requirements higher than the BER requirement. As a result, individuals may satisfy the education requirements with a BTEC or SCOTVEC Higher National Diploma or an Engineering Council-approved Bachelor of Technology (BTech) degree.

Stage 2 - Not less than two years on a structured, approved program, longer if the training is informal.

Stage 3 - Not less than two years in which the individual's education and training are applied at an appropriate level.

Upon satisfying Stage 3 requirements and undergoing a professional review interview, an individual may be entered on the Register as an Incorporated Engineer and use the designation, "IEng."

The *Professional Engineer* section requires the following:

Stage 1 - The main route is a BER/Engineering Council-accredited first degree in engineering–a Bachelor of Engineering (BEng) or Master of Engineering (MEng).

Optional routes are completion of the Engineering Council Part 2 Examination, completion of a BER part-accredited program with additional engineering studies, or a BER-approved BTech award and additional engineering studies. BER part-accredited degree programs are at honours degree level but lack sufficient engineering content. "However, no honours degree course can achieve part-accredited status unless it is deemed possible by the BER for the graduates to make good the academic gaps, in relation to Stage 1 registration, within one year of fulltime study." (The Engineering Council 1990, 16)

Stage 2 - From two years on a formally structured, approved program to about four years of informal training and experience.

Stage 3 - At least two years of appropriate engineering experience.

An individual may be entered on the Register upon satisfying Stage 3 requirements and undergoing a professional review, consisting of an interview and the submission of a written report. However, members of a professional engineering institution of Nominated Body status are entitled to call themselves Chartered Engineers and use the designation, "CEng." Those who register directly with the Council and do not belong to an institution with Nominated Body status may describe themselves only as entered on the professional section of the Engineering Council Register, not as Chartered Engineers.

The U.K. Chartered Engineer (CEng) also may register with the Federation Europeenne d'Associations Nationales d'Ingenieurs (FEANI). Such registration leads to the title European Engineer (EurIng).

Engineering Council Examinations

Generally, most individuals seeking engineering qualifications at the level of a Professional Engineer satisfy educational requirements through a BER-approved engineering degree from a British university or the Council for National Academic Awards (CNAA). However, the Engineering Council examination is an alternate route to the academic standards of Stage 1. It is designed for "those whose circumstances prevent them from qualifying through the normal route," and individuals who have engineering degrees from programs not approved by the BER.

The examination is held each May at locations around the world. Preparation courses are available at many polytechnics and colleges in the U.K. as well as overseas. The examination is in two parts. The entrance requirements and an outline of each part of the Examination are given below.

Part One Examination. Minimally, two GCE A-level passes, preferably for the A-levels in science subjects. There also are acceptable equivalent qualifications–e.g., a Full CGLI Technological Certificate–recognized by the Council for this purpose.

According to the Engineering Council, the scope and standard of the Part One Examination is set at about one third of the way through a British engineering degree course. The examination consists of six subjects–four compulsory and two optional selected from a list of four. The compulsory examination subjects are mathematics, mechanics (solids bias or fluid bias), properties of materials, and presentation of engineering information. The optional examination subjects are electrotechnics, electronics, chemistry, or thermodynamics.

Part Two Examination. Pass Part One or obtain a qualification recognized by the Council for exemption from Part One. Several higher certificates and diplomas or degrees in engineering from programs not approved by the BER are acceptable for this purpose. Applicants also must pursue formal studies for the subjects they intend to take, including appropriate laboratory and practical work. According to the Engineering Council, the scope and standard of the Part Two Examination is set at the level of a BER-approved degree in engineering.

The Part Two Examination is divided into three sections: 1) Five technical subjects from a list of 41 subjects are required. Applicants are expected to select subjects appropriate to a particular field of engineering and possibly required by a professional engineering institution for membership. 2) A single subject, "The Engineer in Society," is required. 3) A report on the engineering project the applicant has completed is required. The project must be "experimental or investigatory in nature with associated theoretical treatment."

A certificate, awarded upon successful completion of Part Two, attests that the candidate has met the academic standard for Stage 1 of the Professional Engineer Register. Working through a nominated institution, the candidate then has to satisfy the training and experience requirements to enter the Register as a Professional Engineer.

Complete details on the requirements and conditions for satisfying Part One and Part Two of the Council's examination are available from the Engineering Council's Examination Department in the publication, "Guidance and Rules for Candidates."

THE INSTITUTION OF ELECTRICAL ENGINEERS

History

The Institution of Electrical Engineers (IEE) traces its origins to the founding of the Society of Telegraph Engineers in 1871. A few years later the society expanded its title to the Society of Telegraph Engineers and of Electricians. In 1888 the Society voted to change its name to the Institution of Electrical Engineers. "By the turn of the century the Institution was giving guidance on such matters as standardizing the metric system, wiring rules, fire-risk rules and municipal trading." (IEE 2) In recognition of its contributions to the field of electrical engineering as a learned society and as a professional qualifying body, the IEE was granted a Royal Charter in 1921.

By the 1960s, four divisions of the Institution had been established to cover the fields of electronics, power, control and automation, and a general division concerned with science, education and management. Currently, more than 30 professional groups deal with papers, lectures, conferences and other matters relating to specialized areas of technology. The Institution also provides an information service in physics, electrical and electronic engineering, computers and control. Computer-based and highly sophisticated, the Institution's information service for the physics and engineering communities "collaborates with other societies and organizations overseas...already the information stored by magnetic tape in its data base exceeds 250,000 entries, drawn from the scientific and technological literature of the world." (IEE 3)

In October 1988, the Institution of Electronics and Radio Engineers (IERE) merged with the IEE. All of IERE's membership and professional activities, library, conferences, journal and others have been integrated into the Institution of Electrical Engineers.

As a qualifying body, IEE admits individuals whose education, professional training and experience make them worthy of recognition as Chartered Electrical Engineers. It also approves programs at universities and polytechnics. As a learned society, IEE holds annually more than 800 meetings and over 100 conferences throughout the United Kingdom and abroad. Each year it also publishes 22 periodicals and about 20 books.

Membership

The following levels of full membership are offered by IEE: Fellow (FIEE) and Member (MIEE). Levels below full membership are Companion (Companion IEE), Associate Member (AMIEE), Student, and Associate.

Associate: Individuals are at least 21 years old, have acceptable educational backgrounds and are interested in the advancement of electrical science or engineering.

Student: Individuals are between 17 and 28 years old and are studying for the profession with the intention of satisfying the requirements for Associate Membership (see below).

Associate Member: Candidates must meet the institution's educational requirements. Those admitted may call themselves Associate Members and use the designation, "AMIEE."

Member: Individuals are at least 25 years old, can satisfy the education and training requirements and have held a position of responsibility in electrical, electronic or software engineering for at least two years in addition to the period of time required to meet the training requirements. Candidates must be engaged or associated with engineering and are required to satisfy the Institution's professional review which includes an interview. They also must not take more than seven years to satisfy the above requirements.

Those admitted to Membership may call themselves Chartered Electrical Engineers and use the designation, "MIEE." The IEE is a nominated institution of the Engineering Council. Full members are eligible to enter the Professional Engineers section of the Engineering Council Register. Members who register with the Council may use the designation, "CEng."

Fellow: Candidates are Members (MIEE) who have had held positions of superior responsibility in the field of electrical engineering for at least five years. Those admitted to Fellowship are entitled to call themselves Fellows and use the designation, "FIEE."

Companion: This is an honorary designation for those who have rendered important service to the profession.

Educational, Training and Experience Requirements

IEE's standards are high. Membership requires an educational base that will enable a candidate to contribute to a profession in which the underlying technology is constantly and rapidly advancing. "The assessment of standards is difficult and inevitably complicated. To help reduce this complication IEE has accredited many programs relevant to the profession. Candidates with a minimum standard of a second class honours degree from a program accredited by IEE are automatically accepted as having satisfied the educational requirements of the Institution. Candidates from other courses are assessed individually and this inevitably requires a closer assessment of their educational qualifications." (IEE 1989, 1)

Education Requirements. The methods for satisfying IEE's educational requirements fall into three categories.

1. Candidates with a minimum of a second class honours degree from a program accredited by IEE are eligible to become Associate Members immediately after graduation.

2. Candidates with at least a second class honours degree either from an appropriate non-IEE accredited engineering program or other relevant discipline (e.g., physics, mathematics, computer science and information processing) from institutions in the U.K. and overseas may apply for Associate Membership after they have demonstrated ability in the application of electrical engineering over a period of not less than two years. The Associate Membership Committee must also be satisfied that the intellectual standard of the candidate's degree is at least comparable to that of a second class honours degree from a program accredited by IEE.

Candidates may demonstrate their ability in the application of electrical engineering in a number of ways:

• It may be apparent from the statement of experience on the application that the candidate already has met this requirement.

• Candidates may submit a 500-word curriculum vita covering their experience subsequent to graduation that indicates clearly the electrical engineering aspects of their work. The statement should be certified as correct by a Member of the Institution, based on personal knowledge.

• Candidates may be interviewed if the Associate Membership Committee is unable to reach a decision by means of the above routes.

• Finally, those who have been graduates for at least two years and have satisfied the Institution's training requirements by either satisfactorily completing an IEE-approved training scheme or through experience which exempts them from these requirements are judged to have demonstrated this ability.

3. Candidates with degrees lower than second class honours either in an appropriate engineering subject or other relevant discipline (e.g., physics, mathematics, computer science and information processing) may apply for Associate Membership. In general, they will remain Associate Members, although after not less than five years they will be given the opportunity to demonstrate that the combination of their subsequent education, training and responsible experience makes them eligible to apply for Membership.

Candidates in this category must demonstrate they have satisfied the Institution's training and experience requirements for Membership before the Associate Membership Committee will consider if they have achieved a satisfactory educational level. This may be as a result of a subsequent degree, by the Engineering Council examination, by a thesis submitted through the mature candidate route, or by means of an extended professional test which includes the submission of an extended curriculum vita of approximately 1,000 words and an in-depth interview covering both academic and experiential attainments.

Training Requirements. Training acquaints candidates with as wide a range of organizations as possible and demonstrates how available practical and analytic techniques can best be applied. The general goal is to develop candidates' talents, skills and sense of responsibility; enable them to communicate with others and recognize their qualities and limitations; and recognize and work within financial and economic constraints. This prepares them to undertake engineering projects in the future with due regard to technical, safety, commercial, social and other relevant factors.

Training can be carried out in a number of ways. Preferably candidates complete two years of approved and registered training. At least six months of the training should follow the completion of an engineering degree. The method of training may vary; many undergraduates move from one department to another. In all cases, the training tutor must be a Chartered Engineer appointed by the Institution.

The following training elements are required in all training programs:

1. Induction: a short period to help in the transition from academic to industrial life. The goals and content of the training program are discussed.

2. Practical skills: Three weeks to three months of instruction in basic skills such as assembly, wiring, soldering and the use of components, instruments and computers.

3. General engineering training: A 12- to 15-month introduction to work done in a number of departments, in one of which a trainee subsequently may be employed. Eight areas of general engineering training have been identified, six of which are covered in the training period: product and/or service specification; design and development; documentation and data preparation; procurement, manufacture and testing; application (system) engineering; installation, commissioning, operation and maintenance; marketing and sales; and company or service organization, including finance and management. In addition, two other areas included in the training are health and safety, and communication skills.

4. Directed objective training: A major part of the second year of training, it is designed to be a direct application of skills to the activity that trainees intend to follow after training. Trainees are expected to work on actual projects and are given increasing responsibility for their own work to stimulate their interest and establish confidence.

Shortly before the end of the registered training, a Training Assessment Form is sent to the Training Tutor for completion by the trainee and the tutor. IEE may examine the log book that the trainee is required to keep during the training period.

Guidelines provided by IEE for the accreditation of company training schemes are general descriptions of some of the features that a training program should have. They are not intended to be prescriptive as the Institution recognizes that there are many different kinds of organizations representing the various aspects of electrical technology.

The Institution offers the following as desirable elements of an acceptable company training scheme:

- top management support for the training scheme;

- evidence that an important aim of the scheme is to contribute to the formation of a professional engineer;

- a detailed program of activities, each of which has an identifiable training objective;

- an environment in which a potential Chartered Electrical Engineer can undergo professional training. This means that the scheme must be suitable for entrants who have fulfilled the Institution's educational requirements and must provide contact with technology and working practices which will be relevant both to immediate employment and to a lifetime career in the profession;

- a program of training containing the four training elements described above;

- a means of recording the training received;

- involvement of professional engineers in the design, development and monitoring of the training scheme;

- a tutoring system in which trainees are guided and supported by responsible senior Chartered Electrical Engineers;

- a system of assessing the development of trainees which insures that only those who demonstrate the potential to become Chartered Engineers complete the training successfully;

- adequate staff and resources to support the scheme.

According to IEE, the main objective of accreditation is to encourage a high standard of training in all aspects of the profession.

> by a quality control process which examines the main features of the scheme and compares them with the Institution's training requirements. In doing this, the Training Committee will interpret the training requirements and objectives in a broad and flexible way to take account of the wide range of activities and technologies covered by the profession. Where appropriate the Training Committee has drawn on its experience in the accreditation of university and polytechnic degree courses...The Institution holds the view that the ability of the scheme to fulfill the training requirements cannot be assessed without a visit to the site where the majority of the training takes place. (IEE 1989, 5)

Experience. Acceptable experience can range from the engineering manager controlling staff to an individual worker developing new technology. The work should not be of a routine nature that could be carried out by a technician engineer. The experience must be primarily within the broad discipline of electrical engineering, must involve the application of the theoretical and practical skills acquired during and after the education and training period and the exercise of engineering judgment (not merely working to rules or to instructions established by superiors) and professional responsibility.

A record of the candidate's training and professional experience is reviewed by the Institution before an interview is conducted to assess the candidate's experience.

The Mature Candidate Scheme

IEE also provides a mature candidate scheme for those who do not have the required formal academic qualifications but who have "achieved a standard of engineering competence comparable to that of their contemporaries who became corporate (full) members by a normal route." (IEE 1987, 1) IEE considers examinations an inappropriate measure of a mature candidate's competence.

The candidate must be at least 35 years old, have had experience in posts of increasing responsibility in electrical engineering over a period of at least 15 years, and have satisfied the Institution's requirements for responsible experience.

Candidates who have met the entry requirements are required to prepare a synopsis of the paper they propose to submit as evidence of academic competence. With the approval of the synopsis, the candidate is given up to two years to submit a 5,000- to 10,000-word paper based upon work that has been completed or previously published by the candidate. If the paper is accepted, the candidate is required to take an oral examination. Those who pass the interview are put up for election to full membership in the Institution at the level of Member.

The Accreditation of Education Programs

The IEE considers the following features in accrediting a program:

- the quality of the students (entry standards, motivation, etc.) and staff (qualifications, research, publications, etc.);

- aims and philosophy of the course;

- structure and content of the course (balanced up-to-date curriculum, inclusion of nontechnical subjects and current industrial practices);

- inclusion of design (CAD/CAM, reliability, maintainability, marketability, etc.) and engineering applications (materials and projects);

- assessment (level and style of examinations, role of projects, communication skills, etc.);

- industrial contact (industrial visits/lectures, liaison); and

- resources (library, computing, laboratories, support staff).

A list of accredited programs at universities and polytechnics in the U.K. is available from the Schools Liaison Service of the Institution of Electrical Engineers. The list is updated annually.

THE INSTITUTION OF ELECTRONICS AND ELECTRICAL INCORPORATED ENGINEERS

The Institution of Electronics and Electrical Incorporated Engineers (IEEIE) was created in April 1990 by the amalgamation of the Institution of Electrical and Electronics Incorporated Engineers and the Society of Electronic and Radio Technicians. IEEIE is the only institution serving the professional interests of Incorporated Engineers (Electrical and Electronics) and Engineering Technicians engaged in electronic and electrical engineering at a technical or managerial level. With 30,000 members, its members are found in every sphere of activity involving electronic or electrical technology.

Incorporated Engineers (Electronics and Electrical) are practical engineers, often having managerial responsibility for a team or working individually with a large amount of complex equipment. "Fundamentally, they are concerned with maintaining and managing existing technology at peak efficiency." (IEEIE 1988) Engineering Technicians usually work as a member of an engineering team, applying proven techniques and procedures to solve problems of a practical nature. They also have a certain amount of technical responsibility, frequently under the guidance of engineers.

Membership

The following classes of full membership are offered by IEEIE: Fellow (FIEIE) and Member (MIEIE). Levels below full membership are Graduate (Graduate IEIE), Associate Member (AMIEIE), Associate Technician (Associate Technician IEIE), Associate (Associate IEIE), and Student (Student IEIE).

Student: Individuals are studying in a course of further or higher education approved by the IEEIE Council and intending to satisfy the academic requirements for the Graduate or Associate Technician classification.

Associate: Individuals are employed in electronic or electrical engineering for at least five years and, as a result of their connection with the Institution, are working toward a general advancement of electronic or electrical engineering. Those admitted may call themselves Associates and use the designation, "Associate IEIE." Associates may transfer to the class of Member by submitting a technical paper.

Associate Technician: Individuals have obtained one of the following:

1. Ordinary National Certificate or Diploma in Engineering (with acceptable engineering subjects);

2. BTEC National Certificate or Diploma in one of the following: electrical engineering, electronics, telecommunications, building services (electrical). Each of these certificates or diplomas must include a coherent group of units at Pass standard or above, and each candidate must have obtained a minimum of three relevant Level III units, excluding a project, two of these being electrical/electronic related. In addition to programs covering the above sectors, the Council of the Institution gives special consideration to other programs related to electrical/electronic engineering;

3. SCOTVEC National Certificate in electrical and electronic engineering;

4. Part II Certificates of the CGLI in the same fields listed under the requirements for Graduate membership.

Those admitted may use the designation, "Associate Technician IEIE."

Associate Member: Individuals are at least 21 years old who have attained the educational requirements for Associate Technician, completed a minimum of two years of training, and have had at least three years' work experience in electronic or electrical engineering, with at least two as an electronic or electrical technician. Those admitted may call themselves Engineering Technicians and use the designation, "AMIEIE." Associate Members of IEEIE who at Stage 3 register with the Engineering Council as Engineering Technicians may use the designation, "EngTech."

Graduate: Individuals who have attained one of the following educational levels:

1. a university or CNAA degree in electrical and/or electronic engineering;

2. BTEC Higher National Diploma (HND) in electrical and electronic engineering;

3. BTEC Higher National Certificate (HNC) with a minimum of the following:

• 11 (eight for those qualifying before July 1990) units relevant to electrical and electronic engineering, which must include mathematics and project work listed below under b and c, and may include a unit of management/supervisory studies;

- one BTEC unit of mathematics or equivalent content in the core subjects;

- an engineering project, essential for integrating the work in a course, which may be group or individually based but must be individually assessed, and at least equivalent to one BTEC unit;

- computing, preferably with assignment work relating to engineering, and equivalent to one BTEC unit;

- practical training or experience comparable to a standard of the Engineering Applications (EA1 and EA2) components of a Higher National Diploma course;

4. SCOTVEC Higher National Certificate or Diploma in Electrical and Electronic Engineering with a pass grade at 5 or above in each of the three Level V units included in the award;

5. a full CGLI Technological Certificate. IEEIE will accept the following fields: Telecommunication Technicians, Radio, Television and Electronics Technicians, Electrical Technicians, Electrical Engineering Practice, and Electrical Installation Technicians.

Those satisfying one of the above requirements are eligible for Graduateship and can use the designation, "Graduate IEIE."

Member: Candidates are at least 25 years old, have attained the educational level for the classification of Graduate, have completed approved training for a period of not less than two years, and have been employed in electronic or electrical engineering for at least five years with at least two years of responsibility at the Incorporated Engineer level. Those admitted may call themselves Incorporated Engineers (Electronic and Electrical) and use the designation, "MIEIE."

Members of IEEIE are also eligible to register at Stage 3 of the Incorporated Engineers section of the Engineering Council Register. Those who choose to register with the Council may use the designation "IEng."

Fellow: Candidates are at least 30 years old, have been Members for at least three years, and have been employed in electronic or electrical engineering for at least 10 years with involvement in superior respon-

sibility for at least five years. Those admitted may call themselves Fellows (Electronic and Electrical) and use the designation, "FIEIE."

ACCOUNTANCY

Great Britain's leading role in industrial development during the industrial revolution saw corresponding developments in the practice of accounting. The expansion of industry required large amounts of money and new types of organizational structures. Corporations emerged, based on the type of organization used in the earlier trading companies. Their need to assure investors that their risk was limited to the amount of money invested in shares led to the creation of the limited liability company. The development of balance sheets and profit/loss statements gave shareholders and creditors information on a corporation's business activities. Eventually, withdrawal of money by shareholders was restricted legally to the amount of profit earned by a company. Accountants were required to exercise a great deal of judgment, as the method of calculating business transactions could affect the value placed on a company's assets and profits. The introduction of the income tax at the end of the eighteenth century required that accountants calculate income and profits. In the nineteenth century as companies determined the minimum cost of production, accountants were called upon to analyze cost components. This led to the development of cost accounting.

With the increased demand for accounting services and the developments in accounting work in the nineteenth century, a professional organization was needed to assure high standards of skill and promote the interests of those working in the field. The Institute of Chartered Accountants of Scotland was established in 1850 (see Appendix D) and the Institute of Chartered Accountants in England and Wales a few years later. Other organizations such as the Association of Certified and Corporate Accountants and the Institute of Cost and Works Accountants were established later to meet the needs of individuals working in these specialized areas of accounting.

Early in its development as a profession, the training of accountants basically depended on the passing of knowledge in a master/apprentice relationship. To a large extent, this pattern of education and practice existed up to the 1950s.

The normal path to membership of ICAEW involved leaving school at the age of 16...and signing 'articles' for employment by a principal member of the Institute in professional practice. The period of articled service would be five years....Three examinations set by the Institute had to be passed or avoided by exemption. First, there was the preliminary examination, a basic test of general education, from which a majority gained exemption by passing five subjects at GCE O-level at one attempt or six subjects at two attempts. There followed two professional examinations, intermediate and final, involving together 36 hours of examination. The examinations were quite demanding but emphasized technical knowledge rather than analytical ability. Study for the majority of students was by correspondence course, in the evenings, except that short leave of absence for study was allowed before each examination.

The contract of articles imposed obligations on the principal as well as on the clerk. The principal had to give personal supervision in the training of (the) articled clerks...and there was no formal control by the Institute. Acceptance into membership...was usually a formality once the examinations had been passed and the articled service completed. The principal had to submit a report on the practical experience gained by the clerk under articles. (Turner and Rushton 1976, 10)

Most of the other professional accounting bodies followed similar education and training routes to membership.

A plan for a new educational path for accountants was introduced in 1944. Known as the McNair scheme, it was designed to encourage the development of accounting in the universities. Graduates who had studied accounting, economics and law could receive exemptions from the intermediate examinations of the ICAEW. From this beginning, a majority of those individuals now seeking membership in one of the professional accounting bodies have university or CNAA degrees.

There are four areas of professional accounting in the U.K. with corresponding professional bodies overseeing the qualifications for each area. The four areas are chartered accountancy, certified accountancy, cost and management accountancy and public sector accountancy.

Chartered Accountancy: Chartered Accountants work in specialized accounting firms which provide services to outside clients, individuals and businesses. They prepare financial accounts, audits and advise in tax matters. The professional associations for Chartered Accountants are the Institute of Chartered Accountants in England and Wales (ICAEW), the Institute of Chartered Accountants in Ireland (ICAI) and the Institute of Chartered Accountants of Scotland (ICAS).

Certified Accountancy: Certified Accountants may work in both managerial and financial accounting with a specialized accounting firm or in an industrial or commercial company. The professional association is the Chartered Association of Certified Accountants (ACCA).

Cost and Management Accountancy: Cost and Management Accountants work for industry and commerce, producing data and statistics to help solve management problems. They also provide information needed for the efficient operation of a business. The professional association is the Chartered Institute of Management Accountants (CIMA).

Public Sector Accountancy: Public Sector Accountants work for public bodies–central or local government, the National Health Service, etc. They are involved with the financial management of large organizations, the development of financial policies and the use of resources. The professional association is the Chartered Institute of Public Finance and Accountancy (CIPFA).

The accounting profession is not regulated in the U.K. Membership in a professional accounting body is not a license to practice. It is an indication that standards of education and training have been met. However, according to the 1985 Companies Act, only members of the following chartered institutions are permitted to carry out the statutory annual audit of the financial records of a company: Institute of Chartered Accountants in England and Wales; Institute of Chartered Accountants in Ireland; Institute of Chartered Accountants of Scotland; and the Chartered Association of Certified Accountants.

The Consultative Committee of Accountancy Bodies (CCAB) is a loose federation of the six professional accounting bodies. The CCAB supports and sponsors the Association of Accounting Technicians

(AAT), which provides accounting qualifications at a technician rather than professional level.

The CCAB has established a committee which evaluates and approves programs of higher education with an accounting specialization. Known as the Board of Accreditation of Educational Courses (BAEC), it determines whether programs at institutions provide relevant background education for the accountancy bodies and provides students with a guide to suitable accounting programs, as well as a guide to examination exemptions their accounting education may yield. This information is provided in the BAEC publication "Approved Courses for Accountancy Education: Degree and Other Courses of Higher Education Approved by the Principal Accountancy Bodies in the British Isles as Relevant Background Education" and is updated regularly.

There are two stages of program recognition by the BAEC: Foundation Education and Professional Education. Foundation Education programs have a substantial accounting component and offer subjects supporting accounting, such as economic reasoning, legal concepts, quantitative methods and data processing, and may be considered for exemption from the foundation stage requirements of the participating bodies (BAEC 1989, 1). Professional Education programs that satisfy the requirements for Foundation Education and provide a more complete accounting curriculum may grant exemption from professional examinations of individual accountancy bodies.

THE INSTITUTE OF CHARTERED ACCOUNTANTS IN ENGLAND AND WALES

The Institute of Chartered Accountants in England and Wales (ICAEW) received its Royal Charter in 1880. Its principal objectives are to advance the theory and practice of all aspects of accountancy, including, in particular, auditing, financial management, and taxation; to recruit, educate, and train members skilled in these arts; to preserve at all times the professional independence of accountants in whatever capacities they may be serving; to maintain high standards of practice and professional conduct among all its members; and to advance the profession of accountancy in relation to public practice, industry, commerce, and the public service.

Membership

The following levels of full membership are offered by ICAEW: Fellow (FCA) and Associate (ACA).

Associate: The three stages in the process of becoming an Associate are foundation education, approved training and the examinations. All candidates must pass the Professional Examination 1 and the Professional Examination 2. Individuals who complete all three stages are eligible for Associateship. Those admitted can call themselves Associates and use the designation, "ACA."

Fellow: Individuals must have been Associate members for 10 years and have satisfied the ICAEW Council that they have maintained continuing professional education (CPE) through both structured and unstructured educational experiences. Acceptable CPE may range from keeping abreast of current literature on accounting to formal seminars, conferences, or courses. Regardless of the means chosen to accomplish CPE, detailed records are required by ICAEW. Those admitted can call themselves Fellows and use the designation, "FCA."

Educational and Experience Requirements

There are three methods by which students normally satisfy the educational, training and experience requirements for Associateship:

1. An individual with an ICAEW-accredited accountancy degree enters and completes a three-year training contract with a firm of Chartered Accountants. Professional Examination 1 is taken in the second year of the training contract, Professional Examination 2 in the third year.

2. An individual with a nonrelevant degree at a U.K. university or polytechnic enters and completes a three-year training contract with a firm of Chartered Accountants during which an ICAEW-approved conversion course is completed, usually during the first year. Professional Examination 1 is taken in the second year of the training contract; Professional Examination 2 in the third year.

3. Individuals who are not degree holders but have at a minimum the requirements for entry to a university or CNAA degree program or other qualifications and educational attainments accepted by the Institute (members or students of the Association of Accounting Technicians who are at least 21 years old and have passed the Final membership Examination of

AAT with distinction) may complete a one-year ICAEW-approved accounting foundation course at a polytechnic or college. Upon successful completion of the foundation course, they enter and complete a four-year training contract with a firm of Chartered Accountants. Professional Examination 1 is taken in the second year of the contract, Professional Examination 2 in the fourth year.

While it is possible to qualify by method 3, many accounting firms restrict the awarding of training contracts to those with degrees. At present, approximately 90% of the individuals completing ICAEW requirements are degree holders. Of these, 20% hold Accountancy degrees, having satisfied the qualification requirements by methods 1 or 2.

Foundation Education. The foundation education stage ensures that students have a sound and appropriate base for the education, training and work experience that lead to ICAEW qualification. Six subject areas–financial accounting, management accounting, data processing, economics and the business environment, law, and quantitative techniques–comprise the required components of an acceptable foundation education, whether it is an accounting degree, a nonrelevant degree plus a conversion course or a foundation course. Accounting foundation and conversion courses offered at polytechnics and colleges cover the six subject areas of the required foundation education. Some institutions include additional topics such as business organization and behavioral studies. Some also require that prior to starting an accounting foundation course, a student must have made provisional arrangements for ICAEW-approved training.

Training. ICAEW-approved training is obtained under a training contract with an authorized training office at an accounting firm where a member of the Institute practices as a public accountant. Approved training may only be completed in the United Kingdom. Approved training offices have met ICAEW standards and are able to provide the required elements of approved training.

Examinations. The goal of ICAEW's examinations is to confirm that candidates for membership possess the professional knowledge, skill and understanding to undertake work as chartered accountants. The subjects that make up Professional Examination 1 are auditing 1, financial accounting 1, law, management accounting and financial management 1 and taxation 1. The subjects making up Professional Examination 2 are auditing 2, financial accounting 2, management accounting and financial management 2, and taxation 2.

THE CHARTERED ASSOCIATION OF CERTIFIED ACCOUNTANTS

The Chartered Association of Certified Accountants (ACCA) was founded in 1904 and received its Royal Charter in 1974. As one of the professional accounting bodies in the U.K., the Association has contributed to the training and development of services in the field of accounting, providing a route to qualification as a Certified Accountant.

Membership

ACCA offers the following levels of full membership: Fellow (FCCA) and Associate (ACCA). The Association also provides a Registered Student classification.

Registered Student: Candidates are at least 18 years old, have had a standard of education equal to that required for admission to a U.K. university. The ACCA-required level is five GCE/GCSE passes in five separate subjects with two at GCE A-level. (Two AS-levels are accepted as one A-level). As a further condition, the passes must include English language and mathematics, minimally at O-level standard. Passes in the GCSE examinations at Grade C or higher are accepted in lieu of passes at GCE O-level.

Holders of a BTEC National or Higher National Certificate or Diploma may be entitled to exemptions on a subject-for-subject basis from some, or all, of the papers in the Level 1 - Preliminary Examination. Holders of the Association of Accounting Technicians (AAT) qualification may receive exemptions from some or all of the Level 1 examination. In addition, holders of other qualifications recognized by the Association are eligible for student registration and may also receive exemptions.

External Student: Individuals who are at least 21 years old but do not meet the minimum entry requirements for Registered Student status may become External Students through the Mature Student Entry Route (MSER). An external student may become a Registered Student upon passing two of the Level 1 - Preliminary Examinations: accounting and cost and management accounting I. These must be passed within four consecutive examination sessions after becoming an external student.

Upon passing the two examinations and transferring to Registered Student status, candidates must complete the remaining examinations of the Level 1 - Preliminary Examinations within the next three consecutive examination sessions, approximately a year and a half. Those who fail to meet this requirement must retake the examinations for accounting and cost and management accounting I.

Associate: Candidates have completed ACCA's examinations and satisfied the accountancy experience requirement. Those admitted may call themselves Associates or Certified Accountants and use the designation, "ACCA."

Fellow: Associates may advance to the level of Fellow after having been Associates for five years. Those admitted to Fellowship may call themselves Fellows and use the designation, "FCCA."

Methods of Satisfying the Membership Requirements

There are several methods by which candidates may satisfy the requirements for membership.

1. The individual completes a degree and becomes a Registered Student with ACCA and is exempted from the Preliminary Examination. Those with relevant degrees (accounting or business studies) may also receive exemptions from some papers of the Level 2 examination. Degree holders study for and complete the remaining papers of Level 2 and Level 3 in three to four years by day-release, evening or correspondence course, or ACCA's open learning program (see study methods below) while obtaining three years of approved accountancy experience in industry, commerce, public sector or public practice.

2. An individual completes a one-year fulltime Foundation Level 1 course at a college or polytechnic and becomes a Registered Student, gaining exemption from the Level 1 Examination. The individual then takes a two-year fulltime course for the Level 2 and 3 Examinations after which a three-year program of approved accountancy experience in industry, commerce, public sector or public practice is undertaken.

3. Another option is to study for the Level 2 and 3 Examinations by day-release, evening or correspondence course, or ACCA's open learning program while obtaining four years of approved account-

ancy experience in industry, commerce, public sector or public practice.

4. A person takes a two-year fulltime or three-year part-time BTEC HND or two-year part-time HNC of the Business and Finance Board, then follows a two-year fulltime course for the Level 2 and 3 Examinations. Once this is accomplished, three years of approved accountancy experience in industry, commerce, public sector or public practice are required.

5. An individual obtains employment of an approved accountancy nature in industry, commerce, public sector or private sector and registers with the Association; then studies for examinations in a day-release, evening or correspondence course, or ACCA's open learning program. The training is completed in four years and the examinations in five to six years.

Examination and Experience Requirements. The three levels of examinations offered by ACCA are Level 1 Preliminary Examination, Level 2 Professional Examination and Level 3 Final Examination. The lower level examination must be completed before the next level is attempted. Exemptions may be granted for papers in Level 1 and Level 2, based on degrees in accounting or equivalent qualifications. No exemptions are given to the Level 3 Final Examinations. All papers for Level 3 must be attempted at one sitting.

Level 1 Preliminary has five sections: accounting, cost and management accounting I, economics, law, business mathematics.

Level 2 Professional has nine sections: auditing, company law, taxation, cost and management accounting II, quantitative analysis, information systems in development and operation, the regulatory framework of accounting, advanced accounting practice (a two-part paper), and one from the following: executorship and trust law and accounts; organization and management; managerial economics; U.K. public sector financial management; and insolvency.

Level 3 Final has four sections: advanced financial accounting, financial management, advanced taxation, and auditing and investigations.

Study Methods. Individuals may prepare for the ACCA qualifying examinations in various ways. Fulltime courses at colleges or polytechnics for the Level 1 and Level 2 Examinations may be internally or externally examined. Fulltime courses for all three of the Association's examinations normally take three years.

Part-time day-release, evening or correspondence courses usually take a minimum of five years.

Internally examined courses are those ACCA assesses as adequately covering the syllabuses of its examinations. Successful completion of an internally examined fulltime course enables the Registered Student to claim exemption from equivalent ACCA examinations. However, exemptions must be applied for within six months of completing the course. Externally examined courses are those which have not been assessed by the ACCA. After completing a course, students sit for the ACCA examinations at one of the ACCA external examining centers.

The ACCA Open Learning Program began in 1989 and provides preparation for the Level 1 Examinations. The program uses workbooks and audio cassettes with optional tutoring available. The workbooks contain self-assessment exercises and assignments for computer marking.

Correspondence courses are an option for those unable to study by other methods and are offered usually by private organizations.

Experience and Training Requirements. The required experience may be obtained before, during, or after preparing for the ACCA qualifying examinations and may vary in length from three to five years, depending on a candidate's educational background. Training may take place in an accounting department in the office of a practicing accountant recognized by statute to conduct an audit of company accounts, or in commerce, industry, local government or public service. Individuals are not required to enter formal training contracts in the U.K., as for the Institute of Chartered Accountants in England and Wales, with the result that overseas candidates are able to satisfy membership requirements of the ACCA.

THE ASSOCIATION OF ACCOUNTING TECHNICIANS

The Association of Accounting Technicians (AAT) was established in 1980 in response to the need for a professional structure for accounting support staff. AAT is sponsored and governed in part by nominated representatives of the following professional accounting bodies: the Chartered Association of Certified Accountants, the Chartered Institute of Public Finance and Accountancy, the Institute of Chartered Accountants in England and Wales, the Chartered Institute of Management Accountants and the Institute of Chartered Accountants of Scotland. The Association states that Accounting Technicians are the skilled support staff working in accounting and finance, whose positions range from accounts clerks to finance managers.

Membership

The AAT offers the following levels of full membership: Senior Accounting Technician (SAT) and Member (MAAT). The Association also provides a Registered Student classification.

Registered Student: There are two categories of Registered Student.

1. Individuals under 21 years of age who must satisfy either a or b below.

a. At least four different subjects at any of the following levels:

- GCSE examination of any of the approved examining bodies in England and Wales at Grades A, B or C;

- GCE examination of any approved examining bodies in England and Wales at Grades A, B or C at Ordinary level;

- CSE examination of any of the approved examination bodies in England and Wales at Grade 1;

- Scottish Certificate of Education at Standard Grades 1, 2 or 3;

- Royal Society of Arts examinations at Stage II (Intermediate);

- London Chamber of Commerce and Industry examinations at Second Level.

   The subjects must include English language and a numerate subject (mathematics, statistics, or accounting). No more than one craft subject is counted. Three subjects are acceptable if one is at least at GCE AS-level, and the English Language and numerate subject requirements have been fulfilled.

b. The following also are acceptable: the AAT Certificate in Accounting, a BTEC First Diploma, a BTEC National Award.

2. Those over 21 years of age who do not meet the entry requirements stated in a and b above. Individuals may be accepted as Registered Students at the discretion of the Council if one of the following is presented: evidence of an O-level or acceptable equivalent in English Language or a numerate subject; a letter of recommendation from the student's employer confirming experience in an accounting or financial function; or a letter of recommendation from a college prepared to enroll the student in a program leading to the Preliminary Examination.

Member: Individuals have passed the Association's membership examinations and completed three years of practical accounting experience. Those admitted may call themselves Members and use the designation, "MAAT."

Senior Accounting Technician. Individuals have been Members of AAT for at least five years and have had senior or specialized experience. Those admitted to this level of membership may call themselves Senior Accounting Technicians and use the designation, "SAT."

The Membership Examinations

There are three levels to the Membership examinations: preliminary, intermediate and final. All papers for the particular examination must be taken at one sitting unless an exemption has been given for one or more of the papers.

The Preliminary Examination requires the following papers: basic accounting, communication, business administration, and numeracy (mathematics) and statistics. The Intermediate Examination requires the following papers: accounting, elements of information systems, business law, and economics and statistics. The Final Examination requires that four papers from one of the following three streams be taken at one sitting.

a. Accounting Practice Stream: financial accounting, cost accounting and budgeting, analysis and design of information systems, organizational and financial control;

b. Industry and Commerce Stream: financial accounting, cost accounting and budgeting, analysis and design of information systems, organization and financial control;

c. Public Sector Stream: cost accounting and budgeting, analysis and design of information systems, public sector accounting and auditing, public sector organization and financial control.

Exemptions from some or all of the Association's examinations may be granted based on membership in other qualifying bodies, education and/or work experience. For example, an individual holding a SCOT-VEC Higher National Certificate in Accounting Technician Studies may apply for exemption from all three levels of the membership examinations.

The Certificate in Accounting

The Certificate in Accounting is designed to meet the needs of those who do not meet the entry requirements for student registration or for individuals who seek a more elementary qualification.

The syllabus is based on the ACCA Preliminary Examination syllabus with the addition of a paper on computer applications in accounting. There are no academic entry requirements for the Certificate. Part-time study to prepare for the examination normally takes one academic year. Individuals who pass the Certificate in Accounting examination are eligible to register as full AAT students, and a credit pass in the Certificate examination gives exemption from the Preliminary Examination.

THE INSTITUTE OF FINANCIAL ACCOUNTANTS

The Institute of Financial Accountants (IFA) began as the Institute of Book-Keepers, incorporated in 1916. In June 1966, the name was changed to the Institute of Bookkeepers and Related Data Processing. In 1974 the name again was changed to the Institute of Administrative Accounting and Data Processing, with a subsequent change in 1982 to the Institute of Administrative Accountants. The current name was registered and approved by the Registrar of Companies in December 1987.

The IFA focuses on internal auditing and will provide for the training and qualification of compliance officers. As a result of the Financial Services Act of 1986 and directives from Brussels relating to the European Community, companies need to insure that they comply with legal requirements. The Institute foresees that compliance officers will need an account-ancy base and therefore plans to increase its efforts to meet this need.

Membership

The following levels of full membership are offered by the IFA: Fellowship (FFA) and Associateship (AFA). Levels below full membership are Licentiateship and Registered Student.

Registered Student: Only Registered Students are permitted to take the Institute's examinations. Individuals with a minimum of either of the following are eligible to register as students: four GCSE passes (English, mathematics or mathematics related subject, and two other academic subjects); a BTEC First Certificate or Diploma in Business and Finance.

Licentiateship: Licentiateship is an intermediate step to becoming an Associate. The requirements are completion of Level 1 and Level 2 Examinations and two years of approved practical experience. Those admitted may call themselves Incorporated Accounting Technicians and use the designation, "LFA." Those holding Licentiateship and continuing for Associateship have to complete only the Level 3 and 4 Examinations and an additional year of approved practical training.

Associateship: Individuals complete the Institute's examinations and three years of approved practical training. Those admitted may call themselves Incorporated Financial Accountants and use the designation, "AFA." See document 5.2.

Fellowship: After obtaining Associate Membership in the Institute, members completing five years in a senior post as an accountant or lecturer in accountancy are eligible to apply as a Fellow of the Institute. Those admitted may call themselves Fellows and use the designation, "FFA."

Examinations

Subjects covered in the four levels of examinations offered by the Institute are:

Level 1: accounting 1, introduction to law, business administration 1, and economics;

Level 2: accounting 2, commercial law, business administration 2, and cost accounting;

Level 3: accounting 3, company law and practice, personnel administration, and taxation;

Level 4: advanced financial accounting, techniques and functions of management, financial information systems, and integrated case study.

Individuals may apply for exemption from some or all of the Institute's examinations based on education or other qualifications. For example, those who have completed a BTEC National Certificate or Diploma in Business and Finance, including the Accounting Unit, may receive exemptions from the Level 1 and 2 Examinations.

The Diploma in Accounting Technology

There are no anterior requirements to sit for the Diploma in Accounting Technology (DipAT). The requirements for the diploma are two papers each for the Level 1 and Level 2 Examinations: accounting 1 and 2, economics and cost accounting. Upon passing the examinations, the DipAT is awarded. Holders of the Diploma then are eligible for exemptions from the appropriate papers of the Level 1 and Level 2 Examinations if they choose to pursue full membership in the Institute.

MANAGEMENT

Management is not an easily defined profession. As pointed out by Peter Moore,

> Management is not a recognized profession in the sense that medicine is, or accounting or the law. These professions are controlled by governing bodies which themselves have defined legal status, and the title of, for example, solicitor has a recognized definition in official parlance, whilst a doctor to practice must be on the official register of the General Medical Council. Engineers have been for some time in the same position as managers, with the title widely used for a wide variety of activities...The lack of professional status (as opposed to professionalism)

has very significant implications in the case of management education. Anybody can call himself or herself a manager, so that the term manager can just as easily denote somebody in charge of a small (candy) shop as the boss of a multi-national company... (Goodlad 1985, 74)

Because management is not a profession in the same sense as others and because there is an absence of management qualifying associations that represent the entire field, management does not fit the same pattern seen with other areas of this report. The institutes and associations presented in this section represent only components or aspects of management; they do not define the field of management. The Institute of Administrative Management and the Institute of Personnel Management represent aspects of management. Two other qualifying bodies, the Chartered Institute of Banking and the Chartered Institute of Marketing, are related to management. Even though it does not currently function as a qualifying body, the British Institute of Management plays a leading role in the recent research and discussions about the state of management education and training in the U.K. and is frequently mentioned.

The provision of management education and training recently has been the subject of much study in the U.K., resulting in several reports and initiatives. The first report was published in 1984 by the Institute of Manpower Studies (IMS). The IMS report, *Competence and Competition,* focused on vocational education and training in three of the U.K.'s main competitors: Japan, the United States and West Germany. IMS concluded that while the provision for education and training was different in the three countries, "...there was a clear perceived link between investment in education and training and competitive success–a perception that was absent in the U.K. Moreover, the other countries were concerned with developing effective performance at work in its widest sense, rather than concentrating on narrow skills development." (Deloitte, Haskins and Sells 1989, 7) The IMS report helped develop an awareness of the importance of management training and highlighted the need for government and industry to act to improve the situation in the U.K.

A year after the IMS report, a management consulting firm was commissioned by the Manpower Services Commission (MSC) to assess the status of training in British industry. Their report, *A Challenge to Complacency,* "...showed that there was widespread ignorance amongst top management of how their company's training performance compared with their

competitors; that many senior executives had only a limited knowledge of the scale of resources directed to training within their company; that training was not seen as an important contributor to competitiveness and profitability, but rather as an overhead to be cut when profits were under pressure." (Deloitte, Haskins and Sells 1989, 7)

As with the IMS study, the MSC report raised serious concerns about management education and training in the U.K. Following the MSC report, Professor Charles Handy studied management education, training and development in France, Japan, the United Kingdom, the United States and West Germany. Published in 1987, *The Making of Managers* concluded that with the exception of the U.K., management groups

> ...are more likely to have been educated to a higher level, and are more likely to have benefitted from formal and systematic policies for continuing education and development...Britain's system (of management education and training) was in a muddle. Handy suggested that Britain should aim to implement a...plan that drew on the best practice in other countries...He suggested particularly that leading organizations act as role models of good practice; and that individuals should secure greater levels of education. (Deloitte, Haskins and Sells 1989, 7)

Concurrent with the Handy report, the Department of Education and Science (DES) and the Department of Trade and Industry (DTI) commissioned a comprehensive assessment of management education and training. The review was conducted under the auspices of the British Institute of Management and the Confederation of British Industry. Known as the Constable-McCormick report, *The Making of British Managers* (1987) again pointed out major areas where the United Kingdom has fallen behind other countries in the training and education of managers and recommended several courses of action. These are the most significant of the report's findings and recommendations:

- Effective management is recognized as a key factor in economic growth. Britain's managers lack the development, education and training opportunities of their competitors but are generally willing to consider new approaches to each of these areas.

- The U.K. has about 2.75 million people who exercise managerial positions (about 1.1 million in middle and senior management). About 90,000 people enter management roles each year, although the great majority lack formal management education and training.

- About 12,300 people graduate each year with an undergraduate degree, a postgraduate degree in business and management studies, or a Diploma in Management Studies or a Higher National Diploma.

- Management-oriented professional institutes make a valuable contribution to the education and training of managers in specific functional skills.

- Management education and training has grown over the past 25 years, especially in-company development programs.

- The private sector provides post-experience management training although the universities, polytechnics and colleges provide the bulk of these programs.

- Major deficiencies in the supply of management education and training relative to this anticipated growth in demand are likely.

- A new Diploma in Business Administration that provides a foundation in management should be created. It would be taken by young people during their first three years of work, primarily part-time, following completion of higher education. It would also be available to those who were entering a managerial career without having completed higher education. However, the level would be based on the completion of a higher education program. The eventual target would be an output of at least 35,000 per year.

- The new Diploma should not be created by "repackaging" the existing Diploma in Management Studies. Management-oriented professional institutes should adopt the new diploma as part of their qualification requirements. It should be the primary qualification for membership in the British Institute of Management.

- Management schools should remain within parent academic institutions but should have greater managerial and financial autonomy. Employers do not support the wholesale privatization of management schools.

- Legislation should be introduced to eliminate bogus degrees in business and management. (BIM 1987)

With respect to the last recommendation, bogus degrees should not be confused with "diploma mills." The reference is to associations and institutes that offer qualifications, examinations and memberships that have little or no relationship to the "mainstream" of management education available in the public or private sector. In other words, the "qualification" offered by the Institute has little or no real currency in terms of providing a qualification in management.

Concurrent with the release of *The Making of British Managers* and drawing on the recommendations of the Handy and Constable-McCormick reports, the Management Charter Initiative (MCI) was inaugurated. Under the guidance of the Confederation of British Industry and the British Institute of Management, the Council for Management Education and Development (CMED) was created primarily to set up the Management Charter Initiative. The initial purpose of MCI was the preparation of a code of practice to which businesses must subscribe as a pre-condition to becoming a member organization. In July 1988, a code of practice was adopted with more than 200 organizations pledging support. The main thrust of MCI at this stage has been to increase the awareness that, contrary to past practice, management education and training are vital components in establishing a competitive edge in the marketplace.

THE BRITISH INSTITUTE OF MANAGEMENT

The British Institute of Management (BIM), formed in 1948, is not an examining body. It exists to foster and encourage the highest standards of professional excellence at every level of management. Membership in the Institute is recognition of an individual's status as a manager, management qualifications having been obtained by education and/or experience. While the Institute is not an examining body, it conducts short courses mainly as continuing education for those already in management positions, not as education for those working toward a management qualification.

Membership

The BIM offers the following levels of full membership: Companionship (CBIM), Fellow (FBIM), and Member (MBIM). Levels below full membership are Associate (ABIM) and Affiliate.

Affiliate: This level of membership is for those pursuing careers related to management who wish to be associated with the aims of the Institute. Affiliate membership is available for those who do not plan on becoming full members.

Associate: Eligibility is open to individuals who meet the educational requirements of Members but do not have sufficient management experience, and who intend to become Members in a reasonable amount of time. This also applies to those who have appropriate management experience but have not completed the educational requirements. Those admitted may call themselves Associates and use the designation, "ABIM."

Member: Individuals have a recognized qualification in management--for example, the CNAA Diploma in Management Studies or a master's degree in management--and at least one year of approved management experience. BIM will also consider those with a first degree in a nonmanagement subject or membership by examination in a professional management or associated body with a longer period of management experience required. Those admitted may call themselves Members and use the designation, "MBIM."

Fellow: The criterion for Fellowship is an extended period in a post as general manager or director of substantial scope and duration at board level in organizations of significant size. As an alternative, those who have had a progressive management career over an extended period and have achieved a policy-making board appointment or exercise wide management responsibilities in their specialist field are eligible to become Fellows. Those admitted may call themselves Fellows and use the designation, "FBIM."

Companionship: Membership is by invitation only for individuals the Institute chooses to recognize for their achievements as managers. There are approximately 1,500 individuals holding this honorary title. Those admitted may call themselves Companions and use the designation, "CBIM."

THE INSTITUTE OF ADMINISTRATIVE MANAGEMENT

Established in 1915, the Institute of Administrative Management (IAM) is the only organization in the United Kingdom specializing in the promotion of administrative management in the fields of industry, commerce and government. The Institute promotes high standards of administrative management; helps business improve administrative efficiency; develops the science of administrative management; encourages the attainment of professional management qualifications; provides information to enable members to keep up-to-date with the latest techniques and developments in the field of administrative management.

Membership

The IAM offers the following levels of full membership: Fellow (FInstAM), and Member (MInstAM). Levels below full membership are Associate (AInstAM), and Student.

Student: Candidates must have, minimally, four GCE O-level or GCSE passes, one of which must be English, and one pass at A-level, or three years of administrative management work experience.

Associate: Individuals must pass the certificate examination, or be at least 28 years old and have at least three years of administrative management experience. Those admitted may call themselves Associates and use the designation, "AInstAM."

Member: Applicants must be at least 30 years old with at least five years of administrative management experience, or pass the Institute's Diploma examination. Those admitted may call themselves Members and use the designation, "MInstAM." Those admitted who have passed the Diploma examination may use the letters "MInstAm(Dip)."

Fellow: Individuals have had Member status for at least five years, and have held a senior position within the Institute or been recognized for distinguished service. Those admitted may call themselves Fellows and use the designation, "FInstAM."

The IAM Qualifications

The Foundation Certificate. The Foundation Certificate program is made up of the first three modules or subjects of the certificate examination and is mainly for candidates who do not meet any of the requirements for entry to the certificate examination. However, the Institute views the Foundation Certificate as a qualification in its own right. An applicant for the Certificate must have a recommendation from a college tutor or full member of the Institute. Upon successful completion of the Foundation Certificate, individuals may choose to complete the remaining modules of the certificate examinations to obtain the Certificate in Administrative Management.

The Certificate in Administrative Management. The Certificate in Administrative Management consists of six modules–administration in the office, office systems, manpower administration, office planning and control, information technology, administrative data and technology–and a case study. Individuals must pass all six modules to obtain the certificate. Entry requires any one of the following:

1. four GCSE Grade A, B or C and one subject at A-level. One subject must be English. O-levels or CSE Grade 1 are also accepted;

2. any National Council for Vocational Qualifications (NCVQ)-approved qualification at Level 3 in appropriate subjects;

3. a BTEC or SCOTVEC National Certificate or Diploma in appropriate subjects;

4. in exceptional cases, at least three years of relevant work experience.

Diploma in Administrative Management. Six required modules, two optional modules and a case study constitute the program for the Diploma in Administrative Management. The required modules are: administrative management 1 and 2, human resources management, organizational analysis, advanced methods and systems - integration, and advanced methods and systems - development. The optional modules are financial and quantitative methods, office automation, facilities management, public sector management and telecommunications management. Entry requires any of the following:

1. the Certificate in Administrative Management;

2. Associate IAM Membership awarded on a vocational basis;

3. a U.K. first degree;

4. a U.K. Higher National Certificate or Diploma in approved subjects;

5. other qualifications recognized and approved by the Institute for direct entry to the Diploma, e.g., five years of acceptable and relevant work experience.

THE INSTITUTE OF PERSONNEL MANAGEMENT

The Institute of Personnel Management (IPM) began as the Welfare Workers Association in 1913. There were several subsequent name changes, ranging from the Central Association of Welfare Workers and Welfare Workers Institute to the Institute of Labour Management. The present name was adopted in 1946. The Institute's goals are to provide an association of professional standing for its members; develop a continuously evolving body of professional knowledge to help members do their jobs more effectively in response to changing demands and conditions; develop and maintain professional standards of competence; encourage investigation and research in personnel management and subjects related to it; and present a national viewpoint on personnel management; and establish and develop links with other bodies, both national and international, concerned with personnel management.

The Institute seeks to achieve its goals by making the continuously developing body of information and knowledge available to members and management in general through an active information service, conferences, courses, publications and by any other available means; providing high standards of training for the profession and entry into full membership of the Institute through examinations conducted by the Institute and objectively assessed experience; and taking positive steps to encourage investigation and research in personnel management and subjects related to it.

Membership

The following levels of membership are offered by the IPM: Companionship (CIPM), Fellow (FIPM) and Member (MIPM). Levels below full membership are

Graduate (GradIPM), Student Member and Affiliateship.

Affiliateship: Candidates hold a post in personnel management or in an occupation where knowledge of the principles of personnel management is desirable and valuable.

Student Member: Individuals are normally at least 20 years old and have met the entry requirements. Students must also be following an Institute-recognized course of study in personnel management. The entry requirement for student membership is any of the following:

1. five GCSE/GCE passes in different subjects with at least two subjects at A-level (O-level passes must be at grade C or above);

2. in Scotland, three SCE O grade passes at band C or above and three Higher grade passes;

3. equivalent or higher level awards from nationally recognized U.K. or Irish educational or professional bodies;

4. successful completion of the Certificate in Personnel Practice; or

5. for those who have completed secondary education outside the U.K., academic or experiential qualifications recognized by the Institute as comparable to the entry requirements stated above and acceptance to an approved course of study.

Graduate: Graduates have passed Stage 1 and 2 of the Institute's education scheme or equivalent exams approved by the Institute. In exceptional cases, those holding a Master's degree may seek direct admission to Graduateship if their studies have covered the content of Stages 1 and 2 and if they have had relevant personnel management experience. Those satisfying the requirements may call themselves Graduates and use the designation, "GradIPM."

Member: Candidates have Graduate status and have had executive and/or advisory duties in the personnel function of management for at least three years. Those admitted may call themselves Members and use the designation, "MIPM." Individuals with at least 10 years of appropriate experience at a middle management level or above may be eligible for membership through the Management Entry scheme.

Fellow: Candidates have Member status and at least 10 years in an executive and/or a supporting position in personnel management. Those admitted may call themselves Fellows and use the designation, "FIPM."

Companionship: This is an honorary designation for Fellows or Members who have made significant contributions to the development of personnel management and the Institute. Those admitted may call themselves Companions and use the designation, "CIPM."

The IPM Education Scheme

Individuals wishing to complete the Institute professional education scheme must first hold Student Membership for a maximum of five years. Students are expected to complete Stage 1 within the first year of admission to Student Membership and Stage 2 within three years of admission.

Stage 1: Introduction to Personnel Management is comprised of three subjects: personnel management in context, introduction to organizational behavior, and personnel information and decision making. Stage 1 introduces the relevant aspects of the main academic disciplines underlying the practice of personnel management; the range and scope of personnel management including its organization, functions and development; and the major factors—economic, political, social, financial and legal—influencing the operation of the personnel management function.

Individuals granted exemptions for the following qualifications may proceed directly to Stage 2 with the approval of the Institute:

1. IPM-approved university or CNAA degrees or postgraduate diplomas in management, public administration or business studies;

2. nationally recognized British professional qualifications which prescribe study subjects reasonably equated in content and length to the three Stage 1 subjects;

3. IPM-approved BTEC Higher National Awards which include the study of appropriate core and optional units related to Stage 1 subjects;

4. Open University's Professional Diploma in Management subject "The Effective Manager" or Henley's Human Resource Management course, "Effective Management."

For the college-based students, exemptions are granted at the discretion of the course tutor. Independent and correspondence students must apply directly to the Institute to receive exemptions.

Stage 2: The Personnel Management Function is comprised of several subjects or modules. Individuals are required to complete three core modules and then choose three additional ones. They must also complete an additional component of five assignments and one management report. Stage 2 develops the knowledge and understanding of personnel management through in-depth studies of the major elements which make up the function of personnel management. No partial exemptions are given for Stage 2 requirements. In exceptional instances, individuals who hold a first degree or who complete a postgraduate program might qualify for complete exemption from Stage 2.

The Certificate in Personnel Practice

The Certificate in Personnel Practice is open entry and, as a result, requires no formal academic qualifications for admission. The program includes core topics such as interpersonal and interviewing skills, instructional techniques, employment legislation, personnel records, and options which may be core subjects studied in greater depth or broader areas of personnel management. The Certificate in Personnel Practice also provides for the development of basic personnel skills and examines key functional areas such as manpower planning, recruitment, training, industrial relations, wage/salary administration and employee services.

THE CHARTERED INSTITUTE OF BANKERS

The purpose of the Chartered Institute of Bankers (CIB) has changed little since its founding in 1879. As stated in its Royal Charter granted in 1987, the goal of the Institute is the "advancement of knowledge of and education in the principles and practice of banking for the benefit of the public." (CIB 1988, 15) To this end, the Institute views its primary role to be the "provision of qualifying examinations of demanding standards."

Membership

The CIB offers the following levels of full membership: Fellow (FCIB) and Associate (ACIB). Ordinary Membership is the only level below full membership.

Ordinary Member: Employment in banking or a relevant position for at least three years.

Associate: Candidates have completed the Banking Diploma and have at least three years of banking or relevant work experience. Those admitted may call themselves Associates and use the designation, "ACIB."

Fellow: Candidates are Associates who hold managerial positions in banking. Those elected may call themselves Fellows and use the designation, "FCIB."

The Institute's Examinations

A major review of the Institute's activities was conducted when the Royal Charter was granted. To strengthen employers' use of the Institute's qualifying examinations in the promotion of employees to management positions and out of a general concern for the Institute's image and professional identity, several changes have been made to the examination structure. The descriptions that follow reflect these changes.

There are three levels to the qualifying examination structure: the Banking Certificate, the Associateship Examinations and the Financial Studies Diploma. The first level, the Banking Certificate, is a qualification in its own right. The second level, the Associateship Examinations, is the route to qualification for career bankers and leads to full membership in the Institute at the Associate level. The third level, the Financial Studies Diploma, is a management-level qualification in banking.

The *Banking Certificate,* designed for banking staff at the senior supervisory level, is regarded as a sound basis for progress to the Associateship Examinations. The syllabus is practical and job-related. There are two sections to the Banking Certificate: Preliminary and Final. The Preliminary contains three subjects and the Final six. There are two routes to the Banking Certificate, depending on the qualifications of the candidate.

1. No entry requirements other than student membership. Individuals complete both sections of the Banking Certificate, Preliminary and Final, generally within three years.

2. Individuals with one or more A-levels plus GCSE or O-level in English Language (grades A, B or C) or five years of employment in banking or relevant work are exempted from the Preliminary section and may go directly to the Final section. The normal length of study is two years.

The *Associateship Examinations* previously had three different options: the Banking Diploma, the International Banking Diploma or the Trustee Diploma. As a result of the Institute's concern that individuals were specializing too early, the diplomas were amalgamated and a "core" of subjects was created to provide a common foundation for those seeking Associateship. Specialization now occurs as an option after the core subjects are completed. Entry requires the Banking Certificate, the Foundation Course or other qualification recognized by the Institute as satisfying the first-level educational requirements.

Candidates are required to pass eight papers: four core papers–the financial system, law relating to banking, accountancy, management in banking–and four optional papers selected from a group of 16. Exemptions may be considered on a subject-by-subject basis for those who hold appropriate qualifications.

The Foundation Course is designed to provide access to the Associateship Examinations. Those successfully completing the Foundation Course are eligible to proceed to that level. The subjects of the Foundation Course are economics, structure of accounts, general principles of law, and elements of banking or elements of investment. Entry requires one or more A-levels plus GCSE or O-level in English Language (grades A, B or C), or credit passes of 65% or higher in the three papers of the Preliminary section of the Banking Certificate in only one sitting.

The *Financial Studies Diploma* is designed for individuals seeking senior management positions. The course contents include advanced banking and management subjects. Entry requires an Associateship in CIB or a CIB-recognized degree or professional qualification. There are two sections of the Financial Studies Diploma. The contents of Section One are finance for business customers, human aspects of management, and business planning and control. The contents of Section Two are marketing of financial services, corporate finance and a project. Exemptions may be granted on a subject-by-subject basis for those who hold academic or professional qualifications of not less than U.K. degree standard, as determined by the Institute.

THE CHARTERED INSTITUTE OF MARKETING

The Chartered Institute of Marketing (CIM) began as the Sales Managers Association. Incorporated in 1911, the Association started to function as an examin-

ing body in 1928. At that time, individuals employed in sales would take evening programs to prepare for the Association's examinations. With the Association's qualification, individuals could hope to advance their careers in sales. As a result of the natural ties between sales and marketing, the Association began to focus on marketing and started to offer executive training programs in marketing around 1950. By the 1960s, the Sales Managers Association had become the Institute of Marketing. In 1981 the Institute decided to restrict its membership to those who could clearly satisfy academic requirements and demonstrate that they had practical experience in marketing. In 1989 the Institute received a Royal Charter and is now the Chartered Institute of Marketing.

Membership

The CIM offers the following full levels of membership: Fellow (FCIM) and Member (MCIM). Levels below full membership are Graduate and Associate.

Associate: Candidates have completed one of the CIM Certificates or one or more CIM-approved qualifications (listed below) and have been employed for at least one year in a recognized marketing management position. Those admitted may call themselves Associates.

Any of the following is approved by CIM as qualifications for Associateship:

1. BTEC/SCOTVEC Higher National Certificate/Diploma with a marketing specialization;

2. U.K. university or CNAA degree or diploma (degree in a business subject, Diploma in Management Studies, postgraduate diploma in business or management);

3. other CIM-approved professional qualifications of equivalent standard.

Graduate: Candidates have completed the CIM Diploma or CIM-approved marketing qualification (listed under the requirements for Membership). They have not completed the requisite practical experience. Those admitted may call themselves Graduates.

Member: Candidates have completed the CIM Diploma or a CIM-recognized marketing qualification (listed below) and have at least three years' employment in a recognized area of marketing. In addition, individuals must have been employed for a minimum of one year either in a recognized marketing management position or in a position of marketing or sales training. Those admitted may call themselves Members and use the designation, "MCIM."

The following are CIM-approved marketing qualifications for Membership:

1. U.K. university or CNAA degree or diploma (degree in a business subject with a marketing specialization, Post-Graduate Diploma in Business or Management with a marketing specialization; Diploma in Management Studies with a marketing specialization);

2. other CIM-approved professional qualifications of equivalent standard.

Fellow: Candidates have made an outstanding contribution to marketing education or practice and have a clearly proven record of expertise, experience and success in marketing management on a national or international scale. Election to Fellowship may take place on entry or after a period of membership if the individual qualifies for membership under the current membership requirements and has been in a position as chief executive, executive director, senior marketing executive, professor of marketing or senior academic for a minimum of three years. Those admitted may call themselves Fellows and use the designation, "FCIM."

Examinations

The Diploma examination demonstrates that the individual has acquired ability and skill in the application of basic marketing knowledge and techniques. Four required subjects for the Diploma are international marketing, marketing planning and control, marketing communications and marketing management (analysis and decision case study).

Individuals seeking registration for the Diploma must have one of the following:

1. the CIM Certificate in Marketing or Sales Management;

2. U.K. postgraduate Diploma in Marketing or Management Studies (with CIM-approved marketing module);

3. U.K. degree or postgraduate degree in a business-related subject (with a CIM-approved marketing module);

4. approved BTEC or SCOTVEC Higher Diploma or Certificate award in Business Studies and Finance which includes a CIM-approved marketing option;

5. degree other than those listed above and satisfactory completion of either the Graduate Entry Examination or two Certificate subjects: practice of marketing and financial aspects of marketing.

6. other CIM-recognized equivalent qualifications.

As an alternate route to satisfying the Diploma entry requirements, individuals who have completed the CIM Training Division's Certificate of Sales Management Practice or Marketing Management Practice are eligible for entry to the Diploma and may become registered students of the Institute for the Diploma by paying the appropriate fees. Registration for the Diploma enables the student to be registered for a special one-year period.

Academic qualifications at degree or postgraduate level may provide subject-by-subject exemptions from the diploma examinations. However, the academic qualification must have a substantial marketing management content. Academic qualifications must have been obtained within 10 years to qualify for subject exemptions, not more than six years in the case of U.K. professional qualifications. In either case, individuals do not receive exemptions from marketing management (analysis and decision). Also, students who completed subject examinations prior to 1974 are not able to carry their results forward. Post-1974 results are valid for a period of 10 years.

The *Graduate Entry Examination* prepares those with nonbusiness related degrees who are working in a marketing or sales environment for the Diploma course. The examination is comprised of two papers designed to test the individual's knowledge of marketing and the financial aspects of marketing.

The *Certificate of Marketing* and the *Certificate of Sales Management* provide a comprehensive foundation regarding business organization and the environment in which it operates. Eight subjects are required for either certificate. Seven subjects comprise a common core: fundamentals of marketing, principles and practice of selling, economics, statistics (quantitative studies), business law, behavioral aspects of marketing and financial aspects of marketing.

The option for the Certificate in Marketing is the practice of marketing and the option for the Certificate of Sales Management is the practice of sales management.

Entry requires individuals be at least 18 years old and have one of the following to become registered students:

1. four GCSE passes, plus one pass at A-level. Passes are required in subject areas testing English Language and a branch of Mathematics;

2. applicants from Scotland and Northern Ireland may offer the Scottish Certificate of Education and the Northern Ireland General Certificate of Education, respectively;

3. BTEC or SCOTVEC national award in Business Studies;

4. applicants lacking one of the above may be admitted, provided they have one or more years of fulltime marketing experience and can also offer five GCSE passes including one in math;

5. applicants 21 or over who satisfy none of the above may be registered if they have a minimum of three years of approved fulltime experience and their employer and/or marketing tutor supports their application.

Upon satisfying the above and paying appropriate fees, individuals may become registered students. They then have two years to satisfy all the Certificate examinations. Extensions to the two years may be granted upon payment of a further fee.

The Senior Management Entry Scheme is available to individuals who do not have any of the CIM-recognized marketing qualifications. There are three different routes to Membership by this scheme.

1. Entry by Qualification is for individuals who have been personally responsible for planning and implementing profitable marketing programs for at least five years and who hold a university or CNAA degree in a discipline related to a product or service of the business or profession in which the individual is currently employed.

Another route is for those who have gained membership by examination in one of the recognized Chartered Institutes in a discipline related to the business in which the individual is currently employed. Individuals must also be interviewed by the Senior Management Entry Panel. Examples include BSc(Econ) - Marketing Director for a firm of financial consultants; BPharm - Export Marketing Director for a pharmaceutical manufacturer; CEng - Marketing Director for an engineering company

2. Entry by Management Experience is for individuals who have been personally responsible for planning and implementing profitable marketing programs and have held a senior marketing management position for at least five years. This route requires the submission of a formal paper, for assessment by an academic assessor, which clearly demonstrates the ability to analyze and formalize the practice of marketing. The review of the paper is followed by an interview with the Senior Management Entry Panel.

3. Entry by the Senior Manager's Intensive Diploma Course. This course is carried out over five residential weekends at the CIM Training Center and has been specifically designed to prepare senior managers for the Diploma examinations. Individuals must have had either three years of experience in senior marketing management or six years of experience in a senior management position. Upon passing the Diploma examinations, candidates are eligible for direct entry to Membership as the experience requirements have already been satisfied.

The CIM Certificate of Sales Management Practice and Certificate of Marketing Management Practice are awarded for extensive short-term training programs for individuals employed in various areas of marketing. Those who have attended one of the short-term training programs may accumulate short-term training "credits." After accumulating a number of credits, individuals are eligible for either certificate.

Either certificate then gains an exemption from the Certificate examinations and gives entry to the Diploma program.

NURSING

Introduction

Evolving from the work of Florence Nightingale in the nineteenth century, the history of modern nursing in the United Kingdom dates from the Registration Act of 1919. The legal recognition of nurses established the title State Registered Nurse (SRN). This acknowledgment of nursing as a profession carried with it regulation to protect the public through the establishment of entry requirements, approval of training institutions and the creation of licensing examinations. Subsequent to the 1919 Act, the profession grew rapidly, as evidenced by the increase in recognized nursing schools from six to over 200 by the end of World War II. There was little change for the next 30 years with nursing essentially devoted to servicing the burgeoning National Health Service established in 1946.

The first major change in nursing since 1919 came with the adoption of the Nurses, Midwives and Health Visitors Act of 1979. This Act was a response to the need for changes in nurse training to facilitate compliance with the training requirements established in 1977 by the Council of the European Communities (EEC). The U.K. 1979 Act founded the United Kingdom Central Council for Nursing, Midwifery and Health Visiting and created four National Boards to establish and improve standards of training and professional conduct for nurses, midwives and health visitors. The UKCC and the National Boards of England, Wales, Scotland and Northern Ireland replaced the nine bodies concerned with nursing, midwifery and health visiting.

Following its establishment in 1979, the UKCC developed rules to define the content and standard of training needed to qualify for nursing registration. Called the Nurses, Midwives, and Health Visitors Rules of 1983, the academic qualifications required for admission to training changed from two GCE O-levels to five, expanded areas of study and clinical experience to meet the new European Economic Community guidelines and increased the theoretical component of training from 15% to 30%.

Recognizing that there were still shortfalls in nurse education despite the changes of 1983, the Educational Policy Advisory Committee (EPAC) of the UKCC continued work on identifying the educational needs of the nursing service, looking specifically to the year 2000 and beyond. The work of the Committee resulted in the Nurses, Midwives and Health Visitors Amendment Rules of 1989, referred to as Project 2000 (P2000). Cited as the most significant reform in nursing education since Florence Nightingale, the new program moved control of nursing education from the service to the academic side and has reinforced nursing as a profession. It also expanded education and training from essentially hospital nursing to both hospital and community nursing. The P2000 program also required that nurse training institutions be linked to and validated by institutions of higher education, giving academic currency to nursing education. P2000 also gave student nurses full student status, prohibiting hospitals from including them on duty rosters.

The first P2000 programs were implemented in England in fall 1989 with an intake of some 1,500 students in 13 nurse training institutions. Further im-plementation will be incremental over the next several years and will include the amalgamation of some 200 schools of nursing into about 90, each linked to a university or polytechnic. Wales, with six schools of nursing, and Northern Ireland, with five, will implement P2000 all at once in fall 1991. Scotland will introduce the program into its six schools of nursing in fall 1992.

The United Kingdom Central Council and the National Boards

The United Kingdom Central Council (UKCC), established in 1979, is responsible for setting the requirements for admission to training, the content and standards of training, and the standards of professional conduct. It also maintains a Professional Register for nurses, midwives and health visitors. Responsibility for evaluating and approving training institutions and programs of preparation within those institutions rests with the four National Boards. To receive approval, a program must incorporate all requirements and competencies set down by the UKCC.

The Professional Register

To practice as a nurse, midwife or health visitor in the U.K., an individual practitioner is required to have a current registration on the UKCC Register. The Register is divided into Parts according to various types and levels of qualification as established by the Council. A practitioner may be registered on more than one of the various Parts. Effective with P2000, registration must be renewed every three years and is based on continuing education. In 1989 approximately 600,000 practitioners were on the UKCC Register.

There are two levels of qualification: Registered (first level) and Enrolled (second level). A first-level registration is similar to a Registered Nurse qualification in the United States and a second-level qualification is similar to a U.S. Licensed Practical Nurse.

Effective with the Nurses, Midwives and Health Visitors Rules of 1983 there were 11 Parts of the UKCC Register. The Amendment Rules of 1989 added Parts 12 through 15 to provide for Project 2000 qualifications. A current chart of the complete Register is presented below:

Part	Designation	Abbreviation
1	Registered General Nurse	RGN
2	Enrolled Nurse (General)	EN(G)
3	Registered Mental Nurse	RMN
4	Enrolled Nurse (Mental)	EN(M)
5	Registered Nurse for Mentally Handicapped	RNMH
6	Enrolled Nurse (Mentally Handicapped	EN(MH)
7	Enrolled Nurse (trained in Scotland or Northern Ireland)	EN
8	Registered Sick Children's Nurse	RSCN
9	Registered Fever Nurse (Two-year course not offered since 1976)	RFN
10	Registered Midwife	RM
11	Registered Health Visitor	RHV
12	Registered Adult Nurse	*
13	Registered Mental Health Nurse	*
14	Registered Mental Handicap Nurse	*
15	Registered Children's Nurse	*

Not yet determined

For nurses on one or more Parts of the Register, additional professional qualifications such as District Nurse, Teacher of Nursing, Midwifery or Health Visiting, or Occupational Health Nurse may be recorded.

The National Boards have statutory responsibility to hold, or arrange for others to hold, examinations enabling nurses and midwives to qualify for registration or to obtain additional qualifications. From 1983, the majority of examinations for basic nursing and health visiting have been set and held internally by the training institutions with the standards of the examinations monitored by the National Boards. Currently the Midwifery Qualifying Examination is conducted by the respective Boards, but it is expected that soon this examination also will be delegated to the training institutions.

Assessment in P2000 programs is continuous. Instruction is by unit, and each unit is assessed 20% continuously and 80% by unseen examination. Clinical competence is assessed on a continual basis by qualified ward supervisors.

Enrolled Nurse

An Enrolled Nurse qualification is obtained through satisfactory completion of an 18-month to two-year program which is practically oriented and enables the practitioner to work under the supervision of a first-level nurse. There is no statutory minimum standard for entrance to training, though many schools ask for two subjects at the former GCE O-level or the equivalent on other examinations.

A significant reform of Project 2000 is that there will be only one level of nurse in the U.K. Therefore, no new students are being taken into Enrolled Nurse training and all existing programs will end by October 1992. Transition courses of a minimum of 52 weeks of fulltime study have been put into place to enable practitioners currently on the Register as Enrolled Nurses to upgrade to a first-level qualification. Up to 50% of the 52-week requirement may be waived for experience and/or coursework undertaken since initial qualification.

Registered Nurse: Pre-project 2000

A Registered Nurse qualification–RGN, RMN, RNMH, or RSCN–is obtained through satisfactory completion of a three-year program at a school or college of nursing approved by one of the four National Boards or through completion of a diploma or degree program at a university or polytechnic. Entry requires that students admitted to training at a school or college of nursing be at least 17 1/2 years old. As of January 1, 1986, the entry requirements are:

1. five subjects on the GCSE at grades A, B or C or GCE O-levels at grade A, B or C;

2. five subjects passed on CSE Grade 1 or on Scottish Certificate of Education at Standard Grade, grade 1, 2 or 3 or Ordinary Grade, Bands A, B or C;

3. passing the UKCC DC Educational Test, a one-hour test measuring verbal reasoning, nonverbal reasoning, arithmetic and comprehension skills, if a student does not meet the entry requirement.

Training: Three-year fulltime training programs are required for admission to Parts 1, 3, 5 or 8 of the Register as a first qualification and are taken at schools and colleges of nursing. Nurses with a first qualification may pursue additional one-year fulltime training to qualify for registration on an additional Part or Parts of the Register. Until 1983 nurse training was predominantly clinical, with 15% theory. Effective with the Nurses, Midwives and Health Visitors Rules of 1983, the theoretical component increased to 30%.

General Nurse (RGN) program content–The syllabus is divided into three parts: nursing, the study of the individual, and the nature and cause of illness together with its prevention and cure. Integrated throughout the parts are the subject areas of social, biological and psychological sciences. Specific areas of theoretical study and clinical experience include general medicine, surgery, pediatrics, obstetrics, psychiatry and geriatrics; anatomy and physiology, dietetics and pharmacology; sociology and psychology.

Mental Illness (RMN) program content–The syllabus is divided into four parts: nursing, organizational and management skills, communication and interpersonal skills, and a common foundation subject. Areas of specific study include human growth and development, psychology, sociology, social psychology of the family, human sexuality; anatomy and physiology, pharmacology; acute psychiatry, care of the elderly mentally ill, rehabilitation.

Mentally Handicapped (RNMH) program content– The syllabus falls into three broad areas: the nature and causes of mental handicaps, the development of the individual in and outside the family, and the process of learning. Areas of specific study include human growth and development, anatomy and physiology; education and the mentally handicapped, sociology of organizations, normalization and human rights; developmental, clinical, educational and environmental psychology; causation, nature and effects of mental handicaps, developing care and training programs, rehabilitation.

Sick Children (RSCN) program content: The training covers the full range of nursing skills and knowledge as for the RGN. The nature and causes of disease over the entire life span are considered, but emphasis is on medical and surgical care of children, family relationships, and social, cultural, and physiological influences

on children's development. RSCN programs are generally about eight months longer than RGN programs. It is common for sick children's nurses to enter the field as RGNs with a one-year post-registration course in sick children's nursing.

Registered Nurse: Project 2000

Registration on Parts 12 through 15 of the Register is obtained through successful completion of a three-year program at a school or college of nursing approved by one of the four National Boards and academically linked to a polytechnic or university or through a polytechnic or university degree program. These four Parts of the Register represent the new system of nurse education and training which began implementation in 1989. The major changes from Parts 1, 3, 5 and 8 are:

- all students take a Common Foundation Program (CFP);

- nursing students are fulltime students, no longer employed under contracts of service to hospitals to provide nursing care during their course of preparation;

- programs are academically based, culminating in the Diploma in Higher Education and first-level Registration;

- every school or college of nursing is required to have a memorandum of cooperation with a polytechnic or a university which includes provision for cross use of faculty and facilities and for validation of the academic content of the program at the level of the Diploma in Higher Education (DipHE) (see chapter III for more information on the DipHe);

- programs no longer focus exclusively on hospital nursing but are designed to enable the resulting practitioner to practice across all health care settings, both institutional and in the broader community.

- Entry requirements for training under P2000 remain the same as those established for all nurse training effective January 1, 1986.

Training: P2000 nurse education consists of an 18-month Common Foundation Program (CFP) followed by an 18-month Branch Program in Adult Nursing, Mental Health Nursing, Mental Handicap Nursing, or Children's Nursing. P2000 nurse education is 50% theoretical and 50% practical and clinical. The latter experience is related to the level of theoretical study and is undertaken both in the hospital and in the community

The *Common Foundation Program (CFP):* The curriculum of the CFP provides a body of knowledge embedded in health as well as illness; develops problem solving, observational, communication, caring and assessment skills and the application of these to responsible decision making; exposes the student to a range of settings and provides experience with a variety of persons requiring care; develops critical thinking and prepares the student for further learning. Specific subjects covered in the 18-month CFP are:

1. theory and practice of nursing: values, concepts, ideologies, models, information systems, research methodology and application;

2. communication processes: working with individuals, families, groups, and communities from different racial and ethnic groups, intra- and interprofessional work, counseling skills;

3. social and behavioral sciences: human social development and behavior across all age groups and sexes related to individuals, groups, cultures and communities;

4. life sciences: normal and disordered structure and function, the nature and causation of disease, aspects of microbiology and pharmacology;

5. professional, ethical, and moral issues-codes and dilemmas, boundaries of medical and nursing practice, patient advocacy;

6. organizational structure and statutory framework: statutory, voluntary and private services, working with others involved in care, working in teams, access to and use of information, preparation for managing nursing teams;

7. framework for social care provision and care systems: present provision of care services, theoretical frameworks for care and management of resources.

Branch Programs: Following the Common Foundation Program, students of nursing choose a specialization from among four Branch Programs: Adult Nursing (12), Mental Health Nursing (13), Mental Handicap Nursing (14), or Children's Nursing (15). Branch programs are 18 months in length. Each includes material on legislative and administrative aspects and develops previous learning in social, behavioral and applied sciences, applying this to the specific area of practice in a variety of settings with individuals, families, groups, cultures and communities.

Adult Nursing Branch: Learning in this branch is designed to enable the student to assess, plan, implement and evaluate, across any health care setting, the nursing care of those persons over the age of 16 with an acute or chronic physical illness which impairs their bio-psycho-social functioning.

Subject matter includes theoretical frameworks of health, health promotion, prevention of ill health; models of nursing, priority setting and acute intervention, technical and physical skills, care in a variety of settings; priority setting and long-term support or rehabilitation in a variety of settings; continuing care.

The CFP together with the Branch Program in Adult Nursing meet the requirements of the European Community Nursing Directive on the activities of nurses responsible for general care.

Mental Health Nursing Branch: Learning in this branch is designed to identify a person's emotional responses to physiological, psychological, and environmental stresses and the interplay of the many factors that enhance or inhibit the ability to cope with stress and to systematically provide care in a variety of settings.

Subject matter includes theoretical frameworks of mental health, health promotion, community-based approach to care; psycho-social skills; the nurse as a therapist, counselor and teacher; models of psychiatric care and nursing; crisis intervention; institutionalization; therapeutic milieu; activities of daily living, social skills training, specialized psychotherapeutic techniques.

Mental Handicap Nursing Branch: Learning in this branch is designed to enable the student to assess, plan, implement and evaluate the care required by any individual with a learning difficulty due to a mental handicap, in any setting and within a multidisciplinary framework. "Care" is seen in its widest sense and encompasses the total needs of a client.

Subject matter includes theoretical frameworks of mental handicap, development of care and current policy, attitudes, the principles of social role valorization; models of care and nursing, identification of need, environmental assessment, behavioral analysis and intervention; goal planning, multidisciplinary management, skills development, providing appropriate care settings.

Children's Nursing Branch: Learning in this branch is designed to enable the student to assess, plan, implement and evaluate the nursing care needs of the child within the family; to address issues of health promotion as well as sickness; to assist children in reaching their full developmental potential.

Subject matter includes theoretical frameworks of health and illness in children, models of nursing with the child and the family; health promotion, prevention of ill health, development of physical and psycho-social potential of children; technical and physical skills adapted to meet the maturational needs of children, provision for nursing care in a variety of settings; priority setting, family support systems, setting maturational goals and programs to develop full potential; continuing care.

Registered Midwife

A Registered Midwife is qualified to take professional responsibility for and to plan and provide care as an autonomous practitioner for mothers and babies throughout pregnancy, labor and delivery, and the postpartum period.

There are two ways to qualify as a midwife on Part 10 of the Register: completion of a three-year, direct entry midwife education and training program which does not require previous nurse training, or completion of an 18-month post-registration program which requires previous registration as a general nurse. Increasingly, midwives have qualified through post-registration programs. In 1989 there was only one direct entry program still in existence. However, to preserve their status as independent practitioners, midwives opted to stay out of P2000 and instead to return to and strengthen three-year midwifery education and training programs. Effective fall 1990, seven such programs were in place in England with another seven anticipated in 1991. In addition, the first pre-registration degree program in midwifery was instituted in 1989 at Oxford Polytechnic.

Entry requirements for three-year, direct entry midwifery education and training programs parallel those for any first-level nurse training program, both before and after 1986. The requirement for entry to an 18-month program is a general nursing registration (Part 1 or Part 12).

Training: Midwives are trained in hospital schools of midwifery which have been approved by one of the four National Boards. To be approved, a hospital must have prenatal, postnatal and neonatal clinical areas and must have sufficient qualified midwifery teaching staff. To ensure professional updates and maintenance of good practice, midwives are required to attend an approved refresher course every five years.

Midwife education and training consists of theoretical, clinical and practical instruction in each of the following subjects: physiology and applied anatomy of the body, the female reproductive system, the male reproductive system, the healthy neonate; psychology of child bearing, social and environmental influences, family planning, sexually transmitted diseases, termination of pregnancy; microbiology (its significance in obstetric and neonatal care), management of pregnancy, recognition and treatment of complications of pregnancy; physiology, progress and management of labor, recognition of abnormal conditions, their management, and the midwife's duties; drugs and their modes of administration, indication for use, effects of those in general use in obstetrics and pediatrics, legislation affecting the supply and control of drugs, regulations governing the administration of drugs by midwives.

Advanced Diploma in Midwifery. Prior to 1989, Registered Midwives (RM) could earn an additional professional qualification through programs leading to the Advanced Diploma in Midwifery (in Northern Ireland, the Diploma in Midwifery) offered in midwifery schools or in colleges of further or higher education.

Study for the Advanced Diploma prepared the midwife for movement into midwifery management, education or research. Entry required the RM and two years of post-registration experience (one year in Scotland). The length of the course was a minimum of 100 days fulltime or the part-time equivalent. (In Scotland the length of the course was 300 hours.) The curriculum integrated deepening and broadening knowledge of the subjects of midwifery with indepth study of the theory of professional midwifery practice, the history and development of midwifery and other related professions, and introduction to research methods.

From 1989 the Diploma in Professional Studies in Midwifery (DPSM) began replacing the Advanced Diploma programs. The DPSM is an academic qualification requiring one year of fulltime study in a program offered or validated by a university or a polytechnic.

Midwife Teacher's Diploma. The Midwife Teacher's Diploma qualifies a midwife to teach in midwifery schools or in midwifery programs in colleges of further or higher education.

The entry requirement is the RM plus the Advanced Diploma or the DPSM and at least 12 months of professional practice immediately prior to acceptance to the program. Programs are one academic year, fulltime, or the equivalent and are based in or academically validated by a polytechnic or a university. Course content includes principles and practice of teaching and learning, further study of both new and fundamental areas of midwifery, and a minimum of six weeks' teaching practice.

In Scotland, a midwife may earn a Midwife Clinical Teacher's Certificate to teach clinical subjects in midwifery schools. The entry requirement is both the RGN and the RM plus an advanced midwifery course of at least six months and three years' professional practice within the 10 years immediately preceding entrance to the program. Programs extend over 15 months and are based in midwifery schools. Students later wishing to pursue the Teacher's Diploma may substitute the Clinical Certificate plus six months of clinical teaching for the Advanced Diploma or DPSM entry requirement.

Health Visitor

The Health Visitor is an individual practitioner who works in the community for the promotion of good health and the prevention of ill health. Much of the work is with individual families, both through routine visits to all families with children from birth to school age and through referral from, among others, doctors, social services, and schools. The Health Visitor also collects information about the health of the local population and plays an active role in organizing health-promoting activities for the community.

To qualify as a Health Visitor on Part 11 of the Register, the individual must complete a National Board-approved program of professional preparation. Programs offered in universities or programs with CNAA validation offered in polytechnics lead to the Diploma in Health Visiting, an academic qualification.

The entry requirement is a general nursing registration (Part 1 or Part 12) plus an RM or some obstetric experience as well as entry requirements for the particular institution of higher education offering the program.

Training: The program is fulltime for one academic year followed by nine to 12 weeks of supervised practice. The course of study includes the psychological, physiological and social influences on human growth and development, the social aspects of both health and disease, the impact of social policy on health, the principles and practice of health visiting and community health care.

Post-Registration Diplomas

Opportunities for registered nurses to move into higher education are steadily increasing. Among them are post-registration diploma programs offered in or validated by universities, and post-registration programs offered in polytechnics and validated by the Council for National Academic Awards (CNAA). In addition to the diplomas described in this section there are a growing number of academically validated diploma programs in various aspects of community nursing. Descriptions are available from the respective institutions offering the programs.

Diploma in Nursing - University of London/Wales. The Diploma in Nursing is a three-year part-time program requiring a first-level registration and usually five O-levels or the equivalent for entry. (Most institutions consider mature nurses on a case-by-case basis.) The program is offered in colleges of further or higher education with the validation of the University of London or the University of Wales. The core of the program is an indepth study of man as a biological and psycho-social being, development of an understanding of nursing as an independent discipline and development of skills required to promote effectively individualized patient care.

Diploma in Professional Studies in Nursing (DipPS). This is a two-year part-time program requiring a first-level registration and usually five O-levels or the equivalent for entry. (Many programs consider mature nurses on an individual basis.) The program is offered in colleges of further or higher education, validated by CNAA.

Diploma/Certificate in Nursing Education. Programs which lead to a teaching qualification in nursing are provided by universities, polytechnics and other colleges of higher education. All are academically validated by a university or the CNAA. Programs are one year fulltime, two year part-time, or four-term sandwich courses. In addition to the entry requirements set by the particular institution, all candidates must have a first-level registration, relevant post-registration study of at least six months and three years' experience in the field of nursing in which they will be certified to teach. The National Boards have adopted a policy to move toward an all-graduate teaching profession as rapidly as possible, which means that the minimum academic entry requirement to teaching programs will become the Diploma in Nursing, the DipPS (Nursing), or the DipHE - Nursing. The program of study includes principles of teaching and learning, course development and curriculum management, policy framework for nurse education, and practice teaching.

Degrees in Nursing

Recently there has been a growth in the number of higher education institutions offering degree programs in nursing, a trend which is expected to continue. Some programs are three-year, post-registration degree completion programs designed for those already holding a first-level nursing registration. Other programs are four-year, direct entry programs, leading to both registration and the bachelor's degree. Currently, some institutions are seeking National Board approval for reduction of the four-year direct entry programs to three years, to be consistent with most other British first degrees. Many institutions are developing one-year degree completion programs for the new P2000 nurses who will already hold a Diploma in Higher Education, the equivalent of two years of study toward the three-year British bachelor's degree.

Along with the growth in first degree programs, the number of master's degree programs for nurses, midwives, and health visitors is increasing. Programs may be based on research or taught, or be a combination of the two. Taught programs are generally one year fulltime or two to three years' part-time. The standard entry qualification is a first degree. However, access may be gained directly to a master's degree program, usually through evidence of advanced professional study.

The Royal College of Nursing

The professional association for nurses in the U.K. is the Royal College of Nursing (RCN). The purpose of the RCN is to promote the welfare of nurses and to provide continuing education opportunities for its members. It also houses the Library of Nursing, the foremost source of nursing literature in the U.K. Unlike other professional associations, the RCN is not a qualifying body and therefore plays no direct role in the licensing of practitioners.

The education branch of the RCN, the Institute of Advanced Nursing Education, is a specialist center of higher education offering a range of post-registration programs and short courses leading to diplomas and certificates in various aspects of nursing. These are advanced professional rather than academic qualifications. In addition, the Institute is an approved external center for the University of London Diplomas in Nursing and Nursing Education and the BSc (Hons) in Nursing Studies. The Institute is also an approved external center for the University of Manchester BSc/BSc(Hons) in Nursing Studies and BA/BA(Hons) in Nursing Education.

Placement Recommendations

Note: See "Guide to the Understanding of Placement Recommendations," page 47 and the statement on the role of the National Council on the Evaluation of Foreign Educational Credentials in developing these placement recommendations on page v. Students who have completed some coursework for any of the programs listed below may be considered for undergraduate admission with up to one year of transfer credit, determined through a course-by-course analysis. If length of study is cited, it refers to the standard length of the program when pursued fulltime. The actual period of attendance may be longer.

Credential	Entrance Requirement	Length of Program	Gives Access in United Kingdom to	Placement Recommendation
1. Enrolled Nurse [EN(G), EN(M), EN(MH), EN(Scotland, No. Ireland)] (p. 196)	Completion of 10 years of education	1 1/2 to 2 years	Employment; Registered Nurse conversion scheme	A vocational qualification.
2. Registered Nurse [RGN, RMN, RMHN, RSCN]				
Enrolled Nurse Conversion Scheme (p. 196)	Enrolled Nurse and 1 year experience	1 year	Employment; further study	May be considered for undergraduate admission with transfer credit awarded on the same basis as for students of U.S. hospitals schools of nursing.
Entry pre-1985 (p. 194)	2 subject passes at GCE O-level or CSE, grade 1	3 years	Employment; further study	May be considered for undergraduate admission with transfer credit awarded on the same basis as for students of U.S. hospitals schools of nursing
Entry 1985 to present (pp. 196-99)	5 subject passes at GCE O-level, CSE, grade 1 or GCSE, grades A-C; or UKCC entrance examination	3 years	Employment; further study	May be considered for undergraduate admission with transfer credit awarded on the same basis as for students of U.S. hospitals schools of nursing.

University or CNAA Validated Diplomas

	Entrance Requirements	Length	Leads to	U.S. Equivalency
3. Diploma in Higher Education in Nursing [DipHE (Nurs)] (pp. 57, 197)	5 subject passes at GCE O-level, CSE, grade 1 or GCSE, grades A-C; or UKCC entrance examination	3 years fulltime	UKCC registration; further study	May be considered for up to 2 years of undergraduate transfer credit, determined through a course-by-course analysis.
4. Diploma in Nursing-University of London (1982 curriculum) (p. 200)	UKCC registered nurse registration and 5 subject passes at GCE O-level, CSE, grade 1 or GCSE, grades A-C; or UKCC entrance examination	3 years part-time	Further study	May be considered for up to 2 years of undergraduate transfer credit, determined through a course-by-course analysis.
5. Diplomas in Professional Studies [DipPS] in Nursing, Nursing Studies, Nursing Education, Professional Development in Nursing, Professional Study in Nursing, Midwifery, District Nursing, Health Visiting, Occupational Health Nursing, Health Service Management (pp. 65, 200)	UKCC registered nurse registration and 5 subject passes at GCE O-level, CSE, grade 1 or GCSE, grades A-C; or polytechnic or university entrance examination	1 year fulltime	Employment; further study	May be considered for up to 1 year of undergraduate transfer credit, determined through a course-by-course analysis.
6A. Bachelor in Nursing [BN], Bachelor of Arts [BA] in Nursing, Bachelor of Science [BSc] in Nursing, Bachelor of Science [BSc] in Nursing Science, Bachelor of Science [BSc] in Nursing and Human Services, Bachelor of Science [BSc] in Nursing Studies Bachelor of Science [BSc] in Social Sciences (pp. 58, 201)	5 subject passes, 2-3 at A-level and 2-3 at GCE O-level, CSE, grade 1 or GCSE, grades A-C	4 years fulltime	UKCC registration; further study	May be considered for graduate admission if the program is appropriate preparation.

6B. Bachelor in Nursing (Honours) [BN (Hons)], Bachelor of Arts in Nursing (Honours) [BA (Hons)], Bachelor of Science in Nursing (Honours) [BSc (Hons)], Bachelor of Science in Nursing Science (Honours) [BSc (Hons)], Bachelor of Science in Nursing and Human Services (Honours) [BSc (Hons)], Bachelor of Science in Nursing Studies (Honours) [BSc (Hons)], Bachelor of Science in Social Sciences (Honours) [BSc (Hons)] (pp. 58, 201)	5 subject passes, 2-3 at A-level and 2-3 at GCE O-level, CSE, grade 1 or GCSE, grades A-C	4 years fulltime	UKCC registration; further study	May be considered for graduate admission.
7A. Bachelor of Nursing [BN], Bachelor of Science [BSc] in Nursing, Bachelor of Science [BSc] in Nursing Studies, Bachelor of Science [BSc] in Community Nursing, Bachelor of Science [BSc] in Midwifery, Bachelor of Science [BSc] in Occupational Hygiene, Bachelor of Science [BSc] in Professional Development in Nursing, Bachelor of Arts [BA] in Applied Social Science, Bachelor of Arts [BA] in Nursing Education (pp. 58, 201)	UKCC first-level registration and 5 subject passes, 2-3 at A-level and 2-3 at GCE O-level, CSE, grade 1 or GCSE, grades A-C	3 years fulltime	Further study	May be considered for graduate admission if the program followed is appropriate preparation.

7B. Bachelor of Nursing (Honours) [BN (Hons)], Bachelor of Science in Nursing (Honours) [BSc (Hons)], Bachelor of Science in Nursing Studies (Honours) [BSc (Hons)], Bachelor of Science in Community Nursing (Honours) [BSc (Hons)], Bachelor of Science in Midwifery (Honours) [BSc (Hons)], Bachelor of Science in Occupational Hygiene (Honours) [BSc (Hons)], Bachelor of Science in Professional Development in Nursing (Honours) [BSc (Hons)], Bachelor of Arts in Applied Social Science (Honours) [BA (Hons)], Bachelor of Arts in Nursing Education (Honours) [BA (Hons)] (pp. 58, 201)	UKCC first-level registration and 5 subject passes, 2-3 at A-level and 2-3 at GCE O-level, CSE, grade 1 or GCSE, grades A-C	3 years fulltime	Further study	May be considered for graduate admission.
8A. Bachelor of Science in Nursing [BSc], Bachelor of Science in Nursing Studies [BSc] (pp. 58, 201)	Diploma in Higher Education in Nursing; or the University of London Diploma in Nursing (1982 curriculum)	1 year fulltime	Further study; employment	May be considered for graduate admission if the program is appropriate preparation.
8B. Bachelor of Science in Nursing (Honours) [BSc (Hons)], Bachelor of Science in Nursing Studies (Honours) [BSc (Hons)](pp. 58, 201)	Diploma in Higher Education in Nursing; or the University of London Diploma in Nursing (1982 curriculum)	1 year fulltime	Further study; employment	May be considered for graduate admission if the program is appropriate preparation.

9. Master of Nursing [MN], Master of Science in Nursing [MSc], Master of Science in Advanced Studies in Nursing and Administration [MSc], Master of Science in Nursing Education [MSc], Master of Science in Nursing and Health Care Management [MSc] (pp. 68, 201)	UKCC first-level registration and bachelor's degree or professional equivalent	1 year fulltime; 2-3 years part-time	Employment	May be considered comparable to a U.S. master's degree.

Appendix A. Sample Syllabuses

SAMPLE 1. Diploma in Accountancy (Foundation Course)

Financial Accountancy
Principles of Management Accounting
Principles of Law
Economics
Data Processing and Systems Design
Quantitative Techniques
Business Managment and Environment

Source: Coventry Polytechnic, *1989 Course Syllabus.*

SAMPLE 2. Certificate of Higher Education: Business Administration

Working with People (Managing Taxes)
Personnel Management
Finance for Non-Financial Managers
Using Word Processors
Database Management

Certificate of Higher Education: Computing Studies

Computer Studies
Systems Analysis and Design
COBOL Programming
Computer Language Programming
Expert Systems
Project

Source: West London Institute of Higher Education, *1990 Prospectus.*

SAMPLE 3. ENGINEERING: BEng, BEng Hons and DipHE

The BEng and BEng Hons at Oxford Polytechnic offer the opportunity to study either electronics or mechanical engineering. Students do not have to make a choice until the end of their first year. The work in the first year is common to both programs. This degree program at Oxford Polytechnic is taught on a term basis in a modular format. The curriculum for the two-year full time DipHE program of study comprises the first two years of the BEng Hons in Engineering.

First Year

Electrical Engineering Principles
Mechanical Engineering Principles
Mathematics
Computer-Aided Engineering
Engineering Graphics and Design
Communication, Management and Organization
Materials and Manufacturing
Integrated Engineering Studies; Design Experimentation

Second-Year

Dynamics of Engineering Systems
Instrumentation and Data Acquisition
Mathematics
Engineering Management
Integrated Engineering Studies: Design and Industrial Field course Mini-Projects

Students specializing in Electronics also study:

Electrical and Electronic Circuits
Electronic Devices and Systems
Electronic Computer-Aided Engineering
Material Technology (Electronics)

Students specializing in Mechanical Engineering also study:

Mechanics of Engineering
Mechanical Computer-Aided Engineering
Material Technology (Mechanical)
Engineering Thermodynamics

(Note: The completion of the first and second years will lead to the DipHE should a student wish to discontinue studies at the end of the second year.)

Third Year

Control Engineering
Strategic Management
Management of Manufacture
Project
Integrated Engineering Studies: Design

Students specializing in Electronics also study five from:

Analogue Electronics
Digital Electronics
Opto-Electronics
Digital Communications Systems
Software Engineering

Robotics
Digital Signal Processing
Advanced Microprocessor Architecture

> *Students specializing in Mechanical Engineering
> also study five from:*

Stress Analysis
Heat Transfer
Dynamics of Mechanical Systems
Strength of Components
Robotics
Thermal Power Systems
Joining Technology
CAD/CAM

> (Note: The BEng Ordinary/ Unclassified will be two
> modules short of the BEng Hons in the their/final
> year of study.)

Source: Oxford Polytechnic, *1990 Prospectus.*

SAMPLE 4. BA (Hons) Accounting and Finance

Three-year fulltime study

Year 1

Accounting
Behavior in Organizations
Accounting Information Systems I
Economics I
Business Law I
Quantitative Methods I

Year 2

Financial Reporting
Accounting for Decision Making and Control I
Accounting Information Systems II
Economics II
Business Law II
Quantitative Methods in Business

Year 3

Accounting
Theory and Practice of Taxation
International Financial Management
Information Systems Management
Financial Markets and Institutions
Corporate Strategy
Public Sector Finance and Accounting
Industry, State and the Environment
Industrial Economics

Source: Manchester Polytechnic, *1990 Prospectus.*

SAMPLE 5. Bachelor of Education Degree with Honours (In-Service)

For experienced teachers in primary and middle schools who wish to proceed to a first degree. Students must complete 12 modules.

> *Students must complete the following four modules:*

Teaching and Learning in the Classroom
Language in Primary Education
Primary Mathematics
Science in the Primary School

> *before taking one of the following:*

Perspectives on Special Educational Needs
Communication, Culture and Cognition
Disturbed and Disturbing Children

> *Plus:*

The Management of Curriculum Design
Classroom Enquiry
Curriculum Development and Innovation
Teacher-based Enquiry (worth "2" modules)

> *Plus two other modules from the system, subject to
> discussion with course tutor.*

Refer to individual module descriptions for details.

Source: West London Institute of Higher Education, *1990 Prospectus.*

SAMPLE 6. BEng (Honours) Mechanical Engineering

Year I (35 weeks)	Hours/Week
Basic Mathematics	2.5
Programming and Numerical Methods	1.5
Dynamics and Solid mechanics	2.0
Fluids and Thermodynamics	1.5
Materials Technology	1.5
Technology, Society and Enterprise	0.75
Electrical Engineering	1.5
Manufacturing Technology I	1.5
Engineering Drawing and Design I	1.0
Experimental Methods and Communications	2.5
Practical Element of Engineering Applications	7.0
Year 2 (35 weeks)	
Stress Analysis and Dynamics	2.5
Thermal Systems	2.5
Industrial Economics and Business Policy	2.0

Manufacturing Technology II	3.0
Engineering Design I	2.0
Dynamics of Engineering Systems	1.25
Instrumentation and Control	1.25
Computer and Engineering Applications	4.0
Materials Technology	1.0
Mathematics	1.5

Year 3 (sandwich route) OPTIONAL (36 weeks)

Manufacturing Management	2.5
Engineering Design III	3.0
Advanced Manufacturing Systems	2.0
Project	3.0

Plus four options from:

Advanced CAD/CAM	2.5
Microprocessor Applications	2.5
Equipment Engineering	2.5
Numbering Methods in Engineering	2.5
Noise and Vibration Analysis	2.5
Advanced Stress Analysis	2.5
Structural Analysis and Design	2.5
Robotics and Pneumatics	2.5
Heat Transfer	2.5
Fluid and Particle Mechanics	2.5
Control Systems	2.5
Process Control	2.5

SAMPLE 7. Diploma in Professional Studies in Education

Secondary Education

For experienced teachers in secondary schools who wish to develop further their knowledge and skills in a wide range of areas.

Students should complete 8 modules including the following:

The Management of Curriculum Design
The Management of Curriculum Change
Skills for a Caring Environment
Perspectives on Special Educational Needs
Careers Education and Guidance in the Secondary School

and three other modules from the system which may be selected from:

Learning and Teaching with Computers
An Introduction to Multi-Cultural Education
Disturbed and Disturbing Children

Children and Violence
Drugs, Education and the Adolescent
Personal, Social and Health Education

Refer to individual module descriptions for details.

Source: West London Institute of Higher Education, *1990 Prospectus.*

SAMPLE 8. Post-Graduate Certificate in Education [PGCE]

One year fulltime program

Principles and Methods Teaching

I. Primary: trainees study broad areas of the primary curriculum directed towards the education of children from 4-8 or 7-11;

II. Secondary: trainees study both one main teaching subject chosen from Physical Education or Religious Education and one subsidiary teaching area chosen from Personal and Social Education or children with Special Educational needs;

Teaching Studies
School Experience - one day weekly
Block Teaching Practice - two 6-week periods
Source: West London Institute of Higher Education, *1989-1990 Prospectus*

SAMPLE 9. Diploma in Management Studies-

Two years part-time

Stage I (Year I) (3 terms)

Essential computing
Data Interpretation
Information Systems
Financial Analysis and Management Accounting
Managerial Environment
Personal Effectiveness (2 days)
Managerial Behavior

Stage II (Year II) (3 terms)

Marketing
Policy Analysis
Employee Relations
Corporate Finance
Decision Making
Operations Management
Project Tutorials/Workshops (1 week)

Source: Bristol Polytechnic, *1990 Prospectus.*

Appendix B. Polytechnics in England and Wales

Birmingham Polytechnic, Perry Barr, Birmingham B42 2SU

Brighton Polytechnic, Moulsecoomb, Lewes Road, Brighton BN2 4AT

Bristol Polytechnic, Coldharbour Lane, Frenchay, Bristol BS16 1QY

City of London Polytechnic, Admissions Office, 31 Jewry Street, London EC3N 2EY

Coventry Polytechnic, Priory Street, Coventry CVI 5FB

Hatfield Polytechnic, College Lane, Hatfield, Hertfordshire AL10 9AB

Huddersfield Polytechnic, Queensgates, Huddersfield HD1 3DH

Kingston Polytechnic, Penrhyn Road, Kingston upon Thames, Surrey KT1 2EE

Lancashire Polytechnic, Preston PRI 2TQ

Leeds Polytechnic, Calverley Street, Leeds LE1 3HE

Leicester Polytechnic, PO Box 143, Leicester LE1 9BH

Liverpool Polytechnic, Rodney House, 70 Mount Pleasant, Liverpool L3 5UX

Manchester Polytechnic, All Saints, Manchester M15 6BH

Middlesex Polytechnic, Admissions Enquiries, Trent Park, Cockfosters Road, Barnet, Herfordshire EN4 0PT

Newcastle upon Tyne Polytechnic, Ellison Building, Ellison Place, Newcastle upon Tyne NE1 8ST

Oxford Polytechnic, Headington, Oxford OX3 0BP

Polytechnic of Central London, 309 Regent Street, London WIR 8AL

Plytechnic of East London, Romford Road, London E15 4LZ

Polytechnic of North London, Holloway Road, London N7 8D8

Polytechnic South West, Drake Circus, Plymouth PL4 8AA

Polytechnic of Wales, Pontypridd, Mid Glamorgan CF37 1DL

Portsmouth Polytechnic, Ravelin House, Museum Road, Portsmouth PO1 2QQ

Sheffield City Polytechnic, Pond Street, Sheffield S1 1WB

South Bank Polytechnic, Borough Road, London SE1 OAA

Staffordshire Polytechnic, College Road, Stoke-on-Trent ST4 2DE

Sunderland Polytechnic, Langham Tower, Ryhope Road, Sunderland Tyne and Wear SR2 7EE

Teesside Polytechnic, Borough Road, Middlesbrough, Cleveland TS1 3BA

Thames Polytechnic, Wellington Street, Woolwich, London SE18 6PF

Trent Polytechnic, Burton Street, Nottingham NG1 4BU

Wolverhampton Polytechnic, Molineux Street, Wolverhampton WV1 1SB

Beverley College of Further Education

Appendix B. Colleges of Further Education and Colleges and Institutes of Higher Education

Aberdare College of Further Education
Abingdon College of Further Education
Accrington & Rossendale College
Acton College
Afan College
Airedale & Wharfedale College
Amersham College of Further Education, Art & Design
Anglia Higher Education College
Anglo-European College of Chiropractic
Antrim Technical College
Armagh College of Further Education
Arnold & Carlton College of Further Education
Askham Bryan College of Agriculture & Horticulture
Aylesbury College
Ballymena Technical College
Banbridge College of Further Education
Barking College of Technology
Barnet College
Barnfield College
Barnsley College of Technology
Barrow in Furness College of Further Education
Barry College of Further Education
Besford Hall College of Further Education
Basildon College of Further Education
Basingstoke Technical College
Bath College of Higher Education
Bedford College of Higher Education
Belfast College of Business Studies
Belfast College of Technology
Bell College of Technology
Berkshire College of Agriculture
Berkshire College of Art & Design
Bicton College of Agriculture
Bilston Community College
Birmingham College of Food, Tourism & Creative Studies
Bishop Auckland Technical College
Bishop Burton College of Agriculture
Bishop Grosseteste College
Blackburn College
Blackpool & the Fylde College
Bolton Institute of Higher Education
Bolton Metropolitan College
Boston College of Further Education
Bournemouth & Poole College of Art & Design
Bournemouth & Poole College of Further Education
Bournville College of Further Education
Bracknell College
Bradford & Ilkley Community College
Braintree College of Further Education
Bramley Grange College
Brecon College of Further Education
Bretton Hall College of Higher Education
Bridgend College of Technology
Bridgnorth & South Shropshire College of Further Education
Bridgwater College
Brighton College of Technology
Bristol Nursery Nurses College of Further Education
Brixton College
Brockenhurst College
Bromley College of Technology
Brooklands Technical College
Brooklyn Technical College
Brooksby Agricultural College
Broxtowe College of Further Education
Brunel Technical College
Buckinghamshire College of Higher Education
Buckinghamshire College of Nursing & Midwifery
Burnley College
Burton-upon-Trent Technical College
Bury Metropolitan College
Camberwell School of Art & Crafts
Camborne School of Mines
Cambridge College of Art & Technology
Cambridge College of Further Education
Cambridgeshire College of Agriculture & Horticulture
Cannock Chase Technical College
Canterbury College of Art & Design
Canterbury College of Technology
Capel Manor College of Horticulture & Environmental Further Education College
Carlisle Technical College
Carmarthenshire College of Technology & Art
Carshalton College of Further Education
Cassio College of Further Education
Castlereagh College of Further Education
Central Manchester College
Central St. Martins College of Art & Design
Central School of Speech & Drama
Ceredigion College of Further Education
Charles Keene College of Further Education
Charlotte Mason College of Education
Chelmsford College of Further Education
Chelsea School of Art
Cheltenham & Gloucester College of Higher Education
Cheshire College of Agriculture
Chester College
Chesterfield College of Technology
Chichester College of Technology
Chippenham Technical College
City & East London College
City & Guilds London Art School
City Banking College
City College
City College of Higher Education
City of Bath College of Further Education
Clarendon College of Further Education
Cleveland College of Art & Design

Cleveland Technical College
Coalville Technical College
Coleraine Technical College
Cookstown Further Education College
Cordwainers Technical College
Cornwall College of Further & Higher Education
Conventry Technical College
Craven College
Crawley College of Technology
Crew & Alsager College of Higher Education
Cricklade College
Crosskeys College of Further Education
Croydon College
Cumbria College of Agriculture & Forestry
Cumbria College of Art & Design
Dacorum College
Darligton College of Technology
Dartington College of Arts
Davies Laing & Dick College
De Havilland College
Derbyshire College of Agriculture & Horticulture
Derbyshire College of Higher Education
Derby School of Occupational Therapy
Derwentside Tertiary College
Dewsbury College
Distributive Trades College
Doncaster Metropolitan Institute of Higher Education
Don Valley of Further Education
Dorset College of Agriculture & Horticulture
Dorset Institute
Down College of Further Education
Dudley College of Technology
Dungannon Further Education College
Dunstable College
Durham College of Agriculture & Horticulture
Ealing College of Higher Education
East Birmingham College
Eastbourne College of Arts & Technology
East Devon College of Further Education
East Herts College
East Surrey College
East Warwickshire College
East Yorkshire College of Further Education
Ebbw Vale College of Further Education
Edge Hill College of Higher Education
Elm Park College
Enniskillen Agricultural College
Epsom School of Art & Design
Erith College of Technology
Essex Institute of Higher Education
Evesham College of Further Education
Exeter College
Exeter College of Art & Design
Falmouth School of Art & Design
Farnborough College of Technology
Fermanagh College of Further Education
Filton Technical College
Frome College
Gateshead Technical College

Gloucestershire College of Agriculture & Horticulture
Gloucestershire College of Arts & Technology
Glynllifon College
Gorseinon College
Grantham College of Further Education
Greenhill College
Greenmount College of Agriculture & Horticulture
Greenwich College
Grimsby College of Technology
Great Yarmouth College of Art & Design
Great Yarmouth College of Further Education
Guernesey College of Further Education
Guildford College of Technology
Guildhall School of Music & Drama
Gwent College of Higher Education
Gwynedd Technical College
Hackney College
Hadlow College of Agriculture & Horticulture
Halesowen College
Hall Green College
Halton College of Further Education
Hammersmith & West London College
Handsworth Technical College
Harlow College
Harper Adams Agricultural College
Harrogate College Arts & Technology
Harrow College of Further Education
Hartlepool College of Further Education
Hastings College of Arts & Technology
Havering College of Adult Education
Havering Technical College
Hendon College of Further Education
Herefordshire College of Agriculture
Herefordshire College of Art & Design
Herefordshire Technical College
Hereward College of Further Education
Hertfordshire College of Agriculture & Horticulture
Hertfordshire College of Art & Design
Highbury College of Technology
Highlands College
High Peak College of Further Education
Hillcroft College
Hinkley College of Further Education
Hounslow Borough College
Huddersfield Technical College
Hugh Baird College of Technology
Hull College of Further Education
Humberside College of Higher Education
Isle of Man College of Further Education
Isle of Wright College of Arts & Technology
Jacob Kramer College
Joseph Priestley Institute of Further Education
Keighley College
Kendal College of Further Education
Kent Institute of Art & Design
Kidderminster College of Further Education
Kilburn College
Kilkeel Technical College
King Alfred's College

Kingston College of Further Education
Kingston Polytechnic
Kingsway College
Kirby College of Further Education
Kirkby College of Further Education
Kirkwall Further Education Centre
Kirkwall Further Education Evening Centre
Kitson College Technology
Lackham College of Agriculture
Lancashire College of Agriculture & Horticulture
Lancaster & Morecambe College
Lancaster College of Adult Education
Langley College
Larne College of Further Education
La Sainte Union College of Higher Education
Leeds College of Building
Leeds College of Music
Leek College of Further Education & School of Art
Leigh College
Lewes Technical College
Lews Castle College
Limavady Technical College
Lincolnshire College of Art & Design
Lincolnshire College of Agriculture & Horticulture
Lisburn College Further Education
Liverpool Institute of Higher Education
Llysfasi College Agriculture
London College of Dance
London College of Fashion
London College of Furniture
London College of Music
London College of Printing
London College of Tourism
London Contemporary Dance School
Longlands College of Further Education
Loughborough College of Art & Design
Loughry College of Agriculture & Food Technology
Lowestoft College of Further Education
Lurgan College of Further Education
Luton College of Higher Education
Macclesfield College of Further Education
Magherafelt College of Further Education
Manchester College
Matthew Boulton Technical College
Melton Mowbray College of Further Education
Merrist Wood College of Agriculture & Horticulture
Merthyr Tydil Technical College
Merton College
Mid-Cheshire College of Further Education
Mid-Cornwall College of Further Education
Mid-Glouchestershire Technical College
Mid-Kent College of Higher & Further Education
Mid-Warwickshire College of Further Education
Millbrook College of Further Education
Milton Keynes College
Monkwearmouth College of Education
Montgomery College of Further Education
Neath College
Nelson & Colne College

Nene College
Newark Technical College
Newbury College of Further Education
New College
New College Durham
Newcastle College
Newcastle College of Further Education
Newcastle Polytechnic
Newcastle under Lyme College
New England College
Newman & Westhill Colleges
Newport College of Further Education
Newry & Kilkheel College of Further Education
New Technical College
Newtownabby College of Further Education
Norfolk College of Agriculture & Horticulture
Norfolk College of Arts & Technology
Norfolk Institute of Art & Design
Normal College of Education
North Allerton School of Nursing
Northamptonshire College of Agriculture
Northampton College of Further Education
Northbrook College
North Cheshire College
North Devon College
North Down College of Further Education
North East Derbyshire College of Further Education
North East Surrey College of Technology
North East Wales Institute of Higher Education
North East Worcestershire College
Northern College
Northern Ireland Hotel & Catering College
North Herts College
North Lincs College
North Lindsey College of Technology
North London College
North Manchester College
North Nottinghamshire College of Further Education
North Oxfordshire Technical College & School of Art
North Trafford College of Further Education
North Tyenside College of Further Education
Northumberland College of Arts & Technology
North Warwickshire College of Technology & Art
North West College of Technology
North West Kent College of Technology
North West Kirklees Institute of Adult & Continuing
  Education
Norton-Radstock College of Further Education
Norwich City College
Norwood Hall Institute of Horticulture Education
Nottinghamshire College of Agriculture
Oak Hill College
Oldham College Technology
Omagh College of Further Education
Orpington College of Further Education
Oswestry College
Otley College of Agriculture & Horticulture
Oxford College of Further Education

Paddington College
Padworth College
Park Lane College
Parkwood College
Pathway Further Education Centre
Pembrokeshire College
Pencraig College
People's College of Further Education
Pershore College of Horticulture
Peterborough College of Adult Education
Peterborough Regional College
Peterlee College
Pickering Agriculture Centre
Pitman Central College
Plater College
Plumpton Agriculture College
Plymouth College of Art & Design
Plymouth College of Further Education
Pocklington Institute of Further Education
Polytechnic of Central London
Polytechnic of East London
Polytechnic of North London
Polytechnic of South West
Polytechnic of Wales
Pontypool College
Pontypridd Technical College
Portadown College of Further Education
Portslade Community College
Portsmouth College of Art, Design & Further Education
Portsmouth District School of Nursing
Portsmouth Polytechnic Preston College
Radnor College of Further Education
Ravensbourne College of Design & Communication
Reading College Technology
Redbridge Technical College
Restormel Adult Continuing Education Centre
Rhondda College of Further Education Centre
Rhondda College of Further Education
Richmond Adult & Community College
Richmond-upon-Thames College
Ripon & York St. John College
Royal National Institute of Technology
Rochdale College of Adult Education
Rochdale Valley College of Further Education
Royal Academy of Dramatic Art
Royal Academy of Music
Royal Agriculture College
Royal Botanic Gardens, School of Horticulture
Royal College of Music
Royal College of Nursing
Royal Forest of Dean College
Royal Military College of Science
Royal Naval Engineering College
Royal Northern College of Music
Rumney College of Technology
Rupert Stanley College of Further Education
Ruskin College
Rycotewood College
St. Aldates College

St. Albans College
St. Andrew's College of Education
St. Andrew's Hospital School of Occupational Therapy
St. Clare's
St. Giles College
St. Godric's College
St. Helens College
St. Loye's School of Occupational Therapy
St. Mark & St John College
St. Martin's College
St. Mary's College
St. Peter's Tutorial College
Salford College of Further Education
Salford College of Technology
Salisbury College of Art & Design
Salisbury College of Technology
Sandown College
Sandwell College of Further & Higher Education
Sandy Community College
Scarborough Technical College
Schiller International University
Seale-Hayne College
Shaw College of Beauty Therapy
Shetland College of Further Education
Shipley College
Shrewsbury College of Arts & Technology
Shuttleworth College
Solihull College of Technology
Somerset College of Agriculture & Horticulture
Soudwell College
Southall College of Technology
Southampton Institute of Higher Education
Southampton Technical College
South Bristol College
South Cheshire College
South Devon College of Arts & Technology
South Downs College of Further Education
South East Derbyshire College
South East London College
Southend College Technology
Southern England Nursery Training College
South Fields College of Further Education
Southgate Technical College
South Glamorgan Institute of Higher Education
South Kent College
South Kirklees Institute od Adult Education
South London College
South Manchester Community College
South Mersey College
South Notts College of Further Education
Southpoint College of Art & Technology
South Thames College
South Trafford College of Further Education
South Tyneside College
Southwark College
South Warkshire College of Further Education
South West London College
Sparsholt College Hampshire
Sprugeon's College

Stafford College
Stafford House Tutorial College
Staffordshire College of Agriculture
Stamford College for Further Education
Steiner Beauty School
Stevenage College
Stockport College of Technology
Stockton-Billingham Technical College
Stoke Cauldon College of Further & Higher Education
Stoke Technical College
Stourbridge College of Technology & Art
Stradbroke College
Stanmillis College
Stanraer Agriculture Further Education Centre
Strode College
Stromness Academy Further Education Centre
Suffolk College of Higher & Further Education
Sutton Coldfield College of Further Education
Swansea College
Swindon College
Tameside College of Technology
Tamworth College of Further Education, Arts & Technology
Thomas Danby College
Thrruock Technical College
Tile Hill College of Further Education
Tottenham College of Technology
Tresham College
Trinity & All Saints' College
Trinity College
Trinity College of Music
Trowbridge Technical College
USK College of Agriculture
Uxbridge Technical College
Vauxhall College of Building & Further Education
Wakefield District College
Walford College of Agriculture
Wallace High School Further Education Centre
Walsall College of Art
Walsall College of Technology
Waltham Forest College
Ware College
Warwickshire College of Agriculture
Watford College
Weald College
Wearside College of Further Education
Wellignborough College
Welsh Agriculture College
Welsh College of Horticulture
Welsh College of Music & Drama
West Cheshire College
West Cumbria College
West Dean College
West Glamorgan Institute of Higher Education
West Kent College of Further Education
West London College
West London Institute of Higher Education
West Lothian College of Further Education

West Nottinghamshire College of Further Education
West Oxfordshire Technical College
West Suffolk College of Further Education
West Surrey College of Further Education
West Sussex College of Agriculture & Horticulture
West Sussex Institute of Higher Education
Westminster College
Weston-super-Mare College of Further Education
Weymouth College
Wigan College of Technology
Wigston College of Further Education
Willesden College of Technology
Wimbledon School of Art
Winchester School of Art
Windsor & Maidenhead College
Wirral Metropolitan College
Withernsea Institute of Further Education
Wolverhampton College of Higher Education
Wood Tutorial College
Woolwich College
Worcester College of Higher Education
Worcester Technical College
Worcestershire College of Agriculture
Working Mens College
Worsley College of Further Education
W.R. Tuson College
Writtle Agriculture College
Wulfrun College of Further Education
YMCA National College
Yeovil College
York College of Arts & Technology
Ystrad Mynach College of Further Education

Appendix D. Scottish Professional Business Associations

Although most of the professional business associations in the United Kingdom are national (see Chapter V), three are Scottish: Faculty of Actuaries, Institute of Bankers in Scotland and the Institute of Chartered Accountants of Scotland.

Programs offered by the colleges of further education and the central institutions sometimes are tailored to the requirement of a specific association, such as the program at Napier Polytechnic of Edinburgh, which leads to the Final Professional level 3 examinations of the Chartered Association of Certified Accountants and the part-time course at Robert Gordon's Institute of Technology, which leads to the examinations of the Institute of Marketing.

FACULTY OF ACTUARIES

23 St. Andrew Square, Edinburgh EH2 1AQ; Tel. 031-557-1575

Founded in 1856 and incorporated by Royal Charter in 1868, the Faculty is the Scottish counterpart of the British Institute of Actuaries. The Faculty had 669 Fellows worldwide (1989) compared to the 2,917 Fellows of the Institute. The role of the Faculty according to its charter is to elevate the status and promote the general efficiency of all actuaries and extend and improve the methodology.

Qualifications granted: Fellow (FFA) - Any student of the Faculty who has completed the examinations may be admitted as a Fellow. There is no experience requirement.

Admission requires:

1. A degree from a U.K. university with two years of mathematics; or

2. Three subjects at Higher Grade including Mathematics (Grade A) and English, together with the Certificate of Sixth-Year Studies with Grade A in one and at least a Grade B in another of the papers: I (Algebra and Number Systems); II (Geometry and Calculus); III (A. Probability and Statistics, B. Numerical Analysis and Computer Programming, C. Mathematical Topics in Mechanics) with the requirement that one of the papers should be Paper II; or

3. The GCE/GCSE equivalent of the above including two passes at A-level, one of which must be in a mathematical subject at Grade B or above and the other a Grade C or above; or

4. Such other qualifications as the Faculty considers equivalent to the above.

The *examinations* consist of seven parts with 14 papers as follows:

Part I	Statistics (one paper of 3 hours)
Part II	Mathematics and Finance (one paper of 3 hours)
Part III	Life and other contingencies (two papers, each 3 hours)
Part IV	A. Mortality and related investigations; theory and tests of graduation; actuarial aspects of demography (one paper of 3 hours)
	B. Applied statistics utility functions short-term risk models, loss distribution; credibility theory (one paper of 3 hours)
Part V	Finance and investments (two papers, each 3 hours)
Part VI	Actuarial and administrative problems in relation to office premiums surrender and conversion of contracts issued by life assurance companies and valuation and distribution of surplus in respect of such contracts (three papers, each 3 hours)
Part VII	Actuarial and administrative problems in relation to pension funds; actuarial aspects of social insurance (three papers, each 2 1/2 hours)

Exemption from examinations is granted from (1) Part I of the examinations to degree holders with a first or second class honours degree in statistics and to students who have two years of study in mathematics and in statistics with first or second class results; (2) Parts I-III to students who have a BSc in Actuarial Mathematics and Statistics at Heriot-Watt University; (3) Parts I-IV to students who have graduated BSc with honours in Actuarial Mathematics and Statistics at Heriot-Watt University; (4) Parts I-IVA or Parts II-IVB to students who have graduated with the Diploma in Actuarial Science from Heriot-Watt; 5) Exemptions also are granted to graduates with both an undergraduate degree and a postgraduate diploma in Actuarial Science of City University, London and for completion of certain actuarial courses at London School of Economics; University of Kent at Canterbury; Macquarie University (Australia) and the Universities of Cape Town, Stellenbosch and Witwatersrand (South Africa).

THE INSTITUTE OF BANKERS IN SCOTLAND

20 Rutland Square, Edinburgh EH1 2DE, Tel. 031-229-9869

Started in 1875, the Institute was established "to improve the qualifications of those engaged in banking...."

Qualifications granted:

Fellow (FIB Scot), which is open to Associates of at least 10 years who are currently in a managerial position in banking.

Associate (AIB Scot). Candidates must have passed the Institute's Diploma examinations as well as three additional courses: Management and Business Administration, Management Accounting and Business Finance, Taxation. There are no exemptions from individual subjects.

Study for the Associateship can be either by correspondence or by attendance in block release courses offered by the following colleges: Aberdeen College of Commerce, Clydebank College; Dundee College of Further Education, Napier Polytechnic of Edinburgh, Glasgow College, City of London Polytechnic.

Students attend 12 weeks, divided into two six-week periods of fulltime study. Each college runs two separate groups of blocks:

A   Mid-September to end of October; early January to mid-February

B   Early November to mid-December; mid-February to end of March

Diploma (DipIB[Scot]). Requires three years of study in day release. The program for the Diploma consists of two stages: Stage 1 (introductory course) consists of three required courses and Stage 2 consists of eight required courses. All should be completed within the statutory time limit of five years. The course are as follows:

Stage 1	Introduction to Accounting, Introduction to Banking, and Introduction to Commercial Law
Stage 2	Law and Practice of Banking I, Economics, Business Accounting I
Year 2	Money and Banking, Business Accounting II, Investment
Year 3	Foreign Business, Law and Practice of Banking II

Admission to the Diploma course is open to those who have a U.K. degree or three SCE Higher grades or two GCE A-level passes, or a National Certificate. Students who have fewer than three Higher grades on the SCE may qualify for admission by taking a SCOTVEC National Certificate (with 12 mandated modules in accounting, economics, banking, law, and English) or similar courses of the London Chamber of Commerce and Industry (LCCI). This program generally requires two years of study but the students then will be exempt from the Introductory Course.

THE INSTITUTE OF CHARTERED ACCOUNTANTS OF SCOTLAND

27 Queen Street, Edinburgh EH2 1LA Tel. 031-225-5673, FAX 031-225-3813

The Institute of Chartered Accountants of Scotland (ICAS) is the Scottish counterpart of the Institute of Chartered Accountants of England and Wales. The Institute both teaches and examines its students and classes are offered on a block release basis at the Institute's own education centers.

Qualifications awarded:

Member (CA). Candidates must have completed a three-year training contract with a firm of chartered accountants and passed the Institute's Professional Examination and the two-part Test of Professional Competency. Admission is based on receipt of a U.K. degree.

The Institute distinguishes two types of degrees: *fully accredited* (the degree contains approved courses in financial accounting, managerial accounting, business finance, auditing, taxation, information technology, mathematical techniques, economics and business law), and *qualifying* (a degree which does not contain these core subjects but may qualify for other subject examinations). Fully accredited graduates normally are exempted from the Institute's Professional Examination in its entirety while qualifying graduates must take appropriate papers within the professional examination.

The Institute's *examinations* consist of three stages as follows:

Professional:
Financial reporting (two papers)
> Paper I - Financial accounting
> Paper II - Business finance/ Managerial accounting
> Mathematical techniques

> Taxation
> Auditing
> Information technology
> Economics
> Business law

Test of Professional Competence, Part I

Case studies and objective testing in

> Financial reporting
> Auditing
> Taxation
> Information technology

Test of Professional Competence, Part II

A multidiscipline case study designed to test candidates' abilities to apply their theoretical knowledge and practical skills to problems of the type likely to be encountered by the newly qualified accountant.

Appendix E. Frequently Seen Abbreviations of Degrees, Diplomas and Certificates

BA	Bachelor of Arts
BAcc	Bachelor of Accounting
BArch	Bachelor of Architecture
BArchStud	Bachelor in Architectural Studies
BCom	Bachelor of Commerce
BD	Bachelor of Divinity
BDS	Bachelor of Dental Surgery
BEd	Bachelor of Education
BEng	Bachelor of Engineering
BLE	Bachelor of Land Economy
BMed Biol	Bachelor of Medical Biology
BMed Sci	Bachelor of Medical Science
BMSc	Bachelor of Medical Science
BMus	Bachelor of Music
BN	Bachelor of Nursing
BSc	Bachelor of Science
BSc Agr	Bachelor of Science in Agriculture
BScArch	Bachelor of Science in Architecture
BSc Dent Sci	Bachelor of Science in Dental Sciences
BScEng	Bachelor of Science in Engineering
BSc For	Bachelor of Science in Forestry
BSc Med Sci	Bachelor of Science in Medical Sciences
BScVetSci	Bachelor of Science in Veterinary Science
BTechEd	Bachelor of Technical Education
BTh	Bachelor of Theology
BTP	Bachelor of Town Planning
BVM&S	Bachelor of Veterinary Medicine and Surgery
CertEd	Certificate in Education
CertEd-FE	Certificate in Education-Further Education
CertHE	Certificate of Higher Education
ChB	Bachelor of Surgery
ChM	Master of Surgery
DDS	Doctor of Dental Surgery
DDSc	Doctor of Dental Science
DEng	Doctor of Engineering
DipEd	Diploma in Education
DipHE	Diploma of Higher Education
DipNur	Diploma in ...
DipPS	Diploma in Professional Studies
DLitt	Doctor of Letters
DMS	Diploma in Management Studies
DMus	Doctor of Music
DSc	Doctor of Science
DTech	Doctor of Technology
DVM	Doctor of Veterinary Medicine

DVM&S	Doctor of Veterinary Medicine and Surgery
DVS	Doctor of Veterinary Surgery
Grad Dip Mus	Graduate Diploma in Music
LLB	Bachelor of Laws
LLD	Doctor of Laws
LLM	Master of Laws
MA	Master of Arts
MAcc	Master of Accounting
MAppSci	Master of Applied Science
MArch	Master of Architecture
MB	Bachelor of Medicine
MBA	Master of Business Administration
MCC	Master of Community Care
MD	Doctor of Medicine
MDSc	Doctor of Medicine and Science
MDes	Master of Design
MEd	Master of Education
MEng	Master of Engineering
MFA	Master of Fine Arts
MLA	Master of Landscape Architecture
MLE	Master of Land Economy
MLitt	Master of Letters
MMedSci	Master of Medical Science
MMSc	Master of Medical Science
MMus	Master of Music
MN	Master of Nursing
MPH	Master of Public Health
MPhi	IMaster of Philosophy
MSc	Master of Science
MSc MedSci	Master of Science in Medical Science
MSc VetSci	Master of Science in Veterinary Science
MSSc	Master of Social Science
MSW	Master of Social Work
MTh	Master of Theology
MTheol	Master of Theology
MUniv Admin	Master of University Administration
MVM	Master of Veterinary Medicine
PGCE	Postgraduate Certificate in Education
PGD	Postgraduate Diploma
PhD	Doctor of Philosophy

Appendix F. Acronyms

AAT	Association of Accounting Technicians
ACCA	Chartered Association of Certified Accountants
ADES	Association of Directors of Education in Scotland
ALCES	Association of Lecturers in Colleges of Education (Scotland)
APL	Accreditation of Prior Learning (Scotland)
AUTS	Association of University Teachers (Scotland)
BEC	Business Education Council
BER	Board of Engineers' Registration
BIM	British Institute of Management
BTEC	Business and Technicians Education Council
CATS	Credit Accumulation and Transfer Scheme
CCAB	Consultative Committee of Accounting Bodies
CEng	Chartered Engineer
CGLI	City and Guilds of London Institutes
CI	Central Institutions (Scotland)
CIB	Chartered Institute of Banking
CIM	Chartered Institute of Marketing
CNAA	Council on National Academic Awards
COSLA	Convention of Scottish Local Authorities
CPVE	Certificate of Prevocational Education
CPCES	Committee of Principals of Colleges of Education (Scotland)
CSYS	Certificate of Sixth Year Studies (Scotland)
CSE	Certificate of Secondary Education
CTE	Council for Tertiary Education (Scotland)
EA	Education Authority (Scotland)
EC	Engineering Council
EIS	Educational Institute of Scotland
EITB	Engineering Institute Training Board (Scotland)
EN	Enrolled Nurse
FE	Further Education
GCE	General Certificate of Education
GCSE	General Certificate of Secondary Education
GTC	General Teaching Council (Scotland)
HNC	Higher National Certificate
HND	Higher National Diploma
HV	Health Visitor
IAM	Institute of Administrative Management
ICAEW	Institute of Chartered Accountants in England and Wales
ICAI	Institute of Chartered Accountants in Ireland
ICAS	Institute of Chartered Accountants in Scotland
IEE	Institute of Electrical Engineers
IEEIE	Institute of Electronics and Electrical Incorporated Engineers
IFA	Institute of Financial Accountants
IPM	Institute of Personnel Management
LCCI	London Chamber of Commerce and Industry
LEA	Local Education Authority
LMS	Local Management of Schools
MSC	Manpower Services Commission (Scotland)
NC	National Certificate
NCITT	National Committee for In-Service Training of Teachers (Scotland)
NCVQ	National Council for Vocational Qualifications
ND	National Diploma
NVQ	National Vocational Qualification (Scotland)
PEI	Pitman Examination Institute
RM	Registered Midwife
RN	Registered Nurse
RSA	Royal Society of Arts
SCCC	Scottish Consultative Committee on the Curriculum
SCE	Scottish Certificate of Education
SCOSDE	Scottish Committee for Staff Development in Education
SCOTBEC	Scottish Business Education Council
SCOTEC	Scottish Technical Education Council
SCOTVACT	Scottish Council for the Validation of Courses for Teachers
SCOTVEC	Scottish Vocational Eduction Council
SCRE	Scottish Council for Research in Education
SEAC	Secondary School Examination and Assessment Council
SEB	Scottish Examination Board
SECTS	Scottish European Community Transfer Scheme
SEC	Secondary Examinations Council
SED	Scottish Education Department
SFEA	Scottish Further Education Association
STEAC	Scottish Tertiary Education Advisory Council
SUCE	Scottish Universities Council on Entrance
SVQ	Scottish Vocational Qualifications
SWAP	Scottish Wider Access Program
TEACH	Teacher Education Admissions Clearing House (Scotland)
TEC(S)	Technicians Education Council (Scotland)
TEC(S)	Tertiary Education Council (Scotland)
TGAT	Task Group on Assessment and Training
TVEI	Technical and Vocational Education Initiative
UCCA	Universities Central Council on Admissions (Scotland)

Select Bibliography

General Information

Association of Commonwealth Universities. *Commonwealth Universities Yearbook*. 1989. London.

Fisher, Stephen H. 1976. *The United Kingdom of Great Britain and Northern Ireland*. Washington, DC: American Association of Collegiate Registrars and Admissions Officers.

Study Abroad

Ball, Sir Christopher and Eggins, Heather. 1989. *Higher education into the 1990s*. Milton Keynes, U.K.: Open University Press and The Society for Research into Higher Education.

Central Office of Information. 1987. *New policies for higher education in Britain*. London.

Council for Industry and Higher Education. 1989. *Towards a partnership: Higher education-government-industry*. Paper.

Council for National Academic Awards. *Access courses to higher education; A framework of national arrangements for recognition*. London. Paper.

—. 1986. *The Credit Accumulation and Transfer Scheme*. London. Paper.

—. 1989. *The access effect*. Development Services Project Report 20. London. Paper.

Department of Education and Science. 1986. *Projections of demand for higher education in Great Britain 1986-2000*. London: HMSO.

—. 1987. *Changes in structure and national planning for higher education; Universities funding council*. London: HMSO.

—. 1988. *Top up loans for students*. London: HMSO.

Department of Education and Science. 1989. *The English polytechnics*. London: HMSO.

—. 1989. *Shifting the balance of public funding of higher education to fees; A consultation paper.*. *London: HMSO*.

Emerson, Chris and Goddard, Ivor. 1989. *All about the national curriculum*. Oxford: Heinemann.

Institute of Manpower Studies. 1989. *How many graduates in the 21st century?*. Paper.

National Association for Foreign Student Affairs. 1988. *Recording the performance of U.S. undergraduates at British institutions: Guidelines towards standardized reporting for study abroad*. Edited by David Rex and Thomas Roberts. Washington, DC: NAFSA.

Stewart, W.A.C. 1989. *Higher education in postwar Britain*. MacMillan Press.

Trythall, J.W.D. 1990. "The expansion of British higher education" *Academe* (May-June).

Watson, David. 1989. *Managing the modular course*. Milton Keynes, U.K.: Open University Press and The Society for Research into Higher Education.

"The Development of Higher Education into the 1990s" 1985. London: HMSO. Green Paper

Higher Education: Meeting the Challenge. 1987. London: HMSO. White Paper

"British Government Confirms Its Decision to Replace Student Grants With Loans," *The Chronicle of Higher Education* (June 28, 1989)

"Enter the Polyversities," *The Economist* (March 25, 1989).

"Baker's Vision for the Next Twenty Five Years," *The Times Higher Education Supplement* (January 13, 1989).

"Post-Baker Pause," *The Times Higher Education Supplement* (November 3, 1989).

Secondary Education

Associated Examining Board. 1986. *1987 syllabuses*. Guildford.

Department of Education and Science and the Welsh Office. 1985. *GCSE general certificate of secondary education. The national criteria, general*. London: HMSO.

—. 1985. *GCSE general certificate of education. The national criteria, mathematics.* London: HMSO.

—. 1987. *Examination reform for schools.* London: HMSO.

—. 1987. *The National Curriculum: Consultation Document.* Unpublished.

—. 1988. *National curriculum, task group on assessment and testing report.* London: HMSO.

—. 1989. *English in the national curriculum.* London: HMSO.

—. 1989. *Mathematics in the national curriculum.* London: HMSO.

—. 1989. *National curriculum, from policy to practice.* London: HMSO.

—. 1989. *Science in the national curriculum.* London: HMSO.

—. 1990. *Geography in the national curriculum, geography for ages 5 to 16, proposals of the secretaries of state for education and science and the Welsh office.* London: HMSO.

Hughes, James J., ed. 1989. *AS levels: Implications for schools. Examining boards and universities.* East Sussex: The Falmer Press.

International Baccalaureate. 1980. *General guide to the international baccalaureate.* Geneva: International Baccalaureate.

—. *Mathematics subject guide, examinations sessions, 1887 onwards.* London: International Baccalaureate. Photocopy.

Kingdon, Michael and Stobart, Gordon. 1988. *GCSE examined.* East Sussex: The Falmer Press.

Kirk, Gordon. 1986. *The core curriculum.* London: Hodder & Stoughton.

London East Anglia Group. *GCSE, Mathematics (Series 17).* 1989, Summer 1991.

—. LEAG 1989. *GCSE, Mathematics A, Mathematics B.* Summer 1991, Winter 1991.

Maclure, Stuart. 1988. *Education re-formed: a guide to the education reform act 1988.* London: Hodder & Stoughton.

National Curriculum Council. *National curriculum, task group on assessment and testing report. Annual report, 1988-1989.* London: NCC.

—. 1989. *Introducing the national curriculum.*

—. 1989. *Planning the curriculum. Record keeping and assessment. Secondary mathematics. Science in Her Majesty's government. Education reform act.* London: HMSO. Leaflets.

—. 1989. *The national curriculum and the whole curriculum planning: Preliminary guidance (6). Publications on the national curriculum from NCC, DES, HMI, and SEAC (7). Technology in the national curriculum: A digest (8). English in the national curriculum: A digest (9). The national curriculum at key stage 4 (10).* Circulars 6-10.

Roy, Walter. 1986. *The new examination system-GCSE.* Kent: Croom Helm Ltd.

School Examinations Council. 1987. *Current developments in school curriculum and examinations.* HMSO, London, 1987.

School Examination and Assessment Council. 1989. *An introduction to SEAC.* London: HMSO.

—. 1989. *Chief examiners' conference in mathematics.* London: SEAC.

—. 1990. *Examining GCSE: First general scrutiny, report.* London: SEAC.

University of London School Examinations Board. 1989. *GCE regulations and syllabuses, June 1991-January 1992.* London: University of London.

Polytechnics and Colleges

Association of Commonwealth Universities. 1990-91. *Higher Education in the United Kingdom.* Harrow: Longman Group UK Limited.

Business and Technician Education Council. April 1984. *BTEC information sheet.* London.

British Qualifications, 20th Edition. 1989. London: Kogan Page Limited.

Council for National Academic Awards. 1983. *Opportunities in Higher Education for Mature Students.* London.

—. 1986. *Credit Accumulation and Transfer Scheme.* London.

—. 1988. *The Work of the Council.* London.

—. 1989. *Directory of First Degree and Diploma of Higher Education Courses.* London.

—. 1989. *Handbook.* London.

Directory of Technical and Further Education. 1988. Harrow: Longman Group UK Limited.

The English Polytechnic–An HMI Commentary. 1989. London: HMSO.

National Equivalence Information Centre. 1984. *International Guide to Qualifications in Education.* London: Mansell.

Prospectus (catalogs):

Bristol Polytechnic (1990)
Hatfield Polytechnic (1989)
Manchester Polytechnic (1990)
Middlesex Polytechnic (1990)
Oxford Polytechnic (1990)
Polytechnic of North London (1990)
West London Institute of Higher Education (1990)

Scotland

Clark, P. 1987. "Central institutions and their place in higher education–in Scotland." *Scottish Educational Review* (Edinburgh: Scottish Academic Press) 19 (May).

Dearden, R.F. *et al.* 1987. "Education 10-14 in Scotland." *Scottish Educational Review* (Edinburgh: Scottish Academic Press).

Fast forward with further education. n.d. Edinburgh: Scottish Office.

General teaching council Scotland handbook. 1990. Edinburgh: Royal Crescent.

Guide for applicants for entry in October 1990. n.d. Heriot-Watt University.

Kirk, G., ed. *Moray house and professional education, 1935-85.* Edinburgh: Scottish Academic Press.

Public education in Scotland. 1952. Edinburgh: HMSO.

School leavers qualifications in Scotland: A guide for employers. 1988. Edinburgh: Scottish Office.

Scottish Consultative Council on the Curriculum. *Curriculum design for the secondary stages, 1989.* Dundee.

Scottish Council for Staff Development. 1988. *National staff development opportunities (1989-90).* SCOSDE.

Scottish Examination Board. 1990. *Certificate of sixth year studies.* 1990. Dalkeith: SEB.

Copies of SEB publications may be purchased from Robert Gibson and Sons, Glasgow, Ltd., 17 Fitzroy Place, Glasgow G37SF.

—. 1989. *Scottish certificate of education examination: Conditions and arrangements.* Dalkeith: SEB.

—. 1989. *Scottish examination board: Report for 1988.* Dalkeith: SEB.

Scottish Vocational Education Council. 1988. *Guide to equivalencies between SCOTVEC and city guilds.* Glasgow: SCOTVEC Publications.

—. 1988. *National certificate catalogue of module descriptors.* Glasgow: SCOTVEC Publications.

—. 1988. *National certificate guide to modular programmes.* Glasgow: SCOTVEC Publications.

Scottish Universities Council on Entrance. 1989. *Scottish universities entrance guide, 1990.* SUCE, St. Andrews, Fife.

—. 1990. *University entrance: The official guide, 1991.* London: Association of Commonwealth Universities.

Shanks, D. 1987. "The master of education degree in Scotland." *Scottish Educational Review* (Edinburgh: Scottish Academic Press) 19 (November).

Standard grade: Setting new standards for all Scottish pupils. n.d. Edinburgh: Scottish Office.

Stimpson, D.G. 1989. Teacher training regulations and practice in Scotland. Unpublished paper.

Times Educational Supplement (Scotland). May 30, 1986; May 1, 1987; March 11, 1988; June 17, 1988; June 24, 1988; July 29, 1988.

Times Higher Education Supplement. November 3, 1989; December 8, 1989.

Professional Qualifications

Becher, Tony, ed. 1987. *British higher education.* London: Allen & Unwin.

Board of Accreditation of Educational Courses. 1989. *Notes on submission of courses for approval.* London: BAEC.

The British Institute of Management. 1987. *The making of British managers.* London: BIM.

The Chartered Institute of Bankers. 1988. *Report of the committee to review the role and activities of the institute.* London: CIB.

Management challenge for the 1990's. 1987. London: Deloitte, Haskins & Sells.

Department of Trade and Industry. 1989. *Europe open for professions.* London.

The Engineering Council. 1985. *Raising the standard.* London: The Engineering Council.

——. 1989. *The board for engineers' registration.* London: The Engineering Council.

——. 1990. *Standards and routes to registration.* London: The Engineering Council.

Goodlad, Sinclair, ed. 1985. *Education for the professions Quis custodiet...?* University of Surrey: Society for Research into Higher Education & HFER-Nelson.

The Institution of Electrical and Electronics Incorporated Engineers. 1988. *Engineering a career in the electrical and electronics industry.* London: IEEE.

The Institution of Electrical Engineers. n.d. *A brief history of the institution of electrical engineers.* London: IEE.

——. 1989. *Educational requirements.* London: IEE.

——. 1989. *IEE guidelines on accreditation of company training schemes.* London: IEE.

——. 1987. *The mature candidate scheme.* London: IEE.

Renard, Georges. 1968. *Guilds in the middle ages.* New York: Augustus M. Kelley.

Turner, John D. and Rushton, James, eds. 1976. *Education for the professions.* Manchester, England: University of Manchester Press.

Index